# BRITAIN & THE WORLD
## 1815–1986

# BRITAIN & THE WORLD
## 1815–1986

## A Dictionary of International Relations

DAVID WEIGALL

*with editorial assistance
from Christopher Catherwood*

New York
OXFORD UNIVERSITY PRESS
1987

© 1987 BY DAVID WEIGALL

FIRST PUBLISHED IN GREAT BRITAIN IN 1987 BY
B. T. BATSFORD LTD
4 FITZHARDINGE STREET
LONDON W1H 0AH
ENGLAND

FIRST PUBLISHED IN THE UNITED STATES IN 1987 BY
OXFORD UNIVERSITY PRESS, INC
200 MADISON AVENUE
NEW YORK
NY 10016

OXFORD IS A REGISTERED TRADEMARK OF OXFORD UNIVERSITY PRESS

ISBN 0–19–520610–X

LIBRARY OF CONGRESS CATALOGING-IN-PUBLICATION DATA

WEIGALL, DAVID.
  BRITAIN AND THE WORLD, 1815–1986.

  BIBLIOGRAPHY: P.
  INCLUDES INDEX.
  1. GREAT BRITAIN——FOREIGN RELATIONS——DICTIONARIES.
2. INTERNATIONAL RELATIONS——DICTIONARIES.   I. TITLE.
DA45.W45     1987       327.41       87–11133
ISBN 0–19–520610–X

PRINTING (LAST DIGIT): 9 8 7 6 5 4 3 2 1

PRINTED IN GREAT BRITAIN

# CONTENTS

ACKNOWLEDGEMENTS ............................................. 6

LIST OF MAPS ...................................................... 6

PREFACE ............................................................... 7

*Britain and the World 1815–1986* ................. 9

CHRONOLOGICAL TABLE .................................. 227

MAPS ................................................................... 241

# ACKNOWLEDGEMENTS

Particular thanks are due to Dr Paul Stafford and Dr John Wolffe for their invaluable assistance with some parts of this book. I am grateful, too, to Mrs Pippa Temple for her help with the chronology. George Weidenfeld and Nicolson Ltd should be thanked for their permission to reproduce the maps, which are taken from the following Martin Gilbert atlases: *American History Atlas*, *British History Atlas* and *First World War Atlas*. My greatest indebtedness is to my wife and children for their continuous support, understanding and patience.

David Weigall

# LIST OF MAPS

| | | |
|---|---|---|
| 1 | THE AMERICAS 1823–1916 | 241 |
| 2 | BRITAIN AND FRANCE IN AFRICA 1876–1904 | 242 |
| 3 | THE BOER WAR 1899–1902 | 243 |
| 4 | THE ANGLO-RUSSIAN DOMINANCE IN CENTRAL ASIA 1907–1914 | 244 |
| 5 | BRITAIN AND GERMANY IN THE FAR EAST BY 1914 | 245 |
| 6 | BRITISH DIPLOMACY 1904–1914 | 246 |
| 7 | THE FIRST WORLD WAR 1914–1918 | 247 |
| 8 | PEACE TREATIES AND CONFERENCES 1919–1932 | 248 |
| 9 | BRITAIN AND ABYSSINIA 1935 | 249 |
| 10 | BRITISH DIPLOMACY 1939 | 250 |
| 11 | WARTIME CONFERENCES 1941–1945 | 251 |
| 12 | BRITAIN AND THE MIDDLE EAST 1919–1967 | 252 |

# PREFACE

This book, arranged alphabetically, is intended to be used as a standard work of reference on British foreign policy and international relations. It includes historical and biographical entries and definitions of the terms and concepts used in diplomacy and international relations, essential to an understanding of the recent past and the contemporary world. It is hoped that students and teachers of modern history, international relations and world affairs in sixth forms, colleges and universities will find it a constantly valuable companion in their studies and researches. The general reader concerned with these subjects should also find much interest and profitable guidance here.

The study of foreign policy and external relations at once confronts the student or general reader with an – often baffling – abundance of references, allusions, concepts and complexities. This book is written to encourage clarification – to define these concepts and to bring together succinctly and in handy form a mass of information otherwise only accessible through reference to a very wide range of books and other sources.

Recent historical research has added new dimensions to our understanding of external policy, bringing prominently to our attention the role, for instance, of financial, economic and strategic considerations, the influence of public opinion and of domestic political and social concerns. It cannot be said that these new appraisals have made the study of British diplomacy, foreign policy formulation and the motivations behind it more simple, though they have undoubtedly made it more fascinating. As Joseph Frankel commented in his *British Foreign Policy, 1945–1973*:

> With the variety and complexity of her post-imperial commitments, her widespread commercial interests abroad and the sophistication of her domestic political system, Britain's foreign policy is one of the most complex – if not the most complex – of the foreign policies of all countries.

The purpose of the following pages is to evaluate as well as to inform and, without over-simplification, to render these complexities as comprehensible as possible. Whether readers want to find out about the Eastern Question, Britain's relations with Fascist Italy, the Venezuelan Crisis of 1895, Ernest Bevin's contribution to foreign affairs, the Two-Power Standard or the International Monetary Fund, they will find entries here on these topics.

Included among the entries are extended articles on the bilateral relations between Britain and the major powers. These are to be found at the appropriate alphabetical point under the name of the country concerned; e.g. for Anglo-French Relations see: *France, Britain and*. These entries will be found to provide a very helpful framework of reference for many of the other entries.

It must be emphasized that this is not a dictionary of the British Empire and Commonwealth, but of Britain's external relations and of the terms used in international relations. The first – a dictionary of empire – would have been a very different undertaking. The significance of the British Empire and Commonwealth in the history of British foreign policy and international relations is considered, however, in a long entry (see: Empire and Commonwealth, The British) but, for the most part, the domestic developments and internal affairs of the British dependencies and members of the Commonwealth have not been included.

There are numerous biographical entries, including, for example, ones on every British foreign secretary since 1815. These entries concentrate essentially on their subjects' contribution to foreign policy, or influence upon international affairs, and set out to evaluate their significance in this context. Detailed analyses of treaties and diplomatic disputes are given and, as noted above, definitions of the concepts and terms essential for understanding international relations. The Dictionary does not aspire to provide a comprehensive coverage of British warfare over the period since the defeat of Napoleon I, but readers will find articles on the wars in which Britain has been involved, a number of entries on the key engagements, such as the battles of the Atlantic and the Somme, and some biographical entries of relevance here, such as those on Baron Fisher and Earl Haig.

The entries have been comprehensively cross-referenced with asterisks in the text to enable readers to find their way as quickly and efficiently as possible about the book, and to pinpoint further relevant figures, concepts and events. A few very common terms such as 'convention', 'protocol' and 'aggression', though they appear among the entries, are not cross-referenced, because this seemed a needless, and possibly misleading, distraction for readers, who do not need to be referred to the concept of aggression in international law every time they read the word.

Where appropriate, as with very many of the entries, suggested reading available in English is offered for those who want to pursue the topic further. A number of the more substantial entries provide a considerable range of further books for consideration.

The Dictionary concludes with a comprehensive chronology of international relations, followed by maps. Entries in capitals in the chronology indicate those events, treaties and diplomatic engagements in which Britain participated. The maps are annotated to provide maximum historical guidance.

*Cambridge*                                                                                      David Weigall
*May 1986*

# BRITAIN & THE WORLD
## 1815–1986

# A

**ABERDEEN**, George Hamilton-Gordon, Earl of (1784–1860). Conservative Foreign Secretary 1828–30, 1841–6; Colonial Secretary 1834–5; Prime Minister 1852–5. Aberdeen was a close friend of *Castlereagh (1769–1822), who sent him as Ambassador to Vienna in 1813 where, although somewhat dominated by Metternich, he proved himself an effective representative of British interests. His time in Austria combined with extensive European travel to give him a less insular perspective than *Canning (1770–1827) or *Palmerston (1784–1865). During his first period as Foreign Secretary he was overshadowed by *Wellington (1769–1852), but increasingly came to assert his own views, especially in furthering the cause of Greek independence which was guaranteed by France, Russia and Britain in the Protocol of London of 3 February 1830. He also presided at the early sessions of the London Conference on Belgium.

The 1830s, apart from a brief interlude as Colonial Secretary in which Aberdeen made a mark with humane and reforming policies, were spent in active opposition to Palmerston. Returning to the Foreign Office in 1841, Aberdeen inherited a legacy of confrontation from his rival, relations with the United States and France having become particularly strained. Aberdeen made concessions in North America, especially in boundary disputes in Maine and Oregon, which he believed an acceptable price for obtaining harmonious relations with the United States. He enjoyed some success in conciliating France, but relations were threatened by clashes over Morocco and Tahiti in 1844 and Aberdeen's fragile entente was shattered in 1847 by the *Spanish Marriages Affair.

In December 1852 Aberdeen became Prime Minister, heading a coalition of Whigs and Peelite Conservatives. The government was a weak one whose divisions became painfully evident in 1853 in the face of deteriorating relations with Russia. Characteristically Aberdeen, though no pacifist, favoured conciliation, while Palmerston and *Russell (1792–1878) wished to adopt a stronger line against the Tsar. The outbreak of the *Crimean War (1854–6) in March 1854 was therefore a serious blow to Aberdeen's credibility, and subsequent military mismanagement led to the fall of his government in January 1855 when he was succeeded by Palmerston.

This ignominious end to Aberdeen's career led him to be labelled as a weak and incompetent minister who sacrificed essential British interests. There is some justice in this assessment. In eschewing Palmerstonian brinkmanship Aberdeen erred too far in the other direction in failing adequately to appreciate that dissimulation and bluff are integral to diplomacy. Nevertheless he was capable of firm action when he saw the need for it, while his commitment to the peaceful resolution of international differences made him in this respect the political heir of Castlereagh.

CHAMBERLAIN, M. E., *Lord Aberdeen*, Longman, 1983.

CONACHER, J. B., *The Aberdeen Coalition, 1852–1855*, Cambridge University Press, 1968.

**Abyssinian War** (1935–6). The colonial conquest launched without declaration of war by

Fascist Italy. It began when Italian troops invaded Abyssinia on 3 October 1935, moving southwards from Eritrea and northwards from Italian Somaliland. The capture of Addis Ababa by Marshal Badoglio, after a campaign which had included the use of air power and poison gas, on 5 May 1936, led three days later to Mussolini's proclamation of 'a Fascist Empire'.

Even though this proved a test case for the *League of Nations' capacity to enforce *collective security, the Italian dictator Mussolini had judged, correctly, from the outset that neither Britain nor France would wish to run the risk of war. They would not, therefore, impose a blockade or close the *Suez Canal. While the League branded Italy as the aggressor, it only imposed limited sanctions. Loans and imports were prohibited and arms and certain war-related materials were embargoed. Mussolini on the one hand encouraged Western beliefs that a negotiated settlement was possible, while on the other raising the spectre of possible European war if, for instance, oil sanctions were imposed. Britain and France accordingly pursued a negotiated settlement outside the League. The *Hoare–Laval Pact (1935), with its proposals to carve up Abyssinia, which embodied such a settlement, was disowned by the British Government in the face of the strongest parliamentary criticism, not to mention outside pressure, such as that from the *League of Nations Union. The Government was in a dilemma, having only recently staunchly reaffirmed its support for collective security and the League. In fact the idea of collective security under the League suffered from the Abyssinian War a reverse from which it did not recover. Hitler took advantage of the distraction and irresolution of Britain and France to occupy the Rhineland on 6 March 1936 and the war laid the basis for the future understanding between Italy and Germany. Sanctions against Italy were lifted on 4 July 1936. Five years later Britain reconquered Abyssinia and the Emperor Haile Selassie was reinstated.

BAER, G. W., *Test Case: Italy, Ethiopia and the League of Nations*, Hoover Institution, Stanford, California, 1976.

HARDIE, F. M., *The Abyssinian Crisis*, Batsford, 1974.

WALEY, D. P., *British Public Opinion and the Abyssinian War 1935–6*, Temple Smith, 1976.

**Aden.** The port situated at the south-west tip of the Arabian Peninsula. As well as being an important sea port it has historically been of considerable strategic importance as it guards entry into the Red Sea. In the 1820s Britain was very anxious to prevent the designs of *Mehemet Ali, ruler of Egypt, who was at war with his nominal suzerain the Sultan of Constantinople. After the Treaty of *Unkiar-Skelessi (1833), in which Tsar Nicholas I had agreed to protect the Turks against attack, Britain feared that Turkey would fast become a dependant of the Russian Empire. Britain accordingly occupied Aden in 1839. The port was subsequently made into a Crown Colony and the hinterland into a protectorate. Its strategic importance endured as it lay on the imperial sea route to India and beyond. The completion of the *Suez Canal further enhanced its significance. In 1967, after some years of rebel fighting, Aden was granted independence as the Yemen People's Republic.

**Adrianople, Treaty of** (1829). Signed on 14 September following the Russian victory over Turkey in the war of 1828–9. This gave Russia territory down to the Danube, garrison rights in the Principalities (later Rumania) and concessions in the Caucasus. The war arose from the *Greek War of Independence (1821–29). The treaty's terms influenced Britain, who was anxious to prevent Russian expansion at the expense of the Ottoman Empire, to ensure that the boundaries of the new Greek state should not be drawn too widely.

**Afghan Wars.** The First Afghan War broke out in 1839 and lasted until 1842. Britain was afraid of the penetration of Russo–Persian influence in northern India. She had accordingly replaced the existing Barakzay rulers of Kabul and Kandahar by Shah Shuja 'al Mulk, supported by British and Indian troops and advised by a British envoy, Macnaghten. This led to riots and a major insurrection in November 1841. The British garrison from Kabul was destroyed during its retreat to Jalalabad. The Second Afghan War (1879-81) again resulted from Anglo-Russian rivalry. The Afghan ruler, Shir Ali, had received a Russian mission at Kabul and refused to accept a British one. A British force occupied Kabul, expelled the Amir and made the Treaty of Gandamak (1879) with his son and successor, Yaqub. A British Resident, Sir Louis Cavagnari, was installed in Kabul and Britain established control over Afghan foreign relations. Following the murder of Cavagnari and a new uprising, Britain reconquered Afghanistan in a series of campaigns which included General Roberts's celebrated march from Kabul to relieve the garrison at Kandahar. An agreement was subsequently reached with the new Amir, Abd al-Rahman, to exclude Russian influence. During *World War I (1914-18) Afghanistan maintained a position of strict neutrality. The Third Afghan War (1919) resulted from the proclamation of complete independence by the new ruler, Amanullah, which Britain was not disposed to accept. Though his attack on British forces was repelled without difficulty, Britain abandoned her attempt to control Afghan foreign relations in the Treaty of Rawalpindi (1919).

CURZON, G. N., *Russia in Central Asia*, Longmans, 1889.

NORRIS, J. A., *First Afghan War*, Cambridge University Press, 1967.

SPEAR, P., *The Oxford History of India*, 4th ed., Oxford University Press, 1981.

YAPP. M., *Strategies of British India: Britain, Iran and Afghanistan, 1789–1850*, Oxford University Press, 1980.

**Aggression.** In international relations: the use of armed force by a state against the sovereignty, political independence or territorial integrity of another state. It is frequently used as a term in modern diplomacy and international law, but a clear and unequivocal definition has proved elusive. It has been difficult to achieve a consensus on where the distinction lies between aggression and legitimate self-defence. Disarmament talks have, likewise, found the greatest difficulty in reaching an agreed list of 'defensive' as opposed to 'offensive' weapons. Powers have shown great reluctance in accepting the pursuit of their own national interests as 'aggressive'. However, a number of attempts have been made by international bodies or gatherings to fix responsibility for aggression in particular cases.

The *Versailles Treaty (1919) referred to 'the aggression of Germany' and the Covenant of the *League of Nations included the undertaking by members 'to respect and preserve against external aggression the territorial integrity and existing political independence of all members'. The League was provided with sanctions against an aggressor, but its constituent states showed a marked inclination to preserve their own freedom of action. The

*Geneva Protocol (1924), which Britain refused to support, attempted to define aggression in terms of any power rejecting arbitration – but this was not generally accepted. It is sometimes argued that since aggression is an inescapable part of the 'international anarchy' of nation states only a world government with clear laws and respected executive powers (such as the League did not have) could aspire effectively to outlaw it. In a number of cases the League named aggressors, Japan, Italy and the Soviet Union, for instance. As a result these powers left the League and continued their aggressive actions without any effective constraint. After *World War II (1939–45) we find the indictment for aggression also extended to individuals in international relations. Those tried in the Nuremberg and Tokyo trials, for instance, were punished for waging aggressive war and for committing crimes against humanity. The Charter of the *United Nations does not define aggression, contenting itself with the formulation that the Security Council and the General Assembly are authorized to describe specific actions as aggression. It is now common to distinguish between direct aggression between states and indirect aggression, the provision of arms and relief to an existing aggressor.

**Agrément.** Diplomatic term meaning 'consent'. It is used to indicate that a state considers a particular appointment as a diplomatic envoy to be acceptable and is willing to receive him/her from the sending state. The latter requests agrément before accrediting a diplomat.

**Aix-la-Chapelle Congress** (1818). Meeting of Britain, Austria, Russia and Prussia between 29 September and 21 November 1818. The 2nd Peace of *Paris (1815) had imposed on France the payment of 700 million francs over a five year term. Allied armies of occupation had remained to ensure payment and good behaviour by France. The congress settled the question of the remainder of the indemnity payments and arranged the withdrawal of Allied troops. The Treaty of Aix-la-Chapelle was signed by the Allies with France on 9 October 1818. France was formally admitted to the *Concert of Europe as an equal member in a newly constituted Quintuple Alliance (1815). As a safeguard the *Quadruple Alliance (1815) was also secretly renewed. Aix-la-Chapelle can be said finally to have terminated the episode of the Napoleonic wars which had militarily ended at *Waterloo (1815). At the same time it marked the first clear post-war divergence of Britain from her wartime allies. Discussions about future gatherings of the powers raised misgivings in the British Cabinet that the other powers might afford support to reactionary regimes to which British public opinion would be hostile, and involve Britain in actions in which she did not wish to be implicated. Lord *Castlereagh (1769–1822) reflected this concern. He refused to accept a proposal by Tsar Alexander I by which every sovereign would be assured of his throne and territory. This foreshadowed the subsequent rift between Britain and the powers of the *Holy Alliance (1815) over the right of intervention in the domestic affairs of other states.

KISSINGER, H., *A World Restored: Metternich, Castlereagh and the Problem of Peace*, Weidenfeld and Nicolson, 1957.
SKED, A., ed., *Europe's Balance of Power 1815–1848*, Macmillan, 1979

**Alabama Incident** (1864). The *Alabama* was a Confederate raider ship which had been constructed in Liverpool. Between 1862 and 1864 it inflicted very considerable damage on the merchant shipping of the Northern states, destroying, capturing or ransoming no fewer than 64 prizes before being sunk near Cherbourg on 19 June 1864. The United States sought damages from Britain for its depredations, claiming that by allowing her construction and that of other raiders of commerce and allowing them to leave port Britain had abused her neutral status. The *Alabama* incident caused serious strain in Anglo-American relations both during and after the Civil War. In 1871 it was referred with the agreement of *Gladstone (1809–98) to an international tribunal. A compromise settlement was agreed in the Treaty of Washington of 1871, by which Britain was to award £3¼ million pounds in compensation to the United States. This arrangement aroused some protest on both sides of the Atlantic. The sum awarded was only one-third of that claimed in damages, while in Britain Gladstone was criticized for conceding an award at all. It represented, however, an encouraging example of how a major diplomatic dispute could be resolved through *arbitration rather than force.

COOK, A. *The Alabama Claims, American Politics and Anglo-American Relations 1865–1872*, Cornell University Press, New York, 1975.

**Alamein, El, Battle of** (1942). In January 1942, having checked British forces in North Africa, the German commander Marshal Erwin Rommel launched a second offensive which succeeded in pushing the British 8th Army back to the Egyptian frontier at El Alamein, 60 miles west of Alexandria, close to the strategically vital *Suez Canal. With the fall of Tobruk Winston *Churchill (1874–1965) had sacked General Auchinleck and appointed Alexander as Commander-in-Chief with General *Montgomery as 8th Army commander. Montgomery regrouped the 8th Army as a force of 150,000 and waited to launch a counter-attack until he had gained air superiority and massed considerable tank strength. The British forces had the advantage of supplies through the Suez Canal. Rommel's supplies, on the other hand, were dependent on transport by convoys which were being destroyed from the British base in Malta.

The 2nd Battle of El Alamein (23 October–4 November) was a British victory which did much to restore morale at home in Britain after a series of defeats. While it was not of such crucial importance as the larger battles between Germany and Russia on the Eastern Front, its significance should not be underestimated. Though many of the remaining Afrika Corps escaped, the victory meant that Egypt was now secured. The 8th Army advanced over 1,400 miles within six months, ejecting German and Italian forces from North Africa. On 7 November Anglo-American forces landed in French North Africa and British military action was merged into a coalition war against the *Axis.

BARNETT, C., *The Battle of El Alamein: Decision in the Desert*, Macmillan, 1964.

**Alaska Boundary Controversy** (1896–1903). Between Britain and the United States over the Alaskan–Canadian boundary. In 1867 the treaty by which the United States acquired Alaska from Russia upheld the agreed boundary established by the British and Russians (see: *Anglo-Russian Convention (1825)). An unresolved question as to whether the demarcation between Alaska and British Columbia should be measured from the islands in the sea or from the shoreline presented no difficulty until the discovery of gold in the Canadian Klondike in 1896. At this point the issue as to

who controlled the headwaters of the Lynn Canal, the longest inlet into the Klondike region, became very important – since control there would mean a dominant position over its commerce. The controversy was referred in 1903 to a mixed commission in the Hay–Herbert Treaty. The final line was a compromise between the Canadian and United States claims, though the Lynn Canal was allowed to be under United States control. This dispute had a wider significance in removing the last serious obstacle to Anglo-American rapprochement in the early years of the century.
CAMPBELL, C. S., Jr, *Anglo-American Understanding, 1898–1903*, Johns Hopkins Press, Baltimore, 1957.

**ALBERT**, Prince Consort (1819–1861). The younger son of Duke Ernest of Saxe-Coburg, he married Queen *Victoria (1819–1901) in 1840. He held a position technically unknown to the constitution, but exercised great influence over the Queen. While he served as a major architect of constitutional monarchy at home, in foreign affairs he envisaged a more active role for the Crown, maintaining an international outlook and close personal contacts with other European courts. Albert favoured constitutional liberalism and nationalist aspirations, especially in Germany, but was a determined upholder of the dignity of monarchs and a non-interventionist. A serious clash with *Palmerston (1784–1865) thus developed in the late 1840s and the Queen and Prince were instrumental in securing his dismissal by Russell (1792–1878) in December 1851, but relations improved after Palmerston became Prime Minister in 1855. In Germany Albert sought to further the advance of constitutionalism by the marriage in 1858 of his eldest daughter Victoria to Prince Frederick William, the eventual heir to the Prussian throne, a policy which failed owing to the early deaths of Frederick and Albert himself. In 1861 he helped to avert war with the United States by urging on the government a conciliatory attitude in the *Trent Affair.
EYCK, F. *The Prince Consort*, Chatto and Windus (1959).
JAMES, R. R. *Albert, Prince Consort*, Hamish Hamilton, 1983.

**Algeciras Conference** (1906). This followed the 1st *Moroccan Crisis (1905) and dealt with the international issue of the government and policing of Morocco. This had become significant from the 1890s with the decline of the nominally independent empire of the Sultan of Morocco and the growing intervention in its affairs of France and Spain. The conference agreed in the Algeciras Act to a Franco-Spanish police force under a neutral (Swiss) Inspector-General. The preceding crisis had represented a deliberate testing by Germany of the strength of the *Anglo-French Entente (1904). At Algeciras German hopes that the accession of a Liberal ministry in England (in 1905) might weaken the entente were disappointed. Britain, on the contrary, together with Italy and Russia, rallied to France against Germany in the negotiations. The result was to confirm French influence in Morocco and to inflict a diplomatic defeat on Germany. In January 1906 the British Foreign Secretary, Sir Edward *Grey (1862–1933), sanctioned the opening of secret staff talks between the British and French military (see: *Anglo-French Military Conversations (1906–14) ).

**Algiers Conference** (1943). Held between 29 May and 3 June 1943, involving Winston *Churchill (1874–1965) and leading Allied commanders. It discussed Allied strategy following the victory over German forces in the North Africa campaign. There was a division of view between Churchill and the Americans. He pressed for the invasion of the Italian Peninsula after the capture of Sicily, but General George Marshall in particular was apprehensive that this would delay and detract from the effectiveness of the invasion of France. An alternative proposal to take Corsica and Sardinia was rejected. The Algiers deliberations were inconclusive. It was agreed to defer a decision until the battle for Sicily was over.
FEIS, H., *Churchill, Roosevelt, Stalin: The War they Waged and the Peace They Sought*, Princeton University Press, Princeton, N.J., 1967.
MCNEILL, W. H., *America, Britain and Russia: Their Cooperation and Conflict, 1941–46*, Oxford University Press, 1953.

**Alien.** A national of one state residing in another without possessing its nationality or citizenship. The general practice is to concede aliens the right to own property, to contract, to engage in the professions and to allow freedom of speech and religious worship. The alien can become the focus of international dispute when the rights of his person or property are violated. Some states maintain that the standards of the national jurisdiction under which the alien is living should be final, and that he is entitled to no more protection than another citizen. Other countries, including Britain and the United States, argue that if the justice meted out by the national courts is below that standard, then the equality of treatment between the alien and citizen is not sufficient and the government of the state of which the alien is a national may interpose or intervene on his behalf.

**Alma, Battle of the** (1854). The first major military engagement of the *Crimean War (1854–6), which followed the disembarkation of British, French and Turkish forces near Evpatoria on 14 September. The battle was fought on 20 September. The Russian commander Prince Menshikov had entrenched himself with a force of 35,000 on the heights above the Alma River as the invading forces advanced along the Crimean coast towards *Sevastopol. The British contingent under Lord Raglan were 26,000 strong. The Russian forces were driven from their position with the Allies incurring 3,000 casualties. The Allies could have marched on to Sevastopol at this point and taken it because the Russian defences were still inadequately secured. But the allied commanders halted their detachments for a couple of days and then moved eastwards to attack *Balaklava, ignorant of Russian vulnerability at Sevastopol. Had the allies lost the battle they would have been forced to leave the Crimea. In that sense it was the decisive battle of the war.

**AMERY,** Leopold (1873–1955). Conservative statesman and journalist. He was born in India, the son of the head of the Indian Forest Department. As an international correspondent for *The Times* of London (he also edited the *Times History of the South African War*) he became a strong advocate of British imperialism and a lifelong supporter of the policy of *Imperial Preference advanced by Joseph *Chamberlain (1836–1914). He served as Under-Secretary to Sir Alfred (later Viscount) *Milner at the Colonial Office (1919–21), parliamentary and financial secretary to the Admiralty (1921–3), Colonial Secretary (1924–9) and Dominions Secretary (1925–9).

Stanley Baldwin's refusal to adopt Protection served to alienate Amery from the Conservatives and his fervent imperialist enthusiasm

excluded him from the National Government. During the 1930s he became a noted opponent of *appeasement and attacked disarmament. He was dismissive of the concept of effective *collective security through the *League of Nations. The notion of this organization having the power to coerce he described as 'imaginary imperial robes'. He showed some interest in the notion of Paneuropean confederation advanced by Count Coudenhove-Kalergi.

In May 1940 he mounted a celebrated attack on Neville *Chamberlain (1869–1940) in the House of Commons, quoting Oliver Cromwell: 'You have sat too long here for any good you have been doing. Depart, I say, and let us have done with you. In the name of God, go!' When *Churchill (1874–1965) succeeded as Prime Minister Amery accepted office in the Coalition Government as Secretary of State for India and Burma (1940–5). In 1935, unlike Churchill, he had accepted the Government of India Act. He now worked to bring India to independence within the *Commonwealth. His reputation as a strong imperialist, though, made it difficult for him to handle Indian affairs at a time when India was opposed to participation in the war. He was made Companion of Honour in 1945, the year in which he lost his parliamentary seat in the Labour landslide victory.

AMERY, L. C. M. S., *My Political Life* (3 vols), Hutchinson, 1953–5.

BARNES, J. and NICHOLSON, D., eds., *The Leo Amery Diaries, vol. 1, 1896–1929*, Hutchinson, 1980.

**ANGELL,** Sir Norman (1872–1967). Prominent internationalist and publicist. He was educated in France and Switzerland and worked as a labourer in the United States before embarking on a journalistic career. From 1904 to 1912 he edited Lord Northcliffe's *Continental Daily Mail*, which gave him a first-hand appreciation of the problems and tensions of European society during the years leading up to *World War I (1914–18). Though his first book, *Patriotism under Three Flags*, came out in 1903, the work which established his international reputation was *The Great Illusion* (1910) (originally published in 1909 as *Europe's Optical Illusion*). He advanced the view that in modern circumstances with industrially advanced nations and 'credit-dependent wealth' war was economically profitless for the aggressor and that 'on a general realization of this truth depends the

solution of the problem of armaments and warfare'. If conquest, he argued, 'is not to be self-injurious it must respect the enemy's property, in which case it becomes economically futile'. This message was addressed to the Germany of Kaiser William II. Angell's ideas were the object of much misinterpretation; he did not, for instance, argue that war was impossible. Throughout his prolific career as writer and pamphleteer on international affairs his abiding concern was defence. 'Angellism', as it was called, was a significant influence in Britain in the years leading to World War I though as a general idea rather than a concrete proposal for avoiding war. Subsequently he was a prominent advocate of strong international institutions and one of the pioneer influences behind the *League of Nations. His belief in giving forceful backing to international law was clearly articulated, for instance, in *The Unseen Assassins* (1932). His argument that the remedy for the 'international anarchy' was internationalism and education in the acceptance of international institutions underlay the mainstream of liberal thinking between the wars and the concept of *collective security. Briefly, between 1929 and 1931 he was Labour Member of Parliament for North Bradford. In 1933 he was awarded the Nobel Peace Prize.
ANGELL, SIR N., *After All*, Hamish Hamilton, 1951; *The Great Illusion*, Heinemann, 1910. MARRIN, A., *Sir Norman Angell*, Twayne Publishers, Boston, Mass., 1979.

**Anglo-American League.** This was an organization founded in July 1898 by a number of prominent Englishmen including *Asquith (1852–1928) and Rudyard Kipling. Its aim was 'to secure the most cordial and constant co-operation between Britain and the United States' and it reflected the Anglo-American rapprochement of the day. The League was defunct by 1903.

**Anglo-American Relations,** see UNITED STATES, BRITAIN AND THE

**Anglo-French Convention** (1899). Signed on 21 March 1899, this agreement resolved the dispute which had led to the major *Fashoda Crisis the year before. It upheld British control of the Upper Nile and drew up clear British and French *spheres of influence in East Africa. The French climb-down over Fashoda reflected

French official concern at the prospect of finding herself simultaneously in conflict with Britain and Germany. This rapprochement led in 1904 to the *Anglo-French Entente.

**Anglo-French Entente** (1904). Signed by Lord *Lansdowne (1845–1927) and M. Paul Cambon in London on 8 April 1904. It took the form of three conventions settling outstanding matters of colonial dispute and had been preceded in the previous year by the exchange of state visits between King Edward VII and President Loubet.

The heart of the agreement was the French recognition of Egypt as a sphere of British influence in return for acceptance of France's predominance in Morocco. (France undertook at the same time that no fortifications should be constructed which might threaten *Gibraltar.) This trade-off had originally been suggested by Lord *Salisbury (1830–1903) and had attracted the growing support of the French colonial party. Other areas of colonial rivalry were included – Newfoundland fishing-rights, Siam, the New Hebrides and Madagascar – in this measure of reconciliation. From the British point of view it meant a welcome reduction of overseas liabilities, particularly welcome in view of the Russo-Japanese War which could have threatened the risk of a conflict between Russia and Britain as Japan's ally. Though this was not its original purpose, the entente increasingly came to be seen as a deliberate counterweight to the growing power and ambition of Wilhelmine Germany. It was tested by Germany during the 1st and 2nd *Moroccan Crises (1905, 1911) and transformed into an alliance on 3 September 1914 at the beginning of *World War I (1914–18). In 1907 the Anglo-French Entente was expanded by the inclusion of Russia. The new grouping became known as the Triple Entente (during World War I the term Entente Powers was commonly used as a synonym for the Anglo-French-Russian alliance against the *Central Powers). The Anglo-French Entente was followed by *Anglo-French Military Conversations (1906–14). The Foreign Secretary, Sir Edward *Grey (1862–1933) was subsequently criticized in some quarters for involving Britain with France through these discussions to an extent which was not recognized until later – the Cabinet were only notified of them in 1911. On the other hand, it was argued elsewhere that the entente was not adequately definite in its commitment to France to dissuade Germany from war against her.

MONGER, G., *The End of Isolation*, Nelson, 1963.

STEINER, Z. S., *Britain and the Origins of the First World War*, Macmillan, 1977.

WILSON, K. M., *The Policy of the Entente: Essays on the Determinants of British Foreign Policy, 1904–14*, Cambridge University Press, 1985.

**Anglo-French Military Conversations** (1906–14). Confidential discussions between January 1906 and the outbreak of hostilities in August 1914. They followed the request made during the 1st *Moroccan Crisis (1905) by the French that the British Government should agree to work out a common strategy in the event of conflict with Germany. Early in 1906 senior British army officers suggested that the despatch of 100,000 British troops to France would be of more value than the Admiralty's plan for a lightning military–naval raid on the German coast. The British Foreign Secretary, Sir Edward *Grey (1862–1933) initially obtained approval for these talks from the Prime Minister, Sir Henry *Campbell-Bannerman (1836–1908), the Chancellor of the Exchequer and the War Minister. At the time when these were instigated Grey was faced with a serious continental crisis and with a pending General Election. These help to explain his secretiveness, but the fact that the existence of the conversations was not divulged to the Cabinet as a whole until 1911 when naval talks were also authorized, as well as the fact that they extended the scope of the *Anglo-French Entente (1904), were the object of much criticism in certain quarters. Grey was at pains to emphasize the hypothetical character of the undertakings, but in the light of the subsequent British involvement in *World War I (1914–18) this seemed disingenuous or dishonest. The conversations meant that – inevitably – the Entente had become something much closer than the original settlement of outstanding colonial differences had implied. Discussions with Belgian staff officers in Brussels also began in 1906.

KENNEDY, P. ed., *The War Plans of the Great Powers, 1880–1914*, Allen and Unwin, 1979.

WILSON, K. M., *The Policy of the Entente: Essays on the Determinants of British Foreign Policy, 1904–14*, Cambridge University Press, 1985.

**Anglo-French Relations,** see FRANCE, BRITAIN AND

**Anglo-French Union** (1940). A proposal issued on 16 June 1940 by the British Prime Minister, Winston *Churchill (1874–1965) to the French Premier, M. Paul Reynaud, for an indissoluble union between the two countries. It was a prototype for complete union and would have involved the surrender of national sovereignty. It provided for joint defence (a single war cabinet to be entrusted with direction of British and French forces), foreign and economic policies, a formal association of the two parliaments and joint citizenship. Resources were to be pooled for peacetime reconstruction, and the proposal also appealed to the United States to increase economic and material assistance.

On the face of it, the offer represented a dramatic departure from the insular traditions of British foreign policy and the chequered history of Anglo-French relations. In fact, though, it was a last desperate effort to keep France in the war against Nazi Germany. On the British side the proposal was not the expression of any long-term political aspiration towards European unity. With the collapse of France Britain wanted her consent to a French armistice with Germany conditional on the sailing of the French fleet to British ports. De Gaulle, the leader of the Free French, had reported to the British War Cabinet a conversation with the French Prime Minister which indicated that an offer of union would dissuade the French Cabinet from concluding an armistice. Without discussing the mooted arrangements with Britain, the French Cabinet voted for armistice and Reynaud resigned. When in 1945 Churchill was asked in Parliament whether the offer still represented the policy of the British Government, Churchill unequivocally replied that it did not.

GATES, E. M., *End of the Affair: The Collapse of the Anglo-French Alliance, 1939–40*, University of California Press, Berkeley, 1981.

**Anglo-German Agreement** (1899). A settlement of rival colonial claims in the Pacific. This agreement provided for Britain's surrender of her interests in Samoa and led the following year to the sharing-out of the islands between Germany and the United States. The local background to this settlement was the breakdown of the tripartite condominium of

Britain, Germany and the United States over Samoa on the death of King Malietoa Laupepe in 1898 and the outbreak of civil war, with the British and American consuls and the German consul throwing their support behind rival factions. At this point the powers despatched a commission to Samoa to restore peace, form a temporary government and research a final settlement of their own conflicting interests.

The international context of this was the growing imperial rivalry between Britain and Germany, Britain's diplomatic isolation and her conflict with the Boers. Both the British Colonial Secretary, Joseph *Chamberlain (1836–1914) and the German foreign ministry were eager to come to a quick resolution of the Samoan problem and to reduce tension between their countries. Negotiations were held between September and November 1899. Britain yielded its Samoan interest in return for a strengthening of its position in Tonga and some territorial gain in the Solomon Islands. The agreement ended nominal Samoan sovereignty over the islands.

**Anglo-German Naval Agreement** (1935). The London naval agreement concluded on 18 June by an exchange of notes between Sir Samuel *Hoare and *Ribbentrop (1899–1945). Britain was anxious to limit the liabilities of her own naval defence commitments at a time when Japan in particular had refused to prolong her own naval limitation treaties. In the 1935 agreement Germany undertook not to build beyond 35% of British naval strength. She was, though, permitted to reach 45% of British submarine strength and in an emergency to have an equal number of submarines. This was a clear repudiation of the naval clauses of the Treaty of *Versailles (1919). While Hitler construed it as an indication of appeasing weakness on the part of the British government, an embittered France claimed that it undermined the solidarity of the *Stresa Front of Britain, France and Italy. The agreement contributed to very serious French distrust of Britain at a juncture when cooperation between the two powers against the growing German threat was essential.

MEDLICOTT, W. N., *Britain and Germany: The Search for Agreement, 1930–37*, Athlone Press, 1969.

**Anglo-German Navy Race.** A major rivalry in the period leading to *World War I (1914–18).

Since 1889 British naval construction had been governed by the requirements of the *Two-Power Standard. This demanded that the British navy should be stronger than the combined fleets of the next two naval powers. The expansionist German naval policy (*Flottenpolitik) embodied in the Navy Laws of 1898 and 1900 and the construction of Dreadnoughts from 1907, when combined with growing overseas trade, colonialism, demands for a German world role (*Weltpolitik) and German hostility towards the continued dominance of the British *Empire, convinced Britain that her position in the world was being gravely challenged. Enthusiastically supported by Kaiser William II and masterminded by Admiral von Tirpitz, the German naval construction programme had very great repercussions on both foreign and domestic policy in the two countries. Tirpitz believed that once the navy programme was through the 'danger zone' – the period in which it would be vulnerable to a British pre-emptive strike (see: *Copenhagen Complex) – it would make Germany sufficiently strong at sea for Britain not to risk a confrontation. He hoped that Britain could not challenge a navy which could inflict damage on such a scale that even if she emerged victorious she would be so weakened as not to be able to match the requirements of the Two-Power Standard any more.

These hopes were to prove illusory. Germany found that Britain, seeing the *Flottenpolitik* as a major threat to her imperial position and to the world *balance of power, increased the rate of her own naval construction so that the pace of naval armament was constantly accelerating with dramatic impact on national budgets in both countries. Britain introduced Dreadnoughts in 1906. In the *Anglo-French Entente (1904) and the *Anglo-Russian Convention (1907) she moved to rule out the prospect of conflict with France and Russia, her major rivals in the previous century. Various attempts were made to halt or slow the navy race but this proved impossible in the circumstances and climate of the time. Britain tended to regard the German navy as (in Winston Churchill's words) a 'luxury' while considering her own a vital necessity. Germany refused to cut back on naval programmes unless Britain gave a promise of neutrality in the event of a European war (see: *Haldane Mission (1912) ). While the German attempt to influence Britain by the construction of a large fleet failed to fulfil

Tirpitz's hopes it did much to contribute to the Anglo-German antagonism of the period and to the mood which made war possible in 1914. In the event, the kind of construction programme the two powers had undertaken turned out to be inappropriate to the war at sea as actually waged – as the Battle of *Jutland (1916) showed.

KENNEDY, P. M., *The Rise of the Anglo-German Antagonism 1860–1914*, Allen and Unwin, 1980.

MARDER, A. J., *From the Dreadnought to Scapa Flow: The Royal Navy in the Fisher Era 1904– 1919*, Vol. I. Oxford University Press, 1961.

WOODWARD, E. L., *Great Britain and the German Navy*, Oxford University Press, 1935.

**Anglo-German Relations**, see GERMANY, BRITAIN AND

**Anglo-Irish Treaty** (1921). Signed on 6 December, this provided for Ireland to become a self-governing dominion within the British *Empire, with the same constitutional status as Canada. This was given effect in English law when the 1922 Irish Free State Act repealed the 1920 Government of Ireland Act which had created a Northern Irish Parliament in Belfast and a Southern Irish one in Dublin. Although the treaty, remarkably, was between 'Great Britain and Ireland', it did not recognize the Dublin Parliament's right to speak for all of Ireland. Special provision was made for Ulster which could, and duly did, retain its status within the United Kingdom under the 1920 act by request from the Belfast parliament that Ulster should be excluded from Dublin's authority. If Belfast did so request, a tripartite commission was to re-adjust the boundary between the two parts of Ireland; and in negotiations before the treaty *Lloyd George (1863–1945) had led the Irish representatives to believe that the result would be to reduce Ulster so that it could not continue as a separate political unit. This did not happen, and a tripartite agreement of 1925 recognized the 1920 boundary.

Nationalist critics of the treaty within Ireland complained not only of partition, but also of the denial of republican status, towards which Dublin was progressively moving. Irish pressure was important in bringing about the Statute of *Westminster (1931), which conferred full parliamentary sovereignty on the Dominion legislatures. In 1937 the Free State

was renamed 'Eire', and declared the national territory to be the whole of Ireland. In 1938, to pre-empt unilateral action by Eire and improve relations with the De Valera government, Neville *Chamberlain (1869–1940) surrendered Britain's rights under the 1921 treaty to use the three west coast 'treaty ports' (Queenstown, Berehaven, and Lough Swilly) for the navy. Remaining constitutional links were ended in 1948.

GALLAGHER, F., *The Anglo-Irish Treaty*, Hutchinson, 1965.

MARTIN, G., 'The Irish Free State and the Evolution of the Commonwealth, 1921–49' in HYAM, R. and MARTIN, G., *Reappraisals in British Imperial History*, Macmillan, 1975.

**Anglo-Italian Mediterranean Pact** (1938). This was the result of long negotiations prompted by the British Prime Minister Neville *Chamberlain (1869–1940), who wanted to end international intervention in the *Spanish Civil War (1936–9). It was agreed on 16 April 1938 and it specified that Italy would withdraw her troops from Spain where they had in large numbers been supporting the rebel cause of General Franco, once the war had ended. Following this, Britain and Italy should help to preserve the status quo in the Mediterranean. Chamberlain was also keen to achieve a reconciliation with Italy after the rupture of the *Abyssinian War (1935–6) and hoped to draw Mussolini away from dependence on Germany. Italy appears to have seen the agreement in different terms: as a simple way of gaining international credit by agreeing to the end of her involvement while at the same time gaining Britain's acquiescence in her maintenance of troops in Spain until the nationalist cause had triumphed.

**Anglo-Italian Relations**, see ITALIAN UNIFICATION, BRITAIN AND, and also ITALY, FASCIST, BRITAIN AND

**Anglo-Japanese Alliance** (1902). This alliance played a major role in developments in the Far East especially in the period up to *World War I (1914–18). Signed on 30 January 1902 it was, initially, to continue in force for five years and provided for joint action if Russia in concert with any fourth power encroached on either British or Japanese interests. The British Foreign Secretary, Lord *Lansdowne (1845–1927) was backed by the First Lord of the Admiralty, whose advisers insisted that Britain needed the assistance of Japan if she were to maintain her position in the Far East against Russian and French ambitions. It was therefore advanced as a necessary reduction of Britain's burdensome strategic liabilities, and has commonly been presented as ending the period of so-called 'splendid isolation'. Britain and Japan agreed to recognize each other's special privileges and interests in China as well as Japan's interests in Korea.

Through the alliance Britain was able to assure herself of Japanese cooperation in maintaining a *balance of power among those nations vying for economic and political influence in China. Great care was taken in Britain to emphasize its defensive character. Later in 1902 the allies worked out a plan for major joint operations, apprehensive as they were of Russian pressure on northern China and Manchuria. These provisions did not come into effect during the Russo-Japanese War (1904–5) since the Russians fought without allies. Britain undoubtedly hoped by means of this alliance to reduce the risk of military conflict in the Far East. It arguably had the opposite effect, giving the Japanese confidence in the outcome of the war against Russia.

In August 1905 the terms of the alliance were broadened to provide for the defence of British interests in India and a more precise recognition of Japan's hegemony over Korea. Its term was extended to ten years. When it was still further modified in 1911 Britain was absolved from any obligation to support her ally against the United States in the event of a Japanese–United States conflict. The Japanese subsequently joined the Allies in World War I, their navy campaigning in the Mediterranean as well as eastern waters. After 1918 pressures mounted on Britain to terminate the alliance. Various factors were responsible: a rising fear of Japanese commerce, criticism from the United States and China of Japan's expansionist ambitions and domestic revulsion in Britain against the old alliance system which many tended to feel had contributed strongly to the outbreak of war in 1914. *Lloyd George (1863–1945) and *Curzon (1859–1925) were in favour of maintaining it (it had after all helped Britain to advance its interests in China while reducing the expense of its imperial commitment). However, it was terminated with the Four-Power Treaty of 1921.

LOWE, P. C., *Great Britain and Japan, 1911–15,* Macmillan, 1969.

NISH, I. H., *The Anglo-Japanese Alliance, 1894–1907,* Greenwood, 1977.
*Alliance in Decline, 1908–1923,* Athlone Press, 1972.

**Anglo-Japanese Commercial Treaty** (1894). This marked Japan's first major success in removing the commercial inequalities imposed by the Western trading nations in the *Ansei Commercial Treaties (1858). It was signed on 16 July 1894 but did not come into effect until 17 July 1899. It ended British rights to *extraterritoriality and partly restored Japanese rights to tariff autonomy. Other Western powers soon followed Britain in concluding similar agreements.

**Anglo-Polish Alliance** (1939). A Treaty of Mutual Assistance was signed on 25 August 1939. It followed the British guarantee to Poland of 31 March 1939 and formalized British assurances of military assistance to Poland in the event of her suffering aggression from 'a European power'. When Germany invaded Poland on 1 September, this provided the justification for Britain's declaration of war two days later. In March Neville *Chamberlain (1869–1940) had announced to the Commons: 'In the event of any action which clearly threatened Polish independence ... H. M. G. would feel themselves bound at once to lend the Polish Government all support in their power'. The bilateral treaty signed by Lord *Halifax (1881–1959) and Colonel Beck on 6 April had marked a new departure in British policy, for the first time guaranteeing an Eastern European state. As Duff *Cooper (1890–1954) put it: 'We left in the hands of one of the smaller powers whether or not Great Britain goes to war'.

Chamberlain's original guarantee was prompted by rumours in March that Poland and Rumania were about to be attacked by Hitler. There was a growing momentum of opposition at home against any further *appeasement of the dictators. Chamberlain was also aware of the accusation that Britain had encouraged the *Central Powers in 1914 by failing to make unequivocally clear the circumstances under which she would go to war against Germany. He attempted to negotiate a joint declaration involving Russia to uphold Polish and Rumanian independence. He allowed himself to be thwarted in this by the Polish refusal to admit Russian troops across

Poland. This made an effective guarantee impossible of fulfilment. Britain did little to supply Poland with war matériel after March and consistently pressed the Polish Government to negotiate with Germany over the issue of *Danzig and the *Polish Corridor. The formal alliance was only concluded after the *Molotov–Ribbentrop Pact (1939), which suggested that Hitler would direct his aggressions against the West. The treaty did not make it plain that Danzig would be regarded as a *casus belli, though a pledge to defend its status was contained in the secret protocol attached to it.

The treaty pledged reciprocal support against direct aggression and aggression in a sphere of security including Belgium and Holland. The protocol also suggested that Britain reserved the right to conclude an agreement with the Soviet Union. The pledge to Poland angered Hitler but failed to convince him that Britain would stand by her if attacked. On the other hand, it emboldened Poland to resist Hitler's demands.

NEWMAN, S., The British Guarantee to Poland: A Study in the Continuity of British Foreign Policy, Clarendon Press, 1976.

THORNE, C., The Approach of War 1938–39, Macmillan, 1967.

**Anglo-Russian Convention** (1825). Signed in St Petersburg on 6 February 1825, this agreement determined the boundary between British and Russian possessions in North America (now Canada and Alaska). It extended northwest from 56 north latitude and 130 west longitude along the summits of coastal mountains to 141 west longitude and along the meridian to the Arctic Ocean. The Hay–Herbert Treaty of 1903 between Britain and the United States set up a commission to clarify some points of dispute that still remained over the boundary.

**Anglo-Russian Convention** (1907). The agreement concluded on 31 August 1907 between Britain and the Russian Empire, which was the culmination of long negotiations to improve relations that had begun with the abortive proposals of Lord *Salisbury (1830–1903) in 1898. Its purpose was to settle mutual claims and rivalry between the two powers in Persia, Afghanistan and Tibet and, in the words of the preamble, to remove 'all causes of misunderstanding'.

Both parties disclaimed any desire to annex territory in Persia but accepted the idea of *spheres of influence in which each power gave the other a free hand. In the central, neutral zone Britain and Russia undertook not to oppose concessions to either side. The settlement served British purposes by impeding the extension of Russian influence to the Gulf and, therefore, offering further strategic protection to British control of India. As the more powerful economic force of the two Britain stood the better chance of exploiting the opportunities in the neutral zone, particularly the oil of Abadan. Russia, weakened by defeat at the hands of the Japanese and revolution at home, conceded Afghanistan as a British sphere of influence. Britain promised she would not annex it, but Russia agreed to deal with Kabul on all major matters only through London. Britain's special interests as well as China's sovereign rights were also recognized in the *buffer state of Tibet, where British commercial agents were granted special status. There was no mention in the convention of European affairs, though the Russians were notified that Britain would no longer oppose Russian ambitions to control the Bosphorus and *Dardanelles provided the other powers agreed (see: *Straits Question). It did not lead to an Anglo-Russian partnership over Balkan affairs as some in the *Foreign Office had hoped and was never as close a liaison as the *Anglo-French Entente (1904). It aroused considerable political controversy in Britain and criticism of the Foreign Secretary, Sir Edward *Grey (1862–1933). Radicals objected to Tsarist domestic policies, especially their oppression of the Jews, while Conservatives and imperialists took the view that too much had been conceded to Russia and that the Convention did not prevent further Russian intrigues in Persia. Nevertheless, it resulted in a general easing of the Anglo-Russian rivalry and it assisted those who were now increasingly preoccupied by the need to contain the rise of German power. It furthered the process of the grouping of the entente powers which were to fight against Germany and Austria-Hungary in 1914, a process which was interpreted by the Kaiser and German public opinion as one of deliberate encirclement (see: *Encirclement, Theory of).

CHURCHILL, R. P., The Anglo-Russian Convention of 1907, Torch Press, Cedar Rapids, 1939.

KAZEMZADEH, F., *Russia and Britain in Persia, 1864–1914*, Yale University Press, 1968.
STEINER, Z. S., *Britain and the Origins of the First World War*, Macmillan, 1977.

**Anglo-Russian Relations,** see RUSSIA AND THE SOVIET UNION, BRITAIN AND

**Anglo-Russian Trade Agreement** (1921). Signed on 16 March, this agreement ended the blockade against Russia after the *Russian Civil War (1917–21). Both countries undertook to refrain from hostile propaganda against each other and to release each other's subjects from detention. Russian ports were reopened to British ships and British commercial and official representatives were admitted. Russia also accepted in principle its liability to pay compensation whenever sums owing for goods and services supplied to Russia remained unpaid. These terms were Britain's essential conditions for a *de jure* recognition of the Soviet government. The agreement was an indication of Lenin's New Economic Policy which encouraged a measure of free enterprise investment and commerce in Russia.

**Anglo-Russian Unity Committee** (1925–7). This was also known as the 'Anglo-Russian Trade Union Council'. It was an organization created by Soviet and British trade unions in April 1925 to coordinate an international trade union movement, to urge the growth of British–Soviet trade and to work for peaceful relations between Britain and the Soviet Union. Influenced by the seeming possibility of greater international rapprochement following the introduction of the New Economic Policy by Lenin, this group called in the first instance for friendship between Western labour groups and the Soviet Union. The committee was disbanded in September 1927 following the Conservative electoral victory and the public outcry excited by the *Zinoviev Letter (1924), which led London to sever relations with the Soviet Union.

**Anglo-Soviet Treaty** (1942). A mutual aid treaty following Hitler's invasion of the Soviet Union in 1941. It ruled out either party making a separate peace with Nazi Germany. In the second part, which was specified to run for 20 years, the powers provided for post-war co-operation. The Soviet Union had pressed for recognition of her incorporation of Estonia, Latvia and Lithuania and a new frontier favourable to the Soviet Union with Poland. Britain accepted the former but rejected the latter (see also: *Polish Government-in-Exile). All mention of territorial claims in the treaty was dropped on the insistence of the United States which considered them incompatible with the *Atlantic Charter (1941). The Soviet foreign minister Molotov pressed for a *second front, but this was ruled out as an immediate prospect. *Churchill (1874–1965) commented that he would not commit Britain to such an effort until it was 'sound and sensible', adding that 'wars are not won by unsuccessful operations'.

**Anglo-Soviet–Iranian Treaty** (1942). An agreement to allow anti-Nazi powers to maintain a military presence in Iran. In 1941 Britain and the Soviet Union had sent troops into Iran to prevent Germany using that country as a base for operations and supplies. On 29 January 1942 the Anglo-Soviet–Iranian Treaty approved the Anglo-Soviet presence in Iran and pledged that the two powers would preserve her sovereignty and independence. Britain and the Soviet Union were given the right to maintain land, air and naval forces there but were committed not to involve her in military engagements. They were to withdraw their forces not later than six months after the ending of the war against Germany. Iran for her part promised not to establish relations with other powers which were hostile to their interests. The British and Soviet forces were finally withdrawn from Iranian territory by May 1946. Soviet slowness in withdrawing caused British apprehension and was an early focus of *Cold War tension.

**Anglo-Soviet Relations,** see RUSSIA AND THE SOVIET UNION, BRITAIN AND

**Anglo-US Relations,** see UNITED STATES, BRITAIN AND THE

**Angola Treaty** (1898). A treaty between Britain and Germany establishing *spheres of influence. It was signed on 30 August 1898 in London. German economic predominance in Angola was accepted in return for German recognition of Mozambique as in the British sphere. Should Portugal abandon her colonies it was agreed that they were to be divided between Britain and Germany. Imperialist hopes were dimmed, however, when Britain stressed her respect for Portuguese sovereignty over her colonies in the Windsor Treaty of 1899. In 1913–14 Britain resumed negotiations with a Germany anxious to have her aspirations to Angola confirmed. The outbreak of *World War I (1914–18), though, ruined the possibility of a supplementary treaty.

**Anschluss** (1938). The term used for the union of Austria with Germany which was proclaimed on 13 March 1938 after Hitler's occupation: Austria became a province of the Third Reich. Such a union had been forbidden by the peace treaties after *World War I (1914–18), though this veto conflicted with the principle of *self-determination pronounced in Woodrow Wilson's *Fourteen Points.

The Anschluss followed an earlier failed Nazi putsch in Austria, which had occasioned the assassination of Chancellor Dollfuss (1934), persistent pressure by the Austrian-born Hitler and threats of military action. When the Austrian Chancellor, Schuschnigg, called a plebiscite on Austria's future, Hitler forced his resignation. After President Miklas had refused to name the Nazi Seyss-Inquart as Chancellor, Austria was occupied.

This time German action had the acquiesence of Mussolini who had been estranged from Britain and France over the *Abyssinian War (1935–6). Invasion of Austria was followed by a Nazi-controlled plebiscite on 10 April. This returned a 99.75% vote in favour of union. The official British position was that nothing could be done to prevent the takeover. On 11 March Lord *Halifax (1881–1959), the Foreign Secretary, had informed the Austrians that he could not advise 'any course of action which might expose (Austria) to dangers to which His Majesty's Government are unable to guarantee protection'. Winston *Churchill (1874–1965), however, called for a Grand Alliance to resist further German aggrandizement, warning that Europe was 'confronted with a programme of aggression, nicely calculated and timed, unfolding stage by stage'. Both the Government and its critics recognized that the position of Czechoslovakia vis-à-vis Germany was gravely weakened as a result of the Anschluss.

GEHL, J., *Austria, Germany and the Anschluss 1931–38*, Oxford University Press, 1963.
THORNE, C., *The Approach of War, 1938–39*, Macmillan, 1967.

**Ansei Commercial Treaties** (1858). Trade agreements concluded by the Western Powers, Britain, Russia, France, the Netherlands and the United States, with Japan. They opened several Japanese cities including Edo (Tokyo) and Osaka to unrestricted trade and provided for the exchange of diplomatic representatives. They sanctioned the principle of *extraterritoriality, assigned special areas to foreign residents and set tariff rates, which were reduced to 5% in 1886. The treaties are of particular significance because they drew Japan, for the first time in 250 years, into economic relationship with the West. They were strongly resented by the Japanese, and imperial ratification was only finally accorded in 1865 after a Western display of naval strength. They remained an important diplomatic issue throughout the rest of the nineteenth century. Modifications beneficial to Japan were introduced in the *Anglo-Japanese Commercial Treaty (1894).

**Anti-Comintern Pact** (1936). A treaty concluded between Germany and Japan on 25 November 1936. It required both parties to provide information to each other on the activities of the Comintern and to take counsel on defence measures. A secret supplementary clause bound the powers to neutrality in the event of either of them coming into conflict with Russia. Italy entered the pact in 1937. While it was signed with a view to checking the activities of the Communist International (Comintern), no specific anti-Communist action was taken on the strength of the pact. Rather it was a demonstration of the political cooperation of the three signatories against the Soviet Union and the Western democracies. Subsequently a number of smaller states in sympathy with, or dependent upon, the original signatories joined the pact. Spain, for instance, did so in 1939. Adherence to the pact was a precondition of admission to the Axis system.

**Apartheid.** The Afrikaans word meaning 'apartness' – the South African doctrine and practice of racial segregation. It was propounded in the 1948 election campaign of Dr Malan's National Party. Its supporters claimed that it was based on the principle of trusteeship for the Bantu (African) people and that only apartheid could ensure the future of 'white civilization'. Apartheid was codified in such legislation as the Prohibition of Mixed Marriages Act (1949), the Group Areas Act

(1950) and the Ninety Day Law (1963). It envisaged the creation of self-governing African states (Bantustans) in South Africa, though these were to have limited independence. Outside these areas Africans have been deprived of civil and political rights and treated as temporary labour. The system has been widely denounced by world opinion and sanctions have been imposed against South Africa, though Britain, the United States, West Germany and Japan, among other powers, have continued to trade with South Africa.

In 1960 the Nationalists gained a majority in a referendum for the transformation of South Africa into a republic. Commonwealth precedent required that when a member country became a republic it should make formal application for renewed membership of the Commonwealth. When the Commonwealth Prime Ministers met for their 1961 conference the African and Asian members, supported by Canada, insisted that their communiqué should include a condemnation of apartheid. The background to this was of mounting tension. In 1960 anti-apartheid riots at Sharpeville had led to the deaths of a number of Africans and there was widespread revulsion in Britain and the Commonwealth as well as in the world at large. The South African Prime Minister, Mr Verwoerd, announced that he would rather leave the Commonwealth than change the policy of apartheid. South Africa accordingly became an independent republic on 31 May 1961. Harold *Macmillan (1894–1986), the British Prime Minister at the time, worked hard to avoid South African withdrawal from the Commonwealth. Some Conservatives in Britain argued that the attack on apartheid was outside the scope of the Commonwealth Conference since it involved interference in a member state's internal affairs, but such considerations carried little weight in the growing climate of opposition towards racial discrimination in the 1960s. Boycotts of South African goods have been mounted and she has also been excluded from the Olympic Games and other sporting events. The question of Britain's relations with South Africa came to a head in the Commonwealth Conference of January 1971. There most of the Black African states tried to dissuade the British Prime Minister, Edward *Heath (1916–    ) from resuming the sale of arms to South Africa. The Government accepted the obligation under the Simonstown Agreement of 1955, signed by Britain and South Africa, to supply South Africa with naval equipment. Mr Heath believed that Anglo-South African naval cooperation was necessary to keep open the sea lanes of the Persian Gulf and Indian Ocean and denied that this implied conferring a certificate of respectability on what he admitted was an unacceptable regime.

The issue of sanctions against South Africa was the dominant question of the Commonwealth Summit of August 1986, with the British Prime Minister resisting strong international pressure to impose tough sanctions. The month before, a peace mission by the British Foreign Secretary, Sir Geoffrey *Howe (1926–    ) on behalf of the European Community failed to yield any results.

**Appeasement.** The name given to the policy of negotiation with and concession to Germany and Italy by Britain and France in the 1930s. As a policy of averting conflicts with rival states through satisfying their grievances and through compromise, it can be traced back far earlier. Until the *Munich Agreement (1938) the word did not carry a pejorative connotation in the public mind.

In Britain after *World War I (1914–18) there was a popular feeling that 'never again' must such a terrible conflict occur. This was coupled with the widespread view that the terms of the *Versailles Treaty (1919) were unduly harsh on Germany. Britain's armaments were drastically reduced in the 1920s, and rearmament did not recommence until 1932. Pacifist sentiment remained high throughout the 1930s and many looked to the *League of Nations to solve international disputes through mediation. During the 1930s the international situation deteriorated, especially after Hitler came to power in Germany in 1933, with the pledge to revise Versailles. In 1935 Italy, hitherto thought friendly towards Britain, invaded Abyssinia (see: *Abyssinian War (1935–6) ), potentially endangering British lines of communication to India and beyond. Similarly Japanese expansionism threatened British possessions in the Far East. The Service Chiefs of Staff pointed out to the British Government that Britain was not equipped to fight three enemies simultaneously. Her policy had therefore become one of 'limited liability' – of restricting commitments to home and imperial defence and ruling out military action on the Continent.

This meant that priority in rearmament, which began in earnest in 1935, would concentrate on the Air Force and Navy, ruling out a continental field force for the Army. Consequently, Britain was in no position militarily to resist German expansion, especially after the remilitarization of the *Rhineland in March 1936, until her own rearmament programme was sufficiently advanced. The British had, thus, no realistic option but to negotiate – 'appease' the demands made by Hitler, and to appease Mussolini in the hope that he would once again join Britain and France in counterbalancing the rising power of Germany, something made more difficult by Mussolini's support for Franco in the *Spanish Civil War (1936–9).

The best-known act of appeasement was the Munich Agreement in which Britain and France conceded the *Sudetenland to Hitler. When Germany occupied the rest of Czechoslovakia in March 1939, British public opinion, as well as that of the Dominions (which had strongly opposed the idea of Britain again becoming involved in a continental war) turned in favour of a policy of resisting further German demands. At the official level (though appeasing initiatives still continued behind the scenes) appeasement was replaced by a policy of 'guarantees', by which the British and French pledged themselves to aid Poland, Rumania and Greece should any of these countries be attacked. The breathing-space for rearmament provided by Munich meant that Britain was able to declare war on Germany in September 1939, following Hitler's refusal to withdraw his invading armies from Poland. Several politicians, most prominently Winston *Churchill (1874–1965), loudly denounced the appeasement policy, arguing that Britain should have rearmed both faster and sooner and resisted German demands. The chief appeasers, Neville *Chamberlain (1869–1940), *Halifax (1881–1959) and *Hoare (1880–1959), were later condemned by public opinion while *Eden (1897–1977), an appeaser of Germany but not of Italy, largely escaped blame. The word 'appeasement' has, since the 1930s, become a byword for any similar policy of yielding to aggression and expansionism, particularly the encroachment upon weaker neighbours by a powerful neighbour, in order to buy peace. It is now used usually in a derogatory and warning sense, though in the longer perspective appeasement has been, in the words of Professor P. M.

Kennedy, 'the "natural" policy for a small island state gradually losing its place in world affairs, shouldering military and economic burdens which were increasingly too great for it, and developing internally from an oligarchic to a more democratic form of political constitution in which sentiments in favour of a pacific and rational settlement of disputes were widely propagated'.

COWLING, M., *The Impact of Hitler: British Politics and British Policy 1933–1940*, Cambridge University Press, 1975.

GILBERT, M., *The Roots of Appeasement*, Weidenfeld and Nicolson, 1966.

HOWARD, M. *The Continental Commitment: The Dilemma of British Defence Policy in the Era of Two World Wars*, Temple Smith, 1972. *War and the Liberal Conscience*, Temple Smith, 1978.

KENNEDY, P. M., 'The Tradition of Appeasement in British Foreign Policy, 1865–1939', in *Strategy and Diplomacy, 1870–1945*, Fontana, 1984.

MOMMSEN, W. J. and KETTENACKER, L., eds., *The Fascist Challenge and the Policy of Appeasement*, Allen and Unwin, 1983.

ROCK, W. R., *British Appeasement in the 1930s*, Edward Arnold, 1977.

**Arab Revolt** (1916). Turkey's entry into *World War I (1914–18) as Germany's ally in October 1914 had serious implications for British imperial security because the Ottoman Empire in the Middle East lay astride the line of communication to India. From Palestine Turkish troops threatened the *Suez Canal in British-occupied Egypt; from the Arabian Peninsula they threatened the Red Sea route; from Mesopotamia they threatened Persia and the Gulf, beyond which lay India itself. Britain had traditionally sought to preserve the Ottoman Empire lest its disintegration draw Russia southwards; but war substituted for the Russian menace a more formidable one from Germany, and it now became important to encourage the Arab peoples disenchanted with Turkish rule to revolt against their masters. This policy, associated with *Kitchener, was pressed with urgency after the initial failure at *Gallipoli (1915) had made it necessary to divert Turkish resources elsewhere. Negotiations between the British High Commissioner in Egypt, McMahon, and Sharif Hussein of Mecca ended in January 1916. Hussein had been told that, subject to certain conditions,

Britain was 'prepared to recognize and support the independence of the Arabs'.

The Arab Revolt began in 1916 in the Hejaz, the north-western section of the Arabian Peninsula. Hussein first captured Mecca itself, then Jedda. With the help of the Royal Navy and British personnel, amongst whom was T. E. Lawrence, his forces moved north along the Red Sea coast and by mid-1917 had taken Aqaba. The large Turkish garrison at Medina was bypassed, and some 30,000 Turkish troops were immobilized along the desert railway which linked Medina to Amman. By 1918 the Arabs were operating on the right flank of Allenby's army as it advanced north through Palestine, and they played a notable role in the capture of Damascus in October. The value of the Arab Revolt to Britain was considerable, although more would have been achieved had Hussein shown more regard for the ruler of the Nejd, Ibn Saud, who controlled much of central Arabia from Riyadh. The peace settlement provoked lasting Arab bitterness because it placed Palestine under British control and Syria under French control – a result anticipated by the *Sykes–Picot Agreement of June 1916 and the *Balfour Declaration of November 1917. These limited Britain's freedom of action to fulfil the ambiguous provisions of the Hussein–McMahon correspondence which the Arabs believed, with some justice, had committed Britain to recognizing Arab control in those areas.

GLUBB, J., *Britain and the Arabs: A Study of Fifty Years 1908–1958*, Hodder and Stoughton, 1959.

KIMCHE, J., *The Second Arab Awakening*, Thames and Hudson, 1970.

STEWART, D., *T. E. Lawrence*, Hamish Hamilton, 1977.

**Arbitration.** The means of resolving a dispute through judges selected by the disputant powers. The judges, who have standing as international jurists, must render a decision or award based on international law. Those who are party to the dispute agree in advance to accept the decision arrived at as binding. Conflicts over what states regard as their lesser interests have often been resolved through arbitration, though normally the powers are reluctant to submit disputes involving their major interests to such a tribunal. Arbitrations may be concerned with questions of international law or facts. When they are primarily concerned with facts, as in pecuniary claims or boundary disputes, the arbitrators are usually termed a commission. A nineteenth-century example of this process is the settlement of the *Alabama* claims following the Treaty of Washington (1871). The *Hague Conference of 1899 set up a Permanent Court of Arbitration. A list of judges from which the parties to a dispute might select a tribunal was provided and the procedure to be followed was laid down. This machinery was used 14 times in the years up to the outbreak of *World War I (1914–18).

**Arcadia Conference** (1942). Convened in Washington from 22 December to 14 January 1942. It was proposed by Winston *Churchill (1874–1965) following the Japanese attack on *Pearl Harbour (1941), and he was accompanied by Lord *Beaverbrook, his Minister of Supply and the British Chiefs-of-Staff. The Prime Minister was anxious to secure continued United States aid to Britain and a commitment to the war against Germany as the priority – rather than that in the Pacific theatre. Churchill was successful in both of these aims. By 2 January 1942, 26 nations had signed the Joint Declaration prepared by the *State Department.

The powers pledged to use their full resources against the *Axis and to forswear any separate peace until its forces were defeated. In addition to these undertakings, the United States agreed to study the British proposal for a landing in French North Africa. The American General George Marshall called for a supreme commander to be appointed to each theatre of operations. The idea of a Combined Chiefs-of-Staff committee was also accepted. The Arcadia Conference had a considerable impact on American public opinion and Churchill used his stay in the United States skilfully to promote pro-British sentiment for the war effort. He was, however, unable to secure subsequent unqualified support from the United States in a number of strategic issues.

FEIS, H., *Churchill, Roosevelt, Stalin: The War They Waged and the Peace They Sought*, Princeton University Press, Princeton, N.J., 1967.

MCNEILL, W. H., *America, Britain and Russia: Their Cooperation and Conflict, 1941–46*, Oxford University Press, 1953.

**ARCOS Raid** (1927). An Anglo-Soviet incident which resulted in the severing of diplomatic relations between Britain and the Soviet Union and the termination of the *Anglo-Russian Trade Agreement of 1921. In May 1927 the government of Stanley *Baldwin (1867–1947) ordered Scotland Yard to search the headquarters of the Soviet trading company ARCOS (the All-Russian Cooperative Society), alleging it had been informed that it was a front for communist spies and subversion. Two hundred police spent six hours ransacking the premises without producing any incriminating evidence (no prosecution of British or Soviet citizens was mounted as a consequence). Police also entered the offices of the Soviet Trade Delegation which according to the 1921 agreement and commonly accepted interpretations of international law enjoyed diplomatic immunity.

Baldwin nevertheless claimed that the captured documents indicated the existence of a worldwide spy network orchestrated from Soviet House. (It had originally been stated that a document containing military secrets had been stolen from the War Office by an employee of ARCOS.) This raid also led to the cancellation of a business deal negotiated by the Soviet Government in which the Midland Bank was to have extended credit for the purchase of British machinery. This incident reflected as much as it caused the tense atmosphere between Britain and the Soviet Union at the time. Anti-British propaganda, especially in the Empire, the Soviet refusal to settle foreign debts and their support for strikers during the General Strike (1926) had aggravated already very cool relations with the Conservative government. The Soviet Union treated the raid as a deliberately contrived justification for ending diplomatic relations and accused Britain of undertaking 'energetic preparations' for war against her. Diplomatic contacts were resumed in October 1929 after the election of the Second Labour Government and ambassadors were exchanged in 1930.

COATES, W. P. and Z. K., *A History of Anglo-Soviet Relations*, Vol. I, Lawrence and Wishart, 1943.

**Armenian Massacres** (1894–6; 1915). The massacre of the Monophysite Christian people living within the Ottoman Empire by Moslem Turkish troops and Kurdish irregulars. Failure on the part of the Sultan, Abdul Hamid, to carry out promised reforms had led the Armenians to form secret terrorist societies in the hope that Turkish repression would arouse European sympathy, as it had in the case of Bulgaria (see: *Bulgarian Massacres (1875–6) ). Approximately 350,000 died as a result of the repression of the Armenians. British Liberals were prominent in protesting. The Sultan promised reforms but, as before, temporized over them, even when under coercion from the British Fleet. In 1896 the Armenian seizure of the Ottoman Bank in Constantinople led to three days of slaughter, which was only halted after strenuous protest from European ambassadors. In the event, however, the European Powers did not support the Armenians to the extent of demanding the independence of the Turkish provinces. Unlike the case of Bulgaria, the Russians were apprehensive of the consequences of Armenian nationalism within their own Caucasian territories.

In 1915 there was a further massacre; the Turks (regarding the Armenians as a dangerous foreign element during a war which had just led to a campaign against the *Dardanelles) resolved to deport the whole Armenian population of about 1¾ million to Syria and Mesopotamia. About 600,000 Armenians died or were massacred en route.

WALKER, C.J., *Armenia: The Survival of a Nation*, Croom Helm, 1980.

**Armistice.** An agreement between warring states to cease hostilities. This may be limited to a particular period of time or be restricted to a specific place; or it may be general in its scope and without time limits. It may be used to describe either an agreement between belligerents or the nature of their relationship during it. Unlike surrender or capitulation, armistice is essentially a bilateral arrangement with mutual concessions and restrictions. It is to be distinguished from a peace treaty in that it does not end the legal state of war. It is valid only when signed by the highest authorities in the belligerent states.

**Arms Control.** Expression introduced in the 1950s by United States strategists. It denotes all the ways in which one or more states may deliberately restrain the development, testing and deployment, and minimize the danger of, armaments. Though it is sometimes used as a synonym for disarmament, it more precisely refers to measures undertaken to prevent surprise attack, the designing and deploying of strategic forces to decrease their vulnerability to first strikes, the lengthening of the time-scale for decision-making in a crisis and the strengthening of command and control over weapons systems. Agreements for restraint have included SALT and unilateral acts, such as the decision by the United States and others in the West in 1969 to suspend research into biological weapons and to destroy stocks of them.

**Arms Race.** Continuous competition between states in arms production. States involve themselves in arms races in order to establish technological and quantitative superiority in weaponry and methods of delivery and to avoid inferiority to actual or perceived rivals. The term is currently used most commonly to describe the armaments programmes of *NATO and the Warsaw Pact countries in the East–West rivalry of the *Cold War.

*Arrow* **War** (1856). The war between Britain, France and China which followed the boarding of the *Arrow*, anchored at Canton, on 8 October 1856. Though the boat was owned by the Chinese and carried a Chinese crew, its captain was British, it was registered at *Hong Kong and it flew the British flag. When the detained crew members were not handed over by the Chinese in precisely the manner stipulated by the British Consul, Harry Parkes, he ordered the navy to fight its way to Canton. The British Government then sent an expeditionary force. They were joined by the French who had their own *casus belli with China because of the execution of a missionary for travelling to the interior of China, a forbidden undertaking for a foreigner. In fact the aims of the Western Powers went further than seeking redress for these two incidents. They wanted more favourable treaty arrangements with China and they wanted the enforcement of the clause providing for Westerners' entry into Canton stipulated in the *Nanking Treaty (1842). The British and French forces took Canton on 29 December 1857 and then proceeded to Tientsin where they secured new terms (see: *Tientsin Treaties (1858) ).
HURD, D., *The Arrow War: An Anglo-Chinese Confusion, 1856–60*, Collins, 1967.
TWITCHETT, D. and FAIRBANK, J. K., *The Cambridge History of China*, Vol. X, Cambridge University Press, 1978.

**ASQUITH**, Herbert Henry, Earl of Oxford and Asquith (created 1925) (1852–1928). Liberal Prime Minister 1908–16. Asquith's main concerns were with domestic issues but he was to be the Prime Minister who led Britain into *World War I (1914–18). He held office as Home Secretary from 1892 to 1895 and emerged as the most important figure of the Liberal Imperialist wing of the party after *Rosebery (1847–1929) resigned the leadership in 1896. Hence he clashed with *Campbell-Bannerman (1836–1908) during the *Boer War (1899–1902), but was willing to serve under him as Chancellor of the Exchequer from 1905 to 1908.

When Campbell-Bannerman died Asquith was the obvious choice to succeed him. When war came in 1914 Asquith, who believed in upholding the *Anglo-French Entente (1904) and in limiting German expansion, realized that British involvement was a regrettable necessity. In the subsequent debates on strategy Asquith tried to preserve a balance between the Westerners and Easterners although he inclined to the former party. In May 1915 criticism of the Government combined with dissension within it to cause Asquith to form a coalition with the Unionists in order to strengthen his position. Asquith's conduct of the war still seemed insufficiently decisive and against the background of casualties on the *Somme he fell victim to the intrigues of *Lloyd George (1863–1945), who replaced him as Prime Minister in December 1916. Now in opposition, in May 1918 Asquith attacked the Lloyd George coalition in the Maurice debate on allegations that the Prime Minister was deliberately keeping the army short of troops. Lloyd George was able to fend off the attack, while the incident hardened the split in the Liberal Party which was to keep Asquith himself out of office, as the leader of a small faction, for the rest of his political life. He had been a successful peace-time Prime Minister who had failed to demonstrate effectively the different qualities requisite in a war leader.
JENKINS, R., *Asquith*, Collins, 1964.
KOSS, S., *Asquith*, St Martin's Press, 1974.
OXFORD AND ASQUITH, EARL OF, *Memories and Reflections*, 2 vols., Cassell, 1928.

**Associated Powers.** This term was used during *World War I (1914–18) and *World War II (1939–45) to indicate strong cooperation for a specific objective, but falling short of a binding alliance. In World War I the United States, which entered the conflict against the *Central Powers in 1917, did not formally join the Allied

Powers. During World War II, after the *Pearl Harbour attack by the Japanese in 1941, the powers in conflict with the Axis were also spoken of as 'Associated Powers' until, at the suggestion of President Roosevelt, the term 'United Nations' was adopted.

**Atlantic, Battle of the.** The long struggle by British, and later also American aircraft and ships to protect the transatlantic sea routes from attacks by German submarines during *World War II (1939–45). The battle was at its height between June 1940 and August 1943. The German strategy was to force surrender on Britain by cutting off her supplies of food and munitions. It was not until the autumn of 1943 that the battle turned conclusively against the Germans. By then bigger and better protected convoys, asdic and radar and long-range aircraft on the Allied side meant that U-boat sinkings started to exceed the rate of replacement. On the other hand, by 1944 the speed of American and British shipbuilding exceeded the rate of merchant ship loss.
ROSKILL, S. W., *The War at Sea, 1939–1945*, 3 vols. HMSO, 1954–61.

**Atlantic Charter** (1941). The result of the Atlantic Conference held at sea in Placentia Bay off Newfoundland by Winston *Churchill (1874–1965) and President F. D. Roosevelt between 9 and 12 August 1941. This was four months before the United States entered the war, at a time when she was still technically a neutral. The Charter has been described as an 'updated *Fourteen Points'. It served as a statement of the ideological basis for Allied cooperation during the war and offered further evidence of the decline of American *isolationism. It was acceded to a month later by the Soviet Union and 14 other nations at war with the *Axis. While it is possible to be sceptical about it in the light of subsequent events, it articulated a genuine idealism beyond any immediate propagandistic use that it had.

The eight clauses included a denial of territorial or other aggrandizement, support for the principle of *self-determination, commitment to equal access for all to raw materials and the resolve to achieve after the war was over the 'abandonment of the use of force' Churchill advanced the idea of an international organization to enforce a 'permanent system of general security'. The statement of 'the rights of all people to live under a government of their own choosing' was interpreted by the United States as applying to all colonial peoples. In September 1942 Churchill, who did not wish to see the principle of self-determination used to undermine the British *Empire, informed the Commons that this statement had no relevance for the future of India. There was considerable disagreement about the interpretation and application of specific clauses and the ultimate objectives of the Charter were never realized. For their part, at the time, the Americans resisted attempts by Britain to secure United States commitment to specific post-war international obligations.
LASH, J., *Roosevelt and Churchill, 1939–41*, Deutsch, 1977.
REYNOLDS, D., *The Creation of the Anglo-American Alliance*, Europa Publications, 1981.
WILSON, T. A., *The First Summit: Roosevelt and Churchill at Placentia Bay, 1941*, Houghton Mifflin, Boston, Mass., 1969.

**Atlantic Community.** Term used to describe the feeling of common identity, springing from common cultural origins, which links North America and Western Europe. It is sometimes employed to designate the whole of the Western Hemisphere as well as Europe. It is, therefore, a vague concept. Beyond the general sense of identity, it is sometimes used, though, to suggest specific common interests on both sides of the Atlantic sufficiently significant to require a common political and economic policy, even to the point of political union (e.g. in the federal concept of Atlantic Union). To some degree *NATO reflects this sentiment.

**ATTLEE,** Clement Richard, 1st Earl Attlee (created 1955) (1883–1967). Educated at Haileybury and University College, Oxford. He was called to the Bar in 1906 but abandoned his intention of practising, opting instead for East End social work and membership of the Fabian Society. After service in *World War I (1914–18), he became Labour MP for Limehouse in 1922 and soon established a reputation for his knowledge of local government. His experience of foreign affairs began in 1927 when as a member of the Simon Commission on India he examined the possibilities of self-government for the sub-continent; in 1930 he became Chancellor of the Duchy of Lancaster, attended the Imperial Conference and witnessed the full extent of disagreement between Labour ministers and Commonwealth leaders over tariff questions. As leader of the Labour Party from 1935 Attlee was deeply critical of the government's foreign policy with regard to Spain and the *League of Nations, and refused to give Labour backing for rearmament. Only in 1938 did this attitude change.

Entry into Churchill's War Cabinet as Lord Privy Seal in May 1940 provided Attlee with further experience of foreign affairs. In 1942–3 as Dominions Secretary in the War Cabinet he ensured that Australia and New Zealand were represented there at a particularly dangerous time. Subsequently, as Lord President, Attlee's close involvement with post-war planning led him to favour a Western bloc and a divided Germany as an insurance policy against German rearmament, American withdrawal from Western Europe, and Soviet control of the East. Anticipating trouble with the Russians on becoming Prime Minister in July 1945, Attlee sent *Bevin (1881–1951) to the *Foreign Office and left the details of policy to him. The similarity of view and closeness between the two men enabled British foreign policy to be conducted with a firmness of purpose as it adjusted to the post-war world and the perceived emerging Soviet threat in Europe and the Middle East. Attlee's distinctive contribution lay first in ensuring that India received independence, in 1947, and that, though a Republic, she remained in the *Commonwealth. Secondly, it was Attlee who decided, with a small group of ministers, that Britain should manufacture her own nuclear weapons – a decision taken in January 1947, when it was not clear that the United States would remain in Europe, nor what the Soviet Union's aims were.

The costly rearmament programme following the outbreak of the Korean War led to the politically damaging resignations from the Cabinet which helped contribute to the government's defeat in the October 1951 election. Attlee remained as leader until December 1955, when he received an earldom.

ATTLEE, C. R. As It Happened, Heinemann, 1954.

WILLIAMS, F., A Prime Minister Remembers: The War and Post-War Memoirs of the Rt. Hon. Earl Attlee, Heinemann, 1961.

**Austrian State Treaty** (1955). Treaty for the Re-establishment of an Independent and Democratic Austria, signed on 15 May 1955 by Britain, the Soviet Union, the United States, France and Austria. It provided for the withdrawal of occupying troops and reaffirmed the ban on the union of Austria and Germany (*Anschluss). It also required the Austrian Parliament to pass a law pledging permanent neutrality. The treaty came into force on 27 July 1955.

**Avon, Earl of,** see EDEN, SIR (ROBERT) ANTHONY (1897–1977)

**Axis.** A term originally used by Mussolini in 1936 to describe the relationship between his country and Nazi Germany established by the October Protocols. During *World War II (1939–45) it was used to describe the powers of the Tripartite Pact (1940) (Germany, Italy and Japan) and those east European states which were allied with them – Bulgaria, Hungary, Rumania and Slovakia.

# —B—

**Baghdad Pact** (1955). The mutual defence pact which originated in the 1955 treaty between Turkey and Iraq. It was intended to afford protection against possible Soviet advance in the region and was later joined by Britain, Iran and Pakistan. The United States hesitated openly to endorse it for fear of alienating the radical Arab opinion which opposed it. With their pressure for a 'northern tier' alliance though, as an analogue to *SEATO in the policy of *containment, they had done much to encourage it, and they participated in its military and economic committees from 1956. After a coup in 1958 Iraq withdrew and the remaining pact members reorganized themselves as the *Central Treaty Organization (CENTO). Britain bore the brunt of Arab, particularly Egyptian, criticsm for participation in the Baghdad Pact. It has been argued that the treaty, rather than blocking, encouraged greater Soviet penetration in the region and the decline of British influence there and that with the heightening of Arab–Israeli tension it helped to contribute to the *Suez Crisis (1956).

**Balaklava, Battle of** (1854). Fought on 25 October between the allied forces of Britain, France and Turkey under Lord Raglan and the Russians in the *Crimean War (1854–6). Balaklava was used as a base by the invading forces who were engaged in the *siege of Sevastopol. The Russian army seized high ground two miles to the northeast of the town and prepared to dislodge the Allies. The Russian advance was halted by the 'thin red line' of Highlanders under Sir Colin Campbell. Then Lord Raglan sent in British cavalry charges against the Russian positions. Lord Lucan, through a staff officer's error, sent his force up a heavily defended valley to the north, the famous 'Charge of the Light Brigade' under Lord Cardigan. Of a brigade of 673 horsemen only 198 returned unhurt from this muddled attempt to capture the Russian guns, an event which provoked General Bosquet's comment: 'C'est magnifique, mais ce n'est pas la guerre'. The Light Brigade's withdrawal was assisted by brilliant action by the French 'Chasseurs d'Afrique'. Prince Menshikov's failure to contribute enough Russian troops to the action meant that the Russians did not secure the capture of Balaklava.

**Balance of Power.** A term which can be used to describe an observed principle of international relations, a particular configuration of states in a given historical situation or a deliberate policy aiming at the preservation of peace. It has been used particularly in the analysis of European diplomatic relations. The pursuit of a balance of power is intended to prevent any one state or alignment of states from attaining hegemony or military preponderance dangerous to the independence and liberty of the others. It rests on the supposition that peace is more likely where potential combatants are of equal power. Britain has traditionally regarded her interests, and those of peace, as best served by playing the role of balancer in a European equilibrium, shifting her weight to the weaker side when the balance was threatened. Hence her traditional opposition to French ambitions and later to German aggrandizement. Since the end of *World War II (1939–45) the predominance of the United States and the Soviet Union has eclipsed the old European balance, with the development of a *balance of terror and a policy of *deterrence.

**Balance of Terror.** An alleged equilibrium between states based on their mutual possession of weapons which allow each side to cause quite unacceptable damage to the other. The term is used to describe the position of nuclear strength of the superpowers, the United States and the Soviet Union, in which neither can launch a first-strike nuclear attack upon the other without suffering intolerable damage in a retaliatory second strike by the other's surviving nuclear force. The strategy of *massive retaliation attempted to equate this equilibrium with the *balance of power, maintaining peace on the basis of the threat of nuclear weapons alone. In fact the traditional balance of power idea involves all sources of strength and weakness in interstate relations and does not rely on any particular military equipment. Recently, the hypothesis of 'limited' nuclear war, of the possibility of a conflict which can be geographically restricted and stop short of massive retaliation, and the introduction of new weapons systems, have called in question the stability of the balance of terror and its efficacy for the maintenance of peace.

**BALDWIN,** Stanley, 1st Earl Baldwin of Bewdley (1867–1947). Educated at Harrow and Trinity College, Cambridge. His father, a Worcestershire ironmaster, was Conservative MP for Bewdley; and Baldwin, following in his father's footsteps, worked in the family firm and represented Bewdley after his father's death in 1908. Baldwin had had an undistinguished parliamentary career when *Bonar Law (1858–1923), a friend of his father, made him his parliamentary private secretary in 1916. In June 1917 Baldwin became Financial Secretary to the Treasury, where he remained until April 1921 when he joined the Lloyd George cabinet as President of the Board of Trade. Horror at what he regarded as the Prime Minister's levity and near-involvement of Britain in war with Turkey in the *Chanak crisis of autumn 1922 led Baldwin to play a leading part in persuading Conservative backbenchers to ditch the Lloyd George coalition. The rebellion made Baldwin a leading figure in the party: in November he became Chancellor in Bonar Law's new government; the following May, with Bonar

Law dying, he succeeded to the premiership. Baldwin was Prime Minister three times: May 1923 to January 1924; November 1924 to June 1929; and June 1935 to May 1937. As Lord President in the National Government from 1931 to 1935, he controlled the largest single party in the Commons.

Baldwin's rise astonished himself as much as it did contemporaries, and having achieved power he had only very general ideas about what to do with it. These included restoring morality to public life and 'binding together all classes of our people in an effort to make life in this country better'. This meant reconciling employers and workforces and taming the Labour Party to the rules of parliamentary government. Between 1923 and 1937, when he dominated British politics, Baldwin did this with success. He saw the country through the General Strike of 1926 and the Abdication Crisis of 1936 more smoothly than any other Conservative leader would have done. With the domestic scene so preoccupying there were long periods when Baldwin had no time for foreign affairs; but in fact he never showed much interest in them. He travelled rarely, except to France on holiday, did not care for foreigners and in a series of farewell speeches reviewing his political career said nothing at all of international problems. With little experience as a departmental minister, poor grasp of detail and unable to take quick decisions, Baldwin was ill equipped to exercise close supervision over foreign policy – which he left instead to the ministers concerned, giving only the most general guidance about what line to follow. *Locarno (1925) was, therefore, the work of Austen *Chamberlain (1863–1937); the 1929 pledge of Dominion status to India was prompted by Irwin; the 1931 Statute of *Westminster, defining Britain's constitutional relationship with the Dominions, was the outcome of a committee headed by *Balfour (1848–1930). The *Ottawa Conference of 1932 over which Baldwin presided was a disappointment because it fell short of the system of imperial economic unity that he wanted, but the principal work on the British side was handled by Neville *Chamberlain (1869–1940). Baldwin favoured the *League of Nations and disarmament, but was not willing to subordinate British interests to the League and had no constructive ideas on the disarmament question as it changed to one of limiting German rearmament to a level acceptable to France.

Baldwin never faced the German problem directly, underestimating the extent of German rearmament and failing to perceive the danger. During the 1935 election he pledged 'no great armaments', yet, after winning it, authorized the greatest peacetime rearmament programme Britain had made. With the *Abyssinian War (1935–6) and the remilitarization of the *Rhineland (1936) the international situation worsened rapidly during his final premiership, but it would be wrong to exaggerate Baldwin's personal responsibility for the mistakes that were made. He was a good deal more sceptical about Hitler than his successor proved to be. Baldwin was made an earl in 1937 and made no further intervention in politics.

BALDWIN, S. *This Torch of Freedom: Speeches and Addresses*, Hodder and Stoughton, 1935.

DILKS, D., 'Baldwin and Chamberlain' in Butler, Lord, *The Conservatives: A History from their Origins to 1965*, Allen and Unwin, 1977.

MIDDLEMAS, K. and BARNES, J., *Baldwin*, Weidenfeld and Nicolson, 1969.

BALFOUR, Arthur James, 1st Earl of Balfour (1848–1930). Balfour was educated at Eton and Trinity College, Cambridge. Encouraged by his uncle, Lord *Salisbury (1830–1903), he entered Parliament as a Conservative in 1874. In 1878, as Salisbury's personal private secretary, he attended the *Congress of Berlin (1878). He achieved ministerial office in June 1885 as President of the Local Government Board; in August 1886 he became Secretary for Scotland, entering the cabinet in November, and moving to become Chief Secretary for Ireland in March 1887. His success in this post brought him the leadership of the Commons as First Lord of the Treasury in 1891, and when Salisbury resigned in July 1902 the premiership passed naturally to him.

Balfour's experience of foreign affairs was already considerable. He had run the *Foreign Office when Salisbury had been away, while the Foreign Secretary since 1900, *Lansdowne (1845–1927) regularly consulted Balfour on all major decisions. Balfour's premiership was notable for three developments affecting Britain's overseas policy: the formation of the *Anglo-Japanese Alliance (1902) and the creation of the *Committee of Imperial Defence in the same year were responses to Britain's isolation and military unpreparedness during the 2nd *Boer War (1899–1902). The 1904

*Anglo-French Entente was designed to eliminate the risk that France, as Russia's ally, and Britain, as Japan's, would find themselves embroiled because of the Russo-Japanese War (1904–5).

The diplomatic measures were designed to preserve Britain's freedom of action rather than to limit it, but they marked the end of Britain's traditional policy of no entangling peacetime alliances, and one of the first acts of the incoming Liberal government of 1906 was to initiate staff talks with France. Whether Balfour would have done the same had he remained in office is doubtful: the limits of his entente policy did not include defence cooperation with France, and he would have preferred a narrowly defined defensive alliance with her.

When war began in 1914, even though he was in opposition and no longer Conservative leader, Balfour was asked by *Asquith (1852–1928) to rejoin the CID. This he did, and from November was a member of the War Council. In the Coalition government of May 1915 Balfour was First Lord; in December 1916, although he had not plotted in Asquith's downfall, he became Lloyd George's Foreign Secretary. This was a trying post to hold because *Lloyd George (1863–1945) intervened regularly in foreign affairs, but Balfour tolerated this as he could still make important contributions of his own. His visit to the United States in April–June 1917 – the first by any British Foreign Secretary – did much to reduce American suspicion of Britain. Pro-American, Balfour was also pro-Zionist and in November persuaded the Cabinet to make the declaration promising a Jewish homeland in Palestine (see: *Balfour Declaration (Palestine) (1917) ). In the same month, although it was not realized at the time, Balfour did not discourage Lansdowne from publishing his 'peace letter' calling for a negotiated settlement with Germany. At the *Paris Peace Conference (1919–20), Balfour played a secondary role to Lloyd George and disapproved of much the latter did. He agreed with *reparations, but not with the crippling of Germany's economy which prevented her from paying them. Exhausted, he resigned in October 1919 from the Foreign Office to become Lord President, in which capacity he led the British delegation to the 1921 *Washington Conference and supported Lloyd George's *Chanak policy which led to the coalition's break-up in 1922. Again Lord President in Baldwin's 1925–9 government,

Balfour chaired the committee which examined the constitutional relationship between Britain and the Dominions. He had been created an earl in 1922 and died in 1930.

BALFOUR, A. J., ed. BLANCHE DUGDALE, *Chapters of Autobiography: Opinions and Arguments from Speeches and Addresses of the Earl of Balfour, 1910–1927*, Hodder and Stoughton, 1930.

EGREMONT, M., *Balfour*, Collins, 1980.

ZEBEL, S. H., *Balfour: A Political Biography*, Cambridge University Press, 1973.

**Balfour Declaration** (Empire) (1926). The resolution moved by Arthur *Balfour (1848–1930), Lord President of the Council and former Prime Minister, at the Imperial Conference of 1926, which was adopted by the representatives of Britain and the self-governing colonies. It defined Britain and the Dominions as 'autonomous communities within the British Empire, equal in status, in no way subordinate to one another in any aspect of their domestic or external affairs, though united by a common allegiance to the Crown and freely associated as members of the British Commonwealth of Nations'. It gave recognition to the national status attained by the Dominions during *World War I (1914–18). In 1931 this resolution was amplified and incorporated in the Statute of *Westminster.

**Balfour Declaration** (Palestine) (1917). The letter sent by the British Foreign Secretary Arthur *Balfour (1848–1930) to Lord Rothschild on 2 November 1917, which became the keystone of the politics of Zionism. It expressed British Government sympathy with Jewish aspirations, stating that it viewed 'with favour the establishment in Palestine of a national home for the Jewish people'. It promised that the British would use 'their best endeavours to facilitate the achievement of this object, it being clearly understood that nothing shall be done which may prejudice the civil and religious rights of existing non-Jewish communities in Palestine or the rights and political status enjoyed by Jews in any other country'.

The declaration represented the successful culmination of attempts by the Zionists to secure the protection of a dominant power in the Middle East and its sponsorship for the idea of a Palestinian settlement. It was the outcome of long negotiations with the British Government by Zionist representatives, foremost among them Dr Chaim Weizmann. Before its announcement it had been approved by President Woodrow Wilson of the United States and it was subsequently endorsed by other Allied governments. In 1920 it was incorporated in the peace treaty with Turkey, the former possessor of Palestine, as it was in the terms of the League Mandate (see: *Mandates) by which the administration of Palestine was entrusted to Britain.

The declaration was made at a critical time for the Western Powers during *World War I (1914–18) and the British Government's motive for making it was not primarily an altruistic one. In part it represented a bid for the support of the influential American Jewish community. The Government also believed that Alexander Kerensky's revolutionary Provisional Government in Russia was under Jewish influence and that such a gesture might help encourage Russia to continue with her war effort against the *Central Powers. It was also realized in London that there were strategic advantages in placing a barrier of a British-protected state between the French in Syria and the *Suez Canal, bearing in mind the tradition of Anglo-French rivalry in this area. The declaration at once met with strong Arab objections, being seen as contradicting pledges made to the Arab peoples. It became the object of major controversy. Under the policy inaugurated by it, Jewish immigration into Palestine grew rapidly, leading ultimately to the emergence of the State of Israel in 1948.

OVENDALE, R., *The Origins of the Arab-Israeli Wars*, Longman, 1984.

WASSERSTEIN, B., *The British in Palestine: the Mandatory Government and the Arab-Israel Conflict 1917–29*, Royal Historical Society, 1978.

ZEBEL, S. H., *Balfour: A Political Biography*, Cambridge University Press, 1973.

**Balfour Note** (1922). A proposal to resolve the interrelated questions of war debts and *reparations arising from *World War I (1914–18). It was addressed by the British Government to the representatives in London of the Allied Powers which owed war debts to Britain. Presented on 1 August 1922, it serves as a clear illustration of Anglo-French differences at this time. It suggested the cancellation of all inter-Allied debts and reparations (Britain was owed £3,400 million and she owed the United States £850 million). This would in the words of the

Note be 'of more value to mankind than any gains that could accrue even from the most successful enforcement of legal obligations'. Failing such a general renunciation, Britain advanced the seemingly very generous offer that she was willing to receive from her Allies and, by way of reparations, from Germany no more than the amount she owed the United States.

The Note was badly timed, despatched only a few days before the opening of the London Conference which had been convened to deal with the German appeal for a moratorium on reparations. It had the effect of hardening French feeling in favour of strong action to compel Germany to pay up, the mood which led to the *Ruhr Invasion of 1923. The French interpreted this as a discrimination in favour of the aggressor, Germany. She was being asked to pay while Britain was considering mitigating Germany's obligations. At the same time the French Premier, Poincaré, and his colleagues reckoned that the less Britain extracted from Germany in reparations the more she would take from France in debt repayment. The French, in rejecting the Note, insisted that Germany's reparations should precede all else. The Note also aroused suspicion in the United States over Britain's motives since (short-sightedly) the former power refused to admit the relationship between war debts and reparations.

**Balkanization.** The division of a region into a number of small autonomous states, often mutually antagonistic. The term was originally used in the nineteenth century to describe the effects of Russian policies on the Balkan states bordering the Romanov Empire. It was later used to denote the effects of World War I (1914–18) on this area. As a deliberate policy, Balkanization eliminates the possibility of a serious military threat by ensuring division and rivalry among neighbouring smaller states.

**BEACONSFIELD,** Earl of, see DISRAELI, BENJAMIN, (1804–81)

**BEAVERBROOK,** William Maxwell Aitken, 1st Baron (created 1917) (1879–1964). Canadian-born newspaper proprietor (owner of the *Daily Express* and other papers), financier, political historian and Cabinet Minister. He championed Imperial Protection, in 1930 launching the Empire Crusade and, without

success, attempted to force his ideas on the Conservative party. During the interwar years he favoured an isolationist foreign policy as far as relations with the Continent were concerned. At the same time he backed rearmament. He supported the *Munich Agreement of September 1938. After the outbreak of war he served under *Churchill (1874–1965) as Minister of Aircraft Production and, later, Minister of Supply and War Production. With great drive and efficiency he speeded the supply of 'Spitfires' and 'Hurricanes' which played such an important part in the Battle of *Britain (1940). He visited Washington to coordinate *Lend-Lease and also helped to arrange the supply of war materials to the Soviet Union, being also an advocate of an early *Second Front. Between 1943 and 1945 he was Lord Privy Seal. After the end of the war he continued to campaign energetically for the cause of the *British Empire, though the process of de-colonization gathered pace. He supported the British intervention in the *Suez Crisis (1956) and, in his last years, mounted a fierce resistance to the attempt by Harold *Macmillan (1894–    ) to take Britain into the Common Market.

TAYLOR, A. J. P., *Beaverbrook*, Hamish Hamilton, 1972.

**BEF,** see BRITISH EXPEDITIONARY FORCE

**Bering Sea Dispute** (1889). Between Britain and the United States over the seal fisheries in the Bering Sea. Britain claimed it to be part of the high seas while the United States argued it was under their jurisdiction. In 1889 American vessels seized eight British ships, upholding the United States view that the Bering Sea was *mare clausum*. The threat of a consequent war receded when the United States Government consented to *arbitration. In 1893 the meeting of arbitrators in Paris found against the United States on all disputed points. The Bering Sea was stated to be open sea, and they paid damages of 473,000 dollars to Britain.

CAMPBELL, C. S., Jr, *Anglo-American Understanding, 1898–1903*, Johns Hopkins Press, Baltimore, 1957.

**Berlin–Baghdad Railway.** The grandiose description for German plans to build a railway from the Bosphorus to the Persian Gulf. On 4 October 1888 the Deutsche Bank had obtained a concession from the Sultan to construct a railway from opposite Constantinople to Ankara with a view to its continuing through northern Anatolia to Baghdad. This and subsequent concessions aroused the suspicions of Britain, France and Russia of German ambitions in the Middle East. These suspicions were further fuelled by the flamboyant visit of Kaiser William II to Constantinople and the Holy Land in 1898. What had begun as an economic enterprise rapidly became a contentious international political and strategic issue.

British views towards the railway construction were initially divided. Some, like *Balfour (1848–1930) and *Lansdowne (1845–1927) saw it as a useful means of blocking the advance of Russian influence in the area. They regarded the Russian threat to India as the greatest problem with which the British *Empire had to contend. They and banking circles were in favour of cooperating with Germany over the project. Others opposed it, notably Joseph *Chamberlain (1836–1914), as a blatant instrument of German aggrandizement. Under diplomatic pressure Germany agreed to recognize Britain's rights in Persia and Mesopotamia and promised to carry the railway only as far as Basra. In 1899 the Sheik of Kuwait promised Britain that he would cede no territory without her consent. Russia remained consistently hostile to the project, which was one factor helping to bring about the understanding between Russia and Britain in 1907 (see: *Anglo-Russian Convention). Only a small section of the railway had been completed by the outbreak of *World War I in 1914.

CHAPMAN, M. K., *Great Britain and the Baghdad Railway, 1888–1914*, Smith College Studies in History, Northampton, Mass., 1948.
KENNEDY, P. M., *The Rise of the Anglo-German Antagonism, 1860–1914*, Allen and Unwin, 1980.

**Berlin Blockade** (1948–9). A major crisis contributing to the heightening of *Cold War tension. This began in June 1948 as a Soviet response to the Western Powers' decision to establish a federal government for their zones in Germany. All land access to the other sectors of Berlin was cut off, isolating a population of two millions in the Russian-occupied zone of Germany. General Lucius Clay, commander in charge of the American zone, recommended a direct challenge to the blockade, but the idea was rejected in favour of supplying Berlin by air. At the same time a counter-blockade was

mounted against the Soviet zone. In the end with the signing of the New York Agreement on 4 May 1949 the Russians lifted the blockade.

This crisis gave an important impetus to the creation of *NATO. When Sir Stafford *Cripps (1889–1952) visited Washington during the crisis he told the United States Secretary of Defence, Forrestal, that 'Britain must be regarded as the main base for the deployment of American power and the chief offensive against Russia must be by air'. Britain and the United States collaborated closely in the airlift and in October 1948 a Combined Airlift Task Force was set up to provide more effective synchronization of the effort. During the blockade more than 200,000 flights were made and 1·5 million tons of supplies carried. The arrival of American B29 Superfortresses in East Anglia had a significant effect on the bilateral defence relationship of Britain and the United States. Originally introduced as a token of American political support for Western Europe, these assumed a new strategic importance when, in 1949–50, they were modified to carry atomic bombs. Contrary to Stalin's intentions, the blockade served to ensure West Germany's emergence as an independent state in political and economic alignment with the West.

DAVISON, W. P., *The Berlin Blockade: A Study in Cold War Politics*, Princeton University Press, Princeton, N.J., 1958.

**Berlin Congo Conference** (1884–5). A gathering of representatives of 15 nations arranged through the joint efforts of the German Chancellor Bismarck and the French Premier Ferry which met between 15 November 1884 and 26 February 1885. It was intended to ease international tension over the partition of Central Africa, to stop slavery and to secure freedom of trade. It agreed to recognize the existence of the 'Congo Free State' as a personal possession of King Leopold II of Belgium. The Berlin agreement illustrated British isolation in the face of the other colonial powers and secured economic advantages for Germany with its creation of a free trade zone in Central Africa. It subsequently proved an obstacle to the British Cape-to-Cairo railway project, against which Germany successfully protested in 1894. In that same year, as a result of his playing off British and French interests against one another, Leopold secured recognition of his claims to a large area of the Congo basin.

**Berlin Congress** (1878). This major international congress resulted from British and Austrian opposition to the gains made by Russia in the Treaty of *San Stefano (1878) at the end of the Russo-Turkish War. Their main objection was to the 'Big Bulgaria' which posed the threat to British imperial interests of a Russian client state which would allow Russia an outlet to the Mediterranean from the Aegean. At Berlin it was agreed that Bulgaria should be trisected, with the northern part remaining independent, Eastern Roumelia created as a new province under Turkish suzerainty but with a Christian ruler, and the remaining areas handed back to Turkey. It was a major diplomatic triumph for Bismarck the German Chancellor as 'honest broker' and it allowed the British Prime Minister *Disraeli (1804–81) to claim 'peace with honour'. Turkey was not evicted from all its European territories, Britain obtained the right to occupy Cyprus, while Austria-Hungary was allowed to administer Bosnia and Herzegovina.

Disraeli was able to claim that major changes had been made to the San Stefano agreement without an Anglo-Russian war and *Salisbury (1830–1903) was allowed to introduce a re-interpretation of the *Straits Convention (1841). Britain was now justified in forcing the Straits if it could be shown that the Sultan was subservient to Russian designs. The long-term benefits of the congress were less evident. Rather than representing a revival of the *Concert of Europe, Berlin inaugurated the period of Bismarckian alliances, beginning with the Austro-German Dual Alliance of 1879. Bulgaria and Eastern Roumelia were united in 1885 while the annexation by Austria of Bosnia-Herzegovina in 1908 precipitated one of the major pre-war crises. Cyprus proved less useful to Britain after the British occupation of Egypt in 1882 and later was to present an intractable international issue.

LANGER, W. L., *European Alliances and Alignments, 1871–1890*, A. Knopf, New York, 1956.

MEDLICOTT, W. N., *The Congress of Berlin and After: A Diplomatic History of the Near Eastern Settlement, 1878–80*, 2nd ed. Cass, 1963.

TAYLOR, A. J. P., *The Struggle for Mastery in Europe, 1848–1918*, Oxford University Press, 1954.

**BEVIN,** Ernest (1881–1951). Born in Somerset, after elementary education he moved to Bristol, where he worked as a van driver and joined the Socialist Society. A leader of the Dockers' Union in 1914, he was active in securing the efficient use of industrial manpower during the war, and by its end had become a national figure, organizing the successful workers' resistance to arms shipments to Poland for use against the Soviet army. In 1922 Bevin became General Secretary of the newly formed and massive Transport and General Workers' Union, a post he held until his death and which gave him a leading voice in Labour Party councils. The contacts with trades unions overseas which his new work entailed stimulated a growing interest in foreign affairs. Not surprisingly, in view of Hitler's treatment of the German unions in 1933, Bevin became one of the earliest proponents of a vigorous foreign policy to oppose the Nazis. In 1936–7 he was chairman of the TUC and in 1938 his visits to Canada, Australia and New Zealand inspired him with the idea of the British *Commonwealth as the nucleus of a new *League of Nations with an economic basis.

In May 1940 *Churchill (1874–1965) appointed Bevin Minister of Labour and National Service, and in October brought him, by now MP for Central Wandsworth, into the War Cabinet. Bevin's ministerial work mobilizing national manpower proved outstanding, and he established a close relationship with *Attlee (1883–1967). When Labour won the 1945 election he hoped to go to the Treasury to direct Britain's industrial and social regeneration. Attlee, however, sent him to the *Foreign Office, certain that the Soviet Union would be aggressive now that war was over and that Bevin, with his standing with the rank and file and his tough power-broking background in trade union politics, was better equipped to cope with this than anyone else.

Bevin's approach to foreign policy was founded on his belief in international economic cooperation as an antidote to nationalism. At the same time he distrusted Soviet Communism: Stalin's regime was as hostile to freedom as Hitler's – not least because it permitted no free trade unions. But this did not lead Bevin to think immediately in terms of Britain aligning herself with the United States against the Soviet Union. The emphasis rather was on maintaining Britain's independence. With much of the world in 1945 lying under Soviet or American control, Britain's withdrawal from her own *sphere of influence would lead to the triumph of Soviet or American power – both, in varying degrees, hostile to Britain's political or trading interests.

The economic reconstruction Bevin aimed at both in Britain and Europe proved impossible in the face of Soviet political and military pressure in the Middle East and, particularly, in Germany. Britain lacked the strength to resist, and Bevin concluded that the Soviets could only be forestalled if the Americans took over the military burdens previously shouldered by Britain. His greatest achievement as Foreign Secretary lay in persuading Washington to do just this. Without Bevin's prompting, there would have been neither the *Truman Doctrine of March 1947 promising American aid to Greece and Turkey, nor the *Marshall Plan of that summer providing economic aid to Western Europe. In the winter of 1947–8 Bevin reached the conclusion that Western Europe's military security against the Soviet Union could not be guaranteed without direct American participation, which he believed should take the form of a new alliance system under American leadership. European willingness to form such an organization, the coup in Czechoslovakia (1948) and the *Berlin Blockade (1948–9) were required before the United States joined NATO in April 1949. The price of American defence for Europe was Britain's subordination to the United States in the alliance, but Bevin expected that Britain could exert a major influence over American policy, and that the American presence in Europe would permit Britain to continue her global role once the economy had revived and despite withdrawal from India and Palestine in 1947–8. Bevin's distaste for European integration (which he considered could interfere with Labour Government programmes in Britain) and enthusiasm for the Commonwealth (which could spread socialist ideas worldwide) remained powerful in the Labour Party for many years after Bevin, exhausted and ill, left office in March 1951.

BULLOCK, A., *Ernest Bevin, Foreign Secretary 1945–51*, Heinemann, 1983.

FRANKEL, J., *British Foreign Policy, 1945–73*, Oxford University Press, 1975.

NORTHEDGE, F. S., *Descent From Power, British Foreign Policy, 1945–73*, Allen and Unwin, 1974.

**Big Three.** The Grand Alliance of Britain, the United States and the Soviet Union against Germany, Italy and Japan between 1941 and 1945. Also the leaders of these powers, the British Prime Minister, Winston *Churchill (1874–1965), the President of the United States, F. D. Roosevelt, and Stalin, the Prime Minister and Marshal of the Soviet Union. The Big Three first met in person at the *Tehran Conference (1943).

**Bizonia.** The entity created by the unification of the British and United States zones of occupation in Germany after *World War II (1939–45). In May 1946, in the face of Soviet refusal to cooperate in the treatment of postwar Germany as an economic unit and their insistence on stripping their own zone not simply of capital goods but also of goods currently produced, Lucius Clay, the general in command of the United States zone, halted reparations to the Soviet Union from his territory and the British followed suit. The economic absurdity of running each zone separately led the Americans in July 1946 to propose the economic merger of their zone with the others. The Russians and French declined this proposal. With Britain's acceptance Bizonia came into existence and with it the *de facto* division of Germany. It involved the coordination of economic and agricultural policies, food distribution, transportation and communications. A formal financial agreement, the Bevin–Byrnes Bizonal Fusion Agreement, was signed in December 1946 and went into effect in January 1947.

In late 1947 and early 1948 talks were held concerning the creation of a political structure for Bizonia. These evolved into more general discussion about the creation of a West German Federal Government. Bizonia was therefore a stepping stone to the limited German self-government which followed with the Basic Law. At the same time the creation of Bizonia meant that the breakdown of any agreed treatment of the vanquished by the victors became explicit and that the community of British and United States policies towards Germany and the Soviet Union became unmistakable.

**Black Sea Clauses.** Important articles in the *Paris Treaty (1856) at the end of the *Crimean War (1854–6). They confirmed the *Straits Convention (1841) and neutralized the Black Sea. This meant that it was to be closed to all warships, though open to merchant vessels. Military arsenals and naval dockyards along its shores were also prohibited. These clauses were aimed against Russia alone and were a major humiliation for her, which she intended to renounce at the earliest opportunity. This Russia did in October 1870, taking the occasion offered by the Franco-Prussian War (1870). A conference of the powers in January 1871 which was convened in London confirmed this unilateral repudiation. It did, however, stipulate that the Turkish authorities should be free to open the Straits to the warships of other powers if the remaining clauses of the Paris Treaty were thought to be at risk (see also: *London Convention (1871) ).

**Blitz** (from the German 'Blitzkrieg', literally 'Lightning-war'). The German raids carried out by night against British cities from September 1940 till May 1941. The raids by the Luftwaffe were often made on the same target areas on several consecutive nights. The Blitz followed the German failure to destroy the RAF fighter force in daylight attacks. The opening of the air offensive against London in September marked a change in policy by the Luftwaffe, with the greater part of its effort going into night bombing. When it became clear that Britain would not be intimidated into speedy surrender, the Germans extended their night attacks to the major ports and industrial centres throughout the country. The worst-hit areas were Birmingham, Bristol, Coventry and Clydeside. The raid on Coventry on 14 November was particularly devastating. Some 500 bombers dropped 500 tons of heavy explosive and nearly 900 incendiary canisters during ten hours of attack. In spite of considerable loss of life (mitigated by the policy of evacuation from the urban centres) and widespread damage to property, the Blitz caused no irreparable harm to the British war effort. The main offensive of the Luftwaffe against Britain ended as German bombers were moved to the Russian front in preparation for Hitler's invasion of the Soviet Union. Aerial bombardment was revived in June 1944 with flying-bomb attacks followed, in September, by the launching of the V2s against London and southern parts of England.
HARRISSON, T., *Living Through the Blitz*, Collins, 1976.
OVERY, R. J., *The Air War, 1939–1945*, Europa Publications, 1980.

**Blockade.** As a naval action, the prevention of the movement of sea traffic to and from an enemy country. According to international law a blockade is valid only if sufficient naval forces are available to make it effective. It may be applied only against enemy shores, not neutral shores, and consequently a blockaded country may obtain imports via neutral countries. For this reason the Allied Powers did not declare a blockade against Germany during the two World Wars, but applied the laws of contraband and reprisals instead. The law of contraband permits the seizure of supplies going to the enemy even when consigned to neutral ports. The law of reprisals is invoked to prevent enemy exports. The law of contraband also permits the search of neutral vessels (see: *Search, Right of). Since the Congress of Paris at the end of the *Crimean War (1854–6) blockade has been subject to complex international laws designed to safeguard the rights of neutrals. British blockade of Germany was highly successful in *World War I (1914–18), though not without considerable losses of British shipping which forced the Admiralty to reintroduce the convoy system. During *World War II (1939–45) the British found that German control of, in particular, France and Norway enabled her both to outflank the British Fleet and to operate her U-boats from bases which gave her extensive range into the Atlantic. Initially Germany's control of the greater part of continental Europe made her relatively invulnerable to Allied blockade, though by mid-1943 Britain had gained the upper hand in the Battle of the *Atlantic. For an example of land blockade see: *Berlin Blockade (1948–9).

**Boer Wars.** (1) The 1st Boer War (1880–1) between Britain and the Boers, the descendants of the Dutch settlers in South Africa, followed the failure of *Gladstone (1809–98) to give the Boers back that independence which they had earlier surrendered in return for protection from the Zulus four years earlier. After British defeats at Laing's Nek and Majuba Hill at the hands of Kruger and the Boers, Britain granted the Transvaal self-government in the *Pretoria Convention (1881) while at the same time preserving ultimate suzerainty and exercising the right of veto over native legislation. By the London Convention (1884) the veto was abandoned and the title 'South African Republic' allowed.

(2) Between this and the 2nd Boer War the discovery of gold on the Witwatersrand (in

1886) led to the migration of many thousands of *Uitlanders (mainly British) to the Transvaal. The background to the second conflict was the refusal of the President of the Transvaal to grant the Uitlanders full political rights and the growing ambition of the British to control the richest part of South Africa. In the view of *Milner (1854–1925), who was sent to South Africa as British High Commissioner in 1897, the British in the Boer republics were treated like helots; on the Boer side there was mounting resentment at the colonial policy of Joseph *Chamberlain (1836–1914). Talks took place between Kruger and Milner in May–June 1899, but Milner broke them off. After the *Jameson Raid (1895) Kruger had used revenue from the gold mines to purchase weapons and had strengthened Boer fortifications. In September the Orange Free State sided with the Transvaal and war broke out on 11 October 1899.

The early part of the war was an almost continuous series of disasters for the British, culminating in 'Black Week'. The Boers reached *Mafeking, besieged it and penetrated far into the Cape, but it was only when General Buller asked for heavy reinforcements in December that the real seriousness of the British position was recognized at home. On 18 December Lord Roberts became Commander-in-Chief with *Kitchener (1850–1916) as his Chief of Staff. The arrival of large British reinforcements brought a reversal of the Boer fortunes with the result that in February 1900 General Piet Cronje was obliged to surrender at Paarderberg. Barely a fortnight later Bloemfontein was taken. The Boers then switched to a war of attrition by guerilla methods. This led to Kitchener's controversial decision to round up the women and children from Boer areas and place them in concentration camps. The war ended in 1902 with the *Vereeniging Treaty. The Boer War revealed major shortcomings in the British Army. This led to the *Haldane Army Reforms. It also conspicuously showed up British diplomatic isolation. Germany, in particular, was sympathetic to the Boer cause, though there was no military intervention on their behalf. At home the war divided Liberal Party opinion. While *Asquith (1852–1928), Sir Edward *Grey (1862–1933) and Lord *Rosebery (1847–1929) supported the war, *Lloyd George (1863–1945) and *Campbell-Bannerman (1836–1908) opposed it. The subsequent Liberal government gave South Africa Dominion status in 1910, and the considerable concessions granted to the Boers, especially as regards the black majority, laid the foundations for the later policy of *apartheid.

AMERY, L., *The Times History of the War in South Africa*, Sampson Low, 1900–9.

PAKENHAM, T., *The Boer War*, Weidenfeld and Nicolson, 1979.

PORTER, A., *The Origins of the South African War: Joseph Chamberlain and the Diplomacy of Imperialism 1895–99*, Manchester University Press, 1980.

**Bolshevik Revolution and Britain,** see RUSSIA AND THE SOVIET UNION, BRITAIN AND, and also RUSSIAN CIVIL WAR, BRITISH INTERVENTION IN THE (1918–20)

**BONAR LAW,** Andrew (1858–1923). Born in Canada, son of a Presbyterian minister; trained in Scotland as a banker. He was originally elected MP for one of the Glasgow constituencies, becoming Parliamentary Secretary to the Board of Trade in 1902. He supported Tariff Reform. When Balfour (1848–1930) resigned the post in 1911 Bonar Law was elected leader of the Conservative Party. He strongly supported the Ulstermen in the crisis of 1912–14 and succeeded in delaying the Home Rule bills. On the resignation of Lord *Fisher (1841–1920) from the Admiralty over the *Dardanelles in 1915, Bonar Law advocated a coalition government. When *Asquith (1852–1928) agreed to this he accepted the post of Colonial Secretary. Later that year he led the group pressing for the evacuation of the Dardanelles. In the new coalition under *Lloyd George (1863–1945) he displayed skill as a financier by successfully issuing a series of war loans and campaigning for national war bonds.

After the Coupon Election of 1918 he became Lord Privy Seal and leader of the Commons. When Lloyd George was attending the peace conferences he was acting Prime Minister. He succeeded Lloyd George when the *Chanak crisis (1922) precipitated the end of his coalition. Bonar Law's period as Prime Minister was brief but it set the fashion for 'safety first' which characterized British Conservatism during the interwar years. He presided over a conference of Allied Prime Ministers to attempt to resolve the question of *reparations, though British and French difference of view ensured the failure of the conference. He was overruled by his colleagues on the question of the American war debt settlement. He resigned through illness and died six months later.

BLAKE, R., *The Unknown Prime Minister*, Eyre and Spottiswoode, 1955.

**Boxer Uprising** (1900). 'Boxer' was the English name for a Chinese secret society, the 'Righteous and Harmonious Fists', which in fact consisted of several uncoordinated groups which were united in their determination to root out foreign influence in China. This outburst of native anger against foreign imperialism was also directed against those Chinese who had collaborated with foreigners. It had the connivance of the Chinese authorities and the active support of the Dowager Empress.

On 10 June 1900 the Boxers burned down the British summer legation in the Western Hills, in the same month pouring into Peking, burning churches and foreign residences, killing Chinese converts and exhuming the bodies of missionaries. The 231 foreigners killed included the German Minister in Peking. A six-nation expeditionary force relieved the embattled foreigners in August 1900. Britain throughout was particularly concerned with the future of her interests in the Yangtse Valley.

In 1901 the Peking Protocol imposed an annual monetary indemnity to be paid by China to the European powers. In the negotiations Britain supported Germany in an attempt to check Russia, while Russia ingratiated herself with the Chinese in the hope of gaining concessions in Manchuria. The allied occupation of Peking and the Russian advance into Manchuria during the turmoil intensified international rivalry and caused the powers to anticipate conflict among themselves and the end of equal economic opportunity in China. Hence, on 16 October 1900 Britain and Germany signed an agreement stipulating that the signatories would refrain from seizing Chinese territory. The Protocol also allowed the powers to station troops in China and to control the diplomatic quarter of Peking if the central Chinese authorities proved themselves powerless. The agreement, which helped further to stimulate Chinese nationalism, was not abrogated until 1943

PURCELL, V., *The Boxer Uprising: A Background Study*, Cambridge University Press, 1963.

TAN, C. C., *The Boxer Catastrophe*, New York, Columbia University Press, 1955.

**Brest-Litovsk Treaty** (1918). The treaty ending the war between Russia, now under Lenin and the Bolsheviks, and the *Central Powers. It was only agreed after much hesitation and prevarication by the revolutionary regime whose chief negotiator was Trotsky, for its terms involved Russia in a massive cession of territory and economic resources – Poland, the Baltic provinces, the Ukraine and the Caucasus. The Western Allies attempted to persuade Lenin to maintain the Eastern Front. His capitulation, forced by recognition of the unwillingness of the Russians to go on fighting, meant now that the Germans could turn their undistracted attention to the Western Front. The final offensive, which brought them within an ace of victory, was mounted on 21 May. The withdrawal of the Bolsheviks from the war was the primary cause of the ill-fated Allied intervention in Russia. The Treaty of Brest-Litovsk was abrogated in the armistice agreement of 11 November 1918 and formally annulled in the Treaty of *Versailles (1919).

**Bretton Woods Conference** (1944). Also known as the United Nations Monetary and Financial Conference, it lasted from 1 to 22 July 1944. The conference established the *International Monetary Fund (IMF) and the International Bank for Reconstruction and Development. These agencies were intended to help with post-war reconstruction and economic stabilization, to lead to a general expansion of world trade and avert a return to the restrictive protectionist policies of the inter-war years. Though it established institutions of major importance to international economic cooperation, the aspirations towards a world-wide economic community which were expressed during the conference were to be disappointed.

**BRIGHT,** John (1811–89). The son of the owner of a Rochdale cotton-mill, Bright was first elected to Parliament in 1843. He agitated against the Corn Laws and generally shared many of the views of his close friend Richard *Cobden (1804–65), by whom he was overshadowed during the early part of his career. In the mid-1850s his energetic opposition to the *Crimean War (1854–6), expressed most effectively in a series of powerful speeches in the Commons, gave him an independent stature. Bright was a Quaker, but by no means a total pacifist. He believed that wars of self-defence were justified and strongly supported the cause of the North in the American Civil War.

Bright outlived Cobden by nearly a quarter of a century and continued to represent his views, although he proved to be more conservative than his friend and lacked something of the breadth of Cobden's vision. He was prominent in opposing Disraeli's Turkish policy in the 1870s and held Cabinet office under *Gladstone (1809–98), but resigned in 1882 over British intervention in Egypt.

READ, D., *Cobden and Bright*, Edward Arnold, 1967.

TAYLOR, A. J. P., *John Bright and the Crimean War*, Manchester University Press, 1954.

TREVELYAN, G. M., *The Life of John Bright*, Constable, 1913.

**Brinkmanship.** Term originating in the *Cold War confrontations of the 1950s and linked with the presumed deterrence of the United States strategy of *massive retaliation advanced by the American Secretary of State John Foster Dulles. It was cited by Dulles as 'the necessary art' in modern diplomacy and defined as 'the ability to get to the verge without getting into war'. Its objective was to avoid allowing a rival power to gain its ends by a war of nerves. The United States would go to the brink of war in order to uphold its interests, forcing the rival (in this case the Soviet Union) to accept its non-negotiable position, thereby avoiding capitulation disguised as compromise. Dulles claimed in 1956 that this forthright Cold War tactic had more than once averted war in the East–West confrontation.

**Britain, Battle of** (1940). The contest between the RAF and the Luftwaffe (German air force) in the summer and autumn of 1940. Its outcome ensured that Britain would not be invaded by Hitler. It began with a German attack by over 1,350 bombers and 1,200 fighters on airfields, shipping and towns. The principal British air defence was the fighter force of 'Hurricanes' and 'Spitfires'. The turning-point was 15 September. Subsequently, though, Germany resorted to intensive bombing of British cities. Winston *Churchill (1874–1965) commented on the heroism of the British pilots: 'Never in the field of human conflict was so much owed by so many to so few'.

**British Battalion.** The 2,000 volunteers from Britain fighting for the Spanish Republic against the Nationalists during the *Spanish Civil War (1936–9). The battalion consisted of a mixture of working-class radicals and middle-class intellectuals and sustained very heavy losses, with 500 dead and 1,200 wounded. (see also: *International Brigades).

**British Empire and Commonwealth,** see EMPIRE AND COMMONWEALTH, THE BRITISH

**British Expeditionary Force** (BEF). In both World Wars Britain dispatched an expeditionary force of regular army formations to continental Europe to support France against the common enemy Germany.

The first BEF, created by *Haldane (1856–1928) in 1907, was a well-equipped, well-trained army of six infantry divisions and one cavalry division which played a notable role in stopping the German advance on Paris at the Battle of the *Marne (1914). The new experience of trench warfare at Ypres in October and November caused such heavy losses that by the end of 1914 the original BEF had gone. The folly of trench warfare produced such revulsion in Britain after the war that politicians were extremely reluctant to accept the Army's demands after 1933 for the creation of a new expeditionary force with a continental role. No decision to create such a force was taken until February 1939, and the BEF which went to France in September consisted of no more than four infantry divisions with some armoured units. Inaction ensued until the German offensive of May 1940, when one more regular division had arrived and five from the Territorial Army. The *Dunkirk evacuation saved nearly all of this force but it lost most of its tanks, guns and equipment.

**British North America.** This term is commonly used to refer to the British colonies in North America in the period between the acknowledgement of the independence of the United States in 1783 and the creation of the Dominion of Canada in 1867. During this period the interests of the various mainland colonies differed markedly and they had little communication with one another. Newfoundland maintained its isolated existence until 1949.

**BROWN,** George, Baron George Alfred George-Brown (created 1970) (1914–1985). A Transport Worker's Union official, George

Brown became Labour MP for Belper in 1945 and was Minister of Works under *Attlee (1883–1967) from April to October 1951. He was Secretary of State for Economic Affairs under *Wilson (1916–    ) between October 1964 and August 1966 when the Prime Minister, finding his support for devaluation inconvenient, appointed him Foreign Secretary. This delighted Brown, who intended to assert his independence and authority vis-à-vis Wilson. Like *Bevin (1881–1951) Brown was pragmatic, anti-communist and a supporter of the *United Nations, but had no 'socialist' foreign policy. He was a convinced European, believing that Europe with Britain in it was an essential counterbalance to the superpowers. But efforts to join the *EEC were blocked by De Gaulle (see: *Western Europe since 1945, Britain and), while the global role Brown advocated was effectively destroyed by the 1967 economic crisis and the decision, most painful to him, to withdraw from *East of Suez. Foreseeing the disruption to Britain's oil supplies if the Suez Canal were closed, Brown did much to improve relations with Egypt in an attempt to head off the 1967 Arab–Israeli war. His resignation in March 1968 came over arms sales to South Africa. Pretoria's cooperation in guarding the sea route round the Cape, perhaps in getting a Rhodesian settlement and in financing jobs in British defence industries led Brown into conflict with the Prime Minister who, bowing to left-wing pressure, opposed arms sales.

GEORGE-BROWN, G., In My Way, Gollancz, 1971.

SHLAIM, A., JONES, P., SAINSBURY, K., British Foreign Secretaries since 1945, David and Charles, 1977.

**Brussels, Treaty of** (1948). Signed on 17 March 1948 by Britain, France, the Netherlands, Belgium and Luxemburg, a fifty-year defensive alliance in which the powers pledged to render each other 'all military and other aid and assistance' in the event of any of them being attacked in Europe. It further called for co-ordination of military strategies and forces, establishing a Permanent Military Committee and several social and economic sub-committees. While ostensibly it was concluded as a guarantee against revived German aggression, fear of Soviet intentions was uppermost in the minds of its signatories. The treaty was signed in an atmosphere of increasing *Cold War tension following the coup in Czechoslovakia

(February 1948) and soon after it was concluded discussions were held to broaden it by including Iceland, Italy, Denmark, Portugal, Canada and the United States. In April 1949 it evolved into *NATO, to which the Federal Republic of Germany and Italy acceded in 1955. While the Brussels Treaty formed a nucleus for the Western Alliance its economic and social committees marked an advance in the direction of Western European integration. For Britain this indicated the abandonment of a diplomacy of temporary agreements for immediate purposes, in favour of long-term military association in the face of perceived common threat.

**Buffer state.** A buffer state is a small state between two larger powers which serves to forestall clashes between the latter by eliminating a common frontier, and ensures that a strategically important area falls under the domination of neither of these powers. Buffer states exist on the sufferance and with the agreement of their more powerful neighbours. At the same time they easily become the focus of major rivalry. Persia, Afghanistan and Tibet are examples of significant buffer states in the nineteenth and twentieth centuries. They were welcomed by British governments as impeding the encroachment of Russian influence on British interests in the Middle East and India.

**Bulgarian Massacres** (1875–6). These followed an abortive rising of the inhabitants of the Ottoman colony of Bulgaria against the Sultan and led Russia, as the self-appointed defender of the Christians and Slavs in the empire, to declare war on Turkey in 1877. In England the news of the massacres provoked a furious outburst of public indignation. The Prime Minister, *Disraeli (1804–81), insisted that the reports were exaggerated, and pursued, as far as circumstances would allow, the traditional pro-Turkish and anti-Russian foreign policy.

*Gladstone (1809–98), on the other hand, attacked the Turks in speeches and in his celebrated pamphlet The Bulgarian Horrors and the Question of the East (1876). He was widely misinterpreted because of his 'bag and baggage' phrase, as demanding the expulsion of Turkey from Europe altogether. In fact he was only calling for the end of Turkish administration in Bulgaria and Bosnia and Herzegovina. In responding, and appealing to, the force of organized moral indignation in the

ensuing agitation Gladstone re-established himself at the centre of public interest (having in 1875 resigned the leadership of the Liberal Party). As Disraeli saw it, the anti-Turkish mood endangered British interests because it might prevent the Government from taking effective action to counter the Russian occupation of Constantinople. When Russian troops subsequently threatened the Ottoman capital Disraeli ordered the fleet through the *Dardanelles in support of the Turks.

The Russo-Turkish war was ended by the Treaty of *San Stefano (1878), which gave Russia gains in Armenia and created a 'Big Bulgaria' stretching from the Black Sea to the Aegean. This made Disraeli very apprehensive that Bulgaria would become a Russian satellite, thus giving Russia an outlet through the Aegean Sea to the Mediterranean, where British imperial sea routes might be threatened. The treaty was very significantly modified at the *Berlin Congress (1878), by which, among other terms, Bulgaria was divided.

MILLMAN, R., *Britain and the Eastern Question 1875–78*, Oxford University Press, 1979.

SHANNON, R. T., *Gladstone and the Bulgarian Agitation*, Harvester Press, 1975.

**BULWER,** Sir Henry, Baron Dalling and Bulwer (created 1871) (1801–72). Bulwer first made his name in the early 1830s on missions to Belgium, where he played an important part in executing the policy of *Palmerston (1784–1865), which ultimately secured the country's independence and neutrality in 1839. He also served as Secretary to the Embassy at Constantinople where he secured an Anglo-Turkish trade treaty. Meanwhile he also sat in Parliament, establishing a reputation as a Radical orator.

After a period in Paris Bulwer was appointed Ambassador in Madrid in 1843. His efforts to resolve the *Spanish Marriages affair (1846) in Britain's favour were frustrated by Palmerston's precipitancy, and his chief's tendency to lecture the Spanish government combined with his own meddling in internal politics to lead to his expulsion from the country in 1848. A period in Washington followed, during which Bulwer achieved great popularity in America and negotiated the *Clayton–Bulwer treaty (1850), but this proved to be only a superficial

solution to colonial rivalries between Britain and the United States in Central America. From 1852 to 1855 Bulwer served in Tuscany and from 1858 to 1865 was a worthy successor at Constantinople to *Stratford Canning (1786–1880), the only Englishman whose stature as a professional diplomat exceeded his own.

See: Bulwer's own biography of Palmerston, 3 vols, Richard Bentley, 1870–4.

BULLEN, R., 'Anglo-French Rivalry and Spanish Politics', *The English Historical Review*, vol. 88, 1974.

**BUTLER,** Richard Austen, Baron Butler of Saffron Walden (created 1965) (1902–82). Butler was educated at Marlborough College and Pembroke College, Cambridge. He was Tory MP for Saffron Walden from 1929 to 1965. As Parliamentary Under-Secretary for Foreign Affairs between March 1938 and December 1941, he was one of those instrumental in encouraging Neville *Chamberlain (1869–1940) to persist with *appeasement when his senior colleagues had abandoned it. Butler was prepared to concede more to Hitler even than Chamberlain was; but the secrecy of his methods concealed this from contemporaries so that after Chamberlain's disappearance his career was largely unaffected. His success as wartime Education Minister under *Churchill (1874–1965) and as reforming Home Secretary under *Macmillan (1894–1986) did not ensure him the Tory leadership in October 1963, when he took the *Foreign Office as a consolation prize. The Government having only a year to run, Butler could do little with the freedom of action *Home (1903–    ) allowed him. With the United States recovering from the shock of the assassination of J. F. Kennedy, the Soviet Union going through a leadership struggle and France blocking Britain's entry into the *EEC (see: *Western Europe since 1945, Britain and), there was little to be achieved beyond resolving the disputes in Malaysia, southern Arabia and *Cyprus consequent on the withdrawal from *Empire. Butler retired from the Commons in 1965 to become Master of Trinity College, Cambridge.

BUTLER, R. A., *The Art of the Possible: The Memoirs of Lord Butler*, Hamish Hamilton, 1971.

COSGRAVE, P., *R. A. Butler: An English Life*, Quartet, 1983.

Cairo Conference (1943). Allied conference, code-named SEXTANT, which began on 22 November 1943 and whose final session closed on 7 December of the same year. The leading participants were Winston *Churchill (1874–1965), President Roosevelt and Generalissimo Chiang Kai-Shek. It confirmed that Britain would continue its struggle against Japan on the basis of *unconditional surrender after the defeat of Germany. By this time the turn of events in the war was encouraging for the Allies, but it was necessary to orchestrate the future effort against the *Axis. The Cairo Conference agreed that after the war Japan should be stripped of all the conquests she had made since 1894. China, whose status as a world power was confirmed in the Cairo Declaration, was promised Manchuria and Formosa. The Soviet Union was to receive the southern half of Sakhalin and the Kurile Island chain while the United States was to receive the Japanese-mandated islands in the Pacific. It was also agreed that 'in due course' Korea would regain its independence.

MCNEILL, W. H., *America, Britain and Russia: Their Cooperation and Conflict, 1941–46*, Oxford University Press, 1953.

WHEELER-BENNET, J. and NICHOLLS, A., *The Semblance of Peace*, Macmillan, 1972.

CALLAGHAN, (Leonard) James (1912–    ). Educated in Portsmouth, James Callaghan worked for the Inland Revenue and served in the Navy during *World War II (1939–45). He was elected an MP for Cardiff in 1950. He was Chancellor of the Exchequer (1964–7), resigning from this office when Harold *Wilson (1916–    ) insisted on the devaluation of sterling. Subsequently he was Home Secretary (1967–70). Following Wilson's re-election in 1974, he became Foreign Secretary. On Wilson's resignation he became Prime Minister (5 April 1976), defeating Michael Foot, the Left-wing candidate in the contest for the leadership of the Labour Party. Callaghan proved a strong supporter of *NATO and close Anglo-American understanding, and a believer in the British nuclear deterrent. In 1977 he was forced to conclude a pact with the Liberal Party to keep his government in office. In 1979 he received a vote of no confidence in the House of Commons and was defeated by Margaret *Thatcher (1925–    ) in the ensuing general election.

Campaign for Nuclear Disarmament (CND), see UNILATERALISM

CAMPBELL-BANNERMAN, Sir Henry (1836–1908). Liberal Prime Minister 1905–8. After holding junior office in the 1870s and early 1880s, Campbell-Bannerman was Secretary of State for war in the last two Gladstone governments and under *Rosebery (1847–1929), and made necessary, if unspectacular, reforms. In 1898 he became leader of the Liberal Party in succession to Sir William Harcourt. With the onset of the *Boer War (1899–1902), Campbell-Bannerman, who opposed the conflict, found himself struggling not only against the Government, but against the Liberal Imperialist group in his own party. The heated disputes among the Liberals cooled after 1902, a development which was assisted by common opposition to Joseph Chamberlain's proposals for Tariff Reform, and in 1905 Campbell-Bannerman became Prime Minister, with his position secured by a triumphant General Election victory in the next year.

Campbell-Bannerman helped to secure a lasting settlement in South Africa through granting self-government to the Transvaal and the Orange River Colony, but he could hardly have been expected to foresee the later illiberal development of the country. In Europe, while deeply committed to the *Anglo-French Entente of 1904, his peace-loving instincts caused him to desire better relations with Germany, but his aspirations in this matter carried little weight with his own Foreign Secretary, Sir Edward *Grey (1862–1933). A breakdown in his health forced him to retire in favour of *Asquith (1852–1928) and he died shortly afterwards. His shrewd idealism had done much to restore the fortunes of the Liberal Party and to maintain the Gladstonian tradition in foreign affairs.

SPENDER, J. A., *The Life of the Rt Hon Sir Henry Campbell-Bannerman*, Hodder and Stoughton, 1923.

WILSON, J., *CB: A Life of Sir Henry Campbell-Bannerman*, Constable, 1973.

**CANNING,** George (1770–1827). Tory Foreign Secretary 1807–9; 1822–7; Prime Minister 1827. Canning was a protégé of Pitt the Younger (1759–1806) and a man of brilliant abilities and great eloquence who was very popular with the public. However, he damaged his career through an arrogant and headstrong temperament which led many of his Tory colleagues to detest him.

In 1808 he led the way in committing Britain to the support of Portugal and Spain against Napoleon, an important step towards eventual victory. His conduct of relations with the United States was rather less happy, contributing to the deterioration in relations which culminated in the outbreak of the war of 1812. In the period after 1815 he found himself out of sympathy with the *Congress System and when he became Foreign Secretary once more, following the suicide of his great rival *Castlereagh (1769–1822), he brought British involvement in it to an abrupt end. He soon acquired a liberal reputation, being regarded by Metternich, in exaggerated terms, as the evil genius of revolution. Canning supported the independence of Latin America, although this nearly cost

him his job against the more reactionary members of the Cabinet. In European politics he moved away from Austria, made a valuable contribution to the achievement of Greek independence and supported the liberals in Portugal. An awareness of the importance of public opinion led him closely to cultivate the press. He substantially increased the size and efficiency of the *Foreign Office, giving it a character which was to endure throughout the nineteenth century, and he successfully overcame the antagonism of George IV to establish the principle of ministerial authority over the Crown in foreign affairs.

In 1827, after Lord Liverpool (1770–1828) was obliged to retire following a stroke, Canning became Prime Minister, to the consternation of the more hard-line Tories, led by *Wellington (1769–1852), who refused to serve under him, but he died a few months after taking office. On his death the Canningite Tories, of whom *Palmerston (1784–1865) was the most prominent, steered towards the Whigs.

HINDE, W., *George Canning*, Collins, 1973.

ROLO, P. J. V., *George Canning*, Macmillan, 1965.

TEMPERLEY, H. W. V., *The Foreign Policy of Canning 1822–1827*, 2nd ed., Cass, 1966.

**CANNING,** Stratford, see STRATFORD CANNING 1786–1880.

**Cape-to-Cairo Line.** The idea of a railway linking Egypt with South Africa. It was advanced by British imperialists, including Cecil Rhodes, at the turn of the century. Control over such a line would, it was argued, strategically strengthen and consolidate the British imperial role in Africa. The idea never materialized.

**Cardwell Army Reforms.** Edward Cardwell (1813–86), created 1st Viscount Cardwell in 1874, was appointed Secretary of State for War under *Gladstone (1809–98) in 1868. He introduced the most important Army reforms in Britain in the nineteenth century. These remedied the three major deficiencies of the time: the Army's unreadiness in the event of war, its inability to provide adequate colonial garrisons and its antique system of raising officers through purchase of commissions. The infantry battalions of the Army were grouped in the 'Linked Battalion System' – one to remain at home while the other was on service abroad. With associated militia and volunteer battalions he provided a home defence force and the nucleus of an expeditionary corps. Cardwell introduced a system of short-term enlistment, abolished flogging during peacetime and equipped the Army with the Martin Henry breech-loading rifle. The conflict of authority between the Secretary of State for War and the Commander-in-Chief was resolved by making the Minister supreme. The abolition of the institution of purchase of commissions met with strong objections from the Army, the Lords and the Conservatives, but it was now superseded by competitive examination for entry to, and promotion in, the Army. The cumulative effect of these reforms was a comprehensive modernization of the Army which enabled it to fight its colonial campaigns in the later nineteenth century. This modernization was carried further by the *Haldane Army Reforms between 1905 and 1912.

**CARRINGTON,** Peter Alexander Rupert, 6th Baron (1919–    ). Educated at Eton and Sandhurst, he subsequently served in Europe during the war. A Conservative politician, he was First Lord of the Admiralty (1959–63) and Secretary of State for Defence (1970–4). He became Foreign Secretary in 1979 in Mrs Thatcher's first government, where perhaps his most notable achievement was his contribution to the resolution of the question of Rhodesia, which led to the emergence of an independent Zimbabwe. His style and perception differed considerably from those of the Prime Minister, not least on the question of Britain's relations with the *EEC. He resigned as Foreign Secretary following the Argentinian invasion of the *Falkland Islands in April 1982, being succeeded by Francis *Pym (1922–    ). Since 1984 Lord Carrington has been Secretary-General of *NATO.

COSGRAVE, P., *Carrington: A Life and a Policy*, Dent, 1985.

**Casablanca Conference** (1943). Attended by Winston *Churchill (1874–1965) and President Roosevelt and their chiefs of staff, held between 14 and 24 January 1943, by which time the course of the war was turning against the *Axis. Its major significance was the declaration of *unconditional surrender (as opposed to the idea of a negotiated settlement with the enemy). The leaders agreed that peace could come only 'by the total elimination of German and Japanese war power'. They undertook to intensify the war effort, in particular with increased bombing of Germany, and to proceed with the invasion of Sicily. At the same time they decided to postpone the cross-channel invasion for a year. Britain agreed to the transfer of her military resources to the Far East after the defeat of Germany and Italy.

**CASEMENT,** Sir Roger (1864–1916). Having held various commercial and administrative posts in Africa, Casement served in the British consular service from 1895 to 1913. In 1903 he helped to expose atrocities by Europeans against natives in the Congo Free State, thus leading to the end of Belgian rule there, and encouraging generally more humane treatment of natives by colonial powers. In 1910 he performed a similar service for the Putumayo Indians in the Upper Amazon. He was a passionate Irish nationalist and pro-German in his sympathies. When *World War I (1914–18) broke out he was in the United States. He went from there to Germany in the hope of enlisting aid for a rising in Ireland. In April 1916 he was landed in Ireland from a German U-boat, in an unsuccessful attempt to avert the Easter Rising which he judged to be premature. He was captured by the British, tried, convicted of treason and, in spite of an extensive campaign for his reprieve, he was hanged.

INGLIS, B., *Roger Casement*, Hodder and Stoughton, 1973.

**Cash and Carry.** Regulations adopted in the American neutrality legislation of the later 1930s. They reflected the desire of the government and people of the United States to reconcile their trading interests overseas with their wish to avoid involvement in war, and were inspired by the mood of *isolationism and the conviction that international arms credits had been a contributory cause of the participation of their country in *World War I (1914–18). Cash and carry required that goods which were purchased by belligerents should be paid for in cash and transported in foreign vessels. At the same time, arms sales to belligerents were prohibited. In October 1939 these regulations were restricted to the North Atlantic area. They were further relaxed when the Joint Resolution of 4 November 1939 aided the Western Powers, Britain and France, by repealing the embargo on arms.

**CASTLEREAGH,** Robert Stewart, Viscount (1769–1822). Tory Secretary at War 1805, 1807–9; Foreign Secretary 1812–22. Castlereagh was a highly strung and very hardworking man, an excellent diplomatist but a poor orator. His Irish background meant that he entered politics with a strong sense of the vulnerability of political achievements and a pragmatic rather than ideological approach, which meant that his views defied simplistic understanding. In general he considered that British interests were best served by judicious involvement in Europe.

Between 1805 and 1809 Castlereagh made an important contribution to the prosecution of the war against Napoleon, making muchneeded military reforms, showing a sound grasp of grand strategy and sending Wellesley (*Wellington) (1769–1852) to Portugal in 1808. His record was marred by the fiasco of the Walcheren expedition in 1809. As Foreign Secretary his major achievements were the negotiation of the Treaty of Chaumont early in 1814, forming the alliance of the great powers which brought about the downfall of Napoleon, and his subsequent role at the Congress of *Vienna in 1815 as an architect of a European *balance of power which was to endure in essentials for half a century. His influence was especially important in ensuring that, although France was restrained by a ring of *bufferstates, she was not humiliated, and he subsequently supported her re-entry into international affairs. After 1815 he was a leading supporter of the *Congress System aiming to resolve international differences through discussion rather than force, but, unlike the *Holy Alliance powers (Austria, Prussia and Russia), he was a firm non-interventionist, as was evident in his attitude to unrest in Greece and Latin America. He established good relations with the United States, abandoning the arrogant stance which had hitherto characterized British attitudes to her former colonies, although simultaneously seeking to persuade other European countries to outlaw the slave trade.

The tensions within the Congress System led to its breakdown in the early 1820s and it suffered a final blow when Castlereagh himself committed suicide in August 1822. Castlereagh suffered considerable vilification from radicals, who accused him of being implicated in repression at home and reaction abroad, but such a narrow view fails to do justice to the breadth and sophistication of his policies.

BARTLETT, C. J., *Castlereagh*, Macmillan, 1966.
DERRY, J. W., *Castlereagh*, Allen Lane, 1976.
WEBSTER, C. K., *The Foreign Policy of Castlereagh, 1812–15*, Vol 1 (1925), Vol 2 *1815–1822*, Bell, 1931.

***Casus Belli*** and ***Casus Foederis***. The first term means a cause or reason for warfare: an action or provocative behaviour by one state which justifies its adversary in declaring war. *Palmerston (1784–1865) in 1853 described it as 'a case which would justify war'. According to the Charter of the *United Nations the only recognised *casus belli*, apart from those specifically authorized by the Security Council or General Assembly, is self-defence.

*Casus foederis* is a provocative action or behaviour by a state towards another which entitles the aggrieved state to call upon an ally to fulfil the terms of alliance between them, an event compelling treaty partners to come to each other's aid. Sometimes these terms appear to be confused. For example: at the end of the *Crimean War (1854–6) on 15 April 1856 the English, French and Austrian plenipotentiaries signed a convention by which a reciprocal engagement was entered into to regard as *casus belli* any violation of the main Treaty of *Paris (1856) and any encroachment on the independence and integrity of the Ottoman Empire. At the same time it also stipulated the naval and military contingents to be mobilized in the event of this *casus foederis* arising.

**CECIL,** Edgar Algernon Robert Gascoyne, Viscount Cecil of Chelwood (created 1923) (1864–1956). Third son of Lord *Salisbury (1830–1903), educated at Eton and University College Oxford, trained as a lawyer and, from 1906–1910, Conservative MP for East Marylebone. During *World War I (1914–18) he worked for the Red Cross and became Parliamentary Under-Secretary for Foreign Affairs (1915–18), Minister of Blockade (1916–18) and Assistant Secretary of State for Foreign Affairs (1918–19). He helped to prepare the way for the first draft of the Covenant of the *League of Nations, submitting a memorandum making proposals for the avoidance of a future war, including sanctions, blockade and collective resort to military force, which led to the appointment of the Phillimore Committee. Cecil also played a leading part in the debates at the *Paris Peace Conference (1919–20) which preceded the establishment of the League. In

1923 he was put in charge of League affairs in Baldwin's Government as Lord Privy Seal. In 1924 he became Chancellor of the Duchy of Lancaster with a similar responsibility, but in 1926, after a number of disagreements with his colleagues, for instance over the *Geneva Protocol (1924), Cecil resigned when the Cabinet refused to take his advice to accept naval parity with the United States. Under the Labour Government of 1929 he was made chairman of a departmental committee on League matters and British representative to the preparatory disarmament commission. However, the *World Disarmament Conference (1932–4) failed. Cecil hoped to save the League by mobilizing public opinion. He was President of the *League of Nations Union from 1923 to 1945. In 1937 he was awarded the Nobel Peace Prize.

CECIL, 1ST VISCOUNT OF CHELWOOD, *All the Way*, Hodder and Stoughton, 1949. *Great Experiment*, Jonathan Cape, 1941.

**CECIL,** Lord Robert, see SALISBURY, LORD, GASCOYNE-CECIL, ROBERT, 3RD MARQUESS OF SALISBURY (1830–1903).

**CENTO,** see CENTRAL TREATY ORGANIZATION.

**Central Powers.** The collective term used to describe Germany and her allies, Austria, Turkey and Bulgaria in *World War 1 (1914–18). The powers were linked by bilateral treaties and were united in the monarchical principle. Though Germany played the leading role she did not succeed in pressing her war aims upon the other powers – the Central Powers could never agree upon a common foreign policy. Their only coordinated appearance in the public diplomacy of World War I was the peace offer of 12 December 1916 (which was rejected by the Allies) and the negotiations for the *Brest-Litovsk Treaty (1918) with revolutionary Russia. The Central Powers as a bloc were dissolved with the conclusion of the separate armistices in late 1918.

**Central Treaty Organization** (CENTO). This evolved from the *Baghdad Pact (1955) and provided for mutual defence and economic cooperation. Britain, Iran and Pakistan acceded while the United States, though not a member, became associated with the organization. It was designed specifically to counter communist aggression, and the provisions relating to defence were not operative if members were in conflict with other non-communist countries. In 1975 the defence White Paper announced that British forces would no longer be designated for CENTO. It was further weakened by the Iranian revolution from early 1979.

**CHAMBERLAIN,** Sir (Joseph) Austen (1863–1937). Son of Liberal Unionist politician Joseph *Chamberlain (1836–1914) and half-brother of Neville, Austen Chamberlain was educated at Rugby School and Trinity College, Cambridge. After leaving Cambridge he studied in Paris and Berlin, in the process acquiring a passionate liking for France and marked coolness for Germany. In 1892 he entered Parliament as Liberal Unionist MP for East Worcestershire, held junior office in Salisbury's 1895 government and became Financial Secretary to the Treasury in 1900. He was Chancellor of the Exchequer in 1903–5, and in 1911, with Liberal Unionists now indistinguishable from Conservatives, was one of the contenders for the succession to *Balfour (1848–1930). In the summer of 1914 Chamberlain played a leading role in persuading the Asquith Government to support Russia and France against Germany, and in the coalition of 1915 became Secretary of State for India. He resigned in July 1917 after criticisms of the India Office for its role in the disastrous Mesopotamian campaign, but entered the War Cabinet in April 1918, becoming Chancellor once again in the post-war Lloyd George Coalition. In 1921 he succeeded *Bonar Law (1858–1923) as Conservative leader, but his support for *Lloyd George (1863–1945) during the *Chanak Crisis (1922) and his desire to continue with the coalition alienated him from the bulk of his party, so that the Tory revolt which ejected Lloyd George in 1922 also displaced Chamberlain as leader. However, this did not end his ministerial career, for in November 1924 he became Baldwin's Foreign Secretary.

The overriding object of British diplomacy since 1918 had been to re-establish stability in Europe so that Britain could minimize her involvement there and concentrate on rebuilding her global power. But American withdrawal from Europe and the failure of the *Versailles Settlement (1919) to satisfy French claims for security had led to the crisis of 1923, when the French and Belgian occupation of the *Ruhr had brought Germany close to disintegration from revolutionary forces of Left and Right. *MacDonald's answer to the problem had been the *Geneva Protocol (1924), but neither Chamberlain nor the Cabinet would accept the indeterminate military commitments this entailed. But the danger remained, in Chamberlain's view, of France setting off a new war which could lead to the establishment of Soviet Communism in Germany. An Anglo-French alliance was unacceptable to Chamberlain's colleagues, but rumour of it prompted German enthusiasm for a Western security pact.

The resulting agreement, signed at *Locarno in December 1925, was Chamberlain's creation. Britain, France, Germany, Italy and Belgium recognized the inviolability of the Franco–German and Belgian–German frontiers and the existence of the demilitarized Rhineland zone. The French could not again act as in 1923, even if Germany threatened her eastern neighbours. Chamberlain believed that the measure of harmony established by Locarno would be the basis for cooperation in the future, which would see an agreed readjustment of Germany's eastern frontier. Yet his policy after Locarno had no real success, as Germany's refusal to abandon her friendship with the Soviet Union demonstrated. Chamberlain left the *Foreign Office in 1929 and was disappointed not to return when the National Government was formed in August 1931. Instead he went to the Admiralty and resigned before the year was out. Thereafter he was a constant, if cautious, critic of the National Government's foreign policy, warning against the menace posed by Hitler.

CHAMBERLAIN, SIR J. A., *Down the Years*, Cassell, 1935. *Politics from the Inside, 1906–14*, Cassell, 1936.
PETRIE, SIR C., *The Life and Letters of the Rt. Hon Sir Austen Chamberlain*, 2 vols. Cassell, 1939–40.

**CHAMBERLAIN**, Joseph  (1836–1914). Unionist Colonial Secretary 1895–1903. Chamberlain began his career in local politics in Birmingham, where he was Mayor from 1873 to 1876, before being elected to Parliament as MP for Birmingham in 1876. He was remarkable for combining strongly radical views on domestic policy with a strong commitment to the *Empire. During the second Gladstone Ministry Chamberlain was President of the Board of Trade and pressed in the Cabinet for a firmer line on Egypt. He took office again under

*Gladstone (1809–98) in 1885, but shortly after resigned because of his opposition to Home Rule. From 1892 he was leader of the Liberal Unionists in the House of Commons.

In 1895 Chamberlain became Colonial Secretary in a coalition government of Unionists and Conservatives and achieved great prominence in a post hitherto regarded as something of a backwater. He sought to promote the strength of the Empire through unsuccessful plans for federation and customs union. He promoted capital investment in the colonies and sought to secure an alliance with Germany which he believed would be the best security for Anglo-Saxon world influence, although from 1902 he moved to an anti-German stance.

Chamberlain's period at the Colonial Office was dominated by the *Boer War (1899–1902). Tension between British possessions and the Boer republics of the Transvaal and the Orange Free State was increased by the disastrous *Jameson Raid in 1895 into the Transvaal, in which it was alleged that Chamberlain was implicated. From 1897 Chamberlain and *Milner (1854–1925) moved towards full-scale confrontation with the Boers, adopting a bellicose stance as champions of the *Uitlanders. War broke out in October 1899 and although the British were ultimately victorious, their own military inefficiency condemned them to a tedious struggle which lasted until 1902. After peace had been concluded at *Vereeniging Chamberlain himself made a triumphant tour of South Africa.

In 1903 Chamberlain took up the issue of Tariff Reform, campaigning for the reimposition of customs duties while giving a preference to the products of the Empire. He hoped thereby to cement imperial unity; to further economic growth and full employment at home and to raise money for old age pensions. Chamberlain resigned from the government in order to concentrate on the campaign, which split the Unionists and contributed to their disastrous defeat in the General Election of 1906. Shortly afterwards he suffered a serious stroke which ended his active political career. Though he was to see few of his cherished schemes realized, his compelling determination combined with great capacity to mould public opinion enabled him to exert a major influence on the development of British imperial policy.

GARVIN, J. L. AND AMERY, J., *The Life of Joseph Chamberlain*, (6 vols.) Macmillan, 1932–69.

JUDD, D., *Radical Joe*, Hamish Hamilton, 1977.
PORTER, A. N., *The Origins of the South African War: Joseph Chamberlain and the Diplomacy of Imperialism 1895–99*, Manchester University Press, 1980.

**CHAMBERLAIN**, (Arthur) Neville (1869–1940). Son of the Birmingham politician Joseph *Chamberlain (1836–1914) and half-brother of Austen *Chamberlain (1863–1937), he was educated at Rugby School and, intended by his father for business, studied commerce at Mason College, Birmingham. Sent by his father in 1890 to a remote island in the Bahamas, Chamberlain spent his early manhood vainly trying to grow sisal to improve the family's shaky finances. Seven years of adversity and seclusion in pioneering conditions developed characteristics which remained with Chamberlain throughout life and later proved important to his conduct of foreign policy: shyness and reserve, which could make him seem difficult to work with, and confidence in his own judgement and determination to have his way, which could make him seem arrogant and obstinate. Returning home in 1897, Chamberlain began a successful business career, becoming a leading figure in Birmingham's industrial life and a member of the city council in 1911. His work in improving city amenities was outstanding. In 1916 he was Lord Mayor of Birmingham, and in December that year accepted the invitation from *Lloyd George (1863–1945) to become Director-General of National Service to plan voluntary recruitment of labour for war industries. With responsibility but no power, unfamiliar with the processes of central government, and getting no backing from Lloyd George, Chamberlain could make no progress. Disgusted, he resigned in the summer of 1917 and went back to Birmingham.

Although without conspicuous political ambition hitherto, Chamberlain was now prepared to enter Parliament to provide for a nation debilitated by war the social and civic improvements he had carried out in Birmingham. Entering Parliament as a Conservative in 1918, he supported the coalition but had no confidence in Lloyd George. In Bonar Law's government of 1922 he became Postmaster-General, then Paymaster-General; in March 1923 as Minister of Health he entered the Cabinet; by May he was Chancellor. Chamberlain refused the Chancellorship in Baldwin's second government, preferring instead the Ministry of Health where he introduced important reforms. In November 1931 he became Chancellor of the National Government, and from then on became increasingly involved with foreign affairs.

The international nature of economic problems and the troubled world situation of the early 1930s would have prevented any Chancellor from attending to purely domestic concerns. In 1932 Chamberlain played a leading role at the *Ottawa Conference, establishing *Imperial Preference, and at the Lausanne Conference which ended German *reparations; at the same time Simon's indecision in the face of Japanese aggression obliged his colleagues to spend more time on foreign affairs. By 1934 the Chiefs of Staff were warning of the security risk in the Far East, where Japan posed an immediate threat, and in Europe, where in the longer term Germany would pose a more serious danger. The weakness of Britain's forces meant that to provide adequate security a major rearmament programme was necessary, yet its cost would make recovery from depression impossible. In September 1934, therefore, Chamberlain proposed a comprehensive settlement with Japan; *MacDonald (1866–1937) and the Cabinet vetoed this for fear of antagonizing the United States. Growing extremism in Japan discouraged the British from making any similar approach thereafter.

The size and shape of rearmament were decisively influenced by Chamberlain, who emerged as the most effective figure in the National Cabinet. Naval rearmament was to provide a battle fleet equal to Japan's and, simultaneously, protection in home waters against Germany. But priority was given to the RAF. Chamberlain argued that the cheapest and most effective deterrent was a bomber force. It could be used to attack Germany directly and immediately if Hitler moved east or west; an army, by contrast, would need allies, would operate slowly and would be incapable of producing a decisive result without the bloodletting of 1914–18. The result was that the Army remained the Cinderella of the armed forces, unable to play a continental role, while the RAF proved incapable of fulfilling Chamberlain's role for it because bombers could not be produced in sufficient quality or quantity. By the end of 1938, with the technology of air defence rapidly improving, the emphasis had shifted to the fighter programme.

The defence posture which determined mini-.sterial responses to the dictators' aggression was of Chamberlain's making.

During Baldwin's last premiership (June 1935–May 1937) Chamberlain grew increasingly impatient at the inability of British policy to stop the international situation deteriorating to the point where war seemed likely. The *Abyssinian Crisis (1935–6) alienated Italy and wrecked the basis of the rearmament programme which had assumed she would be neutral or friendly. Nor was any serious attempt made to meet what Chamberlain regarded as the legitimate claims of Hitler to self-determination for those Germans living outside Germany. During the winter of 1936–7, when he knew he would succeed *Baldwin (1867–1947) Chamberlain had decided that of the two elements in what would be his foreign policy, conciliation and rearmament, conciliation would have to be pursued more vigorously to create time to make rearmament effective. The objective, a general settlement with Hitler and Mussolini that would avert war and end the ruinously expensive arms race, assumed that the dictators were rational men, opportunists certainly, but who realized that modern war could only mean the destruction of civilization and the victory of 'Bolshevism'. Chamberlain was probably right about Mussolini; he was quite wrong about Hitler. A Victorian Liberal in outlook, Chamberlain understood neither the nihilism of Nazi ideology nor the near limitless power that Hitler wielded over Germany.

The nature of Chamberlain's character and convictions about foreign policy, his wide experience of government, and his authority over his party meant that after he became Prime Minister in May 1937 British policy towards the dictators became markedly more conciliatory. And it persisted in conciliation despite growing indications that it was not discouraging aggression but encouraging it. Aware that the British *Empire was unlikely to survive a war against Germany, Italy and Japan, the Cabinet initially supported Chamberlain's approach. *Eden (1897–1977), less certain, resigned in February 1938; but, with *Halifax (1881–1959) at the *Foreign Office in his place, Chamberlain's control of policy was strengthened: Chamberlain consulted Halifax, but had usually first formulated his ideas with his confidant (nominally the government's Chief Industrial Adviser) Sir Horace

Wilson. Chamberlain led the Cabinet from the front, and in the closing stages of the crisis over the *Sudetenland came near to ignoring it altogether. The *Munich Agreement (1938) so clouded his judgement, and his success in averting war was so popular in the country, that it was only with difficulty that his colleagues persuaded him to speed up the rearmament programme and refrain from exploring colonial and economic *appeasement.

It was only after Hitler's flouting of self-determination by occupying the rump of Czechoslovakia in March 1939 that Chamberlain abandoned conciliation and issued guarantees to Poland, Rumania, Greece and Turkey. Even so, he did not encourage the Cabinet's attempts to get an alliance with Russia, fearing this would make war with Hitler more likely, not less. He had no hesitation about declaring war in September 1939, but with Hitler controlling Central and Eastern Europe did not believe the Allies were capable of military victory. He hoped for a collapse of the German home front. Hence his Fabian conduct of the war, which provoked Commons dissatisfaction and led to his resignation in May 1940. But he remained Conservative leader and worked closely with *Churchill (1874–1965) as Lord President of the War Cabinet. Cancer forced him to resign in October 1940 and he died in November.

DILKS, D., *Neville Chamberlain*, vol 1, *1869–1929*, Cambridge University Press, 1984.

FEILING, K., *The Life Of Neville Chamberlain*, Macmillan, 1946.

FUCHSER, L. W., *Neville Chamberlain and Appeasement: A Study in the Politics of History*, W. W. Norton, New York, 1982.

**Chanak Crisis** (1922). Anglo-Turkish crisis. The Treaty of Sèvres (1920), which followed the defeat of the Ottoman Empire in *World War I (1914–18), had left the remaining national state of Turkey divided up by the victorious Allies into *spheres of influence, with Allied troops in Constantinople. The Turks had been obliged to cede to Greece not just territory in Thrace but also on the Asiatic side of the Straits, the city of Smyrna and its hinterland, which contained up to half a million ethnic Greeks. This was to be for a period of five years, after which there was to be a plebiscite. This aroused deep Turkish animosity, inspiring nationalist revival under General Mustapha Kemal (later known as Atatürk), the hero of the

*Gallipoli campaign. He began organizing a national resistance movement and in 1920 set up a rival national government in Ankara, proceeding to attack Smyrna.

*Lloyd George (1863–1945), the British Prime Minister, was strongly pro-Greek and after the fall of Smyrna decided to reinforce the British garrison at Constantinople. At the same time, the victorious Turkish army advanced towards British lines, reaching Chanak at the *Dardanelles. The majority of the British Dominions indicated that they would not lend Britain support against the Turks (an illustration of the independence from London that was to become increasingly apparent in the following years). The British commander, General Harrington, was told to issue the Turks with an ultimatum to withdraw their forces. His troops being greatly outnumbered, he decided not to give it. Instead he opened negotiations which resulted in the pact of Mudania, agreed on 11 October 1922. This pledged the return to Turkey of Eastern Thrace and Adrianople, provided the Turks accepted the neutralization of the Dardanelles and Bosphorus. In 1923 the Treaty of *Lausanne was signed with Turkey, ending Allied occupation of Constantinople and conceding Kemal's demands. At the same time, it recognized British interests in the demilitarization of the Straits (see: *Straits Question). At home the Chanak crisis led to the fall of the Lloyd George Government, the Conservative *Bonar Law (1858–1923) breaking the coalition with the Liberals and alleging that Lloyd George had recklessly and irresponsibly very nearly brought Britain to war.

WALDER, D., *The Chanak Affair*, Hutchinson, 1969.

**Chargé d'Affaires.** Normally the second-ranking official of an embassy or legation, he or she takes charge in the absence of an Ambassador or Minister. Though not officially accredited, the Chargé d'Affaires is received by the Foreign Minister of the host country and conducts business as usual during his or her incumbency, which is usually of relatively short duration.

**Christmas Eve, Peace of,** see GHENT, TREATY OF (1814)

**CHURCHILL,** Sir Winston Leonard Spencer (1874–1965). Son of Lord Randolph Churchill,

Winston Churchill was educated at Harrow and Sandhurst. He fought at the battle of Omdurman in 1898, was a war correspondent in South Africa during the 2nd *Boer War (1899–1902) between 1899 and 1900, and was elected Conservative MP for Oldham in 1900. Disagreeing with his party's move towards protectionism, he became a Liberal in 1904, and entered the Cabinet as President of the Board of Trade in 1908. In 1910 he became Home Secretary, and in 1911 First Lord of the Admiralty, where he ended the First Sea Lord's monopoly of knowledge about war plans and achieved a measure of combined planning with the War Office through the *CID. The stalemate of trench warfare and the plight of Russia prompted him early in 1915 to suggest that the navy force the *Dardanelles and enter the Black Sea. If successful, such a move would probably have been decisive: Turkey driven from the war, Russia assisted, and the *Central Powers weakened in the Balkans. But delay and inter-service rivalry resulted in the expedition's failure (see: *Gallipoli (1915)) and in May 1915 Conservative pressure forced *Asquith (1852–1928) to transfer Churchill from the Admiralty to be Chancellor of the Duchy of Lancaster. With nothing to do, he resigned in November 1915 and served on the Western Front until May 1916. He then returned to Westminster, but was out of office until July 1917 when *Lloyd George (1863–1945) made him Minister of Munitions.

From December 1918, as Secretary of State for War and Air, Churchill pressed, unsuccessfully, for active intervention in Russia to suppress the Bolsheviks (see: *Russian Civil War, British Intervention in the (1918–20)). More practically, he suggested that Britain's newly acquired territories in the Middle East should be policed by the RAF. Early in 1921 Churchill became Colonial Secretary, playing a leading part in determining the post-war political order in Transjordan and Iraq, and in 1922 supported Lloyd George in the *Chanak Crisis. Defeated at Dundee in November 1922, Churchill remained out of Parliament until October 1924 when he was returned for Epping as a Conservative. Neville Chamberlain's refusal of the Exchequer led *Baldwin (1867–1947) to approach Churchill, and as Chancellor of the Exchequer until 1929 he helped finance pension increases and new insurance programmes with cutbacks in defence expenditure, in 1927 securing the annual renewal of the cost-cutting rule under which the armed services were to assume that they need prepare for no major war within ten years (see: *Ten Year Rule).

In January 1931 Churchill left the Shadow Cabinet because of Baldwin's willingness to contemplate self-government for India, and he waged an almost isolated campaign against the National Government's India Bill which became law in 1935. Standing by the King in the Abdication Crisis at the end of 1936 further alienated Churchill from his party, and in consequence his warnings about Hitler for long went unheeded. Well informed about German military expansion and the shortcomings of Britain's rearmament programme, Churchill was listened to with increasing respect as German territorial aggrandizement continued. Believing he was less dangerous within the Government than outside, *Chamberlain (1869–1940) brought him into the War Cabinet as First Sea Lord when war began in 1939, and it was Churchill's determination to prosecute the war vigorously that led to the Narvik expedition whose failure, ironically, brought about Chamberlain's resignation and replacement by Churchill in May 1940.

The role of supreme warlord came easily to Churchill, who directed strategy himself and so avoided the military–civilian conflicts which had dogged the 1914–18 war effort and which had begun to emerge again due to his activities as First Lord. At no time after September 1939 did Churchill believe that Britain could make peace with the Nazis, or that she could defeat Germany without active American military support. After France's collapse in June 1940, it was clear that the defeat could only come through an invasion of the Continent. That invasion could only take place in France, the obvious route to Germany, and there must be no question of its failure, nor of casualties on the 1914–18 scale. So it could not be undertaken prematurely. Once Churchill had seen off the threat of Germany invading Britain in summer 1940, his caution dictated a twofold approach: a strategic bombing campaign against Germany, and a peripheral strategy, in the Mediterranean and North Africa, against Italy. The object was so to weaken Germany as to make her vulnerable to military assault. This could never have been attained but for Hitler's invasion of Russia in June 1941 and the declaration of war on the United States in December. Churchill did all he could to help Stalin by redirecting much-needed American supplies to

Russia, but he found it increasingly difficult to satisfy either Washington or Moscow with regard to the *Second Front in Europe which both wanted opened as quickly as possible.

Both in 1942 and 1943 Churchill ensured that the Anglo-American effort focused on the Mediterranean. This placed his close and vital relationship with Roosevelt, and Anglo-American relations generally, under perceptibly increasing, if not serious, strain. He dared not oppose a second front for 1944, yet once it was clear that the invasion of Normandy in June that year had succeeded, Churchill realized that the character of the war was changing. Hitler's defeat was a matter of time; more worrying now was Stalin, whose forces would dominate Eastern Europe and the Balkans when the war ended, threatening Britain's position in the Middle East and an exhausted Western Europe with Soviet Communism. Churchill responded with old-fashioned 'realpolitik'. In October 1944 he saw Stalin and agreed on the 'percentages deal' over British and Soviet *spheres of influence in the Balkans; and soon afterwards he urged Eisenhower, in control of the predominantly American Allied army in Western Europe, to advance eastwards into Germany as far and as fast as possible. Eisenhower refused, and Roosevelt did not want to upset Stalin. By the time he left office in July 1945 Churchill realized how greatly Britain's influence had weakened. The war had ended as he feared. In Europe and the Middle East British interests were vulnerable to the Soviet Union; while in India and Southeast Asia the Japanese, despite their defeat, had effectively dispelled any myths about British invincibility by their destruction of regional British naval power and the capture of Singapore in 1941–2.

As Leader of the Opposition (and MP for Woodford) after 1945, Churchill spoke often of the Soviet threat to Europe and of the need for a united Europe to resist it. His were the images of the Iron Curtain and of Britain lying at the centre of three concentric circles – of the Atlantic alliance, of the Commonwealth and *Empire, and of Europe. His final premiership, from October 1951 to April 1955, revealed what this meant: defence cooperation with the United States was improved; decolonization was halted and European unity was construed in a purely military sense. The decision was taken to manufacture the H-bomb, and Churchill stayed in office, despite severe ill-health, believing that a summit between himself and Eisenhower and Stalin's successors could end the *Cold War.

BARKER, E., *Churchill and Eden at War*, Macmillan, 1978.

CHURCHILL, W. S., *The World Crisis, 1911–18*, 5 vols., Thornton Butterworth, 1923–31. *The Second World War*, 6 vols., Cassell, 1948–54.

GILBERT, M., *W. S. Churchill* (the monumental biography begun by Randolph Churchill with accompanying volumes of correspondence), Heinemann/Macmillan, 1966– .

JAMES, R. R., *Churchill, A Study in Failure 1900–39*, Penguin, 1981.

SELDON, A., *Churchill's Indian Summer: the Conservative Government, 1951–5*, Hodder and Stoughton, 1981.

**CID**, see COMMITTEE OF IMPERIAL DEFENCE

**CLARENDON**, Lord, George William Frederick, 4th Earl of Clarendon (1800–70). Liberal Foreign Secretary (1853–8, 1865–6, 1868–70). Clarendon began his career in the diplomatic service, negotiating a commercial treaty with France in 1831 and serving with distinction as Ambassador in Madrid from 1833 to 1839, during which period he helped to conclude the *Quadruple Alliance of 1834 and obtained a treaty with Spain with regard to the slave trade. On his return to Britain in 1839 he entered Melbourne's Cabinet and soon emerged as a leading critic of Palmerston's Eastern policy.

In 1847 *Russell (1792–1878) appointed him Lord Lieutenant of Ireland, where he handled a very difficult situation with considerable ability. On Palmerston's dismissal in December 1851 Russell offered Clarendon the *Foreign Office. He declined it at this juncture but accepted it from *Aberdeen (1784–1860) in February 1853 after Russell himself resigned the post. The least happy phase of his career immediately followed as he strove unsuccessfully to halt the slide to war with Russia, hampered by imperfect coordination of policy with *Stratford de Redcliffe (1786–1880) at Constantinople and by the disagreements between the 'doves' and 'hawks' in the Cabinet in relation to which Clarendon held a middle position. The Foreign Secretary emerged in a rather better light in 1856 when he took the leading part in negotiating the Treaty of *Paris which ended the *Crimean War (1854–6). This proved a significant, albeit temporary, check on Russian ambitions, while in eschewing undue harshness, Clarendon showed a realistic appreciation of the limits of British power.

In his two short periods at the Foreign Office in the 1860s Clarendon's major problem was the rising power of Prussia under Bismarck. In 1866 he resolutely resisted pressure from the Queen to intervene in the dispute between Prussia and Austria, but after 1868 sought to promote disarmament by France and Prussia. His death in harness in July 1870 removed a significant check on Bismarck, and the Franco-Prussian war broke out a few weeks later.

Clarendon was one of the abler Victorian foreign secretaries, a Free Trader who steered a middle course between Palmerstonian interventionism and Cobdenite idealism. He was also active, as was Russell between 1859 and 1865, in reorganizing the Foreign Office, a development which was symbolized by the occupation of Sir Giles Gilbert Scott's new buildings in 1868.

MAXWELL, H., *The Life and Letters of George William Frederick, Fourth Earl of Clarendon*, 2 vols., Edward Arnold, 1913.

**Clayton–Bulwer Treaty** (1850). A compromise arrangement which was devised to end rivalry between Britain and the United States in Central America. It was ratified on 4 July 1850. In the late 1840s Britain was occupying the Bay Islands, which belonged to Honduras, and also the eastern coast of Central America. After war broke out between the United States and Mexico the British saw that American victory would encourage the United States to construct a canal across the isthmus. Accordingly the British authorities seized the mouth of the San Juan River, the obvious outlet of any future canal. Following the failure of negotiations, Sir Henry *Bulwer (1801–72) was despatched to Washington. The subsequent agreement placed any future isthmian canal under joint Anglo-American control, guaranteed its neutrality and provided for equal tolls for the subjects of both powers. It pledged the signatories not to 'occupy or fortify, or colonize, or assume or exercize any dominion over Nicaragua, Costa Rica, the Mosquito Coast, or any part of Central America'. A disputed clause left Britain in control of her existing protectorates along the east coast of the isthmus, though, under pressure from America, Britain left in 1858–60. The Clayton–Bulwer Treaty was superseded in 1901 by the *Hay–Pauncefote Treaties (1900–1), which gave the United States the exclusive right to construct and operate a canal across the isthmus.

BOURNE, K., 'The Clayton–Bulwer Treaty and the Decline of British Opposition to the Territorial Expansion of the United States, 1857–1860', *Journal of Modern History*, 33, 3, 1961, pp. 287–91.

VAN ALSTYNE, R. W., 'British Diplomacy and the Clayton-Bulwer Treaty, 1850–1860', *Journal of Modern History* 11, 2, 1939, pp. 149–83.

**CND,** see UNILATERALISM

**Coalition.** In international relations: a combination of nation states grouped together for joint action. A coalition of states is normally considered to be more informal, as well as more temporary and limited, than an alliance. The terms are sometimes used interchangeably, though. For instance the World War II Grand Alliance between Britain, the United States and the Soviet Union is sometimes referred to as a coalition.

**COBDEN,** Richard (1804–1865). The son of a Sussex farmer, Cobden travelled widely in his youth before setting up in business as a calicoprinter in Manchester and being elected an MP in 1841. He was a passionate advocate of *Free Trade with a far-reaching vision of the moral consequences which would result as it advanced, 'thrusting aside the antagonism of race and creed and language'. He became a national figure as the leader of the Anti-Corn Law League, which secured most of its objectives in 1846 when *Peel (1788–1850) carried the repeal of the Corn Laws.

Cobden was a leading critic of interventionist Palmerstonian diplomacy, considering that national greatness would be better achieved through peace and prosperity at home rather than through meddling abroad. In the 1850s, working in association with his close friend John Bright (1811–89), he strongly opposed British involvement in the *Crimean War (1854–6), feeling that Turkey was wholly unworthy of support. This was a stance which brought him much unpopularity, as did his attack on *Palmerston (1784–1865) over the *Arrow incident. Cobden carried a motion for a committee of enquiry against the Prime Minister, but when Palmerston called a general election on the issue he won a tremendous victory and both Cobden and Bright lost their seats.

Cobden, however, shortly returned to Parliament and successfully promoted and negotiated a Free Trade treaty with France (see: *Cobden–Chevalier Treaty (1860) ). He took a great interest in America, being sympathetic to the North in the Civil War, but was strongly opposed to violence and anxious that Britain should not intervene.

Cobden never held government office, but acquired great stature as an independent statesman, who presented a view of Britain's role in the world radically different from that of Palmerston and his sympathizers. His adherents, dubbed 'the *Manchester School' by *Disraeli (1804–81), were a significant radical faction in the later nineteenth-century Liberal Party.

BRIGHT, JOHN and THOROLD ROGERS, J. E., eds., *Speeches on Questions of Public Policy by Richard Cobden MP*, Macmillan 2 vols. 1870.
MORLEY, JOHN, *Life of Richard Cobden*, Chapman and Hall 1903.
READ, DONALD, *Cobden and Bright*, Edward Arnold, 1967.

**Cobden–Chevalier Treaty** (1860). The Anglo-French Treaty of Commerce signed on 23 January 1860 following discussions between Richard *Cobden (1804–65), the apostle of *Free Trade and Michel Chevalier, the French economist. Napoleon III had had for a long while an interest in free trade ideas. There was also a diplomatic consideration: he wanted to improve diplomatic relations with Britain because of diplomatic tensions arising from French involvement in Italy (see: *Italian Unification, Britain and).

France agreed to abolish all import bans, removed most raw materials and foodstuffs from customs rates and fixed 'ad valorem' duties on manufactured goods and coal that were not to exceed 30 per cent (25 per cent from 1864). Britain agreed to let in a great number of finished products duty-free and drastically reduced its wine tax. The schedule of goods listed clearly defined the main commercial interests of each country. Britain wished to sell chiefly textiles and cloth, iron, steel, machinery and ships. The French wanted to export wines and luxury goods. The Treaty led within the next few years to a great expansion of trade between the two countries and to many measures of a similar kind elsewhere in Europe. The value of French imports from Britain increased between 1859 and 1869 from 278 million francs to 549 million. Britain's imports from France over the same period grew from 591 million francs to 904 million. British industrialists and traders were better able to derive advantages from it than were the less concentrated and weaker industries of France. Britain and France soon made similar arrangements with other European countries in which Article 19 of the Treaty, the most-favoured-nation clause, was repeated, thereby considerably encouraging multilateral trade in Europe.

**Cod War** (1972–6). The dispute between Britain and Iceland which was sparked off by the latter's unilateral extension of her fishing-limit from 12 to 50 miles. It led to a number of incidents between British trawlers and Icelandic gunboats, with the British Navy sending frigates to protect the trawlers from harassment. The Cod War was resolved by an agreement reached in Oslo on 1 June 1976 by Anthony *Crosland (1918–77), the Foreign Secretary, by which up to 24 trawlers were to be allowed to fish within a 200-mile limit claimed by Iceland. This was regarded as capitulation by many in the British fishing industry. It was also specified at Oslo that any subsequent agreement should not simply be a bilateral one between London and Reykjavik but should be negotiated between Iceland and the *EEC as a whole.

**Cold War.** The state of hostility and rivalry between the Communist and non-Communist blocs since the end of *World War II (1939–45) which has involved diplomatic conflict, a massive arms race, propaganda and hostile measures of every kind short of direct military conflict between the superpowers. It bears many of the features of a traditional inter-state power struggle, though its ideological dimension, which may be traced back to the Russian Revolution of 1917, and its global extent clearly distinguish it from previous hostilities. So, too, does the stalemate produced by the possession of vastly destructive nuclear arsenals by the superpowers. The term 'Cold War', which was publicized by the well-known American journalist Walter Lippmann, was used in the Congress debate on the *Truman Doctrine (1947). The conflict was intensified with the *Berlin Blockade and airlift (1948) and was widened to a global rivalry with the Korean War of 1950–3. Its most dangerous episode was the *Cuban Missile Crisis (1962). The

period after this led to a lessening of tension between the superpowers (see: *Détente), though the decline in East–West relations in the late 1970s led some commentators to speak of a 'new Cold War'. Responsibility for the Cold War has been attributed to various causes. The West have traditionally explained it as the result of a Soviet intention to isolate, weaken and subvert them and to spread the Communist creed throughout the world. According to this view, the Soviet consolidation of control in Eastern Europe was a major aggravating factor. Communists have ascribed it to the aggression of international capitalism and, in particular, to the policies of the United States. Others have emphasized the role of mutual misunderstandings and misperceptions. It is clear, however, that this rivalry would not exist without there being two immensely powerful antagonists, brought geographically and militarily face to face by the collapse of Germany in 1945. The clear bipolar conflict of the early years has been modified and complicated by the emergence of independent Communist states, of which the most important is China.

DOUGLAS, R., *From War to Cold War, 1942–8*, Macmillan, 1981.

GADDIS, J. L., *The United States and the Origins of the Cold War*, Columbia University Press, New York, 1972.

MASTNY, V., *Russia's Road to the Cold War*, Columbia University Press, New York, 1979.

ROSS, G. ed., *The Foreign Office and the Kremlin: British Documents on Anglo-Soviet Relations, 1941–5,,* Cambridge University Press, 1984.

ROTHWELL, V., *Britain and the Cold War 1941–47*, Jonathan Cape, 1982.

**Collective Security.** An arrangement, usually laid down in a treaty or convention, by which the signatory states pledge to cooperate for the maintenance of their mutual security should any one, or more than one of them, be attacked. After *World War I (1914–18) it was widely felt that the pre-1914 alliance system had been largely responsible for the outbreak of war and that a system of collective security should be designed to contain acts of aggression as breaches of the international peace, and to supersede reliance on the *balance of power. In this way, bilateral alliances in defence of national interests would be rendered unnecessary. Accordingly, the *League of Nations enjoined collective responsibility for the security of its members as described, in particular, in Article 10 of the Covenant.

The problem was how to transform the aspiration towards a watertight system of collective security into a reality. In 1923 the Draft Treaty of *Mutual Assistance and, in the following year, the *Geneva Protocol represented the most serious attempt to provide formal machinery for its enactment. They were not ratified, however, because of the difficulty of reaching an agreed definition of aggression and because of the British Government's objection to the degree of military preparedness which they thought inimical to the preservation of peace, and to commitments which might cut across prior Commonwealth obligations. Similar hesitancy by the United States had led it to refuse to ratify the Treaty of *Versailles (1919) and join the League of Nations. Many Americans felt that adherence to a strict rule of collective security might oblige their country to become involved in military action without Congressional consent and in places and at times not of its own choosing. Collective security and *isolationism were not compatible. The idea of collective security was closely linked with that of disarmament in the interwar years. At the same time, the use of economic sanctions to contain aggressors, short of the use of military force, was an idea which won considerable popularity, especially in Britain during the *Abyssinian War (1935–6), though nothing served to discredit the notion of collective security as an effective guarantee of international peace and security as much as Mussolini's successful defiance of the League in his conquest of Abyssinia. Since *World War II (1939–40) the term has been used to refer both to the system of international security which the *United Nations has sought to establish and to more limited alliances such as *NATO, covering *spheres of influence rather than aspiring to be a global peace-keeping system.

**Comity of Nations.** Privileges accorded to one state and its functionaries as a matter of polite deference and courtesy rather than as a matter of legal compliance are spoken of as being grounded in comity: the principle of community spirit, friendliness and good manners between states.

**Committee of Imperial Defence** (CID). This was created in December 1902 in response to the weakness of defence organization revealed by the 2nd *Boer War (1899–1902). The CID's purpose, according to *Balfour (1848–1930), was 'not to take up from time to time questions referred to it by the Cabinet, but to make it its duty to survey as a whole the strategical military needs of the Empire'. The CID had advisory status, which allowed the Cabinet to retain its ultimate powers of decision; and its membership included the Prime Minister (who normally acted as chairman), the service ministers and service chiefs, and any other figure the Prime Minister wished to attend. *Campbell-Bannerman (1836–1908) and *Asquith (1852–1928) lacked Balfour's interest in defence matters and neither of them used the CID as Balfour had intended. Before 1914 the full CID, with a growing membership, rarely met; its important work was done by its secretariat, headed from 1912 by *Hankey, and proliferating sub-committees. Grand strategy was infrequently and inadequately discussed, and the resulting strains on the civil–military relationship were exposed after 1914 when the CID was suspended. Its functions were assumed successively by the War Council, the Dardanelles Committee, the War Committee and the War Cabinet, and it resumed again only in 1922.

The interwar CID came closer to fulfilling Balfour's original intentions in two respects: grand strategy was discussed more regularly and relations between ministers and service chiefs became easier – a development which owed much to Hankey being Secretary to the Cabinet as well as to the CID. Following the Salisbury Committee's recommendation in 1923 that the three service chiefs 'should have an individual and collective responsibility for advising on defence policy as a whole', the Chiefs of Staff Committee was set up and became the most important of the standing sub-committees that the CID spawned. Assisted by a Joint Planning sub-committee formed in 1927 and a Joint Intelligence sub-committee in 1936, the Chiefs of Staff provided a regular flow of strategic appreciations to ministers which ensured that CID recommendations and Cabinet decisions had the benefit of extensive military advice. Criticism that the Prime Minister could not exercise the necessary degree of co-ordination and control led to the appointment in 1936 of a Minister for Co-ordination of Defence to act as the Prime Minister's deputy on the CID and to act closely with the Chiefs of Staff. Inter-service rivalry and civil–military differences were not eliminated by the CID, and fundamental questions often went unasked; but the system provided a more rational and intelligent approach to defence policy than any other major power was capable of in the 1930s. The CID's responsibilities were assumed by the War Cabinet in September 1939, and the organization was not re-created subsequently.

GIBBS, N. N., *Grand Strategy*, vol. I, HMSO, 1976.

JOHNSON, F. A., *Defence by Committee: the British Committee of Imperial Defence 1885–1959*, Oxford University Press, 1960.

**Common Market,** see EUROPEAN COMMUNITY

**Commonwealth,** see EMPIRE AND COMMONWEALTH, THE BRITISH

**Concert of Europe.** The customary acceptance after 1815 that the final arrangement of any changes in the *balance of power in Europe should be brought about only after the Great Powers had been consulted. These were Britain, France, Russia, Austria, Prussia (later Germany) and sometimes Italy and Turkey. This consultation was usually by international conference. The minor powers were invited to participate only when directly involved in the problems under discussion. The Concert of Europe did not embody definite and formal provisions and it was, of its nature, a somewhat vague concept. In practice it meant a hegemony of the Great Powers over the lesser ones. It ceased to function when the European balance of power structure developed into two opposed alliance systems, the Triple Alliance and the Triple Entente in the early twentieth century. The basic idea of the dominance and collaboration of the Great Powers was carried over later into the organization of the *League of Nations and the *United Nations in which the Great Powers (e.g. in the Security Council) were given special prerogatives.

**Congress System** (1815–25). The attempt to preserve peace by periodic meetings of the Great Powers. The wish to settle differences peacefully in the years immediately following the Napoleonic Wars was combined with the concern of those powers to prevent and suppress revolution. In Article 6 of the *Quadruple Alliance (1815) Britain, Austria, Prussia and Russia undertook to uphold the *Vienna Settlement (1815) if needs be by force and to meet from time to time in conference. The Congress of *Aix-la-Chapelle (1818) admitted France to the European concert. With the revolutionary upheavals of 1819–20 in southern Europe and Germany clear divergences opened up between Britain and the powers of the *Holy Alliance. Austria and Russia wanted to use the system to put down these revolts and to justify the intervention of the powers in the internal affairs of other states. This rift became very apparent at the Congresses of *Troppau (1820), Laibach (1821) and *Verona (1822). At Verona Britain withdrew formally from the system following demands by the other powers for intervention in Greece and Spain. Both *Castlereagh (1769–1822) and *Canning (1770–1827), as successive Foreign Secretaries, registered dissent from the system. The State Paper of 5 May 1820 clearly stated Castlereagh's position on the issue of intervention, while Canning stated unequivocally that the Congress System was 'never intended as a union . . . for the superintendence of the internal affairs of other states', and denounced the 'European Areopagus'. Subsequently Canning refused to attend the congress convened at St Petersburg in 1825. The issue of intervention together with rivalries between the powers of the Holy Alliance meant that the system effectively collapsed with the death of Tsar Alexander I in December 1825, though the notion of a *Concert of Europe outlived it.

**Conscription.** Compulsory enlistment for military or other specified services. While most continental countries introduced military conscription during the nineteenth century (in France it had been imposed during the Revolution) it was not instituted in Britain until *World War I (1914–18) by the Military Service Act of January 1916. This first act, in winding up the earlier system of voluntary recruitment, imposed conscription on unmarried men between the ages of 19 and 41. There had been vocal opposition in the pre-war period to the idea and this found expression on the outbreak of war in the No Conscription Fellowship. Labour protested and some 50 Liberals voted against the bill. Opposition was on grounds of humanitarian, liberal or socialist conscience and, in some cases, for strategic reasons too – that it was ill advised for Britain to commit her resources to a European land war. The categories of exemption included 'conscientious objection'. Local tribunals were set up with powers of absolute or conditional exemption. World War I conscription remained in force until April 1920. Its reintroduction in Nazi Germany (March 1935) in contravention of the Treaty of *Versailles (1919) led to demands in Britain for peacetime military training. A new act was introduced in April 1939 for 20- to 21-year-olds. Five months later this was widened to include men between the ages of 19 and 41, and later still (in 1941) the call-up was introduced for 18½-year-olds and single women between the ages of 20 and 30. The employment of labour in essential war industries was also regulated by the government, being termed 'industrial conscription'. With the ending of *World War II (1939–45) conscription was abolished for women and limited to 18 months for men. National service was subsequently extended in September 1950 to two years as a result of Western fears of Soviet intentions during the Korean War (1950–3). Conscription ended in 1960, since when Britain has been one of the very few countries not to have it.

BARKER, R., *Conscience, Government and War: Conscientious Objection in Great Britain, 1939–45*, Routledge and Kegan Paul, 1982.

RAE. J., *Conscience and Politics: The British Government and the Conscientious Objector to Military Service, 1916–19*, Oxford University Press, 1970.

**Constantinople Agreements** (1915). Secret agreements made in March and April 1915 by the Western Allies, Britain and France with the government of Tsar Nicholas II. They offered the Russians annexation of Constantinople and the hinterland of the Bosphorus and *Dardanelles after *World War I (1914–18). This was something which Britain had resisted throughout the nineteenth century, which was the heart of the *Eastern Question. The British Foreign Secretary Sir Edward *Grey (1862–1933) described this promise as 'the richest prize of the entire war'. It was to be granted, according to the understanding, provided Britain and France 'achieved their aims in the Near East and elsewhere'.

At the time traditional Anglo-Russian rivalry, already reduced by the *Anglo-Russian Convention (1907), was forgotten in the struggle against the common enemy. With stalemate and mounting catastrophic losses on the Western Front, Britain and France were afraid that the Russian government might sue for a separate peace with the *Central Powers unless offered sufficient territorial inducement for remaining in the war. The terms of the treaties were revealed by the Bolsheviks early in 1918 (they had already renounced all undertakings made by the pre-revolutionary government). This revelation aroused controversy in the West and encouraged Turkish resistance. Growing criticism was levelled against secret diplomacy, most prominently by President Woodrow Wilson, and against such secret treaties, of which the Treaty of *London (1915) with Italy was another example.

ROTHWELL, V., *British War Aims and Peace Diplomacy, 1914–1918*, Oxford University Press, 1971.

**Constantinople Treaty** (1888) (Suez Canal Convention). Signed by Britain, France, Germany, Italy, Austria and Spain, the Netherlands, Russia and Turkey on 29 October 1888, after an international conference at Paris in 1885 had failed to establish a regime for the Canal. It declared the Canal free and open to merchant and war vessels of all powers in times of war and peace. The Canal was not to be blockaded and no acts of hostility were to be committed within its confines; but the Sultan and Khedive were to be free to take such measures as they 'might find necessary for securing by their own forces the defence of Egypt and the maintenance of public order'. The British Government reversed the application of the convention in so far as its clauses 'might fetter the liberty of their government during the occupation of Egypt by their forces'.

**Consular Jurisdiction.** This is to be distinguished from the mutually enjoyed rights and privileges conferred by *extraterritoriality on foreign diplomats by states. Consular jurisdiction, which was common during the nineteenth century, meant that through grants of 'capitulations' foreign nationals were to be subject to the jurisdiction of their own consuls alone, in both criminal and civil cases. These rights might be mutual, but very often they were not, and were resented. An example of this non-reciprocal arrangement was the Sino-British Supplementary Treaty (1843), by which a system of foreign consular courts was set up but no corresponding rights were granted to Chinese residents living abroad.

**Containment.** The United States foreign policy doctrine, first clearly articulated by George

Kennan, the Chief of Policy Planning Staff of the *Department of State, who defined it as the 'patient, but firm and vigilant, policy of containment of Russian expansive tendencies'. Originally it was intended to apply primarily to Europe and was non-military in character. It was based on the supposition that if Soviet and Chinese expansionism was blocked Communism would, sooner or later, collapse due to its own inherent weaknesses and the frustration of its expansionist ambitions. Phase I, dating from the Greek–Turkish aid programme (see: *Truman Doctrine (1947) ), called for a halt to any further geographical advances by the Soviet Union. Phase II from the late 1940s and early 1950s, particularly after the outbreak of the Korean War, resulted in *NATO (1949), the *Baghdad Pact (1955) and *SEATO (1954). It called for the building of 'situations of strength' through countervailing American power, to force the Soviet leadership to accommodation with the West. It therefore involved the maintenance of military bases around the Communist bloc, an extensive armaments programme, including the rearmament of West Germany and defensive wars against Communist expansion, either by armed intervention, as in Vietnam, or simply through technical and economic assistance.

**Continental League.** The German notion of a continental alliance to be formed against Britain. It was mooted in Germany between 1895 and 1905. It was hoped through such an alliance to bring pressure to bear on Britain to draw her out of her isolation towards an understanding with Germany and to exclude the danger of a war on two fronts – such as she faced in the end in 1914. Moves towards such a league were made by the Kaiser in his correspondence with Tsar Nicholas II and during their meeting at Björko. Any such scheme, however, was thwarted by the formation of the *Entente Cordiale between Britain and France. The German idea reflected her growing awareness of isolation (see: *Encirclement, Theory of). In retrospect we can see it was doomed to failure because of the irreconcilability of German aims and ambitions with those of Britain, France and Russia.

**Convention.** Derived from the Latin 'conventio' (agreement). This word is commonly used to describe agreements to which a large number of states are party, and especially to agreements of a law-making type, for instance the *Geneva Conventions.

**COOPER,** Alfred Duff, 1st Viscount Norwich (created 1952) (1890–1945). Conservative politician and diplomat and a prominent opponent of the policy of *appeasement in the late 1930s. He was at the War Office under Stanley *Baldwin (1867–1947) between 1935 and 1937 and when Neville *Chamberlain (1869–1940) succeeded Baldwin as Prime Minister he was offered the post of First Lord of the Admiralty. After a period in which Cooper had placed some trust in the *League of Nations as an instrument of *collective security, he came increasingly to the view that conflict with Germany was inevitable and that Britain must speedily strengthen herself to resist the threat of Nazi continental hegemony. Chamberlain did not enthusiastically support his efforts to prepare the Navy. When the Czech crisis developed in 1938 he had difficulty in obtaining government approval for the mobilization of the Fleet. On Chamberlain's return from signing the *Munich Agreement (1938) Cooper denounced the terms as meaningless, cowardly and unworkable, and resigned from the Cabinet.

On the assumption of the premiership by Winston *Churchill (1874–1965) in May 1940 Cooper was given the office of Minister of Information. In 1941 he left this, accepting the post of Chancellor of the Duchy of Lancaster. In August of that year he departed for the Far East on behalf of the War Cabinet with orders to examine the arrangements for consultation and coordination among the various British authorities. After the Japanese attack on *Pearl Harbour (1941) he was appointed resident Cabinet Minister at Singapore and instructed to establish a war council. The appointment of Wavell as supreme commander for this region made his efforts there redundant, and he returned to Britain to find that some imputed to him a share in the responsibility for the fall of Singapore to the Japanese. He subsequently served as British representative with the French Committee of National Liberation under General de Gaulle in North Africa. In 1944 he was moved to Paris and in November of that year became Ambassador there. During the three years of his ambassadorship he did much to repair Anglo-French relations, damaged in the Vichy period. His wish to see an alliance between the two powers was rewarded in the Treaty of *Dunkirk (1947).

CHARMLEY, J., *Duff Cooper*, Weidenfeld and Nicolson, 1986.
COOPER, D., *Old Men Forget*, Hart-Davis, 1953.

**Copenhagen complex.** The German fear in the years leading to *World War I (1914–18) of a pre-emptive British strike against their navy. The seizure of the Danish fleet and bombardment of Copenhagen by the British during the Napoleonic War in 1807 (without declaration of war) served as a precedent. This anxiety that Britain might at any moment by such a stroke destroy the growing naval strength of Germany and the aspirations of the Reich to an imperial role in the world (see: *Weltpolitik) played a significant part in the formulation of German policy. It reflected the belief that the British might easily present Germany with an ultimatum to reduce her naval armaments before they seriously threatened the British Empire. The scare of possible Anglo-Russian hostilities over the *Dogger Bank Incident (1904) confirmed these fears. At the same time, when governing circles in Germany were discussing such contingencies as the invasion of France, Belgium and Denmark, Germans were probably not unnaturally anxious that the British government might be contemplating doing to them what they were planning to do to their neighbours.

**Council of Four.** The name applied to the political leaders of Britain, France, Italy and the United States at the *Paris Peace Conference (1919–20). These were, respectively, *Lloyd George (1863–1945), Clemenceau, Orlando and Woodrow Wilson. Known more informally as the 'Big Four', it came into existence as a working group of negotiators in March 1919 at the height of bitter disputes over the central peace terms. By this time it had become clear that only private face-to-face discussions between the national leaders could hope to resolve the most contentious issues.

**Coup d'État.** A sudden and decisive change of government by force carried out by holders of political or military power from within the existing system. It is effected from above, as contrasted with a revolution, which involves the participation of the masses – though coups may subsequently be legitimated through a plebiscite. Coups can be carried out by a head of state himself, such as that by Louis Napoleon in

France in 1851. They have been particularly common in Latin America and in Africa, though the seizure of power by the Greek Colonels in 1967 is a reminder that Western states with an experience of democratic government are not immune. A coup d'état is usually accomplished through the armed seizure of control over key government buildings and transport, and over communications, such as broadcasting-stations.

**CRANBORNE,** Viscount, see SALISBURY, LORD, GASCOYNE-CECIL, ROBERT, 3RD MARQUESS OF SALISBURY (1830–1903)

**Crimean War** (1854–6). This was the most serious crisis in the conduct of the *Eastern Question. Britain was committed to the maintenance of the Ottoman Empire as a buffer against Russian expansion and as a security for her commercial interests in the region. Russia for her part, though not intending gratuitously to pursue an expansionist policy at Turkey's expense, considered that the collapse and dismemberment of the Ottoman Empire was in the long term inevitable and was determined to gain the maximum possible advantage from any subsequent redistribution of territory. In the meantime she guarded jealously against any extension of the influence of other powers at Constantinople.

Events in France, however, served as a catalyst which caused long-standing diplomatic tension to degenerate into military confrontation. Napoleon III, having seized power in December 1851, alarmed Tsar Nicholas I by the revolutionary challenge which he appeared to present to conservative autocracy, while Napoleon's own desire for glory abroad to strengthen his position at home led him actively to intervene in the Near East.

The immediate causes of the conflict were the rival claims of France and Russia to guardianship of the Holy Places for the Roman Catholic and Orthodox Churches respectively. The French bullied the Turks into giving a decision in favour of the Roman Catholics. This alarmed the Tsar, who sent Prince Menshikov as an envoy to Constantinople in February 1853, demanding not only a revised decision of the Holy Places dispute in favour of the Orthodox but the concession of a Russian protectorate over the Orthodox subjects of the Ottoman Empire, a claim spuriously based on the Treaty of Kutchuk-Kainardji of 1774. Following the advice of *Stratford de Redcliffe (1786–1880), the British Ambassador in Constantinople, the Turks accepted the former demand but rejected the latter, as submission on this point would have been inconsistent with the maintenance of their own sovereignty. Menshikov then withdrew Russian diplomats from Constantinople and the British and French fleets were moved up to Besika Bay, outside the *Dardanelles.

On 2 July 1853 Russian forces crossed the Pruth and occupied the Principalities of Moldavia and Wallachia. These territories had, under the Treaty of *Adrianople of 1829, been rendered autonomous but under Turkish suzerainty. The situation now looked grave, but Austria, France, Prussia and Britain tried to obtain a settlement by producing the Vienna Note of 28 July, which was agreed by Russia while Turkey decided she could only accept it if amendments were made. This seemed to place Turkey in the wrong, but Nesselrode, the Russian Chancellor, then squandered this moral advantage by claiming on 7 September that the Vienna Note conceded to Russia a general right of intervention on behalf of the Orthodox Christians. This interpretation was utterly unacceptable not only to Turkey but also to Britain and France, who now sought to demonstrate their resolution by ordering their fleets up to Constantinople.

Stratford, however, tried to buy time by delaying execution of the order, but he was ultimately obliged to comply on 22 October and, on the following day, Turkish troops crossed the Danube and killed some Russians. Russia retaliated on 30 November by destroying a Turkish naval squadron in harbour at Sinope. On 27 February 1854 Britain and France sent an ultimatum demanding that Russia withdraw from the Danubian Principalities. When this was refused they signed an alliance with Turkey and on 31 March declared war on Russia.

The British response to the crisis had been confused by disagreements in the Cabinet between *Russell (1792–1878) and *Palmerston (1784–1865), who had favoured a firm stand against Russia and *Aberdeen (1784–1860) who was predisposed to make concessions in the cause of peace, while *Clarendon (1800–70) as Foreign Secretary found himself in an uncomfortable middle position reduced to dangerous vacillation by conflicting advice. All the time Stratford in Constantinople pursued his own policy with little reference to London.

Meanwhile Tsar Nicholas had misunderstood statements by Aberdeen in 1844 and by Russell in January 1853 which led him to suppose that Britain would cooperate with Russia's actions in Turkey. Whatever willingness to compromise remained in London was overcome by a rising tide of popular Russophobia which attained fever pitch after Sinope which, though a legitimate act of war on Russia's part, was viewed in Britain as a monstrous 'massacre'.

After March 1854 a period of 'phony war' ensued while the attitude of the hitherto neutral powers, Austria and Prussia, was clarified. Russia's occupation of the Danubian Principalities threatened Austria as well as Turkey and the Austrian government, having obtained an undertaking from Prussia to support her in action on the Danube if Russia refused to withdraw, accordingly sent a demand for evacuation to St Petersburg. Austria, France and Britain then agreed a programme of war aims, the *Four Points (July 1854), which were that Russia should renounce her special claims over the Danubian Principalities and the Orthodox Christians of the Ottoman Empire; that there should be 'free' navigation of the Danube and that the *Straits Convention of 1841 which had closed the navigation of the Dardanelles to foreign warships except in time of war should be revised 'in the interests of the Balance of Power in Europe'. Meanwhile, however, Russia, unwilling to force a general war with all the other Great Powers, agreed to back down and withdrew her troops across the Pruth.

Britain and France were thus left in the incongruous position of being at war with Russia but having no obvious theatre in which to fight. They therefore resolved on the invasion of the Crimea in September 1854 with a view to capturing *Sevastopol and thus destroying Russian naval power in the Black Sea. Military deadlock resulted and Sevastopol did not fall until 8 September 1855. Britain, France and Russia between them lost nearly half a million men, the majority from disease and hardship, the highest number of casualties in any European conflict between the Napoleonic Wars and *World War I (1914–18).

Diplomatic efforts to resolve the conflict had continued during the war, most notably in abortive negotiations at Vienna between March and June 1855 which followed the death of Nicholas I and the accession of the less belligerent Alexander II. A settlement was ultimately reached in the Treaty of *Paris (1856). While Russia was clearly defeated and forced to concede on all of the Four Points, the achievements of the victorious powers were transient, apart from the establishment of independence in Moldavia and Wallachia, which were to emerge as a united Rumania in 1878. Turkey was effectively given a breathing-space to reform and strengthen herself, but completely failed to do so. Nevertheless, the war was a significant check on Russian southward expansion and it also shattered the *Holy Alliance of the conservative powers which had dominated European diplomacy since 1815. Neither Britain nor France, although victorious, was strong enough to rebuild international relations according to their own designs. Thus the Crimean War ushered in an era of shifting alignments and more frequent conflicts, which was to continue until a new structure was consolidated, with explosive consequences, in the early years of the twentieth century.

ANDERSON, M. S., *The Eastern Question*, Macmillan, 1966.

BARTLETT, C. J., *Great Britain and Sea Power, 1815–1853*, Oxford University Press, 1963.

HIBBERT, C., *The Destruction of Lord Raglan*, Longmans, 1961.

RICH, N., *Why the Crimean War?*, University Press of New England, 1985.

SCHROEDER, P. W., *Austria, Great Britain and the Crimean War*, Cornell University Press, New York, 1972.

TAYLOR, A. J. P., *The Struggle for Mastery in Europe*, Oxford University Press, 1954.

**CRIPPS**, Sir (Richard) Stafford (1889–1952). Educated at Winchester and University College London, where he studied chemistry. He was called to the Bar in 1913, during the war managed a munitions factory, and returned to his practice in 1919, becoming the youngest K.C. in 1927. Cripps' distinctive characteristics were his Christian faith and formidable intellect, which after his joining the Labour Party in 1929 led to his campaigning for the immediate introduction of socialism as the only correct answer to the problems facing Britain in the depression. In 1930 he became Solicitor-General and was knighted, and in 1931 became Labour MP for Bristol East. He did not join MacDonald's National Government and moved to the far left of the Labour Party. In 1936 he brought Labour and Communist Party workers together in a United Front against fascism and capitalism, and late in 1938 called for a wider grouping to embrace Conservative dissidents and drive Neville *Chamberlain (1869–1940) from office. For this he was expelled from the Labour Party early in 1939, being readmitted only in 1945.

The period from June 1940 to January 1942 marks Cripps' most active involvement with foreign affairs, as ambassador to the Soviet Union. In the winter of 1939–40, when he visited Moscow, Cripps argued that Anglo-French policy had left Russia no choice but to sign the *Molotov–Ribbentrop Pact (1939) with Germany, and he urged that Britain should do all she could to draw the Soviet Union away from Germany. *Churchill (1874–1965) had similar views and soon after becoming Prime Minister sent Cripps to the Moscow embassy to improve Anglo-Soviet relations.

This Cripps failed to do by June 1941, when Germany attacked the Soviet Union in Operation Barbarossa. Instead he became disillusioned as he realized how little his idea of democracy and Soviet totalitarianism had in common.

After the German invasion, however, Cripps took a leading part in negotiating a mutual assistance pact and a 'no separate peace' agreement. He also pressed for increased military supplies to Russia and suggested the joint intervention in Iran which occurred in August–September 1941. Cripps was convinced that the post-war order must be based on an Anglo-American–Soviet accord, and had *Eden (1897–1977) not visited Moscow in December 1941 to begin discussions about this, Cripps would have resigned. In fact he left the embassy in January 1942, finding on his return to Britain that he had become immensely popular amidst the public's enthusiasm for its Russian ally. In February Churchill appointed him Lord Privy Seal in the War Cabinet, in which capacity he went on an official mission to India and recommended the promise of full self-governmnet after the war. Churchill refused this, and in November Cripps left the War Cabinet for the Ministry of Aircraft Production, which he managed effectively until June 1945. In the post-war Labour government Cripps was a leading Cabinet minister, and Chancellor of the Exchequer from November 1947 to October 1950, when he resigned from exhaustion. He died in April 1952.

BURRIDGE, T. D., *British Labour and Hitler's War*, Deutsch, 1976.

COOKE, C., *The Life of Richard Stafford Cripps*, Hodder and Stoughton, 1957.

GORODETSKY, G., *Stafford Cripps' Mission to Moscow, 1940–2*, Cambridge University Press, 1984.

**CROSLAND,** (Charles) Anthony Raven (1918–77). Educated at Highgate School and Trinity College Oxford, he served in Africa and Europe during *World War II (1939–45). After three years as Fellow and economics lecturer at Trinity College (1947–50), he entered the Commons in 1950 as Labour MP for South Gloucestershire, for which he was not re-elected in 1955. In the 1950s he published a significant reappraisal of socialist theory in the light of modern circumstances in *The Future of Socialism*. In 1959 he was elected MP for Grimsby. He supported Hugh Gaitskell, the Leader of the Opposition, in his rejection of *unilateralism, but disagreed with him over Europe, favouring British entry into the *Common Market. In 1964–5, under Harold *Wilson (1916–     ) he was Minister of State in the Department of Economic Affairs, sub-sequently becoming Secretary of State for Education and Science, and then President of the Board of Trade. When Wilson returned to power in 1974 he became Secretary of State for the Environment. Failing in his attempt to succeed Wilson, he became Foreign Secretary under James *Callaghan (1912–     ). He had relatively little previous experience of inter-national, as opposed to domestic affairs (on which he was richly informed), and he held the post for only ten months. The settlement of the *Cod War (1972–6) with Iceland fell during his term of office.

CROSLAND, S., *Tony Crosland*, Cape, 1982.

**CROWE,** Sir Eyre (1864–1925). Permanent Under-Secretary at the *Foreign Office (1920–5). Crowe had been born in Leipzig and had a German wife and mother, but he was to emerge as one of the most prominent opponents of Germany in the Foreign Office. In 1907, when he was Senior Clerk, he drew up a famous 'Memorandum on the Present State of British Relations with France and Germany', which made a great impression on the Foreign Secretary, Sir Edward *Grey (1862–1933). It warned of the expansionist tendency of German policy, which he likened to profession-al blackmail. Friendly relations were desirable, but would only be achieved through firmness not through concessions. He was, accordingly, a strong advocate of the *Anglo-French Entente (1904). In the final crisis in 1914 he was influential in arguing that British interests lay with France and Russia and that a clear stand against Germany was necessary. 'The whole policy of the Entente', he said, 'can have no meaning if it does not signify that in a just quarrel England would stand by her friends.'

After the war he was a British delegate at the *Paris Peace Conference (1919–20) and be-came Permanent Under-Secretary for the last five years of his life. Crowe was formidably industrious with a capacity for penetrating comment and persuasive argument. As well as setting new precedents for the direct influence of professional civil servants in the making of foreign policy, he was responsible for signifi-cant reforms in the organization of the Foreign Office itself.

STEINER, Z. S., *The Foreign Office and Foreign Policy, 1898–1914*, Cambridge University Press, 1969.

**Cuban Missile Crisis** (1962). The confrontation between the United States and the Soviet Union after the discovery from U2 aerial reconnais-sance that the latter power was installing ballis-tic missiles and atomic weapons in Cuba. On 22 October 1962 President Kennedy imposed a quarantine around Cuba to prevent further shipments of weapons and issued a demand to the Soviet Union that the missiles there be dismantled and removed. Having obtained the unanimous support of the Organization of American States and the members of *NATO for this step he warned the Soviet Union against any attempt to break the blockade. After nearly a week of the highest international tension and an exchange of letters between President Kennedy and the Soviet leader Krushchev the Soviet Union agreed on 28 October to stop work on the missile sites and to remove the missiles already there. This was to be under *United Nations supervision and the United States were to promise that Cuba would not be attacked – there was to be no repetition of the 'Bay of Pigs' expedition.

A number of considerations appear to have influenced Krushchev in his original decision to introduce the missiles, not least the desire to reaffirm Soviet leadership in the growing rivalry with Communist China and to improve his bargaining position with the West. During the crisis Britain was responsible for the decision not to call a NATO alert and, through the British Ambassador in Washington, Sir David Ormsby-Gore, for the suggestion, acted upon, that the exclusion zone around Cuba for Soviet vessels should be reduced from 800 to 500 miles to allow the Soviet Union more time to reconsider its position. Though many argued at the time, and afterwards, that Britain was not consulted, there were in fact regular communications between the Prime Minister Harold *Macmillan (1894–1986) and President Kennedy. Britain did exercise an influence. It was however a most graphic demonstration of the imbalance in power and influence between Britain and the United States, and of the limitations imposed on the former when the two superpowers were locked in confrontation which seemed to threaten global nuclear war.

DINERSTEIN, H. S., *The Making of the Missile Crisis*, Johns Hopkins Press, Baltimore, 1976.

DIVINE, R. A., ed., *The Cuban Missile Crisis*, Quadrangle, Chicago, 1971.

**CURZON**, George Nathaniel, Marquess Curzon of Kedleston (1859–1925). Educated at Eton and Balliol College Oxford, a Fellow of All Souls. From 1886 to 1892 he was Conservative MP for the Southport division of Lancashire. From 1887 to 1894 he travelled widely in a succession of journeys through North America, Russia, the Near East and Far East, establishing himself as an authority on Asiatic affairs, publishing *Russia in Central Asia* (1889), *Persia and the Persian Question* (1892) and *Problems of the Far East* (1894). From 1895 to 1898 he was Under-Secretary for Foreign Affairs, though his relations with Lord *Salisbury (1830–1903), a Prime Minister who also retained the Foreign Secretaryship, were not entirely harmonious. Salisbury tended to ignore him, while Curzon was prone to underestimate the European dimension in foreign policy.

In 1898 he was appointed Viceroy of India and created Baron Curzon. He was a strong advocate of a forward policy in Tibet, Afghanistan and the Persian Gulf. To begin with his policies were successful; he was determined to administer even-handed justice to the different nationalities under his control. The Durbar of 1903 was the high point of his splendour as Viceroy, but he was engaged in controversy with the Secretary of State and the home government over a number of matters and when Lord *Kitchener (1850–1916) arrived in India as Commander-in-Chief, two dominating personalities came into conflict over the control of the armed forces in India. The disagreement was resolved by compromise, but Curzon did not take kindly to compromise, and his seven years in India ended with his failure to include Tibet in the British *sphere of interest. There followed 11 years of political isolation and disappointment.

During *World War I (1914–18) he was a member of the coalition government, as Lord Privy Seal in 1915 and, after the fall of *Asquith (1852–1928), as Leader in the House of Lords, Lord President of the Council (1916) and a member of the War Cabinet under *Lloyd George (1863–1945). In 1919 he succeeded Arthur *Balfour (1848–1930) as Foreign Secretary but, once again, found himself in a frustrating position since Lloyd George was apt to conduct his own foreign policy without consulting his Foreign Secretary. Eventually the Prime Minister's anti-Turkish policy convinced Curzon that he could no longer endure to be a member of the Coupon Government. When the Conservatives overthrew Lloyd George and *Bonar Law (1858–1925) became Prime Minister in 1922 Curzon remained Foreign Secretary. The *Lausanne Conference (1922) on the Greco-Turkish issue was a failure, but Curzon dominated its deliberations and helped to restore British prestige in Turkey. Earlier Curzon had decried Balfour's 'unfortunate insistence upon the Jewish National Home in Palestine' (see: *Balfour Declaration (1917) ), advocating an active British role in Persia and Mesopotamia, leading ultimately to the creation of a British-controlled Arab state.

When Bonar Law resigned in 1923 Curzon confidently expected to be summoned to be Prime Minister, but Stanley *Baldwin (1867–1947) was preferred instead. Curzon remained at the *Foreign Office until 1924, when he became Lord President of the Council. In the last part of his career he tried to mediate between France and Germany, strongly denounced the Franco-Belgian *Ruhr occupation (1923), and instigated the moves leading to the *Dawes Plan (1924), which mitigated the German *reparations payments.

DUNDAS, L., 2nd Marquess of Zetland, *The Life of Lord Curzon* (3 vols.), Ernest Benn, 1928.

NICOLSON, H., *Curzon: The Last Phase, 1919–1925*, Constable, 1934.

ROSE, K., *Superior Person*, Weidenfeld and Nicolson, 1969.

**Curzon Line.** The armistice line proposed on 11 July 1920 by the British Foreign Secretary Lord *Curzon (1859–1925) to the Soviet Union, which was then at war with the newly created Polish Republic. *Lloyd George (1863–1945), the Prime Minister, had proposed it and secured the agreement of the Polish Premier. Its description in the note to Moscow, though, gave rise to confusions. This later complicated matters when the Curzon Line became the point of reference for drawing up the Soviet–Polish frontier at the end of *World War II (1939–45). With Polish victories in August 1920 the Curzon Line had ceased to be a realistic boundary and it was ignored in the Treaty of Riga (1921). When the *Polish Government-in-Exile started to negotiate with the Soviet Union in 1941 Moscow stated its wish to restore an 'ethnographic' post-war Poland. The Poles insisted that their eastern boundary should be that agreed in the Treaty of Riga. The Soviet Union soon revealed that they expected to retain all territory they had annexed in 1939 after the *Molotov–Ribbentrop Pact (1939) and the invasion of Poland, with the exception of the Bialystok region. At the *Tehran Conference (1943) Winston *Churchill (1874–1965) agreed to the Curzon Line. At Yalta Stalin conceded the possibility of digressing by up to eight kilometres from the Curzon Line in favour of the Poles and the issue of the Soviet–Polish border was settled. Annex IV of the text of the *Yalta Conference (1945) stated that the *Big Three considered the Curzon Line to be the eastern frontier of Poland.

**Cyprus.** Cyprus assumed strategic significance for Britain with the construction of the *Suez Canal. British troops were stationed in the island from 1878 by agreement with the Ottoman Empire. When the Turks entered *World War I (1914–18) on Germany's side Britain annexed her. The Turks officially recognized British sovereignty over her in the *Lausanne Treaty (1923) and she became a Crown Colony in 1925. Strong nationalistic sentiments subsequently developed, particularly among the majority Greek population who were opposed to the Turkish minority. The Cypriot Greeks demanded union with Greece (Enosis) and at first refused self-government. After a period of riots and demonstrations the British Government invited the two peoples to join in negotiations. In 1955 extremists in the EOKA movement, led by Colonel Grivas, made a series of bomb attacks which launched four years of terrorism and threatened Greek–Turkish conflict. In March 1956 Britain deported the leader of the Greek Cypriot community, Archbishop Makarios, to the Seychelles, allowing him to return a year later to plead the Greek Cypriot cause before the *United Nations. A compromise solution was arrived at in 1959 by which Cyprus became an independent republic within the British *Commonwealth (on 16 August 1960) with a Greek Cypriot President, a Turkish Cypriot Vice-President and a communal structure with a 70/30 ratio of representation for the Greeks and Turks. Britain, Turkey and Greece agreed a Treaty of Guarantee with Cyprus under which British sovereignty was limited to the area of its military base.

Relations between the two communities remained strained, however. By 1970 the Turkish minority had ceased to recognize the legality of the House of Representatives in Nicosia, electing an unofficial chamber of their own in northern Cyprus. An EOKA coup against Makarios in 1974 threw Cyprus into near anarchy, Turkey seizing the opportunity to land an army in north Cyprus which proceeded to occupy two-fifths of the island. Within this area the Turks established a 'Turkish Federated State', forcing out Greek Cypriots and effectively partitioning the island. The de facto partition was formally institutionalized on 15 November 1983 with the proclamation of Turkish Republic of Northern Cyprus.

CRAWSHAW, N., *The Cyprus Revolt: An Account of the Struggle for Union with Greece*, Allen and Unwin, 1978.
POLYVIOU, P. S., *The Cyprus Conflict and Negotiations, 1960–80*, Duckworth, 1980.

# –D–

**'Daily Telegraph Affair'** (1908). The public furore in both Britain and Germany after the publication in the British newspaper *The Daily Telegraph* on 28 October 1908 of an interview with William II of Germany. In this the Kaiser declared himself to be a friend of Britain but stated that this was the feeling of only a minority in an otherwise Anglophobic Germany. He claimed to have prevented a continental league being formed against Britain during the 2nd *Boer War (1899–1902) and to have sent a strategic plan to Queen *Victoria (1819–1901) as a result of which the British had defeated the Boers. The interview, which offended Britain and in particular provoked agitation among naval circles in Britain, had been approved through the negligence of an official in the German Foreign Ministry. The Chancellor Bülow offered his resignation, an offer not accepted by the Kaiser. There were widespread demands in the Reichstag and throughout Germany for checks on the Emperor's powers and William was admonished to restrain his comments in future. The incident served to aggravate Anglo-German relations and shook the reputation of the Kaiser within Germany.

**DALLING AND BULWER, Baron,** see BULWER, SIR HENRY, (1801–72).

**Danzig** (now Gdansk). The Baltic port at the mouth of the Vistula which was established as a Free City under the *League of Nations by the Treaty of *Versailles (1919). It enjoyed self-government under an elected Senate, but Poland controlled its foreign relations and railways. Its purpose, thus constituted, was to afford maritime access to Poland. From the start many, *Lloyd George (1863–1945) included, perceived the fragility of this arrangement, since 95 per cent of the population of Danzig was German. In 1933 the Nazi Party gained a parliamentary majority in the city. In March 1939 Hitler demanded its re-incorporation in Germany and, after the failure of British attempts at mediation, he invaded Poland on 1 September 1939, after which it was united with Germany in the new 'gau' Danzig-West Prussia. After the defeat of Germany it was made over by the Soviet Union to Poland and resettled with a Polish population.

**Dardanelles.** The channel between the Aegean Sea and the Sea of Marmora, the first part of the straits between the Mediterranean and the Black Sea (see: *Straits Question). The British fleet passed through the Dardanelles before the outbreak of the *Crimean War (1854–6) and in 1878 during the Eastern Crisis. The southern-most European shore of the Dardanelles was the place of the *Gallipoli landing (1915).

**Dawes Plan** (1924). The plan worked out by a committee headed by leading United States Republican Charles Dawes for the Allied Reparations Committee. It was designed to provide a modified payment schedule for German *reparations, following the invasion of the *Ruhr by French and Belgian troops to enforce payment. The committee presented its report on 9 April 1924. The London Accord on the Dawes Plan was signed on 30 August 1924. To stabilize the new Rentenmark, in the wake 'of the inflationary collapse of 1923, the Dawes Plan proposed that there should be an 800 million gold mark foreign loan to establish a central gold reserve. Germany was to be given economic control over all her territory. The plan helped to remove some of the intense bitterness aroused by the reparations issue, but it did not set a total amount of borrowing on the part of Germany and was superseded by the *Young Plan (1929).

MARKS, S., 'The Myths of Reparations', *Central European History*, 11, 3, 1978, pp. 231–55.

SCHMIDT, R. J., *Versailles and the Ruhr: Seedbed of World War II*, The Hague, Nijhoff, 1968.

TRACHTENBERG, M., *Reparations in World Politics: France and European Economic Diplomacy 1916–23*, New York, Columbia University Press, 1980.

**D-Day,** see NORMANDY LANDINGS (1944).

**Declarations.** A term which is used in different senses in diplomacy. In the first it indicates an agreement of a binding character. For example, the *Anglo-French Entente (1904) is described as a 'Declaration ... respecting Egypt and Morocco'. Secondly, it is used for unilateral announcement of, for instance, war or neutrality. Finally, it can mean simply a clarification or justification of a line of conduct in foreign relations. In the first sense declarations commonly appear as appendages to treaties. For instance, the Treaty of *Lausanne (1923) carried four declarations relating to amnesties.

*De Facto* **Recognition.** An act or acts implying the acceptance of a political change, but falling short of formal legal recognition. A government may recognize a foreign government 'de facto' as the effective authority over the area concerned as, for example, after a revolution, even though it has no legal right. Full recognition – *de jure* – is not accorded until later – until, for instance, the new authority has shown itself capable of maintaining itself in power, or has undertaken to observe the foreign obligations into which its predecessor has entered.

**Defence Ministry,** see MINISTRY OF DEFENCE

**Defence of the Realm Acts** (DORA). Legislation imposing wartime restrictions in Britain during *World War I (1914–18) and *World War II (1939–45), including censorship and intervention in the economy. The best-known and most controversial clauses have been those allowing the incarceration of any alien from enemy countries and any British citizen considered a threat to national security. During World War II clause 18B of DORA was invoked to imprison Sir Oswald *Mosley (1896–1980), the leader of the British Union of Fascists. In the case of Liversidge v Anderson (1942) the DORA legislation was interpreted as giving the Home Secretary a virtually arbitrary power to intern anyone he believed to be a threat to security without being obliged to present the court with any convincing reason for this belief. This decision, though opposed by civil liberties lawyers, has not been reversed.

*De Jure* **Recognition.** Recognition as a matter of legal right: the formal and binding acceptance by other governments of a political change, such as a new government or new state arising from a revolution, a change of frontiers, or transfer of sovereignty.

**Démarche.** According to the circumstances, an offer, an advance, a demand, a suggestion, an attempt, a proposal, a protestation, a remonstrance, a request, an overture, a warning, a threat, a step, a measure.

**Department of State** (State Department). The principal agency for the formulation and execution of foreign policy, situated in Washington D.C. It was established by Congress in 1789, though a department of foreign affairs had existed since 1781. The Secretary of State is the President's official adviser in this field and ranks first among Cabinet members. His responsibilities include the direction and supervision of policy-making, administration at the State Department and of the diplomatic and consular services. The influence exercised by the State Department and successive Secretaries of State has fluctuated. Some Presidents have tended to bypass their own Secretaries of State, for instance Woodrow Wilson and F. D. Roosevelt, who relied, respectively, more on their advisors Colonel House and Harry Hopkins. Institutional modernization and expansion in the twentieth century, particularly since the American assumption of global responsibilities after 1945, have not meant that the State Department has progressively increased its influence in the conduct of foreign affairs. New, competing agencies such as the National Security Council, have come into existence. There has also been a long-running debate over the role of the Department and the extent to which it should confine itself to policy-making.

**DERBY, 14th Earl of,** see STANLEY, EDWARD (1799–1869)

**DERBY, 15th Earl of,** see STANLEY, EDWARD (1826–93)

**Destroyer-Bases Deal** (1940). The agreement announced in its final form on 3 September 1940. The United States transferred 50 destroyers of World War I vintage to Britain and received in return the rights to 99-year leases on bases in Newfoundland, Bermuda, the Bahamas, Jamaica, Antigua, St Lucia, Trinidad and British Guiana. It followed the request made by Winston *Churchill (1874–1965) to President Roosevelt for 'the loan of forty or fifty of your older destroyers to bridge the gap between what we have now and the large new construction we put in hand at the beginning of the war'. After the fall of France the need was widely perceived in Washington as urgent. The President was forbidden by law, however, from disposing of any matériel of war unless it was certified by the appropriate service chief as no longer of use for American defence. This difficulty was overcome by the acquisition by the United States of naval and air bases in the western Atlantic. The deal could be represented as a clear strengthening of American defence. It was a conspicuous step for the United States in the undeclared resistance towards Nazi Germany.

GOODHART, P., *Fifty Ships that Saved the World: The Foundation of the Anglo-American Alliance*, Doubleday, New York, 1965.

**Détente.** Relaxation of political and military tensions; the foreign policy process concerned in recent years with relations between East and West in the *Cold War. Aspects of détente include the avoidance of confrontation in sensitive areas such as the Middle East, the pursuit of agreement over arms control, increased trade and encouragement of cultural exchanges.

Détente may result from deliberations at *summit conferences, from the conclusion of treaties or from a basic reorientation of the policies of the states concerned. Though the word may validly be used of earlier periods in international relations, for instance to describe the period following *Locarno (1925), it is usually applied now to the emphasis on peaceful coexistence and improved relations between the United States and the Soviet Union, identified with the policies of President Nixon and

Henry Kissinger, which led to the *Strategic Arms Limitation Talks (SALT) and subsequent agreements. Détente has also been perceptible in the rapprochement over recent years between the German Federal Republic and the German Democratic Republic. Détente has not meant, however, an acceptance by either side of the ideological principles of the other. While it has marked a shift from the doctrinaire *containment policy of earlier years to a more flexible diplomacy, the deteriorating relations between East and West after the Soviet invasion of Afghanistan in December 1979 have led to lively controversy over its significance and achievements.

**Deterrence.** The notion of deterrence, based on the assumption that an opponent's intentions will go as far as his capabilities, has always been central to relations between states. It implies that a country's defences are so substantial and well protected that an initial strike by an enemy would not remove its ability to retaliate decisively. It is most commonly used today to describe the strategy of discouraging a nuclear attack by being able to arouse fear of a quite unacceptably damaging reprisal. Political leaders of East and West have argued since 1945 that their countries need nuclear weapons so that peace can be maintained. Potential aggression is prevented by this awareness of consequent devastation (see also: *balance of terror). A number of sophisticated theories have been developed around the notion of deterrence in terms of the vast arsenals of the nuclear powers, such as *massive retaliation, mutually assured destruction, flexible response and second-strike capacity.

**Diplomatic Immunity.** The rule which exempts diplomats from local jurisdictions and which is a necessary consequence of the conditions under which they are sent to other states and received. Since they represent other sovereign states they are considered to owe no allegiance to the state to which they are accredited. If they offend against the laws of the country in which they are residing complaint will be made to their government. Without its permission, though, no proceedings can be taken against them under the jurisdiction of the country. These immunities are granted on the understanding that they will be reciprocal. Immunity from local jurisdiction and taxation is called *extraterritoriality. The Vienna Convention on

Diplomatic Relations (1961) settled the modern practice on many matters of such privileges; and this was given effect in Britain by the Diplomatic and other Privileges Act (1971). Diplomatic privileges are extended also to officials of the *United Nations, the *European Community, the *North Atlantic Treaty Organization, judges of the International Court of Justice and representatives of certain other major organizations.

**Disarmament Conference,** see WORLD DISARM-AMENT CONFERENCE (1932–4)

**Disengagement.** Foreign policy option advanced during the 1950s in the context of the *Cold War. It envisaged the neutralization of certain parts of the world, particularly Central Europe. The forces of the superpowers – the United States and the Soviet Union – were to be withdrawn, while the remaining local forces were neutralized and prevented from acquiring nuclear arsenals, by international agreement. George Kennan, earlier the advocate of the doctrine of *containment, in putting forward the idea of disengagement suggested that German reunification could come about as one of its consequences. Though various plans for limiting armed forces in Central Europe were subsequently suggested, the idea of disengagement was strongly resisted by the government of the United States on the grounds that the Soviet Union would take advantage of the power vacuum which it would create, and that it would encourage a return to American *isolationism.

**DISRAELI,** Benjamin, Earl of Beaconsfield (created 1876) (1804–81). Conservative Prime Minister (1868, 1874–80). Disraeli had most improbable origins for a Victorian Conservative Prime Minister. He was a Jew who was baptized as a Christian in boyhood and first came before the public eye in the 1830s as a novelist. He violently attacked *Peel (1788–1850) for repealing the Corn Laws and in 1849 emerged as leader of the Protectionists in the Commons, in virtue of being the only man of any ability left to the party in the lower house after the schism of 1846. He now saw Protection as a liability and gradually persuaded the party to abandon it, a decision which was reluctantly endorsed by *Derby (1799–1869) in 1852.

When the Conservatives gained office in 1852 it was rumoured that Disraeli might be Foreign Secretary, but in fact he became Chancellor of the Exchequer, a post which he also held in the 1858 and 1866 Derby administrations. He took an active interest in foreign affairs, being critical not only of the policies of the Aberdeen and Palmerston governments, but also, within his own party, of those of Malmesbury and Stanley, feeling that they lacked sufficient vigour.

The weakness of the Conservatives in the two decades after 1846 precluded Disraeli from making a major impact on affairs until the late 1860s. However, after carrying the Second Reform Act, which gave the franchise to all ratepayers in 1867, he succeeded Derby as Prime Minister in February 1868. His first tenure of power was brief, but it provided a hint of things to come in the successful Abyssinian expedition, which suggested a more aggressive imperialist policy than the Conservatives had hitherto adopted.

In terms of foreign policy Disraeli was the political heir of *Palmerston (1784–1865), concerned above all with the extension of British prestige based on 'Imperial spirit' at home and vigorous action abroad, although he lacked the older man's sympathy with liberal movements. While counselling firmness and decisiveness, Disraeli disavowed turbulence and aggression. He stated these views effectively in two great speeches at Manchester and Crystal Palace in 1872 which attacked the Gladstone government, strengthening the current which carried him in 1874 to the first clear Conservative General Election victory for over 30 years.

Disraeli's fascination with foreign affairs, which he regarded as the highest calling for a politician, combined with his impatience at the excessive caution manifested by his Foreign Secretary, the 15th Earl of Derby (1826–93) (see: *Stanley, Edward), to cause him to take a particularly active part in the formulation of policy. In 1875 he arranged the purchase for Britain of the shares of the Suez Canal Company belonging to the bankrupt Khedive of Egypt, thus preventing the French from getting exclusive control of the concern. In the early stages of the Eastern Crisis arising from unrest in Turkish Balkan possessions Disraeli's policy was erratic. He generally favoured the traditional British policy of maintaining Turkey, but his main concern was to disrupt the

*Dreikaiserbund* of Russia, Prussia and Austria. This came under heavy strain, but for reasons largely independent of Disraeli's activities.

In 1876 Disraeli was raised to the House of Lords as Earl of Beaconsfield because his health could no longer stand the strain of leading the party in the Commons. During the summer news reached Britain of savage atrocities by the Turks against the Bulgarians (see: *Bulgarian Massacres). Public outrage grew as *Gladstone (1809–98) denounced the Turks and Beaconsfield's Eastern policy, but the Prime Minister himself felt that the reports from Bulgaria were exaggerated, and derided the agitation at home. Although he acknowledged that the Turks had 'forfeited all sympathy', his main concern was now the containment of Russia, which declared war on Turkey in April 1877. Beaconsfield found his Cabinet bitterly divided, but ultimately, early in 1878, he obtained a decision in favour of a show of naval and military force which deterred Russia from seizing Constantinople and the Straits, thus averting a major war.

At this point Derby resigned and Beaconsfield was able to clarify the direction of foreign policy by appointing the Marquess of *Salisbury (1830–1903) as his successor. Following preliminary agreements with Russia, the Congress of *Berlin met in June 1878. Beaconsfield secured the preservation of the rump of Turkey's European empire and returned home in triumph claiming that he had brought back 'peace with honour'. Although the Berlin settlement reflected Beaconsfield's continuing commitment to the now outdated policy of maintaining Turkey in Europe and it could not prevent the *Eastern Question from continuing to trouble British statesmen in the ensuing decades, it did mark the beginning of a period of peace between the Great Powers in Europe which lasted until 1914.

Imperial affairs brought Beaconsfield rather less glory. In 1877 he made the Queen Empress of India, which pleased her and was helpful in controlling the Indian princes, but caused much controversy at home. In 1878 in both Afghanistan and Zululand aggressive policies by men on the spot led to unnecessary and expensive wars. Beaconsfield's direct responsibility for these incidents was small but, combined with economic depression at home, they served to decrease the popularity of his government, and in the spring of 1880 the Liberals obtained a clear victory over 'Beaconsfieldism' at the polls. Beaconsfield died in the following year, defeated but unbroken, having, even when his limitations are put in the balance, played a major role in restoring the political strength of the Conservative Party and the international standing of Britain.

ADELMAN, P., *Gladstone, Disraeli and Later Victorian Politics*, Longman, 1983.
BLAKE, R., *Disraeli*, Eyre and Spottiswoode, 1966.
SETON-WATSON, R. W., *Disraeli, Gladstone and the Eastern Question*, Cass, 1962.

**Dogger Bank Incident** (1904). Also known as the 'North Sea Incident'. On 21 October 1904 Russia's Second Pacific Squadron en route from the Baltic Sea to the Far East during the Russo-Japanese war fired on a fleet of British trawlers over the Dogger Bank, mistaking them for Japanese torpedo boats. One trawler was sunk and five others damaged. Two British fishermen were killed and six wounded. Outraged opinion in Britain and a hostile mood in Russia could easily have led to a major war over this incident but for the moderation of the British government. The European press in general condemned the Russians; on the other hand, military and nationalistic circles in Russia favoured a showdown with the British, whom they suspected of encouraging the Japanese in their war against Russia. Tsar Nicholas II conveyed his regrets to Edward VII, but not an apology. On 25 October the British government delivered a stern note demanding an explanation, an apology and a promise that the officers responsible would be punished. The same evening the British Admiralty alerted the Mediterranean, Channel and Home fleets. *Balfour (1848–1930), the Prime Minister, and his Foreign Secretary Lord *Lansdowne (1845–1927) at the same time allowed the issue to go before the International Court at The Hague. They were supported in this by those who believed that any conflict with Russia would only benefit Germany in the prevailing international circumstances. An international commission of five admirals representing Britain, Russia, France, Austria-Hungary and the United States upheld Britain's claim for compensation, noting that the British trawlers had committed no hostile act. With the Russian payment of £65,000 the matter was promptly closed. The incident was in certain respects analogous in its consequences to the *Fashoda Crisis (1898). In each case long-standing rivals concluded far-reaching agreements which forged the Triple Entente.

**Domino Theory.** The idea advanced by United States governments from the late 1940s that if òne nation fell under Communist control other neighbouring states would follow in a knock-on effect. This was applied to Greece and Turkey in the *Truman Doctrine (1947) which also pledged American support to any country of 'free peoples who are resisting attempted subjugation by armed minorities or by outside pressures'. It was usually applied however to Southeast Asia and explicitly spelled out by the Eisenhower and subsequent administrations. In the early 1960s growing American concern over South Vietnam, which it was feared would become Communist as a result of North Vietnamese aggression and spread Communism throughout the region, led to increased United States involvement. From 1965 to 1973 United States troops were sent to the aid of South Vietnam. The collapse of South Vietnam in 1975 did not prove the Domino Theory correct, not least because the monolithic view of Communism advanced in the early *Cold War has to be modified in the light of polycentrism and the split into pro-Soviet and pro-Chinese camps. From the beginning British foreign policy makers expressed doubts about the domino effect in Southeast Asia. This both reflected a different reading of the situation and British concern to discourage American over-involvement in Asia, which might be detrimental to British interests by distracting the United States from its commitment to Western European defence.

**Don Pacifico Affair** (1850). A celebrated example of Palmerstonian diplomatic high-handedness. In 1850 Britain unilaterally blockaded the Greek coasts to force compensation for a Portuguese moneylender, David Pacifico, who claimed British protection on account of his Gibraltarian birth. This followed the pillaging of his house in Athens in 1847.

*Palmerston (1784–1865) had long been annoyed by the Greek government because of their failure to attend to the many debts owing to British subjects. He also had a strong aversion to continental despots: he described King Otto of Greece as the 'spoilt child of absolutism'. France and Russia, Greece's co-guarantors, protested at the blockade, accusing Britain of breaking the agreement to protect Greek independence. Liberal opinion at home was also greatly affronted. Palmerston opened discussions with the French but omitted to tell the British Minister in Athens of the new, more lenient compensation terms subsequently worked out – in the hope that the stronger terms might prevail.

France withdrew her ambassador in protest and Palmerston had to give way. When his policy was attacked in the House of Commons, though, he made a vigorous defence of his style of foreign policy. This ended with his famous words: 'As the Roman, in the days of old, held himself free from indignity when he could say "Civis Romanus sum", so also a British subject, in whatever land he may be, shall feel confident that the watchful eye and strong arm of England will protect him against injustice and wrong.' Such a policy was popular with the nation, but not with his colleagues or with Queen *Victoria (1819–1901) and Prince *Albert (1819–61). When, in 1851, Palmerston precipitately congratulated Louis Napoleon on his *coup d'état he was forced to resign.

**DORA,** see DEFENCE OF THE REALM ACTS

**Drago Doctrine.** A principle in international law that no state has the right to resort to armed force against another state simply in order to collect public debts. The doctrine was enunciated in a communication of 29 December 1902 from the Foreign Minister of Argentina, Luis Drago, to the Argentine Minister in Washington. It was sent in response to the blockade of Venezuelan ports in the same months by naval units from Great Britain and Germany, later joined by Italy, to force the government to pay debts owing to their citizens. Drago claimed that this violated the principle of the juridical equality of states and that it was contrary to the *Monroe Doctrine. The Second *Hague Peace Conference (1907) adopted a modified version of this, the Porter Doctrine. This was broader in conception than the Drago Doctrine since it covered *all* contractual debts, but it also sanctioned the use of force if the debtor nation refused international arbitration or neglected to enforce a decision arrived at through such arbitration.

**DRUMMOND,** James Eric, 16th Earl of Perth (1876–1951). Entering the *Foreign Office in 1900, he was Private Secretary to *Asquith (1852–1928) between 1912 and 1915, to *Grey (1862–1933) between 1915 and 1916 and *Balfour (1848–1930) between 1916 and 1918, and in 1918–19 he was a member of the

British delegation to the peace conference. With a reputation for objectivity and mastery of detail and procedure, in April 1919 Drummond was appointed Secretary-General to the newly founded *League of Nations. Caution and discretion were an asset at Geneva, where Drummond served with quiet distinction until 1933, when he left to become British ambassador in Rome. A convert to Catholicism, an Italophile and long accustomed to the role of international conciliator, Drummond lacked the temperament and background to be an effective representative of British interests in Rome after the cooling of Anglo-Italian relations during the *Abyssinian Crisis of 1935. Sympathy with many of Fascism's domestic objectives and long exposure to its propaganda had by 1938 made Drummond Mussolini's apologist in London. Drummond's views were influential with *Halifax (1881–1959) and Neville *Chamberlain (1869–1940), although his retirement in April 1939 was greeted by many Foreign Office officials with relief. He served briefly and unhappily as Director-General of the Ministry of Information in 1939–40.

BARROS, J., *Office without Power: Secretary-General Sir Eric Drummond, 1919–33*, Oxford University Press, 1979.

**Drummond–Wolff Convention** (1887). Between Britain and Turkey, signed on 22 May 1887. The British promised to evacuate Egypt within three years provided conditions were favourable. They retained the right to reoccupy the country, however, if it were menaced by invasion or internal disorder. Under pressure from France and Russia, the Sultan refused to ratify this convention. In fact Russian and French interests differed here: it was the main object of Russian policy, in contrast to the French, to keep the British in Egypt and thereby to sour the latter's relations with Turkey. The non-ratification encouraged the British government to believe that they should remain in Egypt for at least some time.

**DUDLEY**, John William Ward, 1st Earl of (1781–1833). Probably the least-known Foreign Secretary of the nineteenth century. He was appointed to the office by George *Canning (1770–1827), continuing under the Duke of *Wellington (1769–1852). His term only lasted from April 1827 till June 1828 and he resigned with the other Canningites, being succeeded by Lord *Aberdeen (1784–1860). He was chiefly occupied with the Greek question and signed the treaty of 6 July 1827 for the pacification of Greece. He was handicapped by serious ill-health and was painfully aware of his incapacity in the post of Foreign Secretary.

DUDLEY, J. W. W., 1ST EARL OF, *Letters of the Earl of Dudley to the Bishop of Llandaff*, John Murray, 1840.

ROMILLY, S. H., *Letters to 'Ivy' from the 1st Earl of Dudley*, Longman, 1905.

**Dumbarton Oaks Conference** (1944). Held in Georgetown, Washington D.C. between 21 August and 7 October 1944. The leading participants were Britain, the United States, the Soviet Union and China. The conference proposals were intended to establish the framework for postwar cooperation and for an effective international security organization. For the most part these were incorporated in the later Charter of the *United Nations, including the major institutions of the UN – the Security Council, the General Assembly, the Economic and Social Council and the International Court of Justice. The conference showed clear appreciation of the reasons for the failure of the *League of Nations. Peacekeeping responsibilities were to be lodged with the Security Council, where the great powers were to have permanent representation and the right of veto. On the insistence of Winston *Churchill (1874–1965) France was included as a permanent member of the Security Council. Britain differed from the United States and the Soviet Union over the crucial question of the veto power. She wanted disputants in an issue to be barred from the use of the veto. This was not accepted by the other powers. As a result a compromise was arrived at: a complete veto over decisions involving enforcement was upheld, but it was agreed that the party to a dispute could not exercise the veto in respect of questions which involved simply investigations of disputes. A range of issues, including rights of representation for a number of states, were not resolved. The mood of the conference, though, was one of optimism for a future harmonious relationship between the major powers – hopes soon disappointed with the growth of tension in the postwar world between the Communist and non-Communist blocs.

MCNEILL, W. H., *America, Britain and Russia:*

*Their Cooperation and Conflict*, 1941–46, Oxford University Press, 1953.
WHEELER-BENNETT, J. AND NICHOLLS, A., *The Semblance of Peace*, Macmillan, 1972.

**Dunkirk, Battle of** (1940). One of the best-known battles of *World War II (1939–45), fought in May and June 1940 by Germany against British and French forces, the *British Expeditionary Force and the French First Army, which had been cut off and encircled. German troops reached the Channel on 20 May 1940, but the advance was stopped on 24 May, the Germans hoping to destroy the Allied forces by aerial attack. The Luftwaffe failed, however, to prevent the evacuation in boats of all sizes and descriptions of 200,000 British and 140,000 French to Britain by 4 June.

TURNBULL, P., *Dunkirk: Anatomy of a Miracle*, Batsford, 1978.

**Dunkirk, Treaty of** (1947). A 50-year treaty of alliance between Britain and France, signed in March 1947. It called for consultation and joint action against any renewed German aggression. As a treaty of alliance and mutual assistance, it provided for consultation on economic matters as well and pledged to take common action should Germany default on her obligations. It marked the emergence of France again as a major European power after the humiliation of *World War II (1939–45). At that time the British and French governments hoped to revive the *Entente Cordiale independently of any special relationship with the United States. The Dunkirk Treaty served as the nucleus of the *Brussels Treaty (1948) organization.

# E

**Eastern Question.** The dominant European diplomatic issue of the nineteenth century, arising from the progressive decline of the Ottoman Empire and the rival ambitions of its neighbours. While Russia and Austria manoeuvred to ensure that they benefited in the event of its collapse, Britain until 1897 attempted to prop up the empire as a means of preventing Russia from gaining control of the *Dardanelles and Bosphorus. Russia advanced claims of Christian religious and Slav racial affinity to justify its aspiration to be protector of the very substantial non-Moslem minority in the Ottoman Empire. For her part, Britain feared that the disintegration of Turkey would leave the Mediterranean and trading routes to India open to Russian threats (already as early as 1791 Pitt the Younger had sounded a warning against Russian encroachment). The major disputes and crises arising from the Eastern Question were the *Greek War of Independence (1821–9), the *Mehemet Ali crises (1832–3 and 1839–41), the *Crimean War (1854–6), the Eastern Crisis (1875–8) and the Balkan conflicts on the eve of *World War I (1914–18). The *Straits Question was central to the Anglo-Russian rivalry, the Straits for instance being closed to foreign warships by the *Straits Convention (1841).

The Ottoman Empire's repeated failure effectively to reform itself and the massacres of its minorities, such as the *Armenian Massacres (1894–6), lost British sympathy for the Turks and at the end of the century the focus of British attention in the Near East shifted to Egypt. The Eastern Question became further complicated by the rise of national states in the Balkans, particularly Serbia and Rumania who, in 1912, combined to fight against Turkey, and by the growing German interest in the Near East, with Turkey looking to Germany rather than to Britain for support by the early twentieth century. The traditional Eastern Question effectively ended with the collapse of the Ottoman Empire during World War I, with the setting up of the Turkish national state and the Treaty of *Lausanne (1923).

ANDERSON, M. S., *The Eastern Question 1774–1923*, Macmillan, 1966.

CLAYTON, G. D., *Britain and the Eastern Question: Missolonghi to Gallipoli*, Hodder and Stoughton, 1971.

MILLMAN, R., *Britain and the Eastern Question 1875–78*, Oxford University Press, 1979.

MOSSE, W. E., *The Rise and Fall of the Crimean System 1855–71: The Story of a Peace Settlement*, Macmillan, 1963.

**'East of Suez'.** A phrase used particularly in the 1960s to describe Britain's commitments in the Gulf and in Singapore and Malaysia. These British military positions had grown up – very largely – as a result of the need to defend India. To a large extent an 'east of Suez' strategy lost its point with the independence of India and Pakistan in 1948, but the decision to withdraw from these positions was not taken until 20 years later, after Britain had already withdrawn from *Aden in 1967. The decision to end the 'east of Suez' involvement was prompted by the economic difficulties of the Labour Government of Harold *Wilson (1916–    ) in 1967. Following the devaluation of sterling in that year the government announced in January

1968 that all British forces would leave these areas by 1971 (troops were to remain in *Hong Kong). This would, among other things, end the agreements with the Gulf rulers. The government justified this change of policy in the following words: 'Britain had a central role to play in supporting the solidarity, strength and strategy on which the effectiveness of the Atlantic Alliance depends. Our decision to concentrate our defence effort in the *NATO area makes us better able to fulfil this role than in the past.' Its effect was to make Britain henceforward more of a European and Mediterranean power.

As leader of the Opposition, Edward *Heath (1916–    ) and the Conservatives objected strongly to the withdrawal from east of Suez. Back in office in 1970, though, the Conservatives found there was little they could do. Mr Heath attempted to give Britain a further military lease of life in the Gulf and also proposed to create a five-power Commonwealth naval force to be based in Singapore. The Gulf rulers proved unwilling to reverse the alternative arrangements they had already made to meet the situation after the British left; and the policy of withdrawal came to be seen as a realistic reduction of British defence commitments in line with Britain's diminished economic position in the world.

BAYLIS, J., Anglo-American Defence Relations 1939–1984, 2nd ed. Macmillan, 1984.
DARBY, P., British Defence Policy East of Suez 1947–68, Oxford University Press, 1973.

EDEN, Sir (Robert) Anthony, 1st Earl of Avon (1897–1977). Educated at Eton, between 1915 and 1918 he served with distinction on the Western Front, reaching the rank of major. Intending to join the diplomatic service, he read Oriental Languages at Christ Church, Oxford, where he took a First in 1922. But he decided to enter politics instead, and in 1923 became Conservative MP for Warwick and Leamington. From 1926 to 1929 he was Parliamentary Private Secretary to the Foreign Secretary, Sir Austen *Chamberlain (1863–1937), and in November 1931 *Baldwin (1867–1947) secured for him the post of Parliamentatry Under-Secretary at the Foreign Office, where from the end of 1932 he assumed major responsibility for disarmament questions because Sir John *Simon (1873–1954), the Foreign Secretary, was unable to spend the necessary time at Geneva where the *World Disarmament Conference (1932–4) was in session.

To increase his authority at Geneva, in January 1934 Eden was promoted Lord Privy Seal, although he did not enter the Cabinet until June 1935 when he became Minister for League of Nations affairs. Eden therefore served as second departmental minister to two foreign secretaries, Simon and *Hoare (1880–1959) (with neither of whom were relations ever easy) and in the public eye he became associated with the *League of Nations and *collective security. Despite the existence of a few substantial policy differences with them, Eden avoided the public disapproval which fell on Simon and still more on Hoare for their respective parts in the *Stresa Conference and the *Hoare–Laval Plan (1935), and in December 1935 he was Baldwin's natural choice to succeed Hoare. Realizing how much both his predecessors had been influenced by the Permanent Under-Secretary, *Vansittart (1881–1957), Eden immediately made plans to replace Vansittart, but could not achieve this until January 1938. By that time Vansittart's anti-Germanism had been absorbed by Eden in watered-down form, while his experiences in 1935 had made him powerfully anti-Italian. Eden was therefore opposed to conciliating Italy and hesitant about conciliating Germany as the Prime Minister from 1937, Neville *Chamberlain (1869–1940), insisted on doing. This led to Eden's resignation in February 1938 – happily removing him from government during the crisis over the *Sudetenland which his earlier indecisiveness had helped bring about and whose outcome, the *Munich Agreement (1938), he approved.

When war began Chamberlain thought Eden less dangerous inside the government than out and made his half-hearted critic Dominions Secretary. This gave Eden the right to attend War Cabinet meetings but not to say anything. In May 1940 he moved outside the Cabinet to the War Office, which he managed effectively until December, the earliest moment when *Churchill (1874–1965) could bring him back to the Cabinet as Foreign Secretary. The Churchill–Eden wartime relationship was less harmonious than many realized. Until mid-1944, for example, Eden was much friendlier to Russia than Churchill was. In 1941 Eden persuaded a reluctant Churchill to recognize Stalin's 1940 annexation of the Baltic states and to declare war on Finland, Rumania and Hungary. He also wanted a token force of British troops in Russia. This Churchill vetoed.

The revelation of the *Katyn Forest Massacre in 1943 did little to discourage Eden's enthusiasm for the Russians; the Warsaw Uprising of August 1944 did more. But Eden remained unrealistic about Britain's need to secure what terms she could with Russia for the post-war world. Churchill's meeting with Stalin in October 1944 to establish British and Russian spheres of influence in the Balkans he believed unnecessary. Disagreements with Churchill brought Eden on several occasions close to resigning: over the conduct of the war in early 1942, and over the Beveridge report in early 1943. Other disagreements, especially in 1943 about the relative importance of the Mediterranean theatre and the invasion of France, were played out before the Americans and undermined Churchill's ability to influence Allied strategy. From November 1942 Eden was also Leader of the House, which limited the amount of time he could spend in the Foreign Office, weakened his grip on affairs, and subjected him to overwork.

But the public perception that the Churchill–Eden combination had guided the country to victory meant that Eden emerged at the end of the war with his reputation enhanced and regarded as Churchill's successor. Churchill's decision not to retire after losing the 1945 election was therefore a hard blow. Eden went back to the Foreign Office for the 1951–5 government with a wealth of diplomatic expertise but with the mental baggage of lessons from the 1930s and outdated conceptions of Britain's world role. Thus his final period as Foreign Secretary was marked by striking achievements where his negotiating skills produced solutions to urgent problems, and by failure to perceive that Britain was no longer the power she had been before or even during the war. Thus German rearmament, the Trieste dispute and the Indo-China conflict were satisfactorily resolved; but the more fundamental questions about Britain's relations with the *Empire, the United States and Europe, were not. Eden still believed the Empire gave Britain independent world status, perhaps not equal, but certainly just below, the superpowers. This gave rise to his formula of 'Association not Participation' with Europe, whose desire for unity he underestimated while failing to understand the implications for Britain that unification without her would have. With Eden as premier in May 1955, these attitudes kept Britain apart from moves to form the *EEC that

year and plunged her into the *Suez Crisis in 1956, when Eden showed himself incapable of understanding Arab nationalism and equated Nasser with Hitler or Mussolini. The ill-health which had plagued him throughout his career affected his judgement during the Suez Crisis: he appreciated the need to keep on good terms with America but did not anticipate the American reaction to Anglo-French intervention in Egypt. Eden's pretext for occupying the Canal Zone – to separate the combatants in an Egyptian–Israeli war which Britain and France had obviously connived in starting – was singularly unconvincing, to say the least. It lost Britain the moral high ground in world affairs which was usually hers. It split the Cabinet and *Commonwealth and earned the censure of the increasingly important and newly independent non-aligned nations. In January 1957, soon after the withdrawal from Suez, Eden resigned. He was created an earl in 1961 and died in 1977.

ASTER, S. *Anthony Eden*, Weidenfeld and Nicolson, 1976.
AVON, LORD, *The Memoirs of the Rt Hon Sir Anthony Eden* (3 vols.) Cassell, 1960–5. *Another World, 1897–1917*, Allen Lane, 1976.
CARLTON, D. *Anthony Eden*, Allen Lane, 1981.
JAMES R. R., *Anthony Eden*, Weidenfeld and Nicolson, 1986.

EEC, see EUROPEAN COMMUNITY

EFTA, see EUROPEAN FREE TRADE ASSOCIATION

**Eisenhower Doctrine.** This resulted from a Congressional Joint Resolution of 1957. It authorized the President of the United States to use military forces if deemed necessary to defend the states of the Middle East that requested such support against what was described as 'overt armed aggression from any nation controlled by international communism'. With the authority of a Joint Resolution support could include the despatch of United States forces to the threatened country as well as military and economic assistance under the Mutual Security Programme. In 1958 forces were sent to Lebanon and Jordan and within the framework of the doctrine subsequent commitments were made to Turkey, Iran and Pakistan. The Eisenhower Doctrine was a consequence of the *Suez Crisis (1956). Some people at the time regarded it as a rather cynical attempt by the United States to replace British influence in the Middle East, which had suffered such a devastating blow at Suez. Others saw it as a case of second thoughts by the American Administration over its role during Suez and as a responsible attempt to fill the power vacuum in the region which it had helped to create. Whatever the motivation, the operations undertaken in fulfilment of the doctrine involved very close Anglo-American military and logistical cooperation, including the despatch of British paratroops to Jordan.

**Empire and Commonwealth, the British.** Possession of a global empire which at its greatest extent, around 1930, covered over 12 million square miles and included over 500 million people – nearly a quarter of the world's land surface and nearly a quarter of its population – gave Britain's foreign policy throughout the nineteenth century and for much of the twentieth a remarkable continuity of ideas. It was a vast, unwieldy and informal organization; but it had developed from a pattern of expanding trade and influence intended to maximize commercial profit by limiting as far as possible the acquisition of colonial possessions with their attendant responsibility and expense. This practice, commercial rather than political in nature and known as 'informal empire', depended on Britain's pre-eminence as a manufacturing nation and as a global naval power. The *Vienna Settlement (1815) confirmed that she was both, and guaranteed that she would remain so for at least 50 years.

There was a third element on which informal empire rested and which became increasingly important as challenges from other states made the practice anachronistic. This was control of India. Uniquely among British possessions, India provided in her Army a huge resource of political and military power. Britain's own military forces were not negligible, but their dispersal among garrisons worldwide limited her ability to apply military pressure effectively. The Indian Army, some 150,000 strong and paid for out of Indian revenues, made Britain the leading power in the East. As Fieldhouse puts it, 'India enabled Britain to play a role in world affairs which the British tax-payer would not have been willing to pay for: to take a major part in the partition of East Africa and South-East Asia, and to conquer much of the Ottoman Empire during the First World War'.

Possession of empire and the security afforded by her island situation determined Britain's attitude to Europe. Britain had no territorial ambitions there, but she did have major inter-ests. These were commercial and strategic. Europe was one of Britain's largest markets. It was important that she should remain so; and, above all, that she should not be dominated by any single state, for this would not only shut out British goods from Europe but would pose a major threat to Britain's security by placing the European seaboard, from the North Sea to the Bay of Biscay, under the influence of a hostile state. This had been Napoleon's challenge and, as the British were aware, only their maritime supremacy and dominance of world trade had enabled them to defeat it. Thus a *balance of power between the continental states, such as the 1815 settlement achieved, was ideally suited to Britain. Support for the territorial status quo and for the peaceful settlement of disputes was therefore characteristic of British policy in Europe.

Such attitudes meant that for most of the nineteenth century Britain continued to see France as her principal rival. At various times after 1815 France tried to extend her control over areas sensitive to Britain: the Iberian peninsula and the Spanish South American colonies, Belgium and the Levant. Adroit diplomacy and judicious use of naval power enabled Britain to meet these challenges; but they were less effective against Russia. Russian expansion into Central Asia and Russian designs on the decaying Ottoman Empire were seen as threats to India. This 'Great Game in Asia' became a permanent feature of international diplomacy from the 1830s. And it was a game that British statesmen believed they had to win, because the loss of India would result in Britain's demise as a Great Power. Relations with Russia in Europe, therefore, had to be considered in the light of their implications for the defence of India.

Britain's industrial leadership and naval supremacy were progressively undermined as the other powers industrialized, built fleets, and themselves developed interests in overseas trade and colonial expansion. *Free Trade, on which the mid-Victorian empire had flourished, was threatened by competition from protectionist Germany, the United States and Japan. As these and others assumed formal control of territories in Africa and the Far East, the British, to protect what they had, reluctantly did the same. As Lord *Rosebery (1847–1929) glumly observed in 1895, Britain's commerce was so universal that scarcely any question anywhere could arise without involving British interests.

In a world of sharpening international tensions, this was a source of weakness rather than strength. By 1900 the United States had emerged as the dominant power in the Western hemisphere, while Japan was about to establish herself as the leading power in the Far East. By agreement with the United States in 1901 and alliance with Japan in 1902, Britain tacitly acknowledged American and Japanese supremacy in those areas so that she could maintain her narrow margin of superiority over her nearest naval rivals, France and Russia. From the end of 1900, however, Germany, already Europe's leading industrial and military state, set about creating a navy that could take on Britain's own in a bid to achieve not only continental hegemony but the global influence which Britain still precariously enjoyed. This led to Britain smoothing over her extra-European disagreements with an equally nervous France and Russia, and cooperation between the three against Germany.

The decline of their relative position in the world had been apparent to the British since the 1880s. To arrest it, groups such as the Imperial Federation League and leading politicians such as Joseph* Chamberlain (1836–1914) had advocated closer links with the settlement colonies in matters of trade and defence. Yet an imperial customs union was never possible. Britain wanted Free Trade while the colonies wanted preferential tariffs for their goods in Britain. Nor were the colonies, with their legislatures acquiring increased responsibilities and a growing sense of independence, willing to share the financial burden of defence. The Cape, Australia and New Zealand made small contributions to the naval budget after 1887, but only New Zealand continued to do so after 1909. None of the colonies would agree in advance to fight Britain's wars, and none could therefore be reckoned as part of an imperial defence system. *World War I (1914–18), however, saw the Dominions (as the settlement colonies had been known since 1907) assume precisely the role the imperial federationists had envisaged: they exported more to Britain and sent a million men to fight for her; India sent a further one-and-a-half million. This vital contribution to the British war effort allowed the Dominions to influence both the direction of the war and the making of the peace, when they unanimously insisted on retaining the captured German colonies. India meanwhile was transferred in status from permanent dependency to future Dominion when, in response to civil disorder, the Montagu declaration of 1917 promised 'progressive realization of responsible government'.

Soon after the long-term potential of imperial defence had been brought into question, the diplomatic unity of the empire came to an end. In 1923 the Dominions acquired the right to make treaties. With their diplomacy no longer under British control, the Dominions sought to influence British diplomacy to meet their own requirements. Unwilling to fight another European war for Britain, they favoured her disengagement from Europe. Australia and New Zealand, mindful of Japan now that Britain's alliance with her was ended, wished to see Britain an Asiatic power again. Weakened economically and disheartened by Europe, the British were not unresponsive to this, and hoped to reconstitute their strength on its old commercial basis. But this failed both in Europe and the Americas, because of protectionism, and in the Far East, because of Japanese competition. Although the war had long since made the original concept impractical, imperial federation was revived in modified form at the *Ottawa Conference (1932). Here, in the worst phase of world depression, Britain abandoned Free Trade and accepted a system of *Imperial Preference. By reducing the level of British trade with Europe, imperial preference helped to pave the way for Nazi economic and political domination of the Continent after 1933.

Though World War I had brought the Empire further territories, it had also increased the disparity between commitments and capabilities which had existed before 1914. The decline of Britain's naval supremacy continued as Britain observed the international naval limitation agreements of the 1920s. But during the 1930s Britain faced three potential enemies, each with powerful modern navies. Germany threatened the British Isles; Italy the Mediterranean and Middle Eastern Empire; Japan the Far Eastern Empire. Now that consultation with Dominions' representatives on defence and foreign policy questions had become a regular feature of British decision-making, the Dominions urged *appeasement in Europe and the Mediterranean, but resisted it in Africa and the Far East. Important as their influence on British policy was, it was not decisive. Whitehall's disinclination to become involved in a European war was already strong, and the Dominions merely provided additional reasons for doing what would have to be done in any case.

All the Dominions declared war on Germany in September 1939, but Canada did so with reluctance and South Africa only after a political crisis. Again they provided a vital contribution to the British war effort, but the centrifugal pressures which had been at work within the Empire in the 1914–18 war operated now with greater force. The priority which the British had since 1939 given to the European conflict left few resources for the Far East. There the loss of Singapore and the defeats sustained in 1942 under Japanese attack had two effects. First, imperilled Australia and New Zealand had to look to the United States not Britain for support – a development which heralded American post-war predominance in the region. And second, with the Japanese demonstration that the white man was not invincible, the moral and political basis of British rule in India and other Asian territories was irreparably undermined. Renewed disorder in India secured the promise of British withdrawal after the war, but when withdrawal took place in 1947 the Victorians' axiom that Britain could not remain a world power without India was forgotten.

The Attlee government and its successors tried hard to maintain the Empire in the era of the *Cold War, in a world now dominated by the United States and Soviet Union. They believed, with some justification, that precipitate departure from unstable territories under British control would result in power vacuums ultimately damaging to British interests. The Attlee government, more positively, considered itself trustee of an empire whose dependent colonies would be beneficiaries of welfare socialism. The Commonwealth and Empire led by socialist Britain could then become a major force for world peace and the basis for Britain's revival as a world power. Conservatives, paternalist rather than socialist, held basically similar ideas; and for much of the 1950s, with the decolonization process almost at a standstill, the belief persisted that Britain still had the capacity to play a major role at the head of her Commonwealth and Empire.

This had major implications for Britain's post-war attitude to Europe. As a *NATO founder member, Britain played a prominent part in Europe's defence. But she was not prepared to commit herself to European political and economic integration by becoming a member of the *EEC. The necessary severance of Commonwealth trade links would mean not only the loss of cheap imported food but also the loosening of political ties with the Commonwealth – and this was not a price she was yet prepared to pay. The *Suez Crisis (1956), which saw Britain condemned by the entire Commonwealth except New Zealand, was followed by withdrawal from most of the remaining dependent colonies as the British economy became increasingly unable to support the expenditure necessary for their administration, control and defence. The Government's application to join the EEC in 1962 reflected a new conviction that Britain's future lay with Europe, not the Commonwealth. The Commonwealth had shown that it was not an instrument which could provide Britain with the leadership role she desired; and with the dollar now established in what had been the *sterling area, nor could it regenerate the British economy on which that leadership depended.

Today's Commonwealth is a loose association of independent sovereign states, and no longer exclusively a white man's club. It has little influence on British foreign policy, now principally focused on Europe; but elsewhere it can serve as a valuable instrument for it. In 1980, for example, it assisted the British government to effect a legal transfer of power in Zimbabwe. Many states have little in common except their common use of English and their subjection to Britain in the past, and it is arguable that the regular Commonwealth conferences do more to expose divisions between rich and poor members than to promote unity or purpose among them. Yet the Commonwealth is useful as a channel for aid, as a forum for discussion and, from the British point of view, as a platform for expressing British values in the conduct of international affairs.

BOURNE, K., *The Foreign Policy of Victorian England 1830–1902*, Oxford University Press, 1970.

FIELDHOUSE, D. K., *The Colonial Empires*, Weidenfeld and Nicholson, 1966.

HOWARD, M., *The Continental Commitment*, Temple Smith, 1972.

KENNEDY, P. M., *The Realities Behind Diplomacy*, Fontana, 1981.

LLOYD, T. O., *The British Empire*, Oxford University Press, 1984.

OVENDALE, R., '*Appeasement*' *and the English-speaking World*, University of Wales Press, 1975.

**Empire Free Trade.** The idea advanced by Lord *Beaverbrook, Lord Rothermere and others from the end of the 1920s for the removal of trade barriers between the member countries of the British *Empire and for the erection of tariff barriers against outside competition. It was regarded by some as the ultimate goal of *Imperial Preference. Under the banner of a United Empire Party, Empire Free Trade candidates were run with some success against official Conservative candidates in a number of by-elections. It was this challenge to his authority which provoked Stanley *Baldwin (1867–1947) to make his celebrated denunciation of the press barons for seeking power without responsibility, 'the prerogative of the harlot through the ages'. Shortly after this the official government candidate Duff *Cooper (1890–1954) won a by-election at St George's Westminster. The idea of Empire Free Trade was clearly unviable. Its apparent simplicity of conception was complicated by the facts that British farmers wanted protection against Empire agriculture and Empire industrialists did not wish to be exposed to unrestricted competition from British manufacturers.

**EMS,** see EUROPEAN MONETARY SYSTEM

**Encirclement, Theory of.** The theory that Germany was being systematically encircled and hemmed in by the other powers, Britain, France and Russia, through ententes, alliances and military understandings in the years leading to *World War I (1914–18). The expression was first used in this context by the German Chancellor Bülow in a speech to the Reichstag in 1906. Those who have advanced this theory have pointed in particular to the *Anglo-French Entente (1904) and the *Anglo-Russian Convention (1907) and have tended to attribute major blame for the alleged encirclement to British foreign policy and imperial rivalry. Since 1918 the theory has featured prominently in the controversial debate over the origins of World War I (1914–18). It was also revived during *World War II (1939–45).

*Entente Cordiale* (see also ANGLO-FRENCH ENTENTE (1904) ). A phrase applied to periods of Anglo-French cordiality during the nineteenth and twentieth centuries. It was first coined by the French premier M. Guizot to record the improvement in relations between the two governments symbolized by the meet-ing of Queen *Victoria and King Louis-Philippe in 1843. This was at a time when the reciprocal sentiments of British and French public opinion were somewhat less than friendly. The Emperor Napoleon III, in contrast to his famous uncle, set out to continue this policy of rapprochement, which is illustrated by his alliance with Britain during the *Crimean War (1854–6) and in the *Cobden–Chevalier Treaty (1860).

Anglo-French relations continued, nevertheless, to be vexed by continuing global colonial rivalries. The *Fashoda Crisis (1898) brought the powers to the point of armed conflict. Subsequently the growing British desire to limit their overseas defence liabilities and a French wish to resolve colonial difficulties led to its revival in the *Anglo-French Entente (1904). Entente Cordiale has always tended to be less than completely specific. Though military discussions were instigated between the British and French after the 1st *Moroccan Crisis (1905), the entente was not perceived as definitive enough to dissuade leading circles in Germany from believing that Britain would remain neutral in the event of a Franco-German conflict. Since *World War I (1914–18) the entente has been, periodically, severely strained, for instance in 1923 by the *Ruhr invasion and by the sinking of the French Fleet at *Mers-el-Kébir (1940), an action taken to prevent it falling into German hands. In 1947 the attempt was made to revive the entente in the Treaty of *Dunkirk (1947). It has subsequently suffered a number of setbacks, such as that occasioned by General de Gaulle's veto of British membership of the Common Market.

**Ethiopian War,** see ABYSSINIAN WAR (1935–6)

**European Community.** The organization which brings together the executive bodies of the European Economic Community, EURATOM, and the European Coal and Steel Community. Established as such in July 1967, it marked a further rationalization of the institutional system of Western Europe which had been set up between 1951 and 1958 by the Six – Belgium, France, West Germany, Italy, the Netherlands and Luxembourg. The Paris Treaty (1951) had established the Coal and Steel Community and in 1957 the Rome treaties had brought the EEC and EURATOM into existence. Britain, together with Denmark and Eire, joined on 1 January 1973. The best-known aspect of the Community is the EEC (Common

Market). Its aim is to promote a harmonious development of economic activity, a continuous and balanced expansion, a rising living standard and closer relations between the member states. Originally it was anticipated that the customs union would be established over a 12- to 15-year span (in fact this was achieved by 1 July 1968), and it was hoped progressively to harmonize the policies of the member states, leading eventually, for instance, to monetary union.

The main decision-making body of the Community is the Council of Ministers, which consists of representatives of the member states. The Commission in Brussels issues proposals to the Council, puts its decisions into effect and exercises powers of its own in the interests of the Community at large, as contrasted with the pursuit of national and sectional interests, which are frequently tenaciously defended in the Council of Ministers. The members of the Commission undertake, as a requirement of their position, to act independently of their own national interests. The European Parliament, which meets in Strasbourg or Luxembourg, has supervisory and consultative powers. Though it cannot select a new one, it can constitutionally dismiss the Commission and it has some control over the Community budget. Originally, members of the Parliament were nominees of their national assemblies. In June 1979 this arrangement was superseded by direct elections, with an increase of representation from 198 to 410 members. The European Court of Justice is responsible for the interpretation and application of community law and its decisions are binding on the member states. (See also: *Western Europe since 1945, Britain and).

**European Concert,** see CONCERT OF EUROPE

**European Free Trade Association** (EFTA). Also known as 'the outer Seven'. A customs union with headquarters in Geneva, EFTA was established on 20 November 1959 in Stockholm by Britain, Austria, Denmark, Norway, Portugal, Sweden and Switzerland; it was subsequently joined by Iceland and, as an associate member, by Finland. It came into force on 3 May 1960. The aim was to support its members in achieving continuous economic expansion, full employment and financial stabilization, as well as creating a single market embracing the countries of Western Europe. The reciprocal elimination of customs duties between EFTA members for industrial products was realized between 1961 and 1970. Britain secured the omission of foodstuffs from the tariff agreements. She participated originally as an alternative to joining the EEC, desiring a wider free trade area in manufactured goods. The benefits to Britain were fairly limited, however, as there was no powerful industry in the EFTA countries which could offer a competitive thrust to her industry and because the population of the EFTA grouping amounted to only about half that of the Common Market. Britain left EFTA on 31 December 1972 to enter the Common Market and in July 1973 the other EFTA countries signed a Free Trade agreement with the enlarged Community.

**European Monetary System** (EMS). A currency mechanism instituted by the *European Community with the purpose of reducing exchange rate fluctuations among the members and establishing an area of 'monetary stability in Europe'. Britain decided not to participate in exchange rate and intervention arrangements, though she reserved the right to participate fully at a later date. The EMS came into being on 13 March 1979. It represents a partial fulfilment of the Werner Report (1970), which suggested the adoption of a common European currency.

**European Recovery Programme,** see MARSHALL PLAN (1948–52)

**Europe, Western since 1945, Britain and,** see WESTERN EUROPE SINCE 1945, BRITAIN AND

**Extraterritoriality.** The situation in which citizens or subjects of one country are exempted from the legal jurisdiction and law courts of another country in which they are living. Based either on international custom or specific treaty provision, the principle was most frequently applied in China and Japan in the nineteenth century (see, for instance, *Ansei Commercial Treaties (1858) with Japan). During *World War II (1939–45) most European nations and the United States abandoned extraterritoriality. The international practice of exempting diplomatic agents and their families from local jurisdictions is called 'Exterritoriality'.

# —F—

**Falkland Islands.** An archipelago, known in Argentina as 'Islas Malvinas', located 300 miles from the Straits of Magellan. Since the repossession of these islands by Britain in 1833 (so that it could build a naval base to guard an important part of its sea-lanes to Australia and New Zealand), Argentina has disputed British sovereignty of the Falklands and their dependencies, South Georgia and the South Sandwich Islands. The Argentinian claim is based on their earlier occupation and the proximity of the islands to the mainland. The British have emphasized the fact of continuous occupation since 1833 and the rights of *self-determination of the Falklanders, who (as with the Gibraltarians) have consistently expressed their wish to be British.

Following a *United Nations resolution noting the dispute, negotiations began between Britain and Argentina in 1966. Various solutions were discussed, including the possibility of the transfer of sovereignty with a 'lease-back' to the islanders. In spite of apparent progress in the talks, the dispute erupted into military conflict when Argentinian forces invaded the Falklands on 2 April 1982, installing an Argentinian governor, and declaring the 'recovery . . . (of the islands) . . . for the nation'. Britain had not anticipated this and the Foreign Secretary, Lord *Carrington (1919– ) and two other Foreign Office Ministers resigned following the invasion. The government of Mrs *Thatcher (1925– ) despatched a task force to the South Atlantic while negotiations for a peaceful solution continued. The situation, however, presented an impasse. The Argentinian government of General Galtieri refused to drop its claim to sovereignty, while Britain insisted on the departure of the invaders before any settlement could be arrived at. British forces first occupied South Georgia and (after mediation attempts by the Peruvian Government and the Secretary-General of the United Nations had failed) they landed on East Falkland on 21 May. The occupying Argentinian force capitulated on 14 June with the fall of Port Stanley.

British rule was re-imposed and the dispute over sovereignty remains unresolved. The conflict presented an invidious dilemma for the United States, who wished to maintain good relations with both Britain and Latin America. In the event they provided Britain with valuable logistical and intelligence support during the war. Mrs Thatcher has insisted that there can be no discussion about sovereignty. A policy of building up the islands' defences ('Fortress Falklands') has consequently been followed.

CALVERT, P., *The Falklands Crisis: The Rights and Wrongs*, Pinter, 1983.
GOEBEL, J., *The Struggle for the Falkland Islands: A Study in Legal and Diplomatic History*, Kennikat Press, New York, 1971.
HASTINGS, M. and JENKINS, S., *Battle for the Falklands*, Michael Joseph, 1983.

**Fashoda Crisis** (1898). A significant imperial confrontation between Britain and France. A French force of about 200 men had established a post on the Nile near the native village of Fashoda in July 1898. Commanded by Major Marchand, this detachment was ordered to maintain a French presence on the Nile in order to challenge British colonial claims in the region. This was essentially the climax of a long-standing rivalry between the two powers for influence in Egypt. By this time joint Anglo-French control had been superseded by a British protectorate over Egypt. Both powers were keen to consolidate their African interests in the Sudan, and Britain aspired to control over a continuous stretch of territory from Cairo to the Cape. Confronted by *Kitchener and the refusal of Lord *Salisbury (1830–1903) to yield, the French post conceded to the British. In the middle of the crisis the French Premier Hanotaux was toppled from power. His successor Delcassé recalled Marchand from Fashoda on 3 November 1898. On 21 March of the following year an Anglo-French declaration defined the *spheres of influence of the two powers, excluding the French from the Nile. During the confrontation Lord Salisbury attempted to calm matters by offering to trade British interests in Morocco for French interests in Egypt. This division of interests was later to become the basis of the Entente Cordiale (see: *Anglo-French Entente (1904) ). Fashoda had the effect of turning minds in London and Paris towards a settlement of their outstanding colonial rivalries. It emphasized to the French their vulnerability and the need for British goodwill if they were to consolidate their interest, particularly in the event of German hostility.

BATES, D., *The Fashoda Incident of 1898: Encounter on the Nile*, Oxford University Press, 1984.
SANDERSON, G. N., *England, Europe and the Upper Nile 1882–99*, Edinburgh University Press, 1965.

**First World War,** see WORLD WAR I (1914–18)

**FISHER,** John Arbuthnot, 1st Baron Fisher of Kilverstone (created 1910) (1841–1920). It was largely due to Fisher's dynamism and enthusiasm that the Royal Navy was sufficiently modernized to meet the German challenge in *World War I (1914–18). He entered the navy in 1854, serving as a cadet in the Baltic Fleet during the *Crimean War (1854–6). By 1882 he was in command of the *Inflexible*, the greatest battleship of the time, and was in action off Alexandria against Arabi Pasha. Subsequently, from 1892 to 1897 as Third Sea Lord and Controller of the Navy he was responsible for the programme of shipbuilding authorized by the Naval Defence Act (1889). In

1902 he became Second Sea Lord and introduced important administrative reforms including a common entry for training officers at Osborne and the creation of a naval college at Dartmouth. During the period 1904–10, as First Sea Lord, he reorganized the distribution of the Fleet, concentrating it in home waters. In 1906 the first 'Dreadnought' was launched. After the outbreak of *World War I (1914–18) *Churchill (1874–1965) invited Fisher to return as First Sea Lord when Prince Louis of Battenberg resigned. He was responsible for the defeat of Von Spee. Fisher only agreed with reluctance to *Gallipoli (1915). When it became obvious that further naval reinforcements would weaken the Channel Fleet he resigned. This led to Churchill's removal from the Admiralty.

FISHER, J. A., *Memories*, Hodder and Stoughton, 1919.
MARDER, A. J., *From the Dreadnought to Scapa Flow: The Royal Navy in the Fisher Era* (5 vols.), Oxford University Press, 1961–70.

**Five-Power Treaty** (1922). Naval disarmament agreement reached at the *Washington Conference on 6 February 1922. It stipulated the following ratios of naval strength for Britain, the United States, Japan, France and Italy respectively: $5 : 5 : 3 : 1.75 : 1.75$. The three leading naval powers had to scrap some existing vessels to meet the limitations. Its primary significance for Britain was that she now accepted naval equality with the United States – Britain's naval dominance was now admitted to be at an end. The United States, with their two-ocean fleet, hoped that this agreement would help to end naval rivalry and imperial competition and avoid a costly arms race. The signatories agreed on a ten-year 'holiday' for naval construction and the maintenance of the *status quo* in the Pacific. Smaller ships and submarines were excluded from these limitations, after strong French insistence, though the later London Naval Conference (1930) set a ratio for cruisers. The Five-Power Treaty was the most important interwar disarmament treaty, but it was never unreservedly accepted in Japan, and Japan announced her intention of abandoning it in 1934.

ROSKILL, S. W., *Naval Policy Between the Wars, 1919–39*, vol. I, Collins, 1968.

*Flottenpolitik* (see also ANGLO-GERMAN NAVY RACE). The expansionist German naval policy introduced by Kaiser William II and Admiral von Tirpitz in the 1890s which precipitated sharp rivalry with Britain. The campaign in Germany for a strong navy to meet the requirements of a growing world power with colonial interests (see: *Weltpolitik) was launched in 1895. The first Navy Law followed in 1898 and a succeeding one, which projected a doubling of the number of battleships by 1916, was passed in 1900. In 1907 she began the construction of Dreadnoughts. The navy race became the most visible cause of tension between Britain and Germany in the years leading to the outbreak of *World War I (1914–18).

**Foreign Office** (Foreign and Commonwealth Office). In 1782 Charles James Fox was granted the 'sole Direction of the Department for Foreign Affairs'. Three years later the duties of the new department were defined as: 'conducting the correspondence with all Foreign Courts, negotiating with the Ambassadors or Ministers of all the Foreign Courts in Europe, as well as of the United States of America, and receiving and making representations and applications to and from the same, and in corresponding with other principal departments of the State thereupon. . .'. The Secretary of State for Foreign Affairs conducted policies agreed by the Cabinet. In practice a small group of ministers including the Prime Minister and Foreign Secretary tended to be both better informed and more involved in foreign policy decision making than other Cabinet ministers. It was rare for the views of a Foreign Secretary to be overruled, and then only by the PM. The implementation of policies was conducted through a separate diplomatic service, created by Crown patronage and socially exclusive. It was essentially a 'family system'. John *Bright (1811–89) commented in 1858 that foreign affairs was 'a gigantic system of outdoor relief for the aristocracy of Great Britain'. It was not until 1871 that even limited competitive examinations for entry were accepted (a proper system was only developed from 1883). Furthermore, though the Ridley Commission in 1890 recommended that the two services be combined, the diplomatic service and the Foreign Office remained separate until 1919. The years leading to *World War I (1914–18) saw an increasing influence in the role of Foreign Office officials. Senior clerks, such as Eyre *Crowe (1864–1925), author of a famous memorandum on Germany, began the practice of writing minutes for the consideration of the Foreign Secretary. At the same time, the registry system introduced in 1905 allowed more of the clerical tasks to be undertaken by newly recruited junior clerks rather than by executive Foreign Office staff.

Following the MacDonnell Commission (1914), and encouraged by public demand for 'open diplomacy' under parliamentary control, a single 'foreign service' was created in the reforms of 1919–20, which also included the abolition of the private means qualification. These reforms, though, failed to improve the disorganized and inefficient commercial and consular services. For instance, a new commercial diplomatic service was established in 1920 under the joint control of the Foreign Office and Board of Trade. The recently created wartime political intelligence departments were dismantled. At the same time, therefore, as the Foreign Office was emerging as a modern department of state, its relative significance was diminishing and with it the role of Foreign Secretary, as foreign policy became more and more visibly constrained by domestic economic problems and imperial decline.

Recognizing its deficiencies, Anthony *Eden (1897–1977) made important proposals in 1943, designed to ensure that the Foreign Office would be better able to: 'deal with the whole range of international affairs, political, social and economic, and so constitute an adequate instrument for the maintenance of good relations and mutual understanding between the United Kingdom and other countries'. The most significant of his reforms was the amalgamation and complete integration of the Foreign Office, diplomatic service, commercial diplomatic service and consular service into a single foreign service. By the mid-1950s most of his reforms had been realized. Since 1945 Britain's changing role in world affairs and her relative economic decline have encouraged further reappraisal of the role of the Foreign Office. In 1968 it merged with the Commonwealth Office. Though it has changed very considerably, criticisms such as that of the Central Policy Review Staff report (1977) have suggested that the Foreign Office may still, in some respects, be too bound by tradition, though the scale of the new developments in world affairs to which it has had to adjust should not be underestimated. Its authority suffered a conspicuous blow in 1982 when the Foreign

Secretary and two senior Foreign Office Ministers resigned over the *Falkland Islands.
CROMWELL, V. in STEINER, Z. (ed.), *The Times Survey of Foreign Ministries of the World*, pp. 541–75, Times Books, 1982.
STEINER, Z., *The Foreign Office and Foreign Policy, 1898–1914*, Cambridge University Press, 1969.

**Four Freedoms.** The term used to describe the basic human rights by President F. D. Roosevelt in his annual message to Congress on 6 July 1941, in which he advocated support for *Lend-Lease legislation. These were the freedoms: (1) of speech and expression, (2) of religion, (3) from want, (4) from fear.

**Four-Nation Declaration** (1943). Issued at the Moscow Conference in October 1943. Britain, the United States, the Soviet Union and China promised to work jointly in both war and peace. They pledged postwar arms regulations and undertook to avoid armed conflict except where it was in the interests of maintaining peace. In retrospect its most significant point was that the powers agreed to establish as soon as possible 'a general international organization, based on the principles of the sovereign equality of all peace-loving states, and open to membership by all such states, large and small, for the maintenance of international peace and security'. This statement anticipated the postwar *United Nations. At the same time it advanced the notion of a global role for the *Big Four, including China.

**Four Points** (1854). A crucial statement drafted during the *Crimean War (1854–6) by France and Austria in July 1854. Though Britain was not a signatory it was of importance to her since it conditioned the diplomacy of the war and formed the basis for the Treaty of *Paris (1856), which concluded the war. It stipulated that peace between Russia and the Ottoman Empire depended on the replacement of the tsarist protectorate over the Principalities (Moldavia and Wallachia) by a guarantee of the European powers; that there should be freedom of navigation on the Danube; that a revision of the *Straits Convention (1841) should be made in the interest of the *balance of power in Europe; and that there should be a five-power guarantee of religious freedom for the Christian subjects of the Sultan in place of a Russian one. In fact Russia conceded the fourth point in

principle in August 1853 and withdrew from the Principalities in August 1854. The interpretation of the third point became the dominant consideration in the war.

**Fourteen Points.** The peace programme announced by President Woodrow Wilson in an address to Congress on 8 January 1918. Germany and Austria sought an armistice on the basis of these points. They were as follows. (1) Open covenants of peace openly arrived at; the end of secret diplomacy. (2) *Freedom of the seas. (3) Removal, as far as possible, of all economic barriers. (4) Adequate guarantees given and received that national armaments would be reduced to the lowest point consistent with domestic safety. (5) Impartial adjustment of all colonial claims. (6) Evacuation of all Russian territory: Russia independently to determine her political development. (7) Evacuation and restoration of Belgium. (8) Evacuation and restoration of occupied French territory; return of Alsace-Lorraine to France. (9) Readjustment of Italian frontiers along clearly recognizable lines of nationality. (10) The freest opportunity of autonomous development for the peoples of Austria-Hungary. (11) Evacuation of Rumania, Serbia, Montenegro; free access to the sea for Serbia; mutual relations of the Balkan states to be determined by friendly counsel along historically established lines of allegiance and nationality: international guarantees for them. (12) Autonomous development for non-Turkish parts of Turkey; free passage through the *Dardanelles. (13) Erection of an independent Polish state, including the territories inhabited by indisputable Polish populations, with a free and secure access to the sea (see: *Polish Corridor). (14) A general association of nations affording mutual guarantees to great and small states alike (see: *League of Nations).

In sum, these points represented a bid for a new international order and a rejection of the old diplomacy. The European Allies were sceptical and Britain had particular reservations over point two. For his part, the President did not wish to see the British Empire strengthened as a consequence of *World War I (1914–18). Woodrow Wilson was forced to compromise with the European powers in order to secure the incorporation of the Charter of the League of Nations into the peace treaty, so that in the end it embodied traditional policies of national interest. The *Paris Peace Conference (1919–

20) was widely criticized for its departures from the idealism of the Fourteen Points, not least because of its selective violation of the principle of national *self-determination in, for instance, its prohibition of *Anschluss and attempt to fulfil secret promises to Italy offered in the *London Treaty (1915).

**France, Britain and.** Between 1689 and 1815 Britain and France went to war with each other no fewer than eight times. In retrospect we can see that the Napoleonic War marked the end of centuries of traditional military hostility. A dominant imperative of British foreign policy was to prevent any single state exercising a hegemony over the Continent and more particularly gaining control of the ports of the Channel and North Sea. Constantly watchful of French ambitions on the Continent, Britain had also come into conflict with France across the globe as her major imperial rival. Though Britain and France have not fought each other since the Battle of *Waterloo (1815), and an ultimate community of interest between the two powers has tended since then to override points of difference, there have been sharp rivalries between them at times, distrust and very different perspectives on foreign relations. At certain times, too, for instance in the war scare of 1860 and over *Fashoda (1898) war has appeared to threaten.

The 2nd Peace of *Paris and the *Vienna Congress (1815) dealt moderately with France. In spite of some public agitation at home for a severe peace, *Castlereagh (1769–1822) and *Wellington (1769–1852) set out to achieve a 'just equilibrium', a *balance of power which included France, while containing her. Britain's ambitions were primarily colonial, with her gaining among other places at the end of the war the strategically useful Malta and the Cape of Good Hope. French interests remained primarily Continental. So while there were periodic British anxieties over French ambitions in Europe, such as over the French intervention in Spain in 1823 which angered *Canning (1770–1827), or during the *Spanish Marriages Affair (1841–6), or later still, during the unification of Italy, the issues which dominated Anglo-French relations in the nineteenth century were largely outside Europe. So at a time when the phrase *'entente cordiale' was coined and while Britain and France were aligned as constitutional states in juxtaposition to the absolutist monarchies of the *Holy Alliance (1815), their relationship was upset by a series of incidents, including the *Tahiti Incident (1843) and the 2nd Mehemet Ali Crisis (1839–41). The most dramatic was the confrontation of *Kitchener (1850–1916) and Major Marchand at Fashoda in the Egyptian Sudan, when it appeared for a while that the long rivalry of the powers over Egypt would erupt into war. In such disputes the mood of public opinion tended to be markedly less conciliatory than that of their governments. This predisposition to popular Francophobia was clearly identified by Richard *Cobden (1804–65), who regarded the most pressing objective of his Peace Society in the 1850s as being 'to beat down this most wicked spirit towards France'.

The seizure of power by Louis Napoleon on 2 December 1851 and his declaration a year later of the Second Empire aroused fears of a revival of Bonapartist imperialism in Europe. In spite of their alliance during the *Crimean War (1854–6) and their recognition of mutual economic interest in the *Cobden–Chevalier Treaty (1860), considerable alarm was aroused in Britain by the French involvement in Italy, as by the disastrous Mexican adventure. Furthermore, after the Prussian victory over Austria at Sadowa (1866), French demands for compensation, the 'pourboire' which Napoleon had been offered by Bismarck at Biarritz, especially his claim on Luxembourg, were regarded with marked suspicion. The British lack of appreciation of the real respective strengths of Prussia and France led Britain to miscalculate the result of the Franco-Prussian War (1870–1). After Sedan there was as a consequence considerable British sympathy for France and opposition to the Prussian territorial acquisitions. The fall of the Second Empire meant the displacement of France as the leading Continental power, something already implicit in the defeat of Austria. France experienced a growing sense of insecurity, as well as periodic bouts of revanchism, in the face of the rapid growth in power, economic and military, of her eastern neighbour. In the *War-in-Sight Crisis (1875) and subsequently, British apprehension over German dominance started to outweigh traditional concerns with French Continental ambitions. Bismarck astutely encouraged French colonialism as an alternative focus for French energies, to distract the Third Republic from preparations for revenge over Alsace-Lorraine. This necessarily increased the risk of

Anglo-French colonial rivalries at the same time as the advantages of a durable understanding between Britain and France over European matters seemed ever more appealing to the French.

The term *entente cordiale* dated from the reign of Louis Philippe. In 1904 it was embodied in a wide-ranging agreement which attempted to settle the outstanding colonial grievances between Britain and France. The major point was the British acceptance of French dominance in Morocco in return for the French acquiescence in British paramountcy in Egypt. Britain was by this time very much aware of the burdens and vulnerability of her imperial interests, something emphasized by her isolation during the 2nd *Boer War (1899–1902) and something which she had already attempted to remedy in the *Anglo-Japanese Alliance (1902). At the same time French colonialists, disappointed by the failure of their negotiations with Germany and Spain, were all the more eager to reach an understanding with Britain. The scope of the commitment, which was primarily intended to relieve the pressure on tightly stretched imperial resources, was ambiguous, though in private conversations the French were assured that the British would support them against Germany. The Entente came to be seen increasingly as a response to the growth of German ambitions. Germany tried without success in the 1st and 2nd *Moroccan Crises (1905, 1911) to destroy the credibility of the undertaking. However, the British did not contemplate any formal engagement in the form of an alliance and when the Foreign Secretary, Sir Edward *Grey (1862–1933) approved staff talks between Britain and France (see: *Anglo-French Military Conversations (1906–14) ) not even the British Cabinet were informed.

During *World War I (1914–18) it became clear that only the closest cooperation at a supranational level could save the British and French empires and the national independence of the mother countries. The course of the war brought out sharp differences of perception, and while they were in common cause against Germany, there was nevertheless a fair degree of distrust between them. Britain laid great emphasis on economic blockade. Again, with the Western Front in apparent stalemate, it was *Lloyd George (1863–1945) and Winston *Churchill (1874–1965) who advanced the view that the best solution was to attack the

*Central Powers via the east. The French objected to British reluctance to accept unified command under French leadership. They took the view that the British were giving priority to their world-wide imperial interests at the expense of the Western Front and, above all, to guarding British economic interests. Still, economic cooperation and unified command were established. The alliance, though not without vicissitudes, remained intact until the armistice.

## 1918–45

Though very seriously weakened by the war, Britain and France emerged as effectively the strongest powers in the world, with the retreat of the nascent superpower, the United States, into political isolation. They were to shoulder the main responsibility for the application of the peace settlement (see: *Paris Peace Conference (1919–20) ). Their attitudes to the German question differed sharply, however. On balance Britain favoured conciliation while France looked to coercion. The British wish, fundamentally, was for an abiding balance of power in Europe which would leave Britain free to concentrate on her own transoceanic interests. The overriding French demand was for a guarantee of security against a revived Germany. British economic interests as a trading nation called for the recovery of Germany, not her permanent economic subjugation. To some in Britain, French insistence over the Rhineland, Poland and *reparations seemed to suggest an immutable peace settlement which would ensure permanent French claims to superiority in Europe, a 'veiled Napoleonic despotism' under the aegis of the *Versailles Treaty (1919). Lloyd George and the British delegation at the Paris Peace Conference were to make a late and sensational attempt to change the whole nature of the peace treaty when in June 1919 the Prime Minister urged a less punitive approach.

The interwar years witnessed continuing and sometimes very aggrieved disputes between Britain and France (the rivalry was even temporarily to flare up again in the Middle East). British governments were very anxious to avoid specific obligations towards France and were critical of France's hesitations over disarmament. In French eyes this was a contradiction, since security against future German aggression must precede disarmament; and the Anglo-American guarantee to France had lapsed when the United States refused to ratify the Versailles Treaty. The *Ruhr invasion (1923), justified by the French leader Poincaré on the grounds of German failure to meet her scheduled reparations payments, was strongly criticized by Britain and the United States. This underlined France's vulnerability and dependence on British goodwill. Faced with German revival, France was to have no alternative but a policy of entente. This was recognized by Austen *Chamberlain (1863–1937) and led to the *Locarno Pacts (1925), which undertook to uphold the territorial status quo of the Franco-German and Belgian–German frontiers as established at Versailles. Locarno did not end the Franco-British distrust. Nor did it resolve the dilemma of French security. It offered no guarantee against German aggrandizement in Eastern Europe. Confronted with the resurgence of aggressive German nationalism in the 1930s the British and French failed to organize an effective security system for Europe. Hitler's coming to power in 1933, his repudiation of disarmament, withdrawal of Germany from the *League of Nations and then, in 1936, the reoccupation and remilitarization of the *Rhineland undermined the hopes of the Locarno period and dissolved the agreements. The British were very reluctant to accept the idea of relations with France as the heart of their foreign policy, preferring to uphold their international imperial role in very changed, and increasingly disadvantageous circumstances.

The decisive factor bringing Britain and France together in 1939 was the British fear at the beginning of February of a German invasion of the Netherlands. France promised to come to Britain's aid in such an event and Neville *Chamberlain (1869–1940), who had a low estimation of French capabilities, stated: 'The solidarity that united France and Britain is such that any threat to the vital interests of France from whatever direction, must bring about the cooperation of Great Britain'. After the spring of 1939 the British, imparting their military secrets, re-emphasized the *entente cordiale*, supported by the press in both countries. At the same time Britain gave guarantees to Poland, Rumania and Greece. Following Hitler's invasion of Poland on 1 September 1939 Britain and France were accordingly at war with Germany.

The *Phony War was followed by the Nazi victories in Western Europe and the fall of France in 1940. This produced a situation of the utmost gravity for Britain. The proposal for an *Anglo-French Union just before the armistice in 1940 was rejected by the French Government out of hand. Anglo-French relations were inevitably severely damaged and the British attack on the French fleet at *Mers-el-Kébir (1940) led to bitter recriminations. On the British side, the collapse of the French army, the acceptance of armistice without guarantees for the fleet or colonies and open criticism of Britain by Pierre Laval and others only served to endorse the British prejudice that the French were weak and unreliable. After France's surrender Marshal Pétain, a hero of the 1914–18 war, became leader of the so-called Vichy regime. De Gaulle, refusing to accept defeat, fled to London, raising the standard of the Free French movement which he claimed to be the true government of France.

Churchill promised the restoration of France, but his relations with de Gaulle were not easy. British survival was perceived by the Prime Minister as being crucially dependent on the support of the United States. Conflicting attitudes towards the transatlantic superpower were to become a dominant element in Anglo-French relations. De Gaulle resisted, for instance, a plan to install a provisional American military government in France at the end of the war. It should be said, though, that Churchill was anxious to see the restoration of French power after the Nazi defeat. De Gaulle's subsequent emphasis on France's independence and world role after 1958 and his portrayal of Britain, in his rejection of her application for membership of the EEC (see: *Western Europe since 1945, Britain and), as not primarily a European power in her loyalties, can be traced to these earlier wartime differences of opinion. It would be fair to say that a basic community of interest has come to characterize Anglo-French relations. At the same time these are troubled by periodic controversy.

ANDERSON, M. S., *The Eastern Question, 1774–1923*, Macmillan, 1966.

BOURNE, K., *The Foreign Policy of Victorian England, 1830–1902*, Oxford University Press, 1970.

FURNIA, A. H., *The Diplomacy of Appeasement: Anglo-French Relations and the Prelude to World War II, 1931–8*, University Press of Washington, Washington, D.C., 1960.

GATES, E. M., *End of the Affair: Collapse of the Anglo-French Alliance, 1939–40*, Allen and Unwin, 1982.

JORDAN, W. M., *Great Britain, France and the German Problem, 1918–39*, Oxford University Press, 1943.

MONGER, G., *The End of Isolation*, Nelson, 1963.

PICKLES, D., *The Uneasy Entente*, Oxford University Press, 1966.

WAITES, N. ed., *Troubled Neighbours: Franco-British Relations in the Twentieth Century*, Weidenfeld and Nicolson, 1971.

WOLFERS, A., *Britain and France Between Two Wars: Conflicting Strategies of Peace from Versailles to World War II*, W. W. Norton, New York, 1966.

**Franco-Austrian–British Treaty** (1815). Signed on 3 January 1815, following the proposal of Talleyrand, the leading French representative at the *Vienna Congress (1814–15). The powers pledged mutual assistance to each other if attacked. This followed growing apprehensions of the signatories over Russian ambitions in Poland and Prussian claims to Saxony. There seemed the very real threat that war might break out between the Allies over these territories (Prussia had stated that if she felt obliged to annex Saxony any refusal to recognize such an act would be treated by Prussia and Russia as tantamount to a declaration of war). This treaty and the restoration of Allied unity by Napoleon's escape from Elba – Napoleon sent a copy of this secret agreement to the Tsar – served to restrain Russia and Prussia from achieving their full objectives in Central Europe and prevented the outbreak of such a war.

**Freedom of the Seas.** The notion that the seas except for territorial waters are free to all peoples and that no authority, sovereign or state can restrict that freedom. In wartime this means that the citizens of neutral states should be allowed to carry on normal trade without interference or molestation by the belligerents unless their trade is in war goods destined for a belligerent. In his argument against the Dutch jurist Grotius's *Mare Liberum* (1608) the English lawyer Selden had stated in his book *Mare Clausum* (1635) that England should have control of adjacent seas from Spain to the Arctic and without limit to the West. Until the end of the eighteenth century Britain demanded a salute to her flag in 'British seas'. From the nineteenth century there was a general acceptance among the major powers of the principle of the freedom of the seas, outside the limits of territorial waters.

**Free Trade.** A system of unlimited international commerce with no discrimination in favour of domestic products, or interference with exports to favour consumers in the home market. Its classic advocacy was in Adam Smith's *The Wealth of Nations*, published in 1776. It is a system in which no duties or tariffs are charged on foreign goods imported into a country, in the anticipation that other countries will also reduce or abolish their duties, leading to general benefit. The liberalization of trade is now usually attempted by agreements through groups of countries, the purpose being to maximize the growth of international trade.

For most of the nineteenth century Britain was the leading supporter of Free Trade. It had been the first country to industrialize and did not therefore need duties and tariffs to protect its industries from foreign competition. It also had a surplus of manufactured goods for export. In addition it needed cheap raw materials from abroad so that it could produce manufactured goods at low cost, and cheap food so that wages could be held at a modest level. William Huskisson started to abolish some of the duties in the 1820s. The process was continued by Robert *Peel (1788–1850), notably with the repeal of the Corn Laws in 1846, and by *Gladstone (1809–98), particularly in the budgets of 1853 and 1860. A significant further advance for Free Trade was secured with the *Cobden–Chevalier Treaty (1860) between Britain and France.

Free Trade was the prevailing system until the last quarter of the nineteenth century, when the spread of industrialization resulted in the desire of increasing numbers of countries to protect their nascent and growing industries by high tariffs (at this time British agriculture was starting to suffer severe competition from the American prairies). Other countries argued that the English doctrine of Free Trade was designed, selfishly, to maintain a British monopoly position in manufacturing industry. Germany, with measures taken in 1878, and the United States, with those of 1890, emerged as the leading advocates of protectionism. Britain, however, continued to uphold Free Trade until the slump of the interwar years. In 1932 a moderate protective tariff was combined with *Imperial Preference. At the start of the twentieth century Joseph *Chamberlain (1836–1914) had campaigned fruitlessly for a policy of tariff reform, but it was not until his son Neville *Chamberlain (1869–1940) introduced the Import Duties Act that Britain officially ended her Free Trade policy. In the 1930s the chief motive behind protection was the desire to assist employment, keep a favourable balance of trade and increase home production to allow Britain to remain as independent as possible of foreign powers, regarded as a necessary precaution for the defence of the home islands.

The background to this switch from Free Trade was one of ever-increasing foreign tariffs, growing unemployment and world economic depression. After *World War II (1939–45) the move was made to return to Free Trade policy through the *General Agreement on Tariffs and Trade (GATT) of 1947. In 1958 the *EEC came into existence. To start with, Britain with its *Commonwealth links and its large imports of cheap food preferred to stay outside this new grouping and instead helped to set up *EFTA, which still allowed cheap food to be imported. As Britain's trade with members of the EEC became more significant than the Commonwealth link and the benefits of membership of the new market became apparent, Britain applied to join. When she was finally admitted in 1973 her participation meant abandonment of Imperial Preference.

FIELDHOUSE, D. K., *Economics and Empire 1830–1914*, Weidenfeld and Nicolson, 1973.
SEMMEL, B., *The Rise of Free Trade Imperialism*, Cambridge University Press, 1970.

# —G—

**Gallipoli Campaign** (1915–16). The controversial and unsuccessful attempt by British and *Commonwealth forces during *World War I (1914–18) to create a second front by landing on the southern European shore of the *Dardanelles. The intention, by defeating the Turks, was to relieve pressure on Russia and strengthen the Balkan front against the *Central Powers. By forcing a way through the Dardanelles and taking Constantinople the Allied force would free Russian troops in the Caucasus for operations elsewhere and Russian ships would be able to have access to the Mediterranean.

In March 1915 British and French warships bombarded the Turkish forts in the Straits, but withdrew after several Allied ships had been sunk. British, Australian and New Zealand troops then made two landings on the northern shore of the Straits – the Gallipoli peninsula – in April 1915 but suffered heavy casualties, numbering 205,000 out of 410,000 engaged. The remainder of the Allied forces was subsequently evacuated without loss between December 1915 and January 1916. Winston *Churchill (1874–1965) was made scapegoat. It has been argued that a further naval attack would have been successful and that it was not the strategic concept but faulty execution, poor coordination and leadership, which were to blame for the failure. Gallipoli at the time was taken to be a vindication of the 'Westerners', those who argued that in spite of deadlock on the Western Front, it was there alone that the war could be won. It served to deter the British high command from further amphibious operations.

JAMES, R. R., *Gallipoli*, Batsford, 1965.

**GATT,** see GENERAL AGREEMENT ON TARIFFS AND TRADE

**General Agreement on Tariffs and Trade** (GATT). An international organization, affiliated to the *United Nations, which has as its objective the reduction of tariffs and other barriers to trade. Originally intended as an interim institution, pending the creation of a permanent International Trade Organization (ITO) (which the United States Senate declined to confirm), it has developed into a permanent international instrument for the regulation of world trading practices. Its principal achievements include world-wide tariff reductions agreed upon in the 'Dillon Round' (1960–2) under which many customs tariffs were reduced by an average of 20 per cent between the United States and the EEC, the United States and Britain, between Britain and the EEC, as well as between the United States and other countries, with all bilateral concessions being granted to all other GATT members under the *most-favoured-nation principle. In the 'Kennedy Round' (1963–7) there was a reduction of tariffs of over 30 per cent. The most recent negotiations, the 'Tokyo Round' (1973–9) covered other matters as well, such as subsidies and countervailing duties. In the early years of GATT Britain insisted on applying differential rates of import duty between members and non-members of the British *Commonwealth.

**Geneva Conventions.** A series of international conventions on the laws of war for the protection of its victims. The first of these was formulated in 1864 in Geneva and reflected the experience of suffering and medical neglect witnessed during the *Crimean War (1854–6) and the Italian War of Independence of 1859. It was closely related to the rise of the Red Cross. The 1864 and 1906 conventions protect sick and wounded soldiers. These were extended to cover naval personnel by the *Hague Peace Conference of 1907. The *Geneva Protocol (1925) prohibited the use of poison gas or bacteriological warfare. The three conventions of 1929 protect sick and wounded soldiers, sailors and prisoners-of-war. Following the experience of 'total war' in *World War II (1939–45), the 1949 conventions afford protection in addition to certain categories of civilians. The First Protocol of 1977 supplements the 1949 conventions, extending protection to wider groups of civilians, regulating the law of bombing and enlarging the category of war subject to the 1949 arrangements including, for instance, civil wars. Reference to the Geneva Conventions usually relates to the 1949 agreements, which were signed by 59 states and are generally considered to embody the customary international law relating to war. They lack final effective sanction, however, and rest on the constraints of world public opinion and the respective humanitarian ethics of those states involved in war.

**Geneva Protocol** (1924) (Protocol for the Pacific Settlement of International Disputes). A proposed agreement among members of the *League of Nations which was presented by the British Prime Minister Ramsay *MacDonald (1866–1937) and his French counterpart Herriot to its 5th Assembly. It was intended to link the issues of security and disarmament with compulsory arbitration, and to determine who was the aggressor in disputed cases. It was an attempt to reconcile Britain's desire for an easing of international tension in Europe with France's overriding concern to guarantee security in the event of another German attack. The protocol stipulated that the Council of the League should submit all legal disputes between nations to the World Court. If the Council could not agree as to whether a dispute was submissible, it was to be referred to a committee of arbitrators for a binding decision.

It also stated that matters of domestic jurisdiction (formerly outside the scope of the Covenant) should be included under Article 11, and that a disarmament conference should be convened in 1925. Under this arrangement any state which refused to comply in a dispute would be named as an aggressor and any victim of aggression was to receive immediate assistance from the signatories. The Dominions objected to the Geneva Protocol, and the Conservative Party campaigned against it in the 1924 election. Britain consequently rejected it in March 1925. The new Prime Minister, Stanley *Baldwin (1867–1947) was strongly against the principle of compulsory arbitration and resisted Britain's acceptance of wide-ranging security obligations – which might, in his view, among other things have led to conflict with the United States. The American Secretary of State was also opposed to it, envisaging that such an arrangement might in certain circumstances interfere with his country's neutral rights. The proposal collapsed with Britain's emphatic rejection of it.

MARKS, S., *The Illusion of Peace: International Relations in Europe 1918–33*, Macmillan, 1976.
ORDE, A., *Great Britain and International Security, 1920–26*, Royal Historical Society, 1977.

**Geneva Summit Conference** (1955). Held between 18 and 23 July 1955 and consisting of delegations from Britain, the United States, France and the Soviet Union. The powers discussed the issues of disarmament, European security, German reunification and contacts between East and West. The conference reflected the hope of Sir Winston *Churchill (1874–1965) among others that détente between East and West could be assisted by a summit meeting with Stalin's successors Bulganin and Krushchev. A 'thaw' seemed possible since the Austrian Treaty had just been signed (May 1955) and the Soviet Union had advanced proposals for disarmament.

Though the atmosphere of the meeting appeared to promise a reduction of tension the results were meagre. The crucial issue of German reunification was sidestepped with the following statement: 'The Heads of Government have agreed that the settlement of the German question and the reunification of Germany by the means of free elections shall be carried out in conformity with the national interests of the German people and the interests of European security.' A major difficulty was the Soviet insistence that an agreement on German reunification could only be reached if

*NATO were dismantled. President Eisenhower assured the conference that the United States would never wage aggressive war, but he did not take up the Soviet plan for disarmament, which corresponded closely with earlier Anglo-French proposals. He put forward instead the 'open skies' proposal for the verification of armaments by aerial reconnaissance. A directive was issued for a meeting of Foreign Ministers (which convened in October) to carry further the discussion of the same issues, and an agreement was reached on cultural exchanges. However, Eastern Bloc arms deliveries to Egypt, and the *Suez Crisis (1956) and Soviet invasion of Hungary in the same year, served dramatically to worsen relations between East and West.

EUBANK, K., *The Summit Conferences, 1919–1960*, University of Oklahoma Press, Norman, 1966.

**GEORGE-BROWN**, Baron, see BROWN, GEORGE (1914–85)

**Germany, Britain and.** The first three-quarters of the nineteenth century gave little suggestion of the antagonism and rivalry which were to characterize Anglo-German relations at the beginning of the twentieth century. Germany was not united until the 1860s and there were no obvious areas of conflict between Britain and Prussia, though there were differences of view, as over the question of Belgium in the 1830s. During the earlier part of the century Prussia played a relatively minor role in diplomacy. Commercial links between Britain and Prussia grew and Britain offered no objection to the *Zollverein* (customs union) which came into existence in 1834 and which was to make Prussia economically dominant in Germany. Prussian actions during the revolutions of 1848 aroused some apprehension in Britain. When Prussia put herself at the head of the movement for the incorporation of the Danish duchies (see: *Schleswig-Holstein Question) into a new German state both Britain and Russia reacted strongly. *Palmerston (1784–1865) feared the prospect of French or Russian intervention in the dispute with Denmark and regarded Prussian acquisition as against British strategic and commerical interests. Palmerston's overriding concern was to preserve the European *balance of power, but within Germany liberal nationalist opinion tended to blame the British defence of Danish

interests for the prolongation of national disunity. This was a foretaste of the strong nationalist anti-British sentiment which characterized sections of German opinion in the years leading to *World War I (1914–18).

The unification of Germany in the three successive wars of Bismarck against Denmark (1864), Austria (1866) and France (1870) transformed the balance of power in Europe. Britain protested over the seizure of the Duchies, but was powerless to alter the course of events. As *Disraeli (1804–81) commented: 'We have threatened Prussia, and Prussia has defied us'. The destruction of the Second Empire confirmed the new European order, though the French collapse had not been widely anticipated in Britain. Britain gained French and Prussian–German signatures to a guarantee of Belgian neutrality (to be ignored by Germany in 1914). The Russians took the opportunity of war in the West to renounce the *Black Sea Clauses imposed at the end of the *Crimean War (1854–6).

After Sedan the cumulative dominance of the new Reich and its dramatic economic and demographic expansion provoked a reappraisal of British policy. Arguments for a strong British army made themselves heard; the desirability of protectionism as against *Free Trade was advanced in the face of growing commercial competition. Lord *Salisbury (1830–1903), among others, became progressively convinced that Britain should involve herself positively in European affairs again. The *War-in-Sight Crisis (1875) witnessed the diplomatic mobilization of Britain, France, Russia and Austria against Bismarck. It was made clear that Britain would not tolerate German hegemonial aspirations in Europe, and more particularly, could not allow the collapse of France as a Great Power. At the same time, the Eastern Crisis of 1875–8, which pushed Britain, Austria and Prussia to collaborate, and the subsequent *Berlin Congress (1878) indicated that Bismarck and Disraeli were capable of a realistic mutual appreciation of German and British interests.

Before 1900, in fact, public opinion in Britain tended to be decidedly pro-German, in marked contrast with its attitude towards the Russian Empire. At the official level, too, Russia and France were considered a greater potential threat to British imperial interests. The German contribution to culture, its social reforms and perceived efficiency were widely admired. Some people appealed to the idea of racial affinity between German and Anglo-Saxon. In 1897, for instance, Joseph *Chamberlain (1836–1914) spoke of an alliance between Britain, Germany and the United States as one underwritten by nature, and Cecil Rhodes chose to admit Germans together with citizens of the United States and Dominions to the scholarships set up by his will. However, the growth of German power, commerce and imperialist ambitions were soon to make the Anglo-German antagonism the dominant diplomatic reality.

To German nationalist and imperialist opinion the British *Empire was increasingly perceived as the major obstacle to her 'place in the sun'. British capital dominated the most attractive fields for investment. Bismarck's diplomacy had attempted to manipulate foreign relations to impress on Britain the need for German support. His successors were not content to regard Germany as a 'satiated' power. German expansion in the world was bound to conflict with established British interests. British apprehensions were encouraged by the relative decline of her own economy. Whereas at the time of German unification, for instance, Britain had produced twice as much steel as Germany, by the outbreak of the war in 1914 she was producing less than half Germany's output. Demographic projections suggested that within a decade or so Germany would have a population twice that of France. The ebullient German attitude was illustrated in the Kaiser's congratulation to President Kruger of the Transvaal on his defeat of the *Jameson Raid (1895). Again, if Germany's future lay on the oceans, as William II declared when committing Germany to its naval programme three years later (see: *Flottenpolitik), it was bound to lie in direct conflict with Britain as the dominant naval power.

The commercial and naval rivalry (see: *Anglo-German Navy Race) and the awareness of German restiveness and hostility progressively influenced British opinion. The perception of a challenge to Britain's imperial role expressed in the famous Foreign Office memorandum by Eyre *Crowe (1864–1925) in 1907 came to be widely shared, not simply by Conservative and imperialist sections of public opinion, but by the leadership of the Liberal Party including the Foreign Secretary, Sir Edward *Grey (1862–1933) and Winston

*Churchill (1874–1965). Hostility towards Germany was by no means universal, however. On the eve of war in 1914 a group of Britain's most eminent liberal intellectuals pleaded that a war against Germany in the interests of Serbia and Russia would be a 'sin against civilization'. The Governor of the Bank of England stated that the financial and trading interests of the City of London were absolutely opposed to war. The Liberal Cabinet were divided and undecided until the German infringement of Belgian neutrality provided the *casus belli. In the words of Professor Paul Kennedy: 'So far as British and German governments were concerned, the 1914–18 conflict was essentially entered into because the former power wished to preserve the existing status quo whereas the latter, for a mixture of offensive and defensive motives, was taking steps to alter it. In that sense, the wartime struggle between London and Berlin was but a continuation of what had been going on for at least 15 or 20 years before the July Crisis.'

## 1914–39

British propaganda served to encourage violent popular animosity towards Germany as the dreadful casualties of World War I mounted on the Western Front. The call for conciliation was not entirely absent though, as for instance with the *Union of Democratic Control, who appealed for a compromise peace. At the end of the war, in spite of the 'Hang-the-Kaiser' mood of the 'Coupon Election', the arguments for conciliation found increasing acceptance among the British delegation at the *Paris Peace Conference (1919–20). *Lloyd George (1863–1945) fought to reverse the section of the *Versailles Treaty (1919) which provided for the occupation of the Rhineland, and managed to preserve much of Upper Silesia from the demands of the Poles and French. French attempts to turn this treaty and the *League of Nations into instruments to perpetuate victory were bitterly resented and there was a growing liberal internationalist sentiment in Britain against what was perceived as the undue harshness of the settlement, incisively articulated in The Economic Consequences of the Peace by J. M. *Keynes (1883–1946.)

The issues of *reparations and disarmament and the need for Germany economically to revive if the interests of the British economy were to be served, divided the British from the

French over Germany. France was overwhelmingly preoccupied with the question of national security; Britain was most pressingly concerned with her own industrial and commercial revival, and basically wished to see the re-establishment of a balance of power between Germany and France. Britain did not anticipate another European war in the near future. Hence the *Ruhr invasion (1923) by France and Belgium to force Germany to pay overdue reparations evoked grave British and American disapproval. British officials encouraged the subsequent moves towards Franco-German rapprochement, which were embodied in the *Locarno Pacts (1925). Some people in the *Foreign Office regarded France as posing the major Continental problem after 1918. At all events the Continent was considered to be an area inviting British mediation but not involvement.

This view of the British relationship with the Continent tended to persist after the advent of Hitler to power at the end of January 1933. Public opinion tended to be isolationist and also tended to put greater trust in the idea of *collective security under the League of Nations than proved credible. Hitler's wider ambitions for *Lebensraum*, as distinct from the desire to remove the restraints, and redress the grievances of, the Versailles Treaty, were not clearly perceived until the end of the decade, though as early as February 1934 a Cabinet report identified Germany as the major threat, and this led to rearmament. The policy of *appeasement, however, justified at the time on both idealistic/pacifistic and realistic grounds, carried a wide consensus of opinion with it. Large numbers of people were willing to take the view that the 'injustices' of Versailles were reponsible for much of the Nazi success, and argued for a policy of judicious revision. Prominent British visitors to Hitler returned to Britain convinced that he was an Anglophile and that his intentions towards the British Empire were pacific.

The governments of 1933–9 were less influenced by the pressures of opinion inside Parliament and outside for or against appeasement than by the economic and strategic constraints of a relatively declining power. Rearmament was constricted by financial facts as well as by the strength of *isolationism and *pacifism in British public opinion. At the same time, Britain was faced with challenges to its global position from both Japan and Italy. In

1935, after the Italian attack on Abyssinia (see: *Abyssinian War (1935–6) ), British public opinion, particularly as represented in Parliament, forced the Government to jettison the *Hoare–Laval Plan. This war dissolved the *Stresa Front (1935), the emergent grouping of Britain, France and Italy in the face of growing German power. It also destroyed the illusion of effective collective security under the League of Nations. While rearming, Britain at the same time sought an accommodation with Germany. Hitler repudiated the disarmament clauses imposed by the Versailles Treaty, left the League of Nations, in March 1936 reoccupied the *Rhineland and supported the Nationalist forces under Franco in Spain (see: *Spanish Civil War, Britain and the, 1936–9). At the same time Hitler presented his policy as one of attempting to secure British friendship. The *Anglo-German Naval Agreement (1935), for instance, was acclaimed as an earnest of goodwill. In fact it registered a British recognition of the fact that Germany, in contravention of Versailles, was rearming. Pressure from the British Treasury, United States neutrality legislation and the resistance of the Dominions to the idea of British involvement in a Continental war confirmed Neville *Chamberlain (1869–1940) in the strategy of appeasement.

Britain's position as far as Eastern and Central Europe were concerned was this. She was willing to concede a revision of German territorial grievances provided these were secured by diplomatic means in agreement with the powers rather than by force. It was hoped, and intended, that rearmament would add support to this policy so that Germany would be dissuaded from seeking other than a peaceful solution of her claims. In fact British concessions served to persuade Hitler that Britain would not resist Germany by force. In the year after the *Munich Agreement (1938) Hitler assured his military planners and Mussolini that Britain would not intervene to try to frustrate his plans against Poland.

After German troops marched into Prague in March 1939 Chamberlain announced in the Commons that if the Poles, who were now to be the next victims of Hitler's aggression, resisted a threat to their independence, Britain and France 'would at once lend them all the support in their power'. This reflected the growing groundswell of public opinion that appeasement had failed and that Nazi ambitions (which now clearly included the incorporation of non-

German peoples under the control of the Reich) must be checked. The seriousness of Britain's intention to assist the Poles seemed to be attested by her opening of negotiations with the Soviet Union for a pact of mutual assistance. These failed, being forestalled by the surprise announcement of the *Molotov–Ribbentrop Pact (1939).

The German invasion of Poland on 1 September brought the guarantee to Poland into effect and Britain and France declared war on 3 September. For most of the interwar period Britain's imperial commitments had been deemed to rule out the possibility of fighting in Europe. This assumption was now revised. Though Poland was the *casus belli, the essential objective of British intervention was to save France and to save the Continent from German hegemony. In 1939, however, neither Britain nor France was prepared to launch a full-scale war on Germany (see: *World War II (1939–45).

BALFOUR, M., *The Kaiser and His Times*, Cresset Press, 1964.

GANNON. F. R., *The British Press and Germany, 1936–39*, Oxford University Press, 1971.

GILBERT, M., *Britain and Germany between the Wars*, Longman, 1964.

GRANZOW, B., *A Mirror of Nazism: British Opinion and the Emergence of Hitler, 1929–33*, Gollancz, 1964.

GRIFFITHS, R., *Fellow-Travellers of the Right–British Enthusiasts for Nazi Germany*, Oxford University Press, 1983.

HALE, O. J., *Publicity and Diplomacy: With Special Reference to England and Germany, 1890–1914*, Appleton-Century, New York, 1940.

MANDER, J., *Our German Cousins: Anglo-German Relations in the Nineteenth and Twentieth Centuries*, J. Murray, 1974.

KENNEDY, P. M., *The Rise of the Anglo-German Antagonism, 1860–1914*, Allen and Unwin, 1980. 'Idealists and Realists: British Views of Germany, 1864–1939', *Transactions of the Royal Historical Society*, 25, 1975, pp. 137–58.

MEDLICOTT, W. N., *Bismarck, Gladstone and the Concert of Europe*, Athlone Press, 1956. *Britain and Germany: The Search for Agreement, 1930–37*, Athlone Press, 1968.

SONTAG, R. J., *Germany and England: Background of Conflict 1848–94*, Appleton-Century, New York, 1938.

STEINER, Z. S., *Britain and the Origins of the First World War*, Macmillan, 1977.

**Ghent, Treaty of** (1814). Signed on 24 December 1814, also known as 'the Peace of Christmas Eve', this ended the Anglo-American war of 1812–14. No mention was made in it of the highly vexed questions of the rights of neutrals and impressment, and outstanding differences were left unresolved. However, it marked a positive change for the better in relations between the two countries and laid the basis for subsequent agreements. It restored the territorial status quo and incorporated clauses dealing with the cessation of operations against the Indians, and condemning the slave trade. Commissions were set up to settle the Canadian boundary issue. Their reports resulted in the Convention of London (1818), which also resolved outstanding disputes over fishing-rights. The demilitarization of the Great Lakes was established in the *Rush–Bagot Agreement, ratified in the same year (1818).

BEMIS, S. F., *John Quincy Adams and the Foundations of American Foreign Policy*, A. Knopf, New York, 1949.

DANGERFIELD, G., *The Era of Good Feelings*, Harcourt Brace, New York, 1952.

**Gibraltar.** The strategic base on the tip of southern Spain, captured by Britain in 1704 and ceded to her in the Treaty of Utrecht (1713). It developed as the principal British naval base in the western Mediterranean during the early nineteenth century and was declared a Crown Colony in 1830. It was put to major naval use as late as 1942 when the Allied invasion fleet for North Africa assembled there. Sovereignty over Gibraltar has been persistently disputed by Spain, particularly since the end of the *Spanish Civil War in 1939. Gibraltarians were granted a greater measure of self-government in 1964 and in 1967 a referendum was held in which the inhabitants overwhelmingly voted to retain links with Britain. In 1969 it received a new constitution giving it a House of Assembly, executive authority being vested in a Governor representing the Queen. In the same year General Franco closed the frontier between Spain and Gibraltar, claiming the latter as part of Spanish national territory. To the Spanish demands the British have consistently replied by referring to the expressed wish of the Gibraltarians to remain British (as in the question of the *Falkland Islands). Since

1973 Gibraltar has been part of the *EEC by virtue of its relation to Britain.

The death of Franco and the negotiation for, and inclusion of, Spain in the Community have produced an improvement in relations between the two countries. An agreement was reached in Lisbon in 1980 by which the border would be reopened and discussion on the major issue would begin. The Spaniards have argued that the 'sole legal basis' for the British presence in Gibraltar has been Article 10 of the Treaty of Utrecht and that legally the cession of Gibraltar is 'subject to a series of limitations'. They have also alleged that the British have encroached northwards. The frontier between Gibraltar and Spain was reopened by Spain on 4–5 February 1985, following the conclusion of an Anglo-Spanish agreement on 27 November 1984 in which Britain undertook for the first time to discuss the sovereignty of Gibraltar.

BRADFORD, E., *Gibraltar – The History of a Fortress*, Hart-Davis, 1971.

**GLADSTONE,** William Ewart (1809–98). Liberal Prime Minister (1868–74, 1880–5, 1886, 1892–4). Gladstone, the leading Liberal statesman of the later nineteenth century, entered Parliament in 1832 as a Conservative. He served in Peel's governments from 1834 to 1835 and in the 1840s, joining his leader in 1846 in separating from the bulk of the Tory Party in order to carry the repeal of the Corn Laws. During the following years he moved steadily towards the Liberals, although he brought with him a Peelite desire for reorganization and efficiency in government, a commitment to the peaceful resolution of international differences which owed much to *Aberdeen (1784–1865), and, above all, an intense Christian conviction which caused him to see his political career in providential terms and to give a moral colour to the most insignificant decision.

Gladstone's first public pronouncements on foreign affairs were attacks on Palmerston's policies, over the *Opium War in 1840 and *Don Pacifico in 1850. In 1851 Gladstone visited Naples, where he was appalled by the conditions he observed in the prisons, and published attacks on the government of King Ferdinand of the Two Sicilies. In 1852 he became Chancellor of the Exchequer in the Aberdeen coalition and, like the Prime Minister, advocated a conciliatory policy towards Russia. He resigned with Aberdeen in 1855 and subsequently supported Cobden's attacks on the Palmerston government's conduct of foreign affairs. Nevertheless, after an inconclusive interlude as British Commissioner in the Ionian Islands, he accepted the Exchequer from *Palmerston (1784–1865) in 1859 and found a congruence of views with his erstwhile adversary in their common support for Italian independence. However, relations between the two men remained cool, and serious friction was only averted because Gladstone's main concern in this period was with financial reform rather than foreign policy, although he did join with *Russell (1792–1878) in furthering Cobden's plan for a commercial treaty with France.

After Palmerston died in 1865 and Russell retired two years later, Gladstone became leader of the Liberal party and, following victory in the General Election of 1868, Prime Minister. He was to leave the detailed conduct of international relations to his successive foreign secretaries, *Clarendon (1800–70), *Granville (1815–91) and *Rosebery (1847–1929), but at least during his first two ministries, Gladstone maintained an active interest in affairs and was very much concerned with the general direction of policy. Thus Gladstone was fully associated with Granville's conciliatory treatment of Russia and the United States, and his government as a whole shared in the consequent unpopularity which was a cause of the Conservative victory in the General Election of 1874.

Gladstone was now 65 and, depressed by the election defeat, he felt that he had reached the end of his active political career. He relinquished the Liberal leadership in favour of the Marquess of Hartington. He was brought out of retirement in 1876 by his outrage at the conduct of the Turkish government, which had repressed a rebellion in Bulgaria with barbaric savagery. A popular outcry was already gaining momentum in Britain when Gladstone greatly inflamed it by publishing a pamphlet entitled 'Bulgarian Horrors and the Question of the East' (see: *Bulgarian Massacres), which denounced the Turks and the Disraeli ministry for supporting them.

Gladstone renewed his attack on the foreign policy of *Disraeli (1804–81), now Earl of Beaconsfield, in his Midlothian campaign of 1879. In a key speech at West Calder on 27 November he contrasted 'Beaconsfieldism' with the six principles which he considered should underlie British foreign policy. These were the resting of a righteous foreign policy on 'just legislation and economy at home'; the placing of the quest for peace as the first responsibility; the cultivation of the Concert of Powers; the avoidance of needless entanglements; the equality of all peoples and states and, finally, the inspiration of foreign policy by love of freedom. Gladstone's mature ideas as thus expounded showed that the strongest influences upon him were *Canning (1770–1827), Aberdeen and *Cobden (1804–65).

Gladstone and Granville, when they returned to office in 1880, found that the application of broad ideals to the somewhat sordid realities of foreign relations was no easy matter. The muddled policies which resulted were little short of disastrous. Granville was badly discredited and Gladstone's own reputation suffered. The failures of 1880–5 combined with his growing obsession with Irish Home Rule to cause Gladstone to take less interest in foreign affairs during the last decade of his career and Rosebery, Foreign Secretary in his third and fourth ministries, was a Liberal Imperialist. Thus, even in his own government, Gladstone's ideals came to carry little weight. His ultimate resignation in 1894 arose from differences with his Cabinet which was insisting on increased naval appropriations. In 1896, however, Gladstone's call for British intervention against Turkey following the *Armenian Massacres precipitated Rosebery's resignation of the leadership of the Liberal Party.

In addition to an active political career lasting more than 60 years, Gladstone had wide-ranging intellectual interests. It is therefore no coincidence that his greatest contributions to British foreign policy lay in the realm of ideas rather than actual achievement. The principles stated at West Calder have had a strong influence on the conduct of international relations in the twentieth century, although, as Gladstone himself was to find, their implementation has been a long and dispiriting task.

FOOT, M. R. D. and MATTHEW, H. C. G., *The Gladstone Diaries*, Oxford University Press, 1968–82.

KNAPLUND, P., *Gladstone's Foreign Policy*, Cass, 1970.

MAGNUS, P., *Gladstone, A Biography*, John Murray, 1954.

SETON-WATSON, R. W., *Disraeli, Gladstone and the Eastern Question*, Cass, 1962.

SHANNON, R. T., Gladstone, vol. I: 1809–65, Hamish Hamilton, 1982.

**GORDON-WALKER,** Patrick Chrestien, Baron Gordon-Walker of Leyton (created 1974) (1907–1980). Gordon-Walker was educated at Wellington College and Christ Church, Oxford, where he became a History Tutor. Entering Parliament in 1945 as Labour MP for Smethwick, he held junior posts in Attlee's government before coming Secretary of State for Commonwealth Relations in 1950–1. Harold *Wilson (1916–   ) appointed him Shadow Foreign Secretary in 1963 and it was a mark of his esteem by the parliamentary party that in October 1964, despite losing his seat at the election, he became Foreign Secretary. Lacking a seat prevented him from speaking in the Commons and forced him to spend time searching for a vacancy, but otherwise had little impact on his conduct of policy. He was neither a neutralist nor a unilateral nuclear disarmer (see: *Unilateralism). He was unenthusiastic about joining the *EEC, and he believed Britain should go on playing her world role. In December 1964 he played a leading part in dissuading the Johnson administration from pursuing its ideas for a multilateral force, which would have denied Britain independent control of her nuclear deterrent. In January 1965, after losing a by-election, he resigned. He was MP for Leyton from 1966 to 1974 but did not hold office again.

SHLAIM, A., JONES, P., SAINSBURY, K., *British Foreign Secretaries since 1945*, David and Charles, 1977.

**GRANVILLE,** Lord, Leveson-Gower, George, 2nd Earl Granville (1815–91). Liberal Foreign Secretary (1851–2, 1870–4, 1880–5). The son of a distinguished British Ambassador in Paris, Granville was Under-Secretary for Foreign Affairs from 1840 to 1841. In December 1851 *Russell (1792–1878) dismissed *Palmerston (1784–1865) from the *Foreign Office and, after the post had been turned down by *Clarendon (1800–70), Granville accepted it. He was regarded as a sound, albeit unexpected and inexperienced choice. Granville drew up a memorandum on the general principles of foreign policy which showed that he proposed little change of direction from the policies of Palmerston, although he eschewed the extremes of his predecessor which had so often offended Queen *Victoria (1819–1901). He had little time to do more before the Russell government fell in February 1852.

Granville was not to return to the Foreign Office for nearly two decades, but in the mean-

·time he continued to play a prominent role in politics, becoming Liberal leader in the Lords in 1856, a post which he was to hold until his death, with the exception of the years from 1865 to 1868 when he relinquished the position to Russell. In 1859 he attempted unsuccessfully to form a government himself. He maintained an active interest in foreign affairs and here, as in domestic politics, displayed great qualities of tact and patience which were his major assets as a politician and diplomat. He also developed close relations with *Gladstone (1809–98) and came to share many of his views on foreign policy.

Thus when Clarendon died suddenly in office in July 1870 Granville was the obvious choice to succeed him. The new Foreign Secretary immediately faced the crisis which quickly led to the Franco-Prussian War and it is arguable that more decisive action on his part might have averted the conflict. However, he acted firmly to preserve Belgian neutrality. Granville's predisposition towards conciliation was evident in his submission to arbitration of the *Alabama dispute (1864) with the United States which led to payment by Britain of 15.5 million dollars in compensation, and by his agreement to allow Russia to maintain naval forces in the Black Sea, a concession from the position established in the Treaty of *Paris of 1856. Popular dislike of these decisions contributed to Liberal defeat in the General Election of 1874.

Granville's qualities as a conciliator were again in demand in the late 1870s as the Liberal opposition found itself divided as to the wisdom of Gladstone's vigorous attack on the foreign policy of the Disraeli administration. On his return to the Foreign Office in 1880 he had to handle the difficult legacy of Conservative imperialist policies. In southern Africa serious conflict with the Boers was averted for the moment but at the cost of loss of face, while instability in Afghanistan seemed to threaten India and thwarted Granville's endeavours for good relations with Russia. Colonial disputes led to tensions with Germany, and in Egypt Granville, committed to intervention, floundered as he tried to extricate Britain from an expensive and embarrassing situation which strained relations with France. Worse still, General Gordon, sent to Khartoum to report on the situation in the Sudan and to conduct a planned withdrawal, was trapped by the Mahdi and an expedition, tardily sent to relieve him, was too late to avert his death and the capture

of Khartoum. The Government had to handle a public outcry at home, headed by the Queen.

Granville's quiet, patient approach to foreign relations, although exposing him to charges of indolence and weakness, was not without results in periods of relative calm. However, the experience of his final term in office reinforced the opinion created by the Franco-Prussian War, that he was not the man to handle crises with sufficient decisiveness. The most damning reflection on his conduct of affairs after 1880 is that, having set out to build good relations with the other powers, in 1885 he left Britain almost totally isolated.

FITZMAURICE, LORD EDMOND, *The Life of Granville, George Leveson Gower Second Earl Granville, K.G.* 2 vols., 1905.

RAMM, A., ed., *The Political Correspondence of Mr Gladstone and Lord Granville 1876–1886*, Oxford University Press, 2 vols. 1962.

**Great War,** see WORLD WAR I (1914–18)

**Greek War of Independence** (1821–9). The revolt against Ottoman authority which began with the rising of Alexander Hypsilantis – a member of a Phanariot Greek family and a Russian army officer – in Moldavia in March 1821. Within a few days this was followed by a religious and nationalistic uprising in the Morea, which spread to the other Greek islands. At the outset Britain, France and Austria proclaimed a policy of neutrality. Tsar Alexander I of Russia left no doubt that he prized conservative and monarchical solidarity above any advantage to be gained for Russia by supporting the Greeks. George *Canning (1770–1827) favoured Greek independence and there was considerable philhellene sympathy in England. Two years after the outbreak of the revolts he recognized the Greeks as belligerents. Volunteers went to join the Greek cause, notably Byron, who died at Missolonghi in 1824, and Lord Cochrane and Sir Richard Church, who became respectively commanders of Greek sea and land forces. Canning reached an understanding with Russia, the protocol of 4 April which led to the treaty of 7 July 1827 between Britain, France and Russia. This stipulated that Greece was to be established as an autonomous, though tributary, state under Turkish suzerainty. A secret article laid down that if the belligerents refused to accept an armistice the powers would intervene to prevent conflicts. The conflict had been widened when, unable to suppress the rising despite the assistance of rebel Greek divisions, the Sultan called on Mehemet Ali of Egypt to send troops to the Morea. After being joined by the French, British and Russian ships sought to blockade Ottoman forces in the Morea. As a result of misunderstandings, the Ottoman and Egyptian fleets were destroyed at the battle of *Navarino on 20 October 1827.

Canning's successor, the Duke of *Wellington (1769–1852) discontinued his policy of working closely with Russia. At the same time, Russia declared war on the Ottoman Empire and by August 1829 Russian forces had seized Adrianople. Greece became autonomous by the *Adrianople Treaty (1829). Wellington in fact favoured merely an autonomous Morean Greece (he had deplored Navarino as an 'untoward event') and succeded in restricting the frontier of Greece fixed by the protocol of 3 February 1830. After the murder of President Capodistrias, however, in 1831 an enlarged Greek kingdom was established under Otto of Bavaria. By the Constaninople Treaty of July 1832 the Turks recognized Greek independence, renouncing all claims of suzerainty.

ANDERSON, M. S., *The Eastern Question, 1774–1923*, Macmillan, 1966.

CLAYTON, G. D., *Britain and the Eastern Question: Missolonghi to Gallipoli*, Hodder and Stoughton, 1971.

CRAWLEY, C. W., *The Question of Greek Independence: A Study of British Policy in the Near East, 1821–32*, Cambridge University Press, 1930.

**GREY**, Sir Edward, 3rd baronet, and Viscount Grey of Fallodon (1862–1933). Educated at Winchester and Balliol College, Oxford. In 1884 he was private secretary to Sir Evelyn Baring (later Lord Cromer) and then to the Chancellor of the Exchequer, Hugh Childers. In 1885 he became Liberal MP for Berwick-upon-Tweed, which he represented until his elevation to the peerage in 1916. Of Northumberland gentry stock, Grey was a latter-day Whig in the Liberal Party. A country-lover and ornithologist, Grey had no ambition in politics: he was there from a sense of public duty.

Grey's involvement with foreign affairs began with the Liberal governments of 1892–5 as Parliamentary Under-Secretary at the Foreign Office. With his superiors, *Rosebery (1847–1929) and *Kimberley in the Lords, Grey became the chief Liberal foreign affairs spokesman in the Commons. He quickly established his reputation there. The so-called 'Grey Declaration' of March 1895, warning France that the encroachment on the Nile would be regarded as an 'unfriendly act', was improvised during a Commons debate without authorization from above. The country approved, however, and the declaration became an axion of British policy during the *Fashoda Crisis (1898).

As an imperialist in a party where disillusion with empire was growing, Grey found himself with Rosebery, *Asquith (1852–1928) and Haldane backing the Unionist government's policies in South Africa at a time when many Liberals strongly opposed them. The 2nd *Boer War (1899–1902) diminished Grey's enthusiasm for empire, revealing Britain's weakness and isolation and convincing him that government should take steps to protect the empire which involved more than strengthening the navy, important though this was. *Lansdowne (1845–1927) and *Balfour (1848–1930) had reached the same conclusion and their establishment of closer relations with the United States and the *Anglo-Japanese Alliance of 1902 were warmly approved of by Grey, an enthusiast for Anglo-American co-operation and an advocate of concentrating Britain's power in Europe to resist challenges from her rivals there. In 1898 France had seemed the main enemy. By 1902–3 it was Germany. The strength of anti-British feeling there and the details emerging of the German fleet programme left Grey in no doubt of this. Not surprisingly, he welcomed the *Anglo-French Entente (1904) and Balfour's support for it during the 1st *Moroccan crisis (1905).

There was therefore much common ground between Grey and the Conservatives when he became Campbell-Bannerman's Foreign Secretary in December 1905, and the support that he received from them before 1914 strengthened his position both in the country at large and against his radical critics in the Liberal Party. The radicals had not been antagonistic at first: *Campbell-Bannerman (1836–1908), one of them himself, had put Grey at the Foreign Office because Grey was unquestionably a patriot and the Liberals drew much support from the patriotic business class. The structure of power within the Cabinet and the conduct of Cabinet business meant that the Prime Minister alone could exert much authority over his masterful Foreign Secretary;

but Campbell-Bannerman was content to give Grey his head, while his successor in 1908, Asquith (1852–1928), was a Liberal Imperialist. The radical 'Grey-must-go' campaign burst out in 1912, provoked by the 2nd *Moroccan Crisis (1911) and continuing naval expansion; but it proved ineffective. Grey defended himself skilfully in public, while the ministerial radicals *Lloyd George (1863–1945) and *Churchill (1874–1965), had openly sided with Grey in his stand against Germany during 1911, when details of Britain's secret military talks with the French were at last revealed to the Cabinet (see: *Anglo-French Military Conversations (1906–14) ).

Grey took office during the 1st Moroccan Crisis, which resulted not, as the Germans intended, in the disruption of the Anglo-French entente, but in its consolidation. Grey, with Campbell-Bannerman's approval, had set staff talks with France on a regular basis: and France had also been supported by her ally Russia. The crisis convinced Grey that an Anglo-Russian understanding was the necessary complement to the entente and the Franco-Russian Alliance. Grey did not wish to align the three powers against Germany, only to end Anglo-Russian friction and so enhance Britain's ability to resist German threats. If Germany could destroy the entente, Britain would be isolated again. But now, with the growth of the German navy, that isolation could lead to her downfall. In August 1907 Grey secured an agreement with St Petersburg designed to limit Anglo-Russian rivalry in Asia (see: *Anglo-Russian Convention). This agreement might not have endured but for Russo-German differences in the Balkans, which sharpened during the 1908 Bosnian crisis and had become irreconcilable by 1914. Grey's ententes policy was designed to ensure that in the event of war Britain had friends; but above all it was meant to preserve peace. Grey would not convert the ententes into alliances because if France and Russia were assured of British support under all circumstances their policy towards Germany might become dangerously

provocative. Grey was still prepared to make generous concessions to Germany over colonial matters. But the ententes and the military arrangements that accompanied them limited Britain's freedom of action in a way that Grey had not anticipated when his success as mediator in the Balkan Wars could not be repeated in 1914.

Grey's peace efforts in the *July Crisis (1914) meant that Britain entered the war united. Grey, however, sensing failure, loathing war, and with worsening eyesight, wished to resign. But he had become a symbol of national integrity and Asquith persuaded him to stay. His remaining time at the Foreign Office was an anti-climax. A fatalistic belief that in wartime foreign policy must be subordinate to strategy deterred Grey from taking initiatives because there were no military successes to exploit. He did not search for allies in the Balkans lest they captured the Straits first and upset Russia. From early 1915 came unwelcome American mediation attempts which Grey skilfully fended off while maintaining Britain's credit with President Wilson. But Grey's influence with Cabinet colleagues fell, and Lloyd George dismissed him in December 1916. Grey had no regrets. His subsequent role in affairs was not important. He went as ambassador on special mission to Washington in September 1919 to encourage American involvement in the *League of Nations, but with Wilson too ill to see him and widespread anti-British feeling over Ireland he decided to return in January 1920. He died in 1933.

GREY, VISCOUNT, *Twenty-Five Years, 1892–1916*, 2 vols., Hodder and Stoughton, 1925.

HINSLEY, F. H. ed., *British Foreign Policy under Sir Edward Grey*, Cambridge University Press, 1977.

ROBBINS, K., *Sir Edward Grey*, Cassell, 1971.

STEINER, Z. S., *Britain and the Origins of the First World War*, Macmillan, 1977.

TREVELYAN, G. M., *Grey of Fallodon*, Longmans, 1937.

# H

**Hague Peace Conferences** (1899, 1907). These were attempts to achieve international co-operation and arms limitation and the preservation of peace in the period of growing European tension and imperial rivalry which preceded *World War I (1914–18). They were significant in establishing the principle that international problems could be resolved by periodic conferences of the powers, and this influenced the creation after World War I of the *League of Nations.

The first conference was suggested by Tsar Nicholas II, who was apprehensive that Russia could not meet the expenditures of the *arms race at the same time as meeting the need for domestic investment. The second was prompted by President Theodore Roosevelt and again proposed by Russia. The first conference evidenced widespread scepticism among its participants and did nothing to restrain the arms race (its declaration banning the use of poison gas was ignored in 1915). Nevertheless it set up machinery for international commissions of enquiry into disputes between states. This was used to effect by Britain and Russia in resolving the *Dogger Bank Incident (1904). It established a Permanent Court of Arbitration, precursor of the Permanent Court of International Justice and the International Court of Justice. The 1907 conference was attended by no fewer than 44 states. Among other things, it established a single code of land warfare and the *Geneva Convention of 1864 was also applied to war at sea. The conference's declaration against the arms race proved ineffectual. British efforts to secure arms limitation were wrecked by the German Foreign Minister's announced decision to veto any disarmament proposals advanced at The Hague. Germany also rejected the principle of compulsory arbitration in disputes. The political deadlock resulted from the German belief that a large navy was essential to her growing role in the world, and the British insistence that naval superiority was essential to her own imperial position. The lesser powers also tended to bridle at any limitation which consigned them to a position of permanent inferiority. The decision of the Hague Conference to reconvene in 1915 was pre-empted by the outbreak of war in August 1914.

SCOTT, J. B., *The Hague Peace Conferences of 1899 and 1907*, 2 vols., Johns Hopkins Press, Baltimore, 1971.

**HAIG,** Douglas, 1st Earl Haig (1861–1928). Haig began his military life as a cavalry officer. He played important roles both in the Sudan and later in the 2nd *Boer War (1899–1902). In 1906 he went to the War Office, where he was known as one of the advocates of army reform. After two years in India he returned to the post of GOC in Aldershot. When war broke out in 1914, he commanded I Corps, being promoted to command of the First Army in 1915. He did not share General French's optimism about the war and urged Lord *Kitchener (1850–1916) to prepare for a prolonged struggle. In December 1915, following devastating losses on the Western Front, he was made Commander-in-Chief of British forces in France, a post which he held for the rest of the war. The losses continued to be high throughout 1916 and 1917, as during the Battle of the *Somme

(1916). But by 1918, especially after the arrival of American troops, the stalemate in the West ended, resulting in victory in November. Throughout the war Haig was not markedly receptive to creative inventions, refusing in 1915, for instance, to acknowledge the importance of the machine gun and cancelling orders for tanks because of his belief in their low military value. Haig served as Commander in Chief of Home Forces (1919–21) and as President of the British Legion.

TERRAINE, J., *Douglas Haig: the Educated Soldier*, Hutchinson, 1963.

**Haldane Army Reforms.** As Secretary of State for War between 1905 and 1912 Richard Burdon Haldane (created 1st Viscount Haldane in 1911) was responsible for an important series of reforms which represented a significant extension of the *Cardwell Army Reforms. The need for improvements had been clearly indicated by the commissions of enquiry which followed the 2nd *Boer War (1899–1902). The reforms included the formation of a general staff and of an expeditionary force (the *BEF of 1914) of six infantry divisions and one cavalry division which was to be capable of mobilization in 15 days. He also created a territorial army of 14 infantry divisions and 14 cavalry brigades recruited at county level from the old yeomanry and volunteers. Additionally, the volunteer corps at English public schools were reorganized into officers' training corps. Haldane's reforms produced the regular army and reserve which engaged in *World War I (1914–18) and made the army ready, in general, for the contingency of a major war.

**Haldane Mission** (1912). On 8 February 1912 to Berlin in order to improve Anglo-German relations. Haldane suggested that Britain would be willing to accede to German colonial claims in Africa in return for a German undertaking not to increase the size of their fleet. On the German side the Chancellor Bethmann-Hollweg asked for a promise of British neutrality. The background to this mission was the dissatisfaction of some domestic political elements with the policy of Sir Edward *Grey (1862–1933), the British Foreign Secretary, during the 2nd *Moroccan Crisis (1911), and the continuing Russian pressure on Persia, in spite of the *Anglo-Russian Convention (1907). Certain elements in Germany, including Bethmann, were also anxious for a lessening of tension between Britain and Germany.

The mission got off to a bad start since an Additional Naval Bill was published in Berlin only the day before Haldane's arrival. To the British Admiralty the new proposals seemed a formidable measure: not only were three additional German capital ships to be laid down, but the number of vessels in the active fleet was to be raised from 17 battleships and four battle-cruisers to 25 battleships and eight battle-cruisers. The Germans demanded in return for restraint in naval construction a treaty pledging 'benevolent neutrality . . . if either of the high contracting parties becomes entangled in a war with one or more other powers'. Grey was willing to undertake only that Britain would not attack or take part in a *hostile* combination against Germany. The German government – aware that the British would certainly interpret the implementation of the *Schlieffen Plan for the invasion of Belgium and France as an aggressive act – declared Grey's formulation to be quite inadequate. After the failure of the Haldane Mission no fresh attempt was made in the pre-World War I period to discuss a neutrality treaty.

KENNEDY, P. M., *The Rise of the Anglo-German Antagonism, 1860–1914*, Allen and Unwin, 1980.

STEINER, Z. S., *Britain and the Origins of the First World War*, Macmillan, 1977.

**HALIFAX,** Edward Frederick Lindley Wood, 3rd Viscount and 1st Earl of (1881–1959). Educated at Eton and Christ Church, Oxford, in 1903 he became a Fellow of All Souls and in 1910 entered Parliament as Conservative MP for Ripon. He served on the Western Front in *World War I (1914–18), in 1917 leaving to become Assistant Secretary to the Ministry of National Service. In 1921 he served under *Churchill (1874–1965) as Parliamentary Under-Secretary for the Colonies. He entered Bonar Law's Cabinet in 1922 as President of the Board of Education, and in 1924 became Baldwin's Minister of Agriculture. Created Baron Irwin in 1926 he went to India as Viceroy. In October 1929, supported by the Labour government, and to the fury of Churchill and many Conservatives, he announced that dominion status for India was the goal of British policy. He left India in 1931, became President of the Board of Education in the National Cabinet in 1932, moved to the War Office in June 1935 (he had succeeded to the viscountcy in 1934), became Lord Privy Seal in November and Lord President when Neville *Chamberlain (1869–1940) became Prime Minister in May 1937.

Regular involvement with foreign affairs came with Halifax's membership of the Cabinet Foreign Policy Committee in 1936, and it continued under the premiership of Chamberlain, who entrusted the *Foreign Office to him when *Eden (1897–1977) was away. By 1937 there had grown up a friendship between Halifax and Chamberlain which would deepen in succeeding years and which was helped in its early stages by an affinity of outlook on the state of Europe and what British policy towards it should be. A private visit of November 1937 to a hunting exhibition in Berlin provided an opportunity for informal talks with Hitler which Chamberlain and (initially) Eden wanted to exploit. Before he left for Germany, Halifax had told Chamberlain he was 'not happy about our attitude to Austria and Czechoslovakia and would personally like to go much further'. With Chamberlain's approval and to Eden's discomfiture, Halifax told Hitler that, with regard to Austria, Czechoslovakia and *Danzig the British 'were not necessarily concerned to stand for the status quo as today, but we are concerned to avoid such treatment of them as would be likely to cause trouble'. The effect of this was to confirm Hitler's belief that Britain would not fight for Austria or Czechoslovakia.

In February 1938 Eden resigned and Halifax, who had little desire to become Foreign Secretary, took his place. Unlike Eden, he was willing to accept Chamberlain's leadership in foreign affairs. Hitler's annexation of Austria (see: *Anschluss) in March had been an unpleasant shock, but Halifax believed that Britain's military weakness and vulnerability to air attack left no alternative to Chamberlain's policy of accommodating Hitler over the *Sudetenland. Halifax and Chamberlain were at one until 24 September when Hitler was demanding, under threat of war with Czechoslovakia, the immediate transfer to Germany of large areas of Czech territory. Chamberlain argued in Cabinet that the Czechs must be made to accept; Halifax, revolted by Hitler's gunpoint diplomacy and calling Nazism an evil that he wanted destroyed, refused to press the Czechs – and the Cabinet supported the Foreign Secretary. Halifax was ready to fight. War was averted only because Hitler, at the last minute, decided to negotiate. Chamberlain hurried off to see him, taking matters out of the hands of

his Foreign Secretary who remained in London, and the *Munich Agreement (1938) was the result.

Halifax thought Munich 'a horrid business and humiliating . . . yet better than a European war'. Like Chamberlain, he still hoped for a general settlement with Hitler. Unlike Chamberlain, he now distrusted Hitler and wanted an acceleration of rearmament, a National Register as a prelude to *conscription, and the formation of a truly national government with Eden and the Labour Party to create a sense of national solidarity. Chamberlain would have none of this, but Halifax's influence, more than any other factor, was responsible for the shift in the British government's attitude towards Germany in 1939 from one of acquiescence in her claims to resistance. Commenting on Hitler's destruction of Czechoslovakia in March 1939, Chamberlain told the Commons that he would continue his policy of *appeasement. Halifax privately warned him that the country expected the government to tell Hitler his aggression must stop. Only then did Chamberlain accept the change of policy whose outcome was the guarantee to Poland and, ultimately, the declaration of war on Germany. Seen by the British people as a man of principle and integrity, the High Church Foreign Secretary played a vital role in creating a national feeling in September 1939 that war for Danzig was just and necessary.

Halifax endorsed Chamberlain's strategy of inaction during the winter of 1939–40, but was less optimistic than Chamberlain that the German home front would collapse. When Chamberlain resigned after the Norwegian fiasco in May 1940, he wanted Halifax to succeed him; but Halifax declined in favour of Churchill and continued at the Foreign Office. At the end of May, with the French in headlong retreat and the *British Expeditionary Force seemingly about to be captured, Halifax contemplated making peace with Hitler through the good offices of the still neutral Mussolini. But his excessively subtle approaches to the Italian ambassador had no result, and after *Dunkirk the immediate danger passed.

In December 1940, after some argument with Churchill, Halifax went as ambassador to Washington – an important post but one which removed him from the direction of affairs. He knew little of America and his aristocratic demeanour was initially a disadvantage. However, his popularity was quickly established as Americans responded with enthusiasm to his transparently sincere belief, proclaimed in countless speeches, in the principles of democracy and Christianity for which the war was being fought. He was created an earl in 1944 and retired from Washington in May 1946. He died in 1959.

BIRKENHEAD, LORD, *Halifax*, Hamish Hamilton, 1965.

CRASTER, H. H. E., ed., *Earl of Halifax: Speeches on Foreign Policy*, Oxford University Press, 1947.

HALIFAX, LORD, *Fullness of Days*, Collins, 1957.

**HANKEY**, Maurice Pascal Alers, 1st Baron Hankey (1877–1963). Educated at Rugby. In 1895 Hankey entered the Royal Marines Artillery, and after duty with the Mediterranean fleet and in the Naval Intelligence Division of the Admiralty, he was appointed assistant secretary to the *Committee of Imperial Defence in 1908 and became its secretary in 1912. During *World War I (1914–18) he was secretary to the War Council, the Dardanelles Committee, and the War Committee, and, from December 1916, when it was created, the War Cabinet. At the *Paris Peace Conference (1919–20) he was secretary to the British *Empire delegation and to the *Council of Four; throughout the 1920s and 1930s he served in the same capacity at many international conferences.

Until his retirement from official life in the summer of 1938 Hankey remained secretary to both the Cabinet and the CID. These two posts placed him at the very centre of British overseas and defence policy-making machinery. He was, *The Times* noted after his death, 'the greatest backroom figure of our political history'. He was an administrator of prodigious ability but his strong sense of constitutional propriety did not allow unrivalled access to a series of Prime Ministers to tempt him into playing a political role. This was important to his success, for he worked closely with men of such widely differing temperaments as *Asquith (1852–1928), *Lloyd George (1863–1945), *Bonar Law (1858–1923), *Baldwin (1867–1947), *MacDonald (1866–1937) and Neville *Chamberlain (1869–1940). Each found Hankey's experience, knowledge and memory invaluable, and each looked to him for guidance in the sphere of defence policy.

HANKEY, 1ST BARON, *The Supreme Command, 1914–1918*, 2 vols., Allen and Unwin, 1961. *Diplomacy by Conference: Studies in Public Affairs, 1920–1946*, Ernest Benn, 1946.

ROSKILL, S., *Hankey: Man of Secrets*, 3 vols., Collins, 1970–4.

**HARDINGE,** Charles, 1st Baron Hardinge of Penshurst (created 1910) (1858–1944). Charles Hardinge, grandson of a Governor-General of India, was educated at Trinity College, Cambridge and joined the *Foreign Office in 1880. He served in the major embassies of Constantinople, Berlin and Washington and also spent time as Chargé d'Affaires in Sofia before holding posts in Bucharest, Paris, Tehran and St Petersburg, which gave him rich experience in diplomacy. He was Assistant Under-Secretary in the Foreign Office (1903–4) and then in 1904 became British Ambassador to Russia. There he helped to improve Anglo-Russian relations and played a vital role arbitrating in the *Dogger Bank Incident (1904). After his next appointment as Permanent Under-Secretary he negotiated the *Anglo-Russian Convention (1907). Hardinge took the view that it was worthwhile supporting Russia in return for a policy of restraint along the Indian border. Convinced of the threat of German ambitions, he was even willing to consider extending the agreement with Russia to cover the Balkans. In 1910 he was appointed Viceroy of India where, despite the attempt on his life in 1912, he pursued a policy of reconciliation. He increased social welfare and improved Anglo-Afghan relations. When war broke out in 1914 many Indians were to serve on the various fronts. The disaster at Kut led to Hardinge being censured along with Austen *Chamberlain (1863–1937). He returned to the Foreign Office in 1916 and served in 1920–2 as Ambassador in Paris. His relations with *Lloyd George (1863–1945) and *Curzon (1859–1925) were never harmonious.

BUSCH, B. C., *Hardinge of Penshurst: A Study of the Old Diplomacy*, Archon, Hamden, Conn. 1979.

HARDINGE, C., *Old Diplomacy: The Reminiscences of Lord Hardinge of Penshurst*, John Murray, 1947.

**Hay–Pauncefote Treaties** (1900–1). The first of these treaties, signed on 5 February 1900, modified the *Clayton–Bulwer Treaty (1850) and allowed the construction and maintenance of a trans-isthmian canal under the authority of the United States alone. The Senate amended the treaty, giving the United States among other things the right to fortify the canal. British refusal to accept the amendments led to the negotiations of the second Hay–Pauncefote treaty. This was signed on 18 November 1901. Article I stated that it should supersede the Clayton–Bulwer Treaty. Article II provided for the canal to be built under the auspices of the United States, stipulating that it would have all the rights over construction, regulation and management. Article III laid down that navigation of the Canal should be open and free to vessels of all nations 'on terms of entire equality'. Britain further admitted the rights of the United States to fortification. These treaties were significant in that they showed Britain was now willing to concede that the Caribbean was in the United States' *sphere of influence.

CAMPBELL, C. S., *Anglo-American Understanding 1898–1903*. Johns Hopkins Press, Baltimore, 1957.

PERKINS, B., *The Great Rapprochment: England and the United States, 1895–1914*, Atheneum, New York, 1968.

**Heartland Theory.** The idea advanced by the British geographer Sir Halford Mackinder (1869–1947) in his paper 'The geographical pivot of history' (1904) and in his best-known work *Democratic Ideals and Reality – A Study in the Politics of Reconstruction* (1919). His theory evolved from his detailed study of the global relationship between land and sea power. Predicting the growing ascendancy of land over sea power, he argued that the state which could control the human and physical resources of the Eurasian landmass between Germany and central Siberia would be in a position to control the world. He warned his contemporaries that whoever 'rules East Europe commands the Heartland, who rules the Heartland commands the World Island, who rules the World Island commands the World'. He advocated policies aimed at creating an equilibrium of power between the land and sea powers so that no single country would be able to dominate the pivot area. By the time of *World War II (1939–45) he had refined his theory so that it also took account of the development of air power and the growing national power of the United States. In 1919 he warned of the consequences of German control of Russia and in 1943 of the results of Russian

control of Germany. To some extent the Heartland Theory may be taken as a precursor of the post-war policy of *containment.

**HEATH,** Edward Richard George (1916–    ). Educated at Chatham House School, Ramsgate and Balliol College, Oxford. After war service in the army he became Tory MP for Bexley in 1950. He was Parliamentary Secretary to the Treasury 1955–9 and Minister of Labour from October 1959 to July 1960, when he became Lord Privy Seal with Foreign Office responsibilities and sat as second Foreign Office minister in the Cabinet. Heath's task soon became to negotiate the terms of Britain's entry into the *Common Market so that the Commonwealth food supplies would be protected, but in January 1963 De Gaulle vetoed Britain's application and in October Heath moved to be President of the Board of Trade. From 1965 to 1970 he was leader of the Opposition, and Prime Minister from June 1970 to February 1974.

The issue which dominated the Heath Government's foreign policy was Common Market membership. Heath renewed the British application soon after taking office and himself conducted the most important negotiations with President Pompidou. In Heath's eyes the Treaty of Accession of January 1973 was a declaration of intent that henceforth Europe would come first in Britain's priorities, rather than the United States, with which there was widespread disillusionment in Britain because of the Vietnam War. The cooling of Anglo-American relations was evident, too, from Washington's readiness to engage in *détente with Moscow and Pekin without reference to London.

The European bias in Heath's policy was further emphasized by the strained relationship with the *Commonwealth. The Black African states were unimpressed by the government's attempts to settle the Rhodesian problem but they were deeply angered by the decision to sell arms to South Africa. Heath regarded this as part of Britain's obligations under the agreement with South Africa to use the Simonstown naval base, whose strategic importance was considerable when the bulk of Britain's oil imports came via the Cape, and he made it clear that he did not welcome Commonwealth criticism on the matter. Heath ceased to be Conservative leader in 1975, following two electoral defeats. Since then he has constantly stressed the importance of European co-operation and relations with the Third World while remaining guardedly critical of the foreign policy of the United States.

HEATH, E., *The British Approach to European Foreign Policy*, Leeds University Press, 1977.

HURD, D., *An End to Promises, 1970–4*, Collins, 1979.

HUTCHINSON, G., *Edward Heath: A Personal and Political Biography*, Longmans, 1970.

**Heligoland–Zanzibar Treaty** (1890). The Anglo-German agreement on 1 July 1890 which established Britain as the dominant power in East Africa at German expense, a reversal of the previous situation. Germany accepted that Zanzibar should become a British protectorate, withdrew from Witu and recognized Uganda as being within the British sphere. In return for these concessions Germany received Heligoland which had been ceded to Britain by Denmark in 1814 and whose relinquishment Lord *Salisbury (1830–1903) had earlier opposed.

Kaiser William II and the German Chancellor Caprivi believed (rightly in the light of *World War I (1914–18)) that Heligoland would prove of considerable strategic advantage to Germany and were willing to pay a high price for it. Its acquisition would, for instance, prevent the French from blockading the coast and the new Kiel Canal in a future war. At the same time they wanted to bring Britain closer to the Triple Alliance of Germany, Austria-Hungary and Italy and in general to promote the improvement of Anglo-German relations. Salisbury for his part wanted a permanent settlement of the problems of East Africa and was under pressure from British public opinion. The Heligoland–Zanzibar Treaty was wide-ranging and has been described as the 'high point of the so-called Anglo-German "colonial marriage" ', but (unlike the *Anglo-French Entente (1904) ) it did not lead to a significant rapprochement. It was followed in a short time by growing Anglo-German antagonism and distrust, and the German hope of attracting Britain into a quadruple alliance was disappointed.

**Helsinki Conference** (1975). This ratified the agreements of the International Conference on Security and Cooperation in Europe and was concluded with the signing of the Final Act on 1 August 1975, by 33 East and West European states together with the United States and Canada. It was one of the results of the policy of *détente and emphasized the mutual desire for international stability. The Eastern Bloc powers, particularly the Soviet Union, were keen to see the existing political division of Europe and the respective *spheres of influence underwritten by international agreement. The Western delegates concentrated on the question of human rights and the protection of civil liberties in accord with the principles of the *United Nations and the Universal Declaration of Human Rights. The Final Act did not, however, have any international legal force and it was not eligible for registration under Article 102 of the United Nations Charter. Violations of the accords are frequently referred to in the war of words between East and West, particularly as regards human rights in the Eastern Bloc countries.

**HENDERSON,** Arthur (1863–1935). Born in Glasgow, General Secretary of the Labour Party from 1911 to 1934. Unlike Ramsay MacDonald (1866–1937) Henderson supported the Government during *World War I (1914–18) and held War Cabinet office as minister responsible for advising on labour matters. In 1917 he made a visit to Russia with the main pupose of persuading the country in revolution to stay in the war. He subsequently resigned from the Government when *Lloyd George (1863–1945) rejected his advice to send delegates to a conference of international socialists at Stockholm, Henderson being convinced that if Russia was to be kept in the war the British Government should send delegates.

In 1924, though he was Home Secretary at the time, Henderson played a large part in the conference called to implement the *Dawes Plan and he contributed to the working out of the *Geneva Protocol. He became Foreign Secretary in the Second Labour Government and strove to establish British leadership in seeking secure foundations for international peace through the *League of Nations. Though he was working against the background of a steadily deteriorating international situation, he achieved some temporary successes, including the settlement of the German-Polish dispute over Upper Silesia and the agreement at Geneva for a general disarmament conference. During his tenure of office he was also responsible for sending the first British Ambassador to the Soviet Union and, through forcing the resignation of Lord Lloyd, the High Commissioner, reaching agreement on Egyptian independence.

When the German Chancellor Stresemann died in October 1929 Henderson became the dominant figure in the League of Nations. He was trusted by both Germany and France, and when the World Disarmament Conference was convened in 1932 he was elected President. By the time the Conference was held he had ceased to be Foreign Secretary, having resigned when MacDonald decided to form a National Government. From 1932 to 1935, though, he continued to preside over the conference at Geneva and in 1934 was awarded the Nobel Peace Prize. His strongest claim to recognition as a Foreign Secretary was his enthusiastic fidelity to the League of Nations and belief in the idea of *collective security, something not shared by his successors.

CARLTON, D., *MacDonald versus Henderson: The Foreign Policy of the Second Labour Government*, Macmillan, 1970.

**HENDERSON**, Sir Neville Meyrick (1882–1942). Entered the diplomatic service in 1905. After a career which included postings to St Petersburg, Tokyo, Rome, Nish, Paris, Constantinople, Cairo, Belgrade and Buenos Aires he was appointed Ambassador to Germany in 1937. He was critical of the French in foreign policy, tended to be isolationist as far as Britain's role in Europe was concerned, and was sympathetic to Hitler's revisionist claims, believing that Britain could set a tight limit to her European commitments and still manage to play the part of independent arbitrator in continental politics. He saw his role in Berlin as that of reconciler of Britain and Germany, for instance attending the Nuremburg Nazi Party rallies as a gesture of friendship to the Third Reich. He was not, therefore, disposed to offer any warning to Neville *Chamberlain (1869–1940) of the dangers of *appeasement and became disillusioned only when Hitler, following the *Munich Agreement (1938) in March 1939 occupied the rest of Czechoslovakia. At this point he was recalled to London (though he was allowed to return to Berlin five weeks later). He undertook the task of attempting to persuade Hitler not to attack Poland and risk war with Britain and France, returning again to Britain on the outbreak of war in September 1939. He subsequently set out to justify his actions in Berlin and the attitude of the British Government in *Failure of a Mission* (1940) and *Water Under the Bridges* (1945).

HENDERSON, SIR N. M., *Failure of a Mission, Berlin 1937–1939* (1940). *Water Under the Bridges* (1945), Hodder and Stoughton.

**HOARE**, Sir Samuel, 2nd Baronet and Viscount Templewood (1880–1959). Educated at Harrow and New College, Oxford, Hoare entered Parliament in 1910 as Conservative MP for Chelsea, which he represented until his elevation to the peerage in 1944. During *World War I (1914–18) he served as a staff officer in Russia and Italy, and after the peace was one of the leading backbench critics of the Lloyd George Coalition. In 1922 Hoare entered Bonar Law's Cabinet as Secretary of State for Air, a post which he retained in Baldwin's 1923–4 and 1924–9 governments. In 1931 Hoare became the National Government's Secretary of State for India. Committed to a measure of self-government for India, he showed great ability in steering through the Commons in face of stern criticism from *Churchill (1874–1965) and other Conservative backbenchers the complex legislation which became the Government of India Act in 1935.

With MacDonald's resignation and Baldwin's resumption of the premiership in June 1935 Hoare had the choice of going to India as Viceroy or moving to the *Foreign Office. Hoare's preference was for India, but his wife feared that this would prevent him from achieving the prize that both coveted: the premiership. So he accepted the Foreign Office, where what he called his six months 'hard labour' were dogged by ill health.

Hoare had no ambition to go to the Foreign Office. Its atmosphere, after the cosiness of the India Office, came as a rude shock to him. Relations with *Eden (1897–1977) (as Minister for League of Nations Affairs also in the Cabinet) were uneasy and officials were divided over what policy to pursue towards Germany. Hoare had no preconceived ideas on the subject, but immediately fell in with those of his Permanent Under-Secretary, *Vansittart (1881–1957). Vansittart believed in the reports of Hitler's aggressive plans, was certain that only British rearmament could stop them, but that because rearmament would take years to complete the immediate need was to gain time and strengthen the allied front. That this double prescription was fully endorsed by Hoare is reflected in his handling of the two issues associated with his period at the Foreign Office:

the *Anglo-German Naval Agreement (1935) and the *Abyssinian War (1935–6).

Hoare played no part in the drafting of the Naval Agreement which had been prepared under his predecessor, *Simon (1875–1954), but he wholeheartedly backed its signature. By limiting the German fleet to 35 per cent of the British, the agreement was intended to avert a dangerous new navy race and guarantee the Royal Navy superiority in home waters while allowing it to concentrate a battle fleet against Japan in the Far East. The Germans' right to submarine parity did not disturb the Admiralty, which in 1935 believed it had overcome the submarine danger. Hoare regarded the agreement as nothing more than a practical arrangement for gaining time and reducing risks. There was no question of placating Hitler.

The priority in the Abyssinian dispute was to keep Italy together with Britain and France in a united front to contain Germany. Mussolini wanted Abyssinia. This was satisfactory to France and no threat to Britain; and both before and after Mussolini's invasion of Abyssinia in October 1935 Hoare and Vansittart were prepared to go far to meet Mussolini's wishes. Their problem was how to reconcile this with support for the *League of Nations, which was popular with British public opinion and potentially a useful instrument for checking Germany. The Zeila proposals of June 1935 and the *Hoare–Laval Plan of December were attempts to square the circle, but the public outcry and the Cabinet's subsequent repudiation of the Plan, after details leaked in the Paris press, led to Hoare's resignation just before Christmas. Hoare never repudiated the Plan, although he acknowledged his failure to explain the very sound reasons for it to his colleagues and public opinion.

Hoare returned to the Cabinet as First Lord in June 1936, and from May 1937 was Neville Chamberlain's Home Secretary. Close to *Chamberlain (1869–1940) and a member of the Cabinet Foreign Policy Committee, Hoare's involvement with foreign affairs remained considerable. He was one of the small group of ministers whom Chamberlain consulted regularly during the *Sudeten crisis (1938). He supported the *Munich Agreement (1938), believing that Britain was in no position to fight at the time and that it was necessary to gain time for rearmament. After Prague, Hoare strongly favoured alliance with Russia. He was Lord Privy Seal in Chamberlain's War Cabinet after

September 1939, and Secretary of State for Air in April–May 1940, when Churchill sent him as ambassador to Madrid. He played a notable role encouraging Spanish neutrality, and retired in December 1944, dying in 1959.

CROSS, J. A., *Sir Samuel Hoare: A Political Biography*, Jonathan Cape, 1977
TEMPLEWOOD, VISCOUNT, *Nine Troubled Years*, Collins, 1954

**Hoare–Laval Plan** (1935). The controversial attempt to settle the Italo-Abyssinian conflict (see: *Abyssinian War 1935–6) negotiated by Sir Samuel *Hoare (1880–1959), the British Foreign Secretary, and Pierre Laval, Premier of France. Hoare's object was to evade the application of sanctions as required by the *League of Nations (an oil embargo seemed imminent) which might provoke Italian military or naval reprisals. France did not intend to risk a war with the Italy which she and Britain had courted at the *Stresa Conference (1935). Britain was unwilling to take unilateral action against Italy without the guarantee of French naval support. British imperial strategic considerations lent strong support to the idea that Mussolini should be appeased. A Mediterranean conflict would have meant the British Navy having to withdraw ships from Far Eastern waters, inviting Japanese expansion in that area.

The Hoare–Laval terms included the cession of approximately two-thirds of Abyssinia to Italy. If put into effect they would have given Italy 60,000 square miles of African territory and economic control of the southern part of the country, including its most fertile areas. Italy would have 'compensated' Abyssinia with a narrow strip of territory in southern Eritrea, giving her access to the sea in the 'corridor for camels'. These terms were accepted by Stanley *Baldwin (1867–1947) and his Cabinet with a view to their being submitted to the League and the two parties to the conflict. An outcry, particularly strong in Parliament, greeted the plan when it was leaked by the French press. Baldwin disowned the plan and Hoare resigned the Foreign Secretaryship on 18 December. Strong opposition in Parliament can be explained not simply on the grounds that the plan seemed to reward aggression, but because the Government had only very recently been elected with a pledge of support for the idea of *collective security under the League, and Hoare had only just eloquently promised it support in Geneva. The United States also expressed outrage at what they regarded as Old World diplomatic duplicity. In the event Mussolini obtained all Abyssinia by war and the notion of effective collective security through the League was conclusively discredited.

HARDIE, F. M., *The Abyssinian Crisis*, Batsford, 1974.

WALEY, D. P., *British Public Opinion and the Abyssinian War, 1935–6*, Temple Smith, 1976.

**Holy Alliance** (1815). Document signed by Tsar Alexander I of Russia, Francis II of Austria and Frederick William III of Prussia on 26 September 1815 in Paris. It stated that 'the precepts of Justice, Christian Charity and Peace ... must have an immediate influence on the Councils of Princes and guide all their steps'. It specified in Article I that the three monarchs would on all occasions and in all places lend each other aid and assistance. Subsequently the Holy Alliance came to include every European ruler with the exception of the Pope, the Sultan and the Prince Regent. The Prince Regent refused his signature because of the constitutional difficulty of signing without also the signature of a minister, though he sent a letter concurring with the 'sacred maxims'. Lord *Castlereagh (1769–1822) described the alliance as 'a piece of sublime mysticism and nonsense'. While there was nothing in the wording of the Holy Alliance to make it the instrument of anti-liberal policies it became associated with the close identification of the three Eastern Powers with the idea of intervention in the affairs of other independent states and a catchword for reaction, as exemplified in Metternich's Carlsbad Decrees. Metternich was in fact as disparaging about the Holy Alliance as Castlereagh, calling it 'a high-sounding nothing'. The practical basis for intervention was laid in other agreements, particularly the *Quadruple Alliance (1815), and such harmony as there was between the powers of the Holy Alliance was severely upset by the *Greek War of Independence (1821–29), when Russia acted together with the two constitutionalist powers Britain and France, but without Austria, to secure Greek independence.

ALBRECHT-CARRIÉ, *A Diplomatic History of Europe*, Methuen, 1958.

SKED, A. ed., *Europe's Balance of Power 1815–1848*, Macmillan, 1979.

**HOME**, Alexander Frederick Douglas-Home, Baron Home of the Hirsel (created 1974) (1903–    ). Home was educated at Eton and Christ Church, Oxford. In 1931 he became Tory MP for South Lanark, and in 1951 succeeded his father as fourteenth Earl of Home. He was Minister of State at the Scottish Office, 1951–5, Secretary of State for Commonwealth Relations, 1955–60, and Foreign Secretary from July 1960 to October 1963 and from June 1970 to March 1974. The Malaysian emergency, the Berlin crisis and the disputes in Laos and the Congo arose during his first period at the *Foreign Office, and his policy, when necessary, was characterized not only by unambiguous opposition to the Soviet Union but also by willingness to take issue with the United States if this could be done without damaging Western interests as a whole. Home realized earlier than most that Britain should join Europe if she were to hope to continue to play a world role. But De Gaulle prevented her entry into the *EEC in 1963 (see: *Western Europe since 1945, Britain and), and nothing further could be achieved during the year of Home's own premiership (Home being in the Commons once again), which ended in October 1964. From 1970 the issue of joining the EEC dominated and Home was content to let Edward *Heath (1916–    ) lead the negotiations, himself concentrating, though with little success, on a Rhodesian settlement and Britain's attempt to maintain a presence in the Indian Ocean.

DOUGLAS-HOME, A., *The Way the Wind Blows: An Autobiography*, Collins, 1967.

SHLAIM, A., JONES, P., SAINSBURY, K., *British Foreign Secretaries since 1945*, David and Charles, 1977.

**Hong Kong.** An island at the estuary of the Pearl River, it was ceded by China to Britain in 1841. This was confirmed in the *Nanking Treaty (1842) and since then it has been a Crown Colony. It was occupied by the Japanese between December 1941 and August 1945. Hong Kong has had special relations with the Chinese People's Republic since 1949; the flight of refugees from Communist China has led to a fivefold increase in its population. Negotiations between China and Britain about the transfer of the New Territories on the Chinese mainland in 1997 started in 1983. On 26 September 1984 a Sino-British Declaration on Hong Kong was signed in Beijing. It specified that from 1 July 1997 Hong Kong will become a 'special administrative region' of the People's Republic,

enjoying for at least another 50 years a large degree of autonomy in accordance with the 'one country, two systems' doctrine. Until 2047 Hong Kong will have the international status of a free port, with its own customs rules and its own international banking system.
ENDACOTT, G. G., *A History of Hong Kong,* Oxford University Press, 1973.

**'Hot Line' Agreement** (1963). The American–Soviet Memorandum of Understanding which was signed in Geneva on 20 June 1963. It instituted an official teletype communications link between Washington and Moscow to permit direct contact between the United States and the Soviet leadership during an international crisis. Its installation reflected the fear that miscalculation and misunderstanding through lack of proper communication could lead to nuclear war between the superpowers. It was a result of the *Cuban Missile Crisis (October 1962), during which President Kennedy had been forced to use commercial lines to communicate with Nikita Khrushchev. Similar links were established between Paris and Moscow in 1966 and between London and Moscow in 1967.

**House–Grey Memorandum** (1916). The outcome of discussions between President Woodrow Wilson's close adviser Colonel Edward House and the British Foreign Secretary Sir Edward *Grey (1862–1933), disclosed on 22 February 1916. At the time the United States was bringing strong pressure on the belligerents to end *World War I (1914–18). House's personal sympathies were entirely with the British and French and he had come to the conclusion that German submarine warfare would sooner or later make United States entry inevitable. The memorandum stated: 'Wilson was ready, on hearing from France and England that the moment was opportune, to propose that a Conference should be summoned to put an end to the war. Should the Allies accept this proposal, and should Germany refuse it, the United States would probably enter the war against Germany'. The suggested peace terms were: the restoration of Belgium, the cession of Alsace-Lorraine to France and of Constantinople to Russia and the handing over of extra colonies to Germany. Had this plan been acted upon it seems probable the United States would have entered the war in 1916. The British Government, in spite of feigned enthusiasm in some quarters for the idea, was not in favour of a negotiated peace at this time. When the memorandum was presented to the War Committee the offer of mediation was received with no commitment on the part of the British Government, except that it would be discussed. It was clearly stated that Britain could not act without the support of the Allies, and *Asquith (1852–1928) commented that even if the United States were really willing to enter the war it was doubtful whether that was to be welcomed since they favoured a deal with the *Central Powers which the Entente Powers could only regard as a defeat.

**HOWE,** Sir Geoffrey (1926–   ). Educated at Winchester College and Trinity Hall, Cambridge, subsequently qualifying as a barrister. First elected MP (for Bebington) in 1964, he was later MP for Reigate (1970–4), and since then for Surrey East. He was Solicitor General (1970–2) and Minister for Trade and Consumer Affairs (1972–4) in the government of Edward *Heath (1916–   ). With the return of the Conservatives to power in 1979 he became Chancellor of the Exchequer. Following Mrs Thatcher's second general election triumph in 1983 he became Secretary of State for Foreign and Commonwealth Affairs, succeeding Francis *Pym (1922–   ), who had not disguised his dissent from Mrs *Thatcher (1925–   ) over a range of issues.

**Hundred Days** (March–June 1815). The period between Napoleon I's escape from Elba and his defeat at the Battle of *Waterloo (18 June). The Allies – Britain, Austria, Russia and Prussia – at the time meeting at Vienna, declared him an international outlaw and re-formed the Grand Alliance to invade France.

**IDDESLEIGH,** Sir Stafford Henry Northcote, 1st Earl of (1818–87). Educated at Eton and Balliol College, Oxford. Lawyer, Conservative MP. Chancellor of the Exchequer in Disraeli's Ministry of 1874, succeeding *Disraeli (1804–81) as Leader of the House. On the formation of the Second Ministry of Lord *Salisbury (1830–1903) Iddesleigh became Foreign Secretary, a post which he held only from August 1886 till February 1887. He had to deal with the complications in the Balkan states produced by the kidnapping of Prince Alexander of Bulgaria. He proved outspoken about Russian intervention in Sofia and objected to the Prince of Mingrelia's candidature for the Bulgarian throne.

LANG, A., *Life, Letters and Diaries of Stafford Northcote, 1st Earl of Iddesleigh*, Edinburgh, W. Blackwood (1890).

**IMF,** see INTERNATIONAL MONETARY FUND

**Imperial Federation.** A late-nineteenth-century movement among Englishmen and a number of ex-colonials living in Britain who believed that the self-governing dominions should assume imperial responsibilities and work towards federating the British *Empire. An Imperial Federation League was founded in 1884. The League split on the tariff question in 1893 and was dissolved in the following year. It was replaced by the British Empire League, founded in 1895. This movement was active until 1906, after which interest in it appears to have waned.

**Imperial Preference.** In the British *Empire: a system under which Britain and the dominions

and colonies gave each other preferential tariff levels and favourable import quotas. The purpose was to encourage a self-contained trading unit. Since the 1890s the self-governing colonies had given preference to British goods, but Britain and the dependent empire had not reciprocated because Britain continued to uphold a *Free Trade policy. When, in 1931, Britain adopted a moderate protective tariff she was able to offer the dominions preferences if they would reciprocate.

The idea of the empire as an economic unit had been advanced by Joseph *Chamberlain (1836–1914) in 1897, and subsequently through the Tariff Reform Movement. He had hoped that Britain could supply most of the manufactured goods while the dominions and colonies would supply cheap food. This modified form of protectionism interested the colonies, but since it involved the abandonment of the doctrine of Free Trade the idea split the Conservative Party, strongly contributing to the Liberal victory in the General Election of 1906. Chamberlain's arguments were rejected by *Asquith (1852–1928), who declared that Free Trade meant 'a big loaf against the little loaf', no duties on food, maintenance of employment and international goodwill.

During the world depression the National Government adopted Imperial Preference (1931) and signed the *Ottawa Agreements (1932), extending the latter in 1933 to the Crown Colonies. By this time the policy was too late to afford Britain much benefit since the dominions were no longer content merely to supply Britain with cheap raw materials and wanted to buy cheaper manufactured goods from other countries. The concept of Imperial Preference was difficult to reconcile with the idea of the protection by each member of its own manufacturing and agricultural industries. Britain and the dominions were, in fact, increasingly becoming competitors in trade rather than complementary partners. Opponents of Imperial Preference argued that it had an adverse effect on world trade. To be effective it required that Britain restrict her imports from foreign countries. In return they would restrict their imports from her.

The *General Agreement on Tariffs and Trade (GATT) (1947) recognized Imperial Preference, and this was a major consideration in subsequent British approaches to trade agreements. It presented a major obstacle to Britain's wish to join the *EEC and was abandoned when she signed the Treaty of Accession to that organization in January 1972.
DRUMMOND, I. M., *British Economic Policy and the Empire, 1919–1939*, Allen and Unwin, 1972.

**Inkerman, Battle of** (1854). Between the allied British and French forces and the Russians east of *Sevastopol on 24 October, during the *Crimean War (1854–6). The Russians mounted an attack to forestall an impending allied assault on Sevastopol. An attack on the British flank was driven off, but not without difficulty and the help of French reinforcements. The Allies suffered 4,000 as against 15,000 casualties. Though the siege of Sevastopol continued, Inkerman convinced the Allies that a protracted siege rather than a full-scale assault on the city would be the wiser course.

**Inter-Allied Control Council** (Germany). The highest controlling agency of the Allied powers occupying Germany after *World War II (1939–45). It was established in Berlin on 30 August 1945. The idea of a body to enforce the terms of surrender on Germany had been agreed at the *Dumbarton Oaks (1944) and *Yalta (1945) conferences. At a meeting on 5 July 1945 the Allies announced that the Control Council would function as a central government for Germany, would take whatever steps were necessary to assure future peace and security there and would assume uniformity of action in each zone, with all Council decisions to be unanimous. Its brief also included the allocation of reparations and controls on

German industry. The four commanders-in-chief, of Britain, France, the United States and the Soviet Union, sat on the Control Council. Its basic weakness, the veto power of individual members, soon became apparent. Commanders made unilateral decisions for their own zones. France resisted every attempt to re-create the 'central German administration' which had been stipulated at the *Potsdam Conference (1945). Above all, deep divisions opened up between the Western Powers and the Soviet Union. The orders and directives issued by the Council were particularly important for Berlin, where it controlled the Inter-Allied Military Command. The departure of the Soviet commander after the disclosure of plans for the creation of a state comprising the three western zones of Germany brought an abrupt end to activities of the Control Council which did not re-convene after 20 March 1948.

**International Brigades.** The volunteers on the side of the Republic during the *Spanish Civil War (1936–9). The majority came from 11 national groups including approximately 2,000 volunteers from Britain. Communist parties recruited, organized and directed the brigades. The war exercised a particularly potent appeal to the idealism of intellectuals outside Spain, including leading British literary figures. It was often presented in oversimplified terms as a struggle between the forces of fascism and democracy. The leading motive of the volunteers was to stop the spread of fascism before it came to power in other countries or plunged Europe into another world war.
BROME, V., *The International Brigades: Spain, 1936–1939*, Heinemann, 1965.

**International Monetary Fund** (IMF). This was founded at the *Bretton Woods Conference (1944) and came into operation in March 1947 as a Special Agency of the *United Nations. Its purpose is to encourage international monetary cooperation, facilitate the expansion and balanced growth of international trade, promote foreign exchange stability and help member countries with balance-of-payment difficulties. The 'Bretton Woods system' was based on a policy of fixed exchange rates, the elimination of exchange restrictions, currency convertibility and the development of a multilateral system of international payments. A member country in deficit obtains foreign exchange from the fund in return for its own. It is also required to consult with the IMF on what measures are being taken domestically to improve the balance of payments. On several occasions British governments have used the credit fund to offset pressure against sterling.

**Intervention.** The interference of one state in the affairs of another. It may be directed against a single state, elements within it, or may involve interference with the relations between a group of states. Its purpose is to coerce the offending state into modifying its domestic or foreign policy, and it may take the form of military action or political/economic pressure. As a measure short of war, it is usually presented as an extension of the intervening power's right of self-defence, or is justified in terms of preserving a political ideology, on which stability is felt to depend. The Charter of the *United Nations upholds the right of intervention when it means collective action by the international community against acts of aggression. In history most interventions have involved the action of major powers undertaking reprisals against smaller states to protect the rights of their nationals, secure payment of debts, obtain concessions or protect property. Since *World War II (1939–45) ideological considerations have constituted the main basis for interventions, particularly where a major power feels threatened within its own *sphere of influence.

**Iran Crisis** (1946). In 1942 Britain, the United States and the Soviet Union had agreed to the joint occupation of Iran to forestall a German takeover of the oil fields (see: *Anglo-Soviet–Iranian Treaty). The Allies undertook to withdraw their troops within six months after the war was over. In early 1946 Soviet troops were still in northern Iran and their government was pressing the Iranians for oil concessions. The Soviets justified their continued presence on the grounds of a Communist-inspired revolt in the area. Iran appealed to the *United Nations to persuade the Soviet Union to withdraw and the United States sent a strongly worded note to Moscow. In the event the Soviet troops left in March 1946. The Soviet government announced at the same time the formation of an Iranian–Soviet oil company to be ratified by the Iranian parliament. The parliament later rejected this proposed company. This crisis contributed towards the development of *Cold War suspicion and hostility.

DOUGLAS, R., *From War to Cold War*, Macmillan, 1981.
GADDIS, J. L., *The United States and the Origins of the Cold War, 1941–47*, Columbia University Press, New York, 1972.

**Iron Curtain Speech** (1946). The term 'iron curtain', first used by the Nazi propaganda minister Joseph Goebbels, was used by Winston *Churchill (1874–1965) in May 1945 to describe the division of Europe under the forces of the Soviet Union and the West following V-E Day. In his celebrated speech of 5 March 1946 at Fulton, Missouri, Churchill repeated it, drawing world attention to the political division between Western Europe and the states of Eastern Europe, the latter increasingly under Soviet domination. 'From Stettin in the Baltic to Trieste in the Adriatic', he stated, 'an iron curtain has descended across the Continent . . . I do not believe that Soviet Russia desires war. What they desire is the fruits of war and the indefinite expansion of their power and doctrines.' This pronouncement, which led Stalin promptly to castigate Churchill as a warmonger, reflected the termination of the wartime Anglo-Russian cooperation, which had already become apparent the previous summer. Though it dismayed many Americans, Churchill's speech reflected the privately held views of the Truman Administration, then moving towards a 'tougher' policy in relation to the Soviet Union.

**Irredentism.** The desire of the people of one state to annex those adjoining territories which are under another rule or race but which are inhabited by peoples sharing their own language, race or culture. The term is derived from the expression *Italia irredenta* ('unredeemed Italy'). It originally referred to those Italian-speaking communities that remained under foreign rule after 1870, particularly those under the Habsburgs in the Trentino and the Tyrol.

Irredentist demands may occur wherever a state frontier does not coincide with ethnic and linguistic boundaries. They have been a powerful source of conflict in the last two centuries. Other significant examples of irredentas include Alsace-Lorraine, ceded to Germany after the Franco-Prussian War (1870–1), and the *Sudetenland, incorporated in the new succession state of Czechoslovakia after the Treaty of *Versailles (1919). The first was the basis of

French demands for revenge against Germany in the years up to *World War I (1914–18). The latter was the object of Hitler's demands, conceded by the powers at the *Munich Conference (1938). Since *World War II (1939–45) those who have supported the idea of German re-unification have regarded East Germany and those former German territories now part of Poland and the Soviet Union as irredentas. Irredentism remains a major potential source of conflict in, among other places, Africa. This is principally because the former European imperial powers drew their frontiers in the 'scramble for Africa' with little reference to the linguistic, racial or cultural identities of the separate African peoples.

**Isolationism.** A political stance or opinion opposing foreign political or military commitments, based on the belief that the interests of the nation are best served by withdrawal from, or non-involvement in, close connections, alliances or engagements with other states. It is a term which has been applied particularly to the foreign policy of Britain and the United States at various times. British policy during the last part of the nineteenth century was characterized as 'splendid isolation'. Britain did not participate in the major alliances of the Bismarckian period of diplomacy. During the years between *World War I (1914–18) and *World War II (1939–45) she was markedly disinclined to enter into binding bilateral alliances which could lead to war – as can be seen in her relations with France. Isolationism did not mean, however, that Britain was in any way uninterested in the course of world developments which might affect her empire and the interests of home defence.

Historically, the isolationism of the United States has been directed more at Europe than at the Far East or South America. The use of the word to describe American policy has evoked considerable debate among historians. For the most part the term has been used to describe the United States' refusal to join the *League of Nations, or other international organizations, her turning away from active response to world crises and her avoidance for as long as possible of involvement in the two world wars. American isolationism is evidenced in the neutrality legislation of the 1930s. As war approached, a discernible struggle for influence emerged between the isolationists and interventionists. The isolationist stance was combined with continuing American commercial expansion throughout the world and a growing significance in world affairs. Domestic political opposition in the United States to post-World War II global commitments, as, for example, during the Vietnam War, is commonly described as *neo-isolationism*.

**Italian Unification, Britain and.** The Risorgimento was a movement of Italian revival stretching back to the eighteenth century. Between 1859 and 1870 a combination of events and movements, of which Italian nationalism was only one element, resulted in the unification of the peninsula under Piedmont and the expulsion of Austria from Lombardy and Venetia. A number of reasons encouraged British public opinion to support the emergence of a united Italy. They included dislike of the autocracy and oppression of the old order. *Gladstone (1809–98) in a famous indictment had described Naples in 1850 as 'the negation of God erected into a system of government'. Count Cavour, the Piedmontese Prime Minister, was known to be an admirer of British institutions and *Free Trade. Popular Protestantism in Britain warmed to the anti-papal consequences of the Risorgimento. Garibaldi's heroic exploits were regarded with great admiration by the British public.

The attitude and decisions of British governments throughout the process of unification were influenced less, however, by pro-nationalist sentiment than by realistic calculations of the British national interest and implications of events in Italy for the European *balance of power. Britain was primarily concerned with French ambitions, which has led one historian to write: 'In reality England was not pursuing an Italian policy as much as a French policy'. *Palmerston (1784–1865) wanted to see Austria preserve her role as a Great Power, not least as a bulwark against Russian expansion, and saw her occupation of Italy as a burdensome involvement. While he wanted Austria out of it he was determined not to see France gain control or strong influence in the peninsula. During the revolutions of 1848–9 he had hoped that he might be able to secure Lombardy for Piedmont-Sardinia and gain some form of home rule for Venetia. He had therefore suggested joint Anglo-French mediation to guard against any unilateral French action. In the event Austria had re-imposed her control in the peninsula.

Following the Pact of Plombières of July 1858 between Cavour and the Emperor Napoleon III, the French and Piedmontese expelled Austria from Lombardy in the Italian War of Independence of 1859. The pact had stipulated the liberation of Venetia as well, but after the battles of Magenta and Solferino the Armistice of Villafranca was concluded without Italian participation. Palmerston returned to power just before Solferino, having strongly supported the Italian cause in speeches during the election campaign. Napoleon's claim to Savoy and Nice, which Cavour conceded in return for Piedmontese incorporation of the Central Duchies, led Palmerston to condemn France. The cession of these territories was not popular with Italian nationalists. Palmerston thereby attempted to outbid Napoleon as the friend of the Italian cause.

In April 1860 an uprising took place in Palermo. The following month Garibaldi sailed from Genoa to Sicily with his 'Thousand', rapidly gaining control of the island. France was committed to the defence of the Pope. Fearing the development of a new danger to the Papal States which would offend the clerical party in France, she proposed a joint Anglo-French action to prevent Garibaldi from crossing the Straits of Messina to the mainland. Palmerston was tempted to accept the French proposal but was persuaded by Lord John *Russell (1792–1878) and Gladstone to remain neutral. The British view was that if Garibaldi succeeded in crossing the Straits and occupying Naples he must have considerable popular support. The fact that he was not impeded from crossing the Straits was due to the goodwill of the British Government and the British Mediterranean Fleet. The French chose not to intervene alone. Garibaldi was left to conquer the rest of unliberated Italy except for Rome and Venetia, while Piedmontese forces anticipated him, defeating papal forces at Castelfidardo. Subsequently Venetia and Rome fell to Italy as results of the Austro-Prussian and Franco-Prussian wars. In spite of public enthusiasm in Britain for Italian unification and the strong support of some leading political figures, Britain had effectively allowed events to take their course. The outcome was a notable success for the policy of *non-intervention.

BEALES, D., *England and Italy, 1859–60*, Nelson, 1961.

BLAKISTON, H. N. ed., *The Roman Question, Extracts from the Despatches of Odo Russell from Rome, 1858–1870*, Chapman and Hall, 1962.

HEARDER, H., *Italy in the Age of the Risorgimento 1790–1870*, Longman, 1983.

**Italy, Fascist, Britain and.** Britain's relations with Italy between the Risorgimento and Mussolini's coming to power in 1922 were unusual for their absence of controversy. There was no point where British and Italian interests were in serious conflict, while each state regarded the other as a counterweight to France. With their classical education and their interest in Renaissance treasures which drew them to the peninsula, the British ruling classes were especially Italophile. The Italians, for their part, conscious of their long and vulnerable coastline, had no wish for conflict with the strongest Mediterranean naval power.

Mussolini's appearance on the scene gradually changed all this. British attitudes to Italy remained unaltered throughout the 1920s and for much of the 1930s. The British ambassador in Rome from 1921 to 1933, Sir Ronald Graham, and his successor Sir Eric *Drummond (1876–1951), who retired in 1939, were always ready to excuse the reprehensible aspects of Fascism and to justify Mussolini to the *Foreign Office. The material and psychological benefits Fascism brought, they claimed, more than compensated for its restrictions on liberty. And such a view seemed eminently sensible to the many officials and politicians in London who regarded Mussolini as the main reason why Italy had not gone Bolshevik after 1918. Austen *Chamberlain (1863–1937) met Mussolini on a number of occasions as Foreign Secretary and established cordial relations, comparing him with Bismarck. The only threat to Anglo-Italian friendship which Chamberlain saw in the 1920s was a long-term one involving Italy's relations with France. All the areas where Italy wished to increase her influence, Central Europe, the Balkans and the North African coast, touched French interests. A more important source of friction was the presence in France of the *fuorusciti*, the anti-Fascist refugees whom Mussolini thought received support from French politicians and governments. Franco-Italian differences worried Chamberlain lest they 'drive Italy into the arms of Germany'.

The course of Anglo-Italian relations in the 1930s was determined by two developments early in the decade: Mussolini's decision, taken by 1932, to secure control of Abyssinia and consolidate Italy's position in East Africa as part of a long-term process to increase Italian influence in the Mediterranean at French and British expense; and Hitler's accession to the German Chancellorship in 1933, which strengthened the forces throughout Europe wishing to revise the postwar settlement. The pressure such *revisionism put on France and Britain gave Mussolini his opportunity, because the support they wanted from Italy to contain German expansion could be obtained at a price: initially, acquiescence in Italian control of Abyssinia. British foreign policymakers in 1935 were willing to pay this, because it would leave British interests in Africa unaffected; but the outcry against the *Hoare–Laval Plan (1935) frustrated their efforts and *Eden (1897–1977) produced a new Foreign Secretary who despised Mussolini and considered Italians untrustworthy. The Italians, reading British cyphers, knew this, and the alienation from Britain caused by the Abyssinian crisis never healed. The shift in the European *balance of power in Germany's favour prevented reconciliation, because cooperation with Hitler seemed to offer Mussolini Mediterranean expansion at little risk, while cooperation with Britain and France offered nothing except the strong likelihood of dangerous conflict with Germany in the north. Recent Italian historians, not entirely unfairly, have blamed Eden for not doing more in 1936–7 to wean Italy away from her ultimately disastrous partnership with Germany. This would have been the statesmanlike course, but the hostility towards Italy expressed among wide circles of British public opinion and the press for the often brutal

activities of Fascist forces in Abyssinia and Spain would have made it difficult to follow. From 1937 onwards, cautiously but tenaciously, and with the encouragement of Drummond, Neville *Chamberlain (1869–1940) did follow it. Like many in the British government, he wanted to reduce the potential military threat to Britain posed by Germany, Italy and Japan together; but his efforts got nowhere. Mussolini's strident demands for French territory in 1938–9 and his requests for British mediation to achieve it were an attempt to split the democracies which the British dared not encourage, despite Chamberlain's hopes that Mussolini, fearing war because of Italy's weakness, would moderate Hitler's claims on Poland. Italy remained neutral when Germany invaded Poland in September 1939 and the British spent the winter trying to make that neutrality favourable to themselves and France by developing trade contacts. No bargain resembling the 1915 Treaty of *London was attempted. With the surrender of France imminent and Britain's own collapse seemingly not far off, Italy declared war on the Allies on 10 June 1940.

BAER, G., Test Case: Italy, Ethiopia and the League of Nations, Hoover Institution, Stanford, California, 1976.

BARROS, J., The Corfù Incident of 1923: Mussolini and the League of Nations, Princeton University Press, 1965.

HARDIE, F. M., The Abyssinian Crisis, Batsford, 1974.

ROBERTSON, E. M., Mussolini as Empire-Builder: Europe and Africa, 1932–1936, Macmillan, 1977.

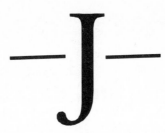

# J

**Jameson Raid** (1895–6). An abortive attempt to overthrow President Kruger's regime in the Transvaal, where the *Uitlanders were restive under a Boer rule which made them pay taxation but denied them the rights of citizenship. Dr Jameson was a South African politician connected with gold-mining interests in the Witwatersrand. He had already, in 1893, engineered a war against the Ndebele and conquered Matabeleland. Cecil Rhodes, Prime Minister of Cape Colony and Director of the British South Africa Company, was implicated in this conspiracy, in which a rising in Johannesburg was to be supported by a force of company police and volunteers from Bechuanaland, and the High Commissioner of Cape Colony, Sir Hercules Robinson, was to be called in as a mediator. The British Colonial Secretary, Joseph *Chamberlain (1836–1914) was aware of the preparations for the raid and was accused of complicity.

The Johannesburg reformers, lacking unity and resolution, postponed their rising. Jameson, though, without waiting for Rhodes's consent, left Pitsani on 29 December 1895 with 500 men, hoping to force the issue. He was taken at Doornkop on 2 January and handed over to the British authorities for trial – he was subsequently brought back to Britain where he was convicted and imprisoned under the Foreign Enlistment Act. Cecil Rhodes resigned the premiership. This episode served to strengthen Afrikaner nationalism. At the same time, British *jingoism was strongly excited by the Kaiser's despatch of the *Kruger Telegram (1896).

PAKENHAM, E., *Jameson's Raid*, Weidenfeld and Nicolson, 1960.

**Jingoism.** Bellicose chauvinism. The term was first applied to those who favoured British intervention on Turkey's behalf during the Russo-Turkish War of 1877–8. It originated from a music-hall song expressive of the mood of the time which had the refrain: 'We don't want to fight, but by jingo if we do – we've got the ships, we've got the men, we've got the money too'.

**July Crisis** (1914). The diplomatic crisis involving the Great Powers which followed the assassination of the Archduke Franz Ferdinand, heir presumptive to the Austrian Habsburg throne, on 28 June 1914 and led to the outbreak of *World War I (1914–18). Austria was determined to humiliate Serbia and suppress Slav nationalism. The crisis turned on the conflicting interests of the Great Powers, particularly following the issue of the so-called 'blank cheque' by which the German Kaiser William II gave assurance of full support to the Austrian envoy on 5–6 July. The Austrians issued an unacceptable ultimatum to Serbia on 23 July. Its refusal precipitated World War I. (See also: *Grey, Sir Edward (1862–1933) ).

GEISS, I., *July 1914: Selected Documents*, Batsford, 1972.

STEINER, Z. S., *Britain and the Origins of the First World War*, Macmillan, 1977.

**Jutland, Battle of** (1916). Off the Danish coast, the principal naval engagement of *World War I (1914–18), fought between the British Grand Fleet and the German High Seas Fleet on 31 May–1 June 1916. German inferiority in Dreadnoughts did not permit a decisive battle to their advantage. The new German navy under Vice-Admiral Scheer aimed at a progressive weakening of the superiority of the British Fleet through a number of sorties. In this case he was particularly keen to engage and defeat Admiral Beatty's battle-cruisers. Jutland was to be the first such sortie. Having intercepted German signals, the entire Grand Fleet was mobilized with a view to a decisive action. Under Admiral Jellicoe, the British lost three battle-cruisers, three cruisers and eight destroyers while the Germans lost one pre-Dreadnought, one battle-cruiser, four cruisers and eight destroyers. Though the Germans inflicted greater losses, they failed to alter the overall situation in their own favour. While they were able to boast their escape from a larger fleet the British command of the sea was confirmed by Jutland and the British continued their blockade. The High Seas Fleet did not come out again to renew the challenge. German frustration at failure to alter this position encouraged pressure within Germany for unrestricted U-boat warfare.

BENNETT, G., *Battle of Jutland*, David and Charles, 1974.

Katyn Forest Massacre (1940). The mass execution of approximately 4,000 Polish prisoners-of-war near Smolensk. The dead were among those who had surrendered to the Soviet Union in the autumn of 1939. A further 11,000 Polish prisoners-of-war were also unaccounted for. The Nazis announced the discovery of the Katyn graves in April 1943. Three commissions identified the time of execution as the spring of 1940, more than a year before the German invasion of the Soviet Union when the Katyn Forest area was in control of the NKVD (Soviet secret police). When the *Polish Government-in-Exile in London requested a further investigation Stalin used this as an excuse to break off relations with them. Britain and the United States refused to support General Sikorski's request to the Soviet government to investigate further the circumstances of the executions. Pressure from *Churchill (1874–1965) and Roosevelt subsequently led the London Poles to withdraw their request. The need to maintain good relations with the Soviet Union which was bearing the main brunt of war against Germany made the Allied leaders unwilling to admit in public the compelling evidence of Soviet responsibility for the massacre. After the war, however, a United States House of Representatives Select Committee on the affair (1952) unanimously voted the Soviet Union responsible.

DOUGLAS, R., *From War to Cold War, 1942–48*, Macmillan, 1982.
KACEWICZ, G. V., *Great Britain, the Soviet Union and the Polish Government-in-Exile, 1939–45*, Nijhoff, The Hague, 1979.

Kellogg–Briand Pact (1928). Multilateral treaty which condemned recourse to war for the settlement of international disputes and renounced it as an instrument of national policy. The French Premier Briand launched the idea in April 1927 in seeking a bilateral Franco-American renunciation of war. The American Secretary of State Kellogg suggested it be broadened to contain all nations. Signed in Paris on 27 August 1928, it initially had 15 signatories and eventually received the adherence of 62 nations. The British government was sceptical of it, seeing it among other things as a move to attract votes to the Republican Party in the United States. Stanley *Baldwin (1867–1947) attempted but failed to modify the draft and only signed with reluctance. The treaty led to the reconvening of the disarmament conference in 1929 and was frequently invoked in subsequent years, such as during the *Manchurian Crisis (1931–3). It contained no provision for sanctions, however, and had a negligible effect on world affairs.

FERRELL, R. H., *Peace in Their Time: The Origins of the Kellogg–Briand Pact*, Yale University Press, New Haven, 1952.

KERR, Philip Henry, see LOTHIAN, MARQUESS OF (1882–1940)

KEYNES, John Maynard, 1st Baron, Lord Keynes of Tilton (created 1942) (1883–1946). Educated at Eton and King's College, Cambridge. After serving in the India Office, during *World War I (1914–18) he did important work at the Treasury on Allied loans. He was subsequently chief representative of the

Treasury at the *Paris Peace Conference (1919–20).

Though his primary achievement was his work as an influential economist, as author of such seminal titles as *The General Theory of Employment, Interest and Money*, he first attained prominence in the national eye with his biting denunciation of the terms of the *Versailles Treaty (1919). He was particularly critical of the *reparations to be imposed on Germany and warned of their likely consequences for the world economy and European peace. His book *The Economic Consequences of the Peace* (1919) was followed in 1922 by *A Revision of the Treaty*. His criticisms helped to encourage the feeling in Britain that Germany had been hard done by, a view regarded with conspicuous disbelief and hostility by the French. In retrospect these criticisms may be seen to have offered support to the arguments in favour of *appeasement, while at the same time their author came to be seen as a prophet of the future conflict.

During *World War II (1939–45) Keynes contributed a great deal to the working-out of economic strategy. In 1940 he published *How to Pay for the War* and was in this period adviser to the Chancellor of the Exchequer. At the end of his life he was chief negotiator of the large United States loan to Britain required at the end of the war. He was instrumental in helping to create a new basis for international monetary and economic cooperation (see: *Bretton Woods Conference (1944) ), which led to the *International Monetary Fund and the International Bank for Reconstruction and Development (The World Bank).

HARROD, R. F., *The Life of John Maynard Keynes*, Macmillan, 1951.

KEYNES, M., ed., *Essays on Maynard Keynes*, Cambridge University Press, 1979.

SKIDELSKY, R., *John Maynard Keynes, vol. I, Hopes Betrayed, 1883–1920*, Macmillan.

KIMBERLEY, John Wodehouse, 1st Earl of (created 1866) (1826–1902). Liberal Colonial Secretary 1870–4, 1880–2; Foreign Secretary 1894–5. During the 1850s Kimberley held junior posts at the *Foreign Office and, after the *Crimean War, which lasted from 1854 to 1856, had a spell as Ambassador in St Petersburg. In 1863 he was sent to Denmark in unsuccessful attempts to resolve the *Schleswig-Holstein question. His periods at the Colonial Office were dominated by prob-

lems in southern Africa, which he handled in an irresolute manner. In 1894 he realized a long-standing ambition when he was appointed Foreign Secretary by *Rosebery (1847–1929). He was an able administrator with a fine grasp of detail, but he pursued Liberal Imperialist policies in a manner which did little to advance the interests of the *Empire. An agreement with Belgium over the Congo damaged relations with Germany and had to be modified. In the face of war between China and Japan, he was unable to maintain any effective diplomatic initiative but contrived to alienate Russia, thus prejudicing British interests in the Near and Middle East. Hence, both at home and abroad, Salisbury's return to office in 1895 was greeted with general relief.

JAMES, R. R., *Rosebery*, Weidenfeld and Nicholson, 1963.

MATTHEW, H. C. G., *The Liberal Imperialists*, Oxford University Press, 1973.

King Cotton diplomacy. Phrase describing the Confederate diplomacy during the American Civil War. By 1850 cotton represented 50 per cent of United States exports, valued at more than 100 million dollars annually. Confederate leaders considered that because Britain and France regarded cotton as vital to their economies they would give recognition and aid to the South. The South brought pressure to bear on the European Powers through embargo, and even destruction of cotton supplies. The strategy failed, however. Britain had built up considerable stocks of cotton before the war, was not disposed to engage in war with the North, and her economic vulnerability was less than the South supposed. She was importing cotton from India and had built up formidable economic strength in the export of other goods, reducing her dependence on cotton goods.

CROOK, D. P., *The North, the South and the Powers, 1861–65*, Wiley, New York, 1974.

OWSLEY, F., *King Cotton Diplomacy*, 2nd ed., University of Chicago Press, 1959.

KITCHENER, Horatio Herbert, Earl Kitchener of Khartoum (created 1914) (1850–1916). Kitchener served as a soldier in the Middle East, rising to become General-in-Chief in Egypt in 1892. He led the reconquest of the Sudan which culminated in victory over the dervishes at Omdurman on 2 September 1898 and a tense but peaceful confrontation with the French at *Fashoda in the same year, an encounter which prevented French expansion in the Nile valley. He then served as Chief-of-Staff to Lord Roberts in the *Boer War (1899–1902) and was himself responsible for the eventual victory over the Boers, although he was strongly criticized for his use of concentration camps. From 1902 to 1909 he was Commander-in-Chief in India, where he quarrelled with the Viceroy, Lord *Curzon (1859–1925) over dual control of the army, but Kitchener ultimately got most of the independence he wanted. From 1911 to 1914 he was British Agent in Egypt, where he made short-lived constitutional changes and important economic reforms.

On the outbreak of hostilities in 1914 *Asquith (1852–1928) appointed Kitchener Secretary of State for War. His immense prestige was vital in boosting national morale and gaining two-and-a-half million volunteers for the Army, while his realization that the country needed to plan for a long war led him to work with great energy in developing the necessary logistical infrastructure. He suffered, however, from an inability to delegate, and his soldierly manner and attitude of mind made him unable to cooperate effectively with his civilian colleagues in the Cabinet. During 1915 he came under mounting criticism because of the inadequate supply of shells to the army in France, the failure of the Dardanelles expedition (see: *Gallipoli (1915) ) and the costly Battle of Loos. Although Kitchener tendered his resignation, Asquith refused to accept it because he needed his name to support the tottering government, but he was relieved of many of his responsibilities. In May 1916, whilst on his way to confer with Tsar Nicholas II, Kitchener was drowned when the ship carrying him hit a mine off the Orkneys.

GREW, E. S., *Field Marshal Lord Kitchener: His Life and Work for the Empire*, 3 vols., Gresham, 1916.

MAGNUS, P., *Kitchener: Portrait of an Imperialist*, John Murray, 1958.

**Kruger Telegram** (1896). Telegram of 3 January from the Emperor William II of Germany to President Kruger of the Transvaal congratulating him on his success in defending the independence of his country against the *Jameson Raid (29 December 1895): 'I sincerely congratulate you that, without appealing for the help of friendly powers, you with your people, by your own energy against the armed hordes which as disturbers of the peace broke into your country, have succeeded in re-establishing peace and maintaining the independence of your country against attacks from without'. The telegram had in fact been suggested by the German diplomat Marschall to forestall even more headstrong action by the Kaiser who, among other things, was toying with the idea of declaring a German protectorate over the Transvaal. However, it caused immense affront in Britain since Germany declared herself a friend of the Boers who were an integral part of the British *Empire. At the same time, Germany was in no position to offer effective military assistance to the Boers.

The Jameson Raid was the culmination of a growing tension in relations between Britain and the Transvaal. The German tactic appears to have been forcefully to demonstrate the high value of German friendship to Britain by threatening her with continuing diplomatic annoyance. This policy misfired. The telegram led to loud demands in Britain for a pact with France and it marked the first violent outbreak of popular hostility between Britain and Germany. The German government had already been warned by Lord Kimberley that South Africa was of crucial strategic significance to the British Empire because of the lines of communication with India. The outcry over the telegram served notice on the German government that a German challenge to the British elsewhere in the world would be likely to provoke a similar response.

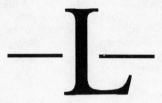

**LANSDOWNE,** Henry Petty-Fitzmaurice, 5th Marquess of (1845–1927). Unionist Foreign Secretary 1900–5. Lansdowne was the last Whig nobleman to hold major government office. Having been a junior minister under *Gladstone (1809–98), he had uneventful periods as Governor-General of Canada from 1883 to 1888 and as Viceroy of India from 1888 to 1894. In 1895 *Salisbury (1830–1903) appointed him Secretary of State for War, and Lansdowne much extended the process of re-organization begun by *Campbell-Bannerman (1836–1908), although the *Boer War (1899–1902) demonstrated that the army was still inadequately prepared for a major conflict, and Lansdowne's reputation suffered accordingly.

In 1900 Salisbury retired from the *Foreign Office and as his successor chose Lansdowne, who was responsible for a series of moves which marked Britain's emergence from 'splendid isolation' (see: *isolationism). This reflected a pragmatic response to events rather than the implementation of a broad strategy. The *Hay–Pauncefote Treaty of 1901 provided for American construction of the Panama Canal and established better relations with the United States at the price of limiting Britain's capacity for influence in the Americas. In 1902 an *Anglo-Japanese Alliance was concluded, followed by the *Anglo-French Entente (1904), which gave France a free hand in Morocco in return for the acceptance of British control in Egypt. Lansdowne was suspicious of Germany but anxious that relations should be as cordial as possible, and in 1901 made attempts to obtain an alliance, which were frustrated by the opposition of his own Cabinet colleagues and by the erratic behaviour of the Kaiser. Growing estrangement between Britain and Germany followed, but Lansdowne failed to foresee the disastrous consequences which were to ensue in 1914.

After the fall of Balfour's government in 1905 Lansdowne continued to lead the Unionists in the House of Lords. In May 1915 he took office in the wartime Asquith coalition as Minister without Portfolio and in November 1916 presented a memorandum criticizing Britain's allies and the military advice given to the government and advocating the consideration of proposals for peace. This contributed to Asquith's fall and in November 1917, Lansdowne, now out of office, made his views public in a letter to the *Daily Telegraph* in which he argued that the continuation of the war would 'spell ruin for the civilized world'. Although Lansdowne's action was strongly criticized, it was welcomed in some quarters, and his views were gaining ground before Germany's military collapse in 1918 eliminated the need to contemplate a negotiated peace. After 1918 Lansdowne took little further part in politics. He was respected as a competent statesman with a cool head in a crisis, although he lacked outstanding intellectual gifts and was limited by his failure to appreciate the importance of public opinion as a tool of foreign policy.

MONGER, G., *The End of Isolation, British Foreign Policy, 1900–1907*, Nelson, 1963.
NEWTON, LORD, *Lord Lansdowne*, Macmillan, 1929.

**Lausanne, Treaty of** (1923). This was a mitigation of the Treaty of *Sèvres (1920) which had imposed harsh terms on the defeated Ottoman Empire after *World War I (1914–18). It was signed on 24 July. Turkey was compelled to recognize the Straits (see: *Straits Question) as demilitarized and to undertake not to claim territory which was not inhabited by Turks – as under Sèvres. Britain retained Cyprus and Italy retained the Dodecanese. The Allies for their part agreed to guarantee the Demilitarized Zones and the Turks received back from Greece all the land in Asia Minor ceded under Sèvres and that in Eastern Thrace. Turkey accepted treaties for the protection of minorities. It was also agreed that there should be an exchange of populations, which led to a million Greeks being forced to leave Turkey. The Treaty of Lausanne was necessitated by the militant Turkish refusal to accept the earlier terms. These had caused a strong nationalist reaction led by the hero of *Gallipoli (1915) General Mustapha Kemal (later known as Atatürk). In 1920 Kemal had established a new nationalist government in the central Anatolian city of Ankara away from allied influence and had proceeded to attack the Greeks. Following the *Chanak Crisis (1922), after the Turkish victory at Smyrna, the Allies were accordingly forced to modify their original peace terms.

BUSCH, B. C., *Mudros to Lausanne: Britain's Frontier in West Asia, 1918–23*, State University of New York Press, New York, 1976.

**League of Nations** (1920–46). An association of independent states for the maintenance of lasting peace and security which reflected the widespread desire to prevent the recurrence of war after the horrors of *World War I (1914–18). The idea of a global peace-keeping body had been advanced by, among others, President Woodrow Wilson in the last of his *Fourteen Points. The League was incorporated in the peace treaties of 1919–20 and came into operation in January 1920 with its seat at Geneva. Britain and all members of the *Empire and Commonwealth were among its original constituent states and the British Sir Eric *Drummond (1876–1951) was its first Secretary-General between 1919 and 1932.

Its two central institutions were the Assembly, a general and representative body, and the small 'executive' Council, which included Britain as one of its permanent members. The Covenant of the League contained elaborate procedures for the peaceful settlement of international disputes by arbitration and a universal guarantee of territorial integrity. It also held out the prospect of eventual universal disarmament. Disputes were to be submitted to the League or other arbitrators, who were to report within six months. If arbitration failed, a further three-month cooling-off period was to be observed before recourse to hostilities. According to Article 16 sanctions could be enforced against any state failing to observe these provisions. Sanctions ranged in severity from severance of trade relations to a military coalition of the League against the aggressor. Supporters of the League were divided among themselves as to whether or not it should reserve to itself the option to use military force.

In March 1920 the US Senate failed to give the Treaty of *Versailles (1919) the two-thirds vote necessary for approval. President Woodrow Wilson refused to accept the reservations on the League, which reflected American isolationist sentiment, put forward under the leadership of Henry Cabot Lodge, Chairman of the Foreign Relations Committee. The consequent refusal of the US to ratify or join the League was to prove a grave blow to that body's credibility, though the US did subsequently send unofficial representatives to its meetings.

The League emerged not as a 'league of democracies' nor a military alliance, but as an association of nations retaining their national sovereignty. Owing to the refusal of the United States to join the League, the belated admission of Germany (1926) and the Soviet Union (1934), and numerous withdrawals, including those of Japan and Italy, it was at no time a fully representative body. It lacked an international armed force by which wayward members could be coerced and was hamstrung by the need for decisions to be unanimous. Its failure to prevent the Japanese invasion and conquest of Manchuria (see: *Manchurian Crisis (1931–3) ) and of Abyssinia by Italy (see: *Abyssinian War (1935–6) ) and its inability to take any decisive steps towards disarmament showed that, as constituted, it was unable to give sanctions against aggression the backing they required. As a peace-keeping body it was discredited long before Hitler resorted to war in 1939. (It also proved unable to stop the Soviet invasion of Finland in 1939). By the late 1930s the major powers were ignoring a League obviously incapable of dealing with the deepening international crisis. Successive British governments gave the League less than wholehearted support. While paying lip-service to it, statesmen such as *Baldwin (1867–1947) and Neville *Chamberlain (1869–1940) were sceptical of the notion of *collective security through the League. They regarded it as a meeting-place rather than an effective body, did not support initiatives to strengthen its authority and gave precedence to imperial commitments. The ambiguity of the British stance was clearly exposed in the *Hoare–Laval Plan (1935).

Other functional organizations and agencies created by the League did much useful and constructive work. These included the International Labour Organization, the International Court of Justice, agencies for relief work among refugees and cultural and technical cooperation, and the supervision of *mandates. In April 1946 the League dissolved itself and transferred its functions and assets to the *United Nations.

EGERTON, G. W., *Great Britain and the Creation of the League of Nations: Strategy, Politics and International Organization 1914–19*, Scolar Press, 1979.

HENIG, R. B., *The League of Nations*, Oliver and Boyd, Edinburgh, 1973.

WALTERS, F. P., *A History of the League of Nations*, 2 vols., Macmillan, 1952.

**League of Nations Union.** Founded in 1918, this British organization incorporated the previous League of Nations Society and the League of Free Nations Association. It worked during subsequent years to promote the aims and objectives of the *League of Nations and to secure the acceptance by the British people of the League as 'the guardian of international right, the organ of international cooperation, the final arbiter in international differences, and the supreme instrument for removing injustices which may threaten the peace of the world'. Its main work was educational. It published materials, organized courses popularizing the ideals of international relations embodied in the League and rejecting the preconceptions of prewar diplomacy. It enjoyed markedly less success among Conservative Party supporters than among those of the Labour and Liberal parties, though the Conservative politician Viscount *Cecil of Chelwood was its President from 1923 to 1945. Another very prominent figure was the Liberal Professor Gilbert Murray.

During the 1930s the League of Nations Union developed as a focus of opposition to the *appeasement policies of the National Govern-ment. Its practical results were modest, how-ever. Pro-League opinion shaped policy, allow-ing German admission to the League in 1926, encouraged the arms embargo during the *Manchurian Crisis (1931–3) and pressed for sanctions against Italy (see: *Abyssinian War (1935–6). It also helped to sponsor the *Peace Ballot. Overall, however, it appears to have had a peripheral influence on the formulation of British foreign policy. The National Government gave lip-service rather than convincing support to the League, and Conservative politicians tended to regard the League conception of *collective security with scepticism. Further-more, supporters of the League were divided between those who called for a 'League with teeth', i.e. with forces at its disposal to compel compliance with its rulings, and those who saw it simply as a moral force.

BIRN, D., *The League of Nations Union, 1918–1945*, Oxford University Press, 1981.

**Lend-Lease.** The American aid programme during *World War II (1939–45) approved on 11 March 1941. It was originally conceived by President Roosevelt as a means of helping Britain in the war against Germany without direct United States military intervention. Lend-Lease further eroded the American position of neutrality, representing a logical extension of Roosevelt's 'arsenal of democracy' speech of the previous December.

Earlier, in 1935, the Johnson Act had for-bidden financial loans to states which had defaulted, as Britain had, on their World War I loans. Lend-Lease came into operation after the evacuation of *Dunkirk (1940), in which Britain had lost considerable quantities of military supplies. It was gradually expanded to include other Allied nations. It provided them with war matériel (later, foodstuffs and other materials, too). The terms of the Act permitted the President to 'sell, transfer title to, exchange, lease or otherwise dispose of' articles of defence to the government of any country whose defence he thought vital to the interests and security of the United States.

The United States was to receive for such aid 'payment or repayment in kind or property, or any other direct or indirect benefit' which the President considered adequate. In fact the goods were not returned, though after the entry of the United States into the war in 1941 the programme of Lend-Lease evolved into a system in which resources were pooled cooperatively for common ends. The Allies made lend-lease agreements among themselves and also supplied goods and services to the United States. The total spent by the United States was 49 billion dollars, of which the British *Empire received 31 billion. The arrangement was terminated in August 1945, with the United States and Britain signing an agreement in March 1946 by which Britain agreed to a liability of 650 million dollars.

KIMBALL, W. F., *The Most Unsordid Act: Lend-Lease, 1939–41*, Johns Hopkins Press, Baltimore, 1969.

LASH, J. P., *Roosevelt and Churchill, 1939–41: The Partnership that Saved the West*, Deutsch, 1977.

**Limited (or Partial) Test Ban Treaty,** see NUCLEAR TEST BAN TREATY (1963)

**Limited War.** Military conflict in which the objective of the participants is something less than the total destruction of the enemy and their *unconditional surrender. A limited war is normally restricted to a circumscribed geographical area, with the conflict exempting the greater part of the territory of some or all of the participants. It is also usually limited in the sense that the adversaries do not use the most potent military equipment at their disposal. The concept of limited war in the post-war period is graphically illustrated by the example of the Korean War (1950–3). During this contest the actual engagement of forces was restricted to Korean territory, though both the United States and China were massively involved, operating respectively from their bases in Japan and Manchuria. Limited war may denote hostilities between small states without intervention by the major powers, or intervention by a nuclear power against a small state without conflict with the other major powers, or further, uprisings against colonial powers in which conventional military support is forthcoming from the superpowers. The term 'limited nuclear war' is also sometimes used and its feasibility debated. This refers to hypothetical conflict in which only tactical nuclear weapons would be used for the destruction specifically of military targets, and in which the powers would not resort to the use of weapons of mass destruction against centres of civilian population.

**LLOYD GEORGE,** David, 1st Earl Lloyd-George of Dwyfor (1863–1945). Brought up in his shoemaker uncle's household in Llanystumdwy, North Wales and educated at the village school, he qualified as a solicitor in 1884 and in 1890 became Liberal MP for Caernarvon Boroughs, which he represented until his elevation to the peerage in 1945. His humble background and upbringing in the nationalist tradition of north Welsh nonconformity profoundly influenced his early political concerns: self-government for Wales, disestablishment of the Anglican church there, and better conditions for disadvantaged rural communities. The creation of a more democratic and egalitarian Britain soon became his objective and remained so throughout his career.

Lloyd George's political connections in the 1890s lay with the nonconformist 'Little Englander' wing of the Liberal Party and his interest in foreign affairs was sporadic. He was not an imperialist – imperialist expansion, he thought, hindered social reform – but on particular issues he had much in common with imperialists. Thus he opposed the French encroachment on the Nile at *Fashoda in 1898, but urged against military solutions. In South Africa, however, he strongly opposed the Salisbury government's policy and claimed that the burden of the war which began in 1899 would fall on the poorer classes. Regarded as a pro-Boer, he was violently unpopular when Britain was suffering military disasters; but as the position improved and anti-war feeling spread in the Liberal Party and the country, he was vindicated. Neither pacifist nor isolationist and arguing that the empire would be strengthened by colonial independence, Lloyd George had become by the end of the war a national figure thought to have statesmanlike qualities.

As the party's leading radical, Lloyd George entered Campbell-Bannerman's Cabinet of 1905 as President of the Board of Trade, and became Asquith's Chancellor of the Exchequer in 1908. His visit to Germany that year to study the social security system gave him firsthand experience of German society and its enthusiasm for naval expansion. His 'People's Budget' of 1909 was designed to provide not only for health and social insurance schemes but also for additional naval construction. In 1910 Lloyd George was privately toying with the idea of *conscription and during the 2nd *Moroccan Crisis (1911), to general surprise, his Mansion House speech warned Germany that to continue intimidating France would mean war with Britain. A member of the

*Committee of Imperial Defence from summer 1911, Lloyd George backed Grey's attempts to improve relations with Germany and opposed increased naval expenditure. Disliking support for Russia, he initially opposed intervention in the 1914 crisis; but the German invasion of Belgium changed his mind, and with his war-time budget of November 1914 and jingoistic speeches that winter he soon established himself as the minister most determined to win the war.

Lloyd George's involvement with foreign affairs still remained limited. The slaughter of trench warfare in autumn 1914 appalled him and convinced him that the war could not be won on the Western Front. As an 'Easterner', who believed that the *Central Powers would be defeated through the Balkans, he favoured the *Gallipoli expedition (1915) and fretted, after its failure, when the generals proved unwilling for further 'sideshows'. As an outstanding Minister of Munitions in the Coalition government of May 1915 Lloyd George ended the shell shortage; as Secretary for War from July 1916 he could not prevail against the General Staff's obsession with the Western Front, and by the autumn, after the destruction of Haig's armies on the *Somme and the failure to help Rumania, feared that the war would be lost if *Asquith (1852–1928) let things continue as they were.

In December 1916 negotiations between senior Coalition politicians to remodel the higher direction of the war unexpectedly led to Asquith's resignation and replacement by Lloyd George. Lloyd George formed a small War Cabinet which he dominated, and began a campaign to wrest power from the generals. It was not until the winter of 1917–18, after Passchendaele, that he succeeded with the creation of the allied Supreme War Council which had authority over the General Staff. Immediately, however, he took control of foreign policy, circumventing the Foreign Secretary, *Balfour (1848–1930), and conducting diplomacy himself through Philip Kerr, later Lord *Lothian (1882–1940), his foreign affairs adviser in the Downing Street 'garden suburb'. Hence he was able to push for the Supreme War Council with the French and make contact with the Central Powers in the winter of 1917–18 when he contemplated a negotiated peace to prevent the spread of Bolshevism.

The autumn of 1918 which brought Germany's unexpected collapse was spent by Lloyd George trying to gain the initiative for the post-war settlement. He got Cabinet backing for large reparations claims against Germany and for an allied military occupation of the Rhineland. Harsh treatment of Germany had a favourable response in the country during the December 1918 election campaign, when Lloyd George himself made several jingoistic speeches. But early in 1919, with the election safely behind him, Lloyd George's attitude changed. The revolutionary discontent which had spread throughout Central Europe in the winter would be fuelled unless post-war Germany could achieve stability. She would be unlikely to, Lloyd George believed, if the far-reaching measures the French had in mind were adopted. At the *Paris Peace Conference (1919–20), therefore, once agreement had been reached to deprive Germany of her navy and her colonies, Lloyd George pressed for her retention of the Rhineland, Silesia and *Danzig. But, to some extent a prisoner of his earlier attitude, he was not wholly successful on any of these issues.

The peace settlement was acceptable to public opinion in Britain but caused endless friction between France and Germany. Unless this was resolved the European economic recovery necessary for Britain's own would never materialize. Lloyd George's priority henceforth was to reconcile French demands for security and German demands for fair treatment by modifying the peace settlement. To do this he promoted a series of international conferences between heads of government in 1921–2 which, despite his efforts, achieved nothing.

In October 1922 an isolated Britain threatening war on Turkey in defence of Greek aspirations in Asia Minor (see: *Chanak Crisis) proved the last straw for many Conservatives dissatisfied with Lloyd George's leadership. Lacking a secure power base, he had to resign. He never took office again, although he remained a formidable political force. In the 1930s he strongly criticized National Governments for not being conciliatory enough with Hitler, whom he met in October 1936 and was apparently deeply impressed by. Anxiety about another Anglo-German war blinded Lloyd George to the realities of Nazism and in early 1940 he was among those wanting to explore a negotiated peace with Hitler. Nevertheless, in December 1940, Churchill offered him the

Washington embassy, which he refused, dying in 1945.

FRY, M. G., *Lloyd George and Foreign Policy*, Vol. I, McGill–Queen's University Press, Montreal, 1977.

LLOYD GEORGE, D., *War Memoirs*, 6 vols. Ivor Nicholson and Watson, 1936. *The Truth about the Peace Treaties*, 2 vols., Victor Gollancz, 1938.

MORGAN, K. O., *Lloyd George*, Weidenfeld and Nicolson, 1974.

**Locarno Pacts** (1925). The series of treaties negotiated by Austen *Chamberlain (1863–1937) for Britain, Aristide Briand for France and Gustav Stresemann for Weimar Germany in October 1925 and signed on 1 December of the same year. They were designed to enhance European stability and French security. The pacts included a Rhineland guarantee, assuring the frontiers between Germany and France and Belgium respectively, to be upheld by Britain, France, Germany, Italy and Belgium. There were identical arbitration and non-aggression conventions between Germany and France and Germany and Belgium; identical arbitration conventions between Germany and Poland and Czechoslovakia respectively and identical guarantee treaties between France and Poland and France and Czechoslovakia.

The signing of the Locarno Pacts was followed in 1926 by Germany's admittance to the *League of Nations. The phrase 'spirit of Locarno' was used until the mid-1930s with the suggestion of an enduring peace. In fact, though, the signatories were motivated by widely differing priorities. Locarno meant that Germany now voluntarily accepted her western frontiers as fixed by the Treaty of *Versailles (1919), but it did not rule out the possibility of treaty revision in the east where there were ethnic German minorities. Austen Chamberlain was anxious to give some guarantee to France but wished to see British involvement and commitment in Europe as circumscribed as possible. He therefore refused to support French demands for an 'Eastern Locarno' – an agreement that would have afforded the same assurances in Eastern Europe as on the Rhine. In March 1936 Hitler's remilitarization of the *Rhineland destroyed this treaty arrangement. Germany announced herself no longer bound by Locarno, citing the Franco-Soviet agreement of 1935 as justification for this volte-face. Later in 1936 Belgium announced her decision to pursue an independent foreign policy, which quashed any suggestion of its renewal.

JACOBSON, J., *Locarno Diplomacy: Germany and the West, 1925–29*, Princeton University Press, Princeton N.J., 1972.

MARKS, S., *The Illusion of Peace: International Relations in Europe 1918–1933*, Macmillan, 1976.

**London Convention** (1827). An agreement signed on 6 July 1827 by Russia, Britain and France during the *Greek War of Independence (1821–29). This called for collective action to be taken against the Porte by the signatories. It was issued in the hope that the Turks could be intimidated into ending their military action against the Greeks. It was further hoped that they would grant Greece autonomy on the understanding that she paid an annual tribute to Turkey. A secret article in the Convention stipulated that should the Turkish authorities refuse, the powers should establish consulates in the most important Greek towns and use military force to bring about an armistice. The Sultan refused to accede to these proposals. This led to the destruction of the Turco-Egyptian fleet at *Navarino (20 October 1827).

**London Convention** (1871). The revision of several articles of the Treaty of *Paris (1856) which had ended the *Crimean War (1854–6). Taking advantage of the Franco-Prussian War, the Russians repudiated the humiliating *Black Sea Clauses on 31 October 1870. Britain attempted to form a coalition to defy the Russians, but Bismarck was only willing to accede to a conference to discuss the situation. Representatives from Britain, Russia, Prussia, Austria, Italy and Turkey assembled in London in January. The resulting Convention which was signed on 13 March 1871 abrogated articles 11, 12 and 13 of the Treaty of Paris. The Black Sea Clauses were replaced by a declaration that both Russia and Turkey had the right to maintain fortresses and naval forces in the Black Sea. Furthermore, the Sultan was to be permitted to open the Straits in peacetime to the navies of allied and friendly powers (see: *Straits Question).

**London Poles,** SEE POLISH GOVERNMENT-IN-EXILE.

**London, Treaty of** (1839). Signed on 19 April 1839. This agreement was between Britain,

France, Russia, Prussia and Austria and settled the dispute between the Dutch and their former Belgian subjects, who had set up an independent monarchy after the overthrow of Dutch rule in 1830. Article 7 affirmed that Belgium was 'an independent and perpetually neutral state' under the collective guarantee of the signatories. The Belgians for their part recognized that Luxemburg should remain a Grand Duchy under the King of Holland and that the river Scheldt should be open to the commerce of both Holland and Belgium. On Britain's insistence, France and Germany subsequently signed an extra treaty, reinforcing the neutrality of Belgium during the Franco-Prussian War. The German infringement of the guarantee of Belgium (described by the German Chancellor Bethmann-Hollweg as 'a scrap of paper') in 1914 was given by Britain as the *casus belli* for her entry into *World War I (1914–18).

**London, Treaty of** (1915). Signed on 26 April 1915, this secret agreement defined the conditions under which Italy, which had been a member of the Triple Alliance with Germany and Austria-Hungary since 1882, would enter *World War I (1914–18) on the side of the Entente Powers. It assured Italy of her irredentist demands (see: *irredentism), which included Trieste, Trentino and the South Tyrol, a large stretch of the Dalmatian coast, some Albanian territory, sovereignty over the Dodecanese Islands, Adalia in Asia Minor, colonial expansion in Africa and a share in any war indemnity. The Allies accepted Italy's claims at a time when there was exasperating military stalemate on the Western Front. They hoped that Italian intervention could help speedily to bring down Austria-Hungary and open the way to Germany.

For the British the agreement created perplexing difficulties. On the one hand there were the Balkan states which were associates in the war effort against the *Central Powers, and whose territory Italy coveted. Support for Italy's claims ran counter, therefore, to the interests of other states whose support the Allies needed. On the other, the promises to Italy obstructed Britain in her wish to detach Austria-Hungary from her alliance with Germany by making a generous peace. Furthermore, Italy suffered repeated military reverses. The terms of the Treaty of London were revealed by the Bolsheviks. They were strongly opposed by President Woodrow Wilson because of their flagrant disregard of the principle of *self-determination. At the *Paris Peace Conference (1919–20) Britain and France reduced their concessions to Italy and she received as a result of the war far less than originally promised. This served to stimulate militant nationalist grievances against the peace settlement and to make Italy a revisionist power in the interwar years.
ROTHWELL, V., *British War Aims and Peace Diplomacy 1914–18*, Oxford University Press, 1971.

**LOTHIAN,** Philip Henry Kerr, 11th Marquess of (1882–1940). Educated at the Oratory School, Edgbaston, and New College, Oxford. In 1904 he went to South Africa as secretary to the lieutenant governor of the Transvaal, becoming a member of Milner's Kindergarten, where he campaigned for union among the South African colonies. After this had taken place in 1909, Kerr returned to England and in 1910 founded and became the first editor of *Round Table*, a magazine promoting organic union of the *Commonwealth. In December 1916 *Lloyd George (1863–1945) appointed him Private Secretary, and he became a leading figure in the so-called 'garden suburb', informing and advising Lloyd George on foreign and imperial affairs. He played a major role in the drafting of the *Versailles Treaty (1919) and was personally responsible for the inclusion of the contentious *War Guilt Clause. He resigned in 1921 to concentrate on his activities for imperial union, returning to government (after succeeding to the title) in August 1931 as Liberal Chancellor of the Duchy of Lancaster in MacDonald's National Cabinet. A free trader, he resigned in 1932 after the *Ottawa Conference.

Lothian's involvement with foreign affairs during the rest of his life was concentrated on Germany and the United States. With many contacts in the press and public life, after 1933 Lothian became one of the most influential advocates of the *appeasement of Germany. Nazi brutality, he wrote in 1935, was 'in considerable measure due to the fact that (Germany's) neighbours were not able to make peaceful revisions in the treaties as war passions died down'. Fairness was a typical motive for appeasement advanced by Liberals. In Lothian's case, fear of Bolshevism was another. Not until Hitler's occupation of Prague in March 1939 did his views change.

Lothian's knowledge of the United States, his belief in Anglo-American cooperation and his skills as a publicist led *Halifax (1881–1959) to offer him the Washington Embassy in August 1938. Foreign Office officials disliked this, but Lothian took up the post on 30 August 1939. The appointment proved an outstanding success. By persuading London to be more open with the United States, Lothian could speak plainly in both public speeches and calculated indiscretions in the right quarters to present Britain's case in terms Americans could readily understand. Using these tactics to explain Britain's financial plight, Lothian created a favourable atmosphere for Roosevelt to move from his *Cash-and-Carry policy to *Lend-Lease in early 1941. Lothian died suddenly, much mourned on both sides of the Atlantic, in December 1940. 'Our greatest Ambassador to the United States', *Churchill (1874–1965) called him.

BUTLER, J. R. M., *Lord Lothian 1882–1940*, Macmillan, 1960.

LOTHIAN, 11TH MARQUESS OF, *The American Speeches of Lord Lothian, July 1939–December 1940*, with a Memoir by Sir Edward Grigg, Royal Institute of International Affairs, 1940.

**Lytton Commission** (1931–1933). A commission of enquiry appointed in December 1931 by the *League of Nations. It was set up to examine the situation and competing nationalist claims in the *Manchurian Crisis (1931–3), which followed the Mukden incident in September 1931 and which led to the seizure of Manchuria by the Japanese army. After visiting government leaders in China and Japan, the five-man commission headed by the Earl of Lytton spent six weeks in Manchuria in the spring of 1932. Japan had accepted the commission with the proviso that it did not preclude any future Japanese military action. In September the Japanese Government recognized Manchukuo, the puppet state created by the army. On 2 October the commission made public its conclusions. While drawing full attention to the complexity of the situation and not exempting China from all blame it stated that Japan had been the aggressor. It argued that Manchukuo should not be recognized and advocated Manchurian autonomy under Chinese sovereignty. When the General Assembly of the League of Nations adopted the Lytton Report the Japanese delegate walked out in protest. In March 1933 Japan withdrew from the League.

LEAGUE OF NATIONS, *Appeal of the Chinese Government: Report of the Commission of Enquiry* (Lytton Report), Geneva, 1932.

THORNE, C., *The Limits of Foreign Policy: The West, the League and the Far Eastern Crisis of 1931–33*, Macmillan, 1972.

# M

MACDONALD, James Ramsay (1866–1937). Born at Lossiemouth, Morayshire, the son of unmarried farmworkers. Brought up in hardship and largely self-educated, he moved to Bristol in 1885 where he came into contact with the Marxist doctrines of the Social Democratic Federation. Soon afterwards he joined the Fabian Society and became private secretary to the prospective Liberal candidate for West Islington. This, and marriage in 1896, brought him into the upper-middle-class circles he found congenial and which helped him to achieve financial independence. The extensive foreign travel this permitted established his authority as a spokesman on foreign affairs after 1906 when, as a Labour Representation Committee candidate, he had been elected MP for Leicester. In 1911 he became chairman of the Labour group in Parliament, where his moderation on social and industrial issues earned him much criticism.

In August 1914 he resigned his chairmanship of the party because it refused to support his opposition to war credits. MacDonald claimed that Britain had been wrong to declare war, but that having done so she should seek peace at the first opportunity on terms allowing for the re-establishment of friendly relations between workers in Europe. In September 1914 he helped found the *Union of Democratic Control, embracing socialists and radicals and whose purpose was a more democratic foreign policy. But he was not a pacifist: he believed that Germany must be defeated and he encouraged enlistment. The popular right-wing press, however, incited by German propaganda, portrayed him as anti-British. His

courage in resisting its vituperative attacks and even physical assaults won him much respect throughout the Labour movement, and in 1922 he resumed the chairmanship of the Parliamentary Labour Party.

In January 1924 Labour took office for the first time as a minority government with MacDonald as both Prime Minister and Foreign Secretary. The combination of roles reflected the priority he attached to foreign affairs and the danger he perceived in the European situation. Since 1919 France and Germany had been locked in endless conflict and recrimination which, if it continued, looked likely to result in another war – and since 1914 MacDonald, according to his biographer, David Marquand, 'had seen the prevention of another war as the greatest single object of his political life'. Moreover, Britain's social and industrial problems seemed largely attributable to unemployment in the export industries, and with important export markets in Central Europe Britain had a primary interest in peace and stability in that area. If MacDonald could succeed in promoting this, when *Lloyd George (1863–1945) and the Conservatives had conspicuously failed, Labour would establish its claim as a responsible party of government and ensure its future electoral advance.

MacDonald was fortunate that by early 1924 both France and Germany were tired of the *Ruhr occupation and that the Dawes Committee, formed to resolve the *reparations question, was reporting. Chairing the London Conference in July 1924, MacDonald skilfully mediated between France and Germany to win their acceptance of the committee's recommendations. The *Dawes Plan prevented France from reoccupying the Ruhr, so to meet French security concerns MacDonald, in August, produced the *Geneva Protocol, a device to draw the French into conciliation and disarmament in return for a promise of support from members of the *League of Nations against aggression. MacDonald did not believe that such a commitment would ever be called upon, but in October the Government fell, over his attempts to improve relations with Russia, before the Protocol could be ratified. The Conservatives, more cautious, rejected it.

In the Second Labour Government (1929–31) MacDonald's assumptions about the international situation were the same. The success of the London Conference was repeated at the Hague in 1929, where the *Young Plan reduced German reparations and led to the withdrawal of the remaining occupation forces. But there was now much greater emphasis on disarmament. This alone, MacDonald believed, provided true security and was more than ever necessary during a world depression. Visiting the United States in October 1929 – the first Prime Minister to do so – MacDonald gave new life to the naval disarmament negotiations deadlocked at Geneva in 1927. In 1930 he presided over a naval conference in London which limited construction of cruisers, destroyers and submarines. In February 1931 a three-party *Committee of Imperial Defence sub-committee, planning for the approaching *World Disarmament Conference (1932–4), accepted the principle that the level of British armaments should be determined by international agreement.

Although not Foreign Secretary in the Second Labour Government, MacDonald had determined foreign policy and continued to do so, though with steadily failing powers, as Prime Minister of the National Government between 1931 and 1935. His new Conservative partners also welcomed disarmament: 'on foreign politics', MacDonald wrote of *Baldwin (1867–1947), 'his personal views are, as near as no matter, the same as mine'. But such views became increasingly difficult to maintain in the face of events in the Far East and Europe. World opinion, on which MacDonald set such store, was shown to be an empty force, disarmament a liability. Britain was too weak to fight Japan and stop her aggression in Manchuria and China; but she could not do nothing. Protests

without force behind them – the course MacDonald took – alienated Japan and did not satisfy the United States.

While MacDonald could see that Hitler and Nazism represented a new and hideously evil force in international affairs, he did not see what could be done about it. By March 1933 he anticipated the failure of the Disarmament Conference, which had started a year before, but he still made desperate efforts to keep it alive – efforts disliked by many of his Cabinet colleagues and, reflecting MacDonald's longstanding suspicion of France, efforts which involved greater concessions to Germany. Under pressure from *Hankey (1877–1963), MacDonald agreed in March 1935 to publish a White Paper on Defence. Drafted by officials of a CID sub-committee, this blamed Germany for the worsening situation and recommended increased expenditure on the armed services. Acknowledging the League's unreliability and the danger of disarmament, it symbolized the collapse of all MacDonald's hopes. In June he resigned and changed places with Baldwin. His subsequent role as Lord President was not important. He resigned in May 1937 and died in November.

CARLTON, D., *MacDonald versus Henderson: The Foreign Policy of the Second Labour Government*, Macmillan, 1970.

MARQUAND, D., *Ramsay MacDonald*, Jonathan Cape, 1977.

MACMILLAN, (Maurice) Harold, 1st Earl of Stockton (created 1984) (1894–1896). Harold Macmillan was educated at Eton and Balliol College, Oxford. After war service in France he entered politics and was Tory MP for Stockton between 1924 and 1929 and 1931 and 1945, and for Bromley 1945–63. Critical of the National Government's domestic and foreign policies, he did not hold office until 1940, and from 1942 to 1945 was Minister Resident in North Africa and Italy. He was active with R. A. *Butler (1908–82) in reshaping post-war Conservatism, and was Minister of Housing (1951–4) and of Defence (1954–5). As Foreign Secretary from May to December 1955 he had little time to adapt the policies of his predecessor *Eden (1897–1977), and so he supported détente, and the Baghdad Pact's extension to secure Britain's position in the Middle East, while accepting the prevailing view that Britain should remain aloof from the negotiations at Messina, where the Six agreed to form a

*Common Market. Uneasy relations with Eden led to Macmillan's transfer to the Treasury, where he showed a distinct coolness for Eden's handling of the *Suez Crisis (1956). On Eden's resignation in January 1957 it fell to Macmillan as Prime Minister to repair relations with the United States and enhance Britain's diminished standing in the world. The first was done easily enough at the meeting with Eisenhower at Bermuda in 1957; the second, in Macmillan's view, could be achieved through an independent thermonuclear deterrent, but it quickly became clear that the missile technology now required could only be obtained from the United States. Eisenhower offered the Skybolt missile, but American cancellation of the programme in 1962 left Britain without a nuclear defence policy. Macmillan's success in obtaining Polaris from Kennedy through the *Nassau Agreement (1962) was a masterpiece of diplomacy but could not disguise the extent of Britain's dependence on the United States.

The liquidation of empire after 1957 saw the emergence of the new Afro-Asian Commonwealth and its condemnation of South African *apartheid. Macmillan's warnings to the Pretoria government, as an attempt to heal the growing breach, proved unavailing, and South Africa left the Commonwealth in 1961. The Commonwealth, reliance on the United States and economic weakness were evidence of the continuing decline of British power which Macmillan had not been able to arrest. In 1961 he decided that the solution to the problem lay in joining the Common Market, which could revive the economy and achieve British leadership of Europe. Skilfully emphasizing the economic rather than the political significance of the move, he obtained the support of his party and acquiescence of the nation and Commonwealth for British membership – only to be frustrated by De Gaulle's veto on British entry immediately after the Nassau meeting. Macmillan resigned through ill-health in October 1963.

FISHER, N., *Harold Macmillan: A Biography*, Weidenfeld and Nicolson, 1982.
MACMILLAN, H., *Winds of Change, 1914–39*, Macmillan, 1966. *The Blast of War, 1914–39*, Macmillan, 1967. *Tides of Fortune, 1945–55*, Macmillan, 1969. *Riding the Storm, 1956–59*, Macmillan, 1971. *Pointing the Way, 1959–61*, Macmillan, 1972. *At the End of the Day, 1961–3*, Macmillan, 1973.

**Mafeking, Siege of** (1899–1900). The siege of a small town on the Bechuanaland border of the Transvaal from which in 1895 the *Jameson Raid had been launched. The siege was defended by the British Colonel Sir Robert Baden-Powell, later founder of the Boy Scout Movement. He held the town with 700 soldiers and 600 civilians against a Boer force under General Piet Cronje, which was initially 5,000 strong. On 17 May 1900 the siege was relieved by Sir Bryan Mahon's cavalry, an event greeted with immense jubilation in Britain (the celebratory carnival in the streets of London gave rise to a new word, 'mafficking'). Strategically, the siege benefited the British campaign since it tied up forces which would have been more dangerous if fighting a mobile campaign against the British.

**MAHAN, Alfred T.** (1840–1914). US admiral and author of the influential analysis of sea power as the basis of imperial power, *The Influence of Sea Power upon History* (1890) and *The Influence of Sea Power upon the French Revolution* (1892). His analysis of British naval history as an explanation of British world power, with its stress on the interdependence of the commercial and military control of the sea, led to the demand in the United States for a strong navy with overseas bases and colonial possessions. He concluded that British naval supremacy was not permanent and that the United States could establish dominance in the Caribbean and Pacific. He was credited with encouraging the navy race. In Britain his ideas were taken as a vindication of the necessity for Britain to continue to command the seas, while they were also influential in Germany, though Mahan predicted the defeat of the *Central Powers and the surrender of the German navy.
MAHAN, A. T., *The Influence of Sea Power upon History, 1660–1783*, Methuen, 1965.

**MAISKY, Ivan** (1884–1975). Soviet diplomat. In 1925–7 he was assigned to the Soviet embassy in London with the rank of Counsellor. There he acted as a liaison between the Soviet authorities and the more militant elements in the British trade union movement. After a subsequent period of service in Finland and Japan he was appointed Ambassador to Britain in 1932. In this capacity he signed the Anglo-Soviet trade agreement of 1934 and the 1937 pact on naval arms limitation. His ambassadorship coincided with the period of the Soviet search for *collective security against Hitler, the great purges in the Soviet Union, the *Munich Agreement (1939), the *Molotov-Ribbentrop Pact (1939), the Russo-Finnish War and the forging of the Grand Alliance. He was also at this time the Soviet representative on the London-based *Non-Intervention Committee for the *Spanish Civil War (1936–9).

His primary mission in London was to persuade the British to take a firm stand against German aggression and, at all costs, to avert the prospect of the Soviet Union having to stand alone against Germany. His attempts to work for collective security suffered a major reverse with the signing of the Molotov-Ribbentrop Pact. After the outbreak of war he tried to convince the British government that the Soviet Union was in fact pursuing an independent rather than a subservient policy and that it had no military alliance with Berlin. In 1941 he passed on information from Sir Anthony *Eden (1897–1977) on the pending German invasion of the Soviet Union. Later in that year he participated in the first inter-allied conference in London. He was recalled to Moscow in 1943.

MAISKY, I., *Before the Storm*, trs. G. Shelley, Hutchinson, 1944. *Journey into the Past*, trs. F. Holt. Hutchinson, 1962. *Memoirs of a Soviet Ambassador, 1939–43*, trs. A. Rothstein, Hutchinson, 1967.

MALMESBURY, Harris, James Howard, 3rd Earl of (1807–1889). Conservative Foreign Secretary (1852, 1858–9). Malmesbury, owing to the weakness of the Conservative Party in the 1850s, was Foreign Secretary only for two short periods and hence fair judgement of his policies is impossible. Although derided as a mediocrity, he was not lacking in energy and common sense. In 1852 he used his friendship with Louis Napoleon to help build good relations with France and in 1858 he handled the Indian Mutiny with moderation. Over Italy he lacked the Liberals' enthusiasm for the nationalist cause, but worked hard to engineer reform and stability. He sent Lord Cowley to Vienna to mediate between France and Austria and, although unable to prevent the outbreak of war in April 1859, Malmesbury helped to contain the conflict.

MALMESBURY, EARL OF, *Memoirs of an Ex-Minister*, Longmans, 2 vols., 1884.
MCINTIRE, C. T., *England Against the Papacy*, 1858–61, Cambridge University Press, 1983.

**Manchester School.** A group which emerged as an effective national voice in Britain in the 1840s. It took its name from the association of its leaders John *Bright (1811–89) and Richard *Cobden (1804–65) with Lancashire industry and more specifically the Manchester Chamber of Commerce (founded in 1820). In domestic politics they supported the Anti-Corn Law League, advocating ideas which came to dominate the Liberal Party in the mid-nineteenth century – free trade, competition and freedom of contract. The economic ideas of the free interchange of the products of commerce and industry were inextricably connected in their view with the achievement of universal peace. International rivalries and mistrust led to the heavy burdens of taxation on industry and furnished an excuse for protectionism. Free trade was seen as the road to peace – as Cobden stated in 1850: 'I believed free trade would have the tendency to unite mankind in the bonds of peace and it was that more than any economic consideration which actuated me in the struggle for free trade'. The logic of this was a policy of military and political non-intervention abroad and the avoidance of entangling alliances. They advanced the view that foreign policy should be based on moral considerations; imperialism and Palmerstonian gunboat diplomacy were to be eschewed. They linked war with the dominance of an innately belligerent aristocratic caste in society. There was some difference of emphasis between Cobden's appeal for international cooperation and Bright's advocacy of the advantages of *isolationism. The influence of this school of thought can be traced in the Little England Movement and in Liberal and pacifist opposition to the 2nd *Boer War (1899–1902) and *World War I (1914–18).

**Manchurian Crisis** (1931–3). The international crisis precipitated by the Japanese field army's conquest of Manchuria between September 1931 and January 1933 following the assault on the Chinese garrison at Mukden. This led to the establishment of the Japanese puppet state of Manchukuo in March 1932. The attack was justified as retribution for an alleged Chinese attempt to destroy the tracks of the South Manchurian Railway. It brought to a head the growing conflict of Chinese and Japanese nationalism over Manchuria. The Chinese wished to reclaim actual as well as nominal control over Manchuria. The Japanese wanted to preserve their rights and properties in South Manchuria by separating Manchuria from China once and for all. The conflict was also encouraged by the severe economic crisis in Japan.

The *League of Nations urged restraint on both countries and appointed a four-man commission headed by Lord Lytton (see: *Lytton Commission). Its verdict in October 1932 was that both parties were to blame and that there should be Manchurian autonomy under Chinese sovereignty. Therefore, though it was intended to be conciliatory towards Japan, it ruled that her political and military restructuring of Manchuria was unjustified. This was approved in the West, but rejected by Japan, who withdrew from the League on 27 March 1933. Britain, essentially, contented herself with the League resolution of 16 February and 11 March 1932 that members should not recognize changes in territorial status brought about by means contrary to the Covenant and the *Kellogg–Briand Pact (1928).

Britain had in 1926 defined her policy towards Japan as 'giving her no excuse for aggression, while affording her the maximum scope for her economic development'. In fact by the time of the Manchurian Crisis little in the way of any special Anglo-Japanese relationship remained. At the *Ottawa Conference (1932) Britain had accepted proposals for *Imperial Preference in trade with her colonies which adversely affected Japan's trade. The Japanese conquest of Manchuria was a severe blow to the credibility of the League of Nations. It also emphasized the vulnerability and growing powerlessness of the British *Empire in Asia and the Pacific and the increasing dependence of Britain on support from the United States, a weakness further underlined by the announcement of Japan's new order in East Asia in November 1938. Subsequent incidents such as the humiliation of British residents by Japanese soldiers in Tientsin in 1939 and the closing of the Burma Road were clear indications that Britain had lost the power effectively to resist Japanese expansion.

BASSETT, R., *Democracy and Foreign Policy: A Case History, the Sino-Japanese Dispute, 1931–1933*, Longmans, 1952.
HAGGIE, P., *Britannia at Bay: The Defence of the British Empire against Japan, 1931–41*, Oxford University Press, 1981.

THORNE, C., *The Limits of Foreign Policy: The West, the League and the Far Eastern Crisis of 1931–33*, Hamish Hamilton, 1972.

**Mandates.** The orders or commissions issued by the *League of Nations to member nations authorizing them to administer dependent territories which had been confiscated from the defeated countries at the end of *World War I (1914–18) on behalf of the League. Jan Smuts (1870–1957) was responsible for the detailed plans. The Mandates system was included in the Covenant of the League of Nations (Article 23) and was a means of dealing with the Ottoman and German empires. Apart from small adjustments, the colonies were administered by the powers which had captured them. The scheme was, therefore, a compromise between those who wanted to annex the territories outright and others, like President Woodrow Wilson, who had wanted to place them under international administration. The Allied and Associated Powers accordingly allotted them to certain states, Britain, France, Belgium, Australia, New Zealand and South Africa, as 'mandated territories'. These states were to be subject to definite obligations to the League and were to report to the Mandate Commission, a body which did not, however, possess coercive powers. Otherwise they were to exercise all the powers of government over them. The chief conditions were freedom of conscience and religion, prohibition of abuses, banning of fortifications, bases or military training for inhabitants for other than purposes of policing, justice to native inhabitants and equality of economic opportunity for all League of Nations members. Group A mandates were formed out of the former Turkish Middle Eastern provinces north of Arabia. These were intended for early independence, Palestine, Iraq and Transjordan being placed under British mandate. Syria and Lebanon in this category went to France. Group B comprising Germany's colonies in Central Africa, Togoland and the Cameroons were partitioned between Britain and France – Tanganyika was also assigned to Britain. Group C consisted principally of the ex-German Pacific territories such as Samoa; South-West Africa in this group was entrusted to South Africa. It was anticipated that the colonies in groups B and C would enjoy longer administration as mandates because of their relative backwardness. In 1945 the Mandate system was superseded by the

Trusteeship system of the *United Nations (see: *Trust Territories). South Africa refused this new arrangement and insisted on maintaining her own position as mandate power in South-West Africa after *World War II (1939–45).

BENTWICH, N., *The Mandates System*, Longmans, 1930.

HALL, H. D., 'The British Commonwealth and the Founding of the League Mandate System', in BOURNE, K. and WATT, D. C., eds., *Studies in International History: Essays presented to W. Norton Medlicott*, Longmans, 1967.

LOUIS, W. R., *Great Britain and Germany's Lost Colonies*, Clarendon Press, Oxford, 1967.

**Marne, Battles of the** (1914, 1918). The Marne represented the point of greatest penetration by the Germans in France. The first battle lasted from 5 to 19 September 1914, when the French and the British Expeditionary Force under General Joffre counter-attacked the German armies of Kluck and Bülow. The so-called 'miracle of the Marne' meant the failure of the *Schlieffen Plan, ending Germany's hope of a rapid victory. But Allied advance was also checked and the war of movement gave way to the stalemate of trench warfare. The second battle was Ludendorff's last offensive, the Germans being held at bay by a Franco-American force under Marshal Foch. This Allied counter-offensive marked the beginning of a general advance that forced Germany to sue for peace, with the strategic advantage passing to the Allies.

**Marshall Plan** (1947–1952). Otherwise known as the European Recovery Programme. It was publicly proposed by the American Secretary of State George Marshall on 5 June 1947 and was funded by the United States, being administered through the Organization for European Economic Co-operation (OEEC). This massive foreign aid programme (1948–52), amounting to 17 billion dollars, 90 per cent of which was in non-repayable loans, sustained the economic recovery of Western Europe after *World War II (1939–45), resolving the acute problem of the 'dollar gap'. By 1951 all recipients of the aid had raised their production capacities beyond prewar levels.

It was intended to encourage European economic collaboration and to contain the spread of Communism (see: *containment). It was also offered to the Soviet Bloc, though Stalin regarded it with the utmost suspicion as a means of strengthening anti-Communist forces in Europe, and the Soviet Foreign Minister Molotov was instructed to reject it. In the first 15 months the aid was spent almost exclusively on non-military items but, following the intensification of the *Cold War with the *Berlin Blockade (1949), it was increasingly directed to military purposes. Though some historians have advanced the view that the Marshall Plan was primarily motivated by United States zeal for the *Open Door Policy, the resulting benefits for American exports, through a strengthened Western European economy, were more of a consequence than an aim. Following the *Truman Doctrine (1947), it served to deepen the East–West division. In 1949 the Soviet Union emphasized this by setting up COMECON. The major significance of Marshall Aid was that it acted as a dramatic stimulant to the reviving Western European economies, particularly that of West Germany.

GIMBEL, J., *The Origins of the Marshall Plan*, Stanford University Press, Stanford, California, 1976.

MILWARD, A. S., *The Reconstruction of Western Europe*, Methuen, 1984.

**Massive Retaliation.** A doctrine of military and international relations first enunciated by the American Secretary of State John Foster Dulles in 1954. Taken literally, it meant the threat to unleash the full thermonuclear force of the United States in retaliation against communist aggression anywhere in the world, and it suggested that the United States would rely on the deterrent power of the Bomb as the main arm of foreign policy in East–West relations. It was argued that the United States should not meet communist aggression locally but rather 'by means and at places of our own choosing'. Massive retaliation was intended to ensure that the West negotiated from a position of strength and that communist aggression would be discouraged by an awareness of its quite unacceptable potential cost. It was a doctrine which on the one hand satisfied Republican demands for a 'hard line' towards the Soviet Union and (since this was anticipated to be cheaper than increased reliance on conventional arms and armies) on the other the demand for balanced budgets. Its critics argued that the rhetoric of massive retaliation limited foreign policy options and in fact Dulles soon took pains to qualify the doctrine by pointing out that local wars, short of nuclear war, were an option. It rapidly lost whatever credibility and efficacy it had when in the later 1950s the Soviet Union developed the capability to strike not only Western Europe but the United States as well. Strategists on both sides of the Atlantic then began to emphasize the need for a graduated deterrence policy with increased flexibility, to avoid the stark choice of nuclear surrender or suicide.

**Mediation.** A diplomatic (rather than legal) procedure for resolving peacefully a dispute in which a third party assists the disputants by producing suggestions for a compromise, with a view to reconciling opposed claims. Mediation may be requested by the parties in conflict or may be offered by the mediator. In international practice disputants are not entitled to regard an offer of mediation as a hostile act, nor are they obliged to accept an unsolicited offer of mediation.

**Mediterranean Agreement, 1st** (1887). Between Britain and Italy, signed on 12 February 1887 and adhered to by Austria and Spain. The agreement took the form of an exchange of notes (Anglo-Italian, Anglo-Austrian and Anglo-Spanish) acceded to by Germany. The German Chancellor, Bismarck, had encouraged the combination, exploiting the Anglo-French tension over Egypt. The notes upheld the status quo in the Mediterranean, including the Aegean and Adriatic seas and the Black Sea. Italy undertook to support British policy in Egypt and Britain the Italian policy in North Africa. The Anglo-Austrian note emphasized the community of interst of the two powers in the Near East. Spain promised not to make an agreement with France regarding North Africa which would be aimed at Italy, Austria or Germany. Britain refused to commit herself to any specific future action but the overall effect of this agreement, which was mainly directed against France, was to provide a basis for common action in the event of any disturbance to the status quo in the Mediterranean.

LOWE, C. J., *Salisbury and the Mediterranean, 1886–96*, Routledge, 1965.

**Mediterranean Agreement, 2nd** (1887). Otherwise known as the Near Eastern Entente. It was signed on 12 December 1887 by Britain, Austria and Italy, the German Chancellor Bismarck having refused conspicuously to participate in it. It restated the principle of the status quo in the Near East and the need to keep Turkey free from foreign domination. Turkey was not to cede its rights in Bulgaria to any other power nor allow occupation of that country by another power. Neither was it to give up any rights in the Straits (see: *Straits Question) or in Asia Minor. If it resisted encroachment the three contracting powers were to agree measures to support it. If it failed to resist, the three powers would consider themselves justified, jointly or separately, in the provisional occupation of such Turkish territory as was thought necessary to secure respect for the treaty. In substance this agreement was anti-Russian. Both it and the *1st Mediterranean Agreement were abandoned after 1892. One of their effects was to encourage Franco-Russian rapprochement.

LOWE, C. J., *Salisbury and the Mediterranean, 1886–96*, Routledge, 1965.

**Mehemet Ali Crises,** 1831–1833 and 1839–1841

(1) Mehemet Ali, Pasha of Egypt, who had carried through extensive reforms and modernization of Egypt and was one of the ablest rulers of his age, launched a war through his son Ibrahim Pasha against the Sultan Mahmud II in November 1831. He had for some time wanted to acquire the pashaliks of Syria, claimed he had not been compensated properly for his part in the suppression of the Greeks during the *Greek War of Independence (1821–9) and was, in any case, increasingly unwilling to accept control by the Sultan.

By 1833 the rebel forces were advancing deep into Asia Minor and it seemed only a matter of time before they would take Constantinople and the Straits. Mahmud appealed to the British Government to rescue him, but she was unable to intervene, her navy at the time being engaged in a blockade to force the King of Holland to accept Belgian independence; and in supporting Queen Maria of Portugal against her uncle Dom Miguel. Britain also had other reasons for hesitation. She was sceptical of the prospects of the Ottoman Empire at this stage and was unwilling openly to collaborate with Austria. France, for her part, had been very considerably involved in the development of Egypt since Napoleon I's time and favoured Mehemet Ali. *Palmerston (1784–1865) was later greatly to regret the British refusal to help the Sultan. Its consequence was that Mahmud turned to Turkey's traditional enemy Russia for support.

By the end of April 1833 14,000 Russian troops had landed at Constantinople and a formal alliance was concluded between the powers (see: *Unkiar-Skelessi Treaty (1833) ). While this saved the Sultan, it gave Russia unprecedented influence over the Ottoman Empire and aroused grave apprehension in British governing circles.

(2) The second crisis was provoked by the Sultan's retributive attack on Mehemet Ali's forces in Syria in 1839. Again, the Sultan's forces were defeated. Russia this time invited the cooperation of Britain. If Britain would agree to the closure of the Straits in wartime, Russia promised not to renew the Unkiar–Skelessi Treaty, a bargain which Palmerston was willing to accept. The difficulty in the second Mehemet Ali crisis was the independent stance of France. Thiers, the French Premier, was willing to gamble on war rather than coerce Mehemet Ali. In July 1840 Palmerston signed a treaty with the Eastern Powers endorsing the previous understanding with Russia and presented Mehemet Ali with an ultimatum to accept the terms. When he refused to capitulate, British naval and military forces drove the Egyptians out of Syria. France climbed down, Thiers being replaced by Guizot, and she signed the *Straits Convention (1841), which stipulated that the Straits must be closed to foreign warships while Turkey was at peace. Mehemet Ali was left with Egypt as a hereditary pashalik.

ANDERSON, M. S., *The Eastern Question, 1774–1923*, Macmillan, 1966.

CLAYTON, G. D., *Britain and the Eastern Question: Missolonghi to Gallipoli*, Hodder and Stoughton, 1971.

**MELBOURNE**, William Lamb, Viscount (1779–1848). Whig Prime Minister 1834, 1835–41. Melbourne, conservative in views and easy-going in manner, was seldom active in foreign affairs, although he was not uninterested in them. He generally allowed a free rein to his obstreperous Foreign Secretary, Lord *Palmerston (1784–1865), while endeavouring in private to restrain his worst extravagances. Melbourne was anxious to avoid any steps which might imperil his government by antagonizing the hostile Tory majority in the House of Lords and recognized that, though public opinion might cheer nationalistic posturing it would be much less content if the country was driven to fortify Palmerston's rash words with money or military action. Matters

came to a head in 1840 when Palmerston's insistence on supporting the Sultan against *Mehemet Ali in the face of French opposition led to serious divisions in the Cabinet and excited complaints from the Queen. Melbourne's tact and skill in patient procrastination eventually enabled him to defuse the situation.

CECIL, LORD DAVID, *Melbourne*, Constable, 1965.

ZIEGLER, P., *Melbourne*, Collins, 1976.

**Mers-El-Kébir** (1940). The naval base on the Gulf of Oran where the Royal Navy on 3 July sank the French Fleet, causing considerable loss of life. With the news of the Franco-German armistice of June 1940 the British War Cabinet resolved not to allow the French Fleet to fall into the hands of the Axis powers. *Churchill (1874–1965) was willing to take ruthless decisions in order to demonstrate his unflinching defiance of Hitler at this critical time. Vice-Admiral Sir James Somerville and Force H confronted French Admiral Marcel Gensoul with a choice: the French either sail with the British, turn their ships over to them, take them to the West Indies for the duration of the war, or sink them. Somerville failed to make clear to the French the alternative of sailing them to American waters. When Gensoul refused to comply with these options the British so destroyed and damaged his fleet as to render it unusable against them. France broke off diplomatic relations, though she did not declare war. Churchill declared the action to be a 'hateful decision, the most unnatural and painful in which I have ever been concerned'. The necessity of the Oran action was subsequently questioned when the French sank their own remaining ships on the German entry into unoccupied France in November 1942.

GATES, E. M., *End of the Affair. The Collapse of the Anglo-French Alliance, 1939–40*, University of California, Berkeley, 1981.

THOMAS, R. T., *Britain and Vichy – The Dilemma of Anglo-French Relations 1940–42*, Macmillan, 1979.

**Metro-Vickers Case** (1933). The trial of six British engineers and 12 Soviet citizens on charges of espionage and sabotage. The engineers were employed by Metropolitan-Vickers Electrical Company, a British firm which the Soviet government had contracted to furnish equipment and to supervise electric power stations. They were arrested in March 1933 and the case attracted international attention. The British government recalled their ambassador, broke off negotiations on a new Anglo-Soviet trade agreement and imposed an embargo on the majority of Soviet imports. Two of the British engineers were sentenced to imprisonment in April; in July their sentences were mitigated to expulsion from the Soviet Union. Accordingly, the British embargo was rescinded and the two countries resumed negotiations on a new trade agreement. The affair contributed to a sharp deterioration in Anglo-Soviet relations, which were in any case poor. The charges appear to have been contrived for domestic political purposes with the presumed aim of blaming Soviet economic failures on foreign conspirators and native enemies of the revolution.

LAMMERS, D. N., 'The engineers' trial (Moscow, 1933) and Anglo-Soviet relations', *South Atlantic Quarterly*, 62, 1963, pp. 256–67.

OWEN, G. L., 'The Metro-Vickers crisis: Anglo-Soviet relations between trade agreements, 1932–34', *Slavonic and East European Review*, 49, 1971, pp. 92–112.

**MILNER**, Alfred, created Viscount Milner (1854–1925). Milner was born and received his schooling in Germany before having a brilliant university career at Balliol College, Oxford. He contemplated becoming a barrister and also worked as a journalist but first made his mark between 1890 and 1892 when he was in charge of Egyptian finances and, at the end of his tour of duty, wrote an able and influential justification of the British role in Egypt. Having served as Chairman of the Board of Inland Revenue, in 1897 he was appointed by Joseph *Chamberlain (1836–1914) British High Commissioner in South Africa. He went out with an open mind, but gradually became convinced that, unless the Boer republics were prepared to reform their treatment of the *Uitlanders, war was inevitable. His views were made clear in a speech at Graaf Reinet on 2 March 1898 and, after talks with Kruger, President of the Transvaal, broke down in June 1899, the *Boer War (1899–1902) began that October. Peace was restored in 1902 and Milner remained as Governor of the Transvaal and the Orange River Colony, organizing much essential reconstruction work. However, he was strongly criticized for permitting the use of imported Chinese labour in the mines, a scandal which

contributed to the defeat of the Unionists in the General Election of 1906.

Milner returned to England in 1905 and began a career in domestic politics, upholding strongly imperialistic views and calling for national service and Tariff Reform. After war broke out in 1914 he was a prominent opponent of the Asquith Government and when it fell in December 1916 Milner himself took office in the Lloyd George War Cabinet, where he had a strong influence on the Prime Minister. He was Secretary of State for War from April 1918 and aroused controversy by his suggestion that Germany should not be weakened too much by the peace settlement in order that she might remain as a bulwark against Russian expansion. Early in 1919 Milner moved to the Colonial Office, where he remained until 1921, but he was now ageing and lacked the energy to push through the imperialist policies he had advocated before the war. In 1920 he participated in the production of a report on Egypt which advocated the regulation of Anglo-Egyptian relations by treaty.

GOLLIN, A. M., *Proconsul in Politics*, Blond, 1964.

HEADLAM, C. , ed., *The Milner Papers 1879–1905*, 2 vols., Cassell, 1931–3.

PORTER, A. N., *The South African War: Joseph Chamberlain and the Diplomacy of Imperialism, 1895–99*, Manchester University Press, 1980.

**Ministry of Defence.** The Ministry of Defence was created in January 1947 as a small department responsible for co-ordination between the three armed services. The extent to which defence policy had been the outcome of inter-service rivalry was to be reduced by giving it central direction. The Defence Minister sat in the Cabinet and the service ministers ceased to do so. But the objective of unified control proved hard to achieve, and in 1958 the Defence Minister's powers were extended so that all major matters of defence policy came under his supervision. The service ministries remained, however, and their ministers were still responsible for the administration of their own forces. Even this failed to produce the degree of control and coherence in policy formulation desired by politicians increasingly concerned to maximize economy, and in 1964 the service ministries were abolished and reduced in status to service boards with ministers of state who were further downgraded to under-secretaries of state in 1967. Minor re-organizations have been carried out since. The vast size of his department and the complexity of defence policy formulation pose formidable challenges to any Secretary of State for Defence, but at least he now possesses the authority and machinery to strike a correct balance between the commitments, resources and roles of the services.

BAYLIS, J., *Anglo-American Defence Relations, 1939–84*, 2nd ed. Macmillan, 1984.

**Minorities Treaties.** The practice of making treaty stipulations which guarantee the rights of minority populations in states has existed since the sixteenth century. It has been particularly prevalent in the present century. As part of the peace settlements of 1919–20, for instance, most Central and Eastern European countries were required to sign treaties or make declarations protecting the rights of their minorities. The treaties guaranteed by the *League of Nations promised racial minorities equal treatment before the law, religious freedom and the right to use their respective languages. Such treaties have frequently proved unenforceable.

**Molotov–Ribbentrop Pact** (1939). The non-aggression treaty signed by the Soviet and Nazi foreign ministers on 24 August 1939. It was specified to last for ten years. Its secret protocol divided Eastern Europe into Russian and German spheres of influence. These were designated by a line following the northern frontier of Lithuania and the *Curzon Line for Poland, which foreshadowed the partition of Poland that took place in September 1939. In military terms the pact offered Germany a temporary security to the east. The Soviet Union welcomed it as guaranteeing a period of peace while she further strengthened herself. It reflected the mutual failure of the Western Powers, Britain and France, and the Soviet Union to achieve a rapprochement in the face of the Nazi threat. It was succeeded by several Russo-German economic agreements in 1940–1. Hitler reneged on the pact, which excluded a war on two fronts, conclusively on 22 July 1941 when he launched Operation Barbarossa.

**Monroe Doctrine** (1823). A fundamental declaration of United States foreign policy announced by President Monroe in his message to Congress on 2 December 1823 and stated in a series of documents between 1817 and 1823.

Claiming that the political system of the Americas was essentially different from that of Europe, it argued that the European nations should not set up new colonies in the Western Hemisphere, that they should not intervene in the affairs of the independent nations of that region and that any attempt by European powers to increase their influence there would be regarded as a threat to peace and security. Monroe also undertook that the United States would not interfere in European affairs or with the existing European colonies.

In part this message was directed against the decree of Tsar Alexander I which had given his Russian subjects exclusive trading rights along the northwest coast of North America to 51 degrees north latitude. It also reflected the growing concern of the President over the intentions of the European powers. During 1823 it had been rumoured that a Franco-Spanish entente (following the French invasion of Spain to restore the authority of King Ferdinand VII) might send an expeditionary force to reimpose Spanish rule over the newly independent Spanish American states, or bring them under French dominion. In August the British Foreign Secretary George *Canning (1770–1827) had asked the American Minister in London whether the United States would be willing to join England in warning France to stay out of the Western Hemisphere. This suggestion was supported by Jefferson and Madison, but the American Secretary of State John Quincy Adams persuaded Monroe to issue a unilateral statement. He also encouraged Monroe to refrain from pledging United States support for Greek revolutionaries seeking independence from Ottoman rule, and instead, reaffirming Washington's policy, to promise that the United States would remain aloof from purely European affairs. He additionally prevented the inclusion of a pledge that the United States would not acquire new territory.

While, therefore, the Monroe Doctrine was intended as a barrier to European intervention, it was subsequently used as a justification for United States intervention in the Western Hemisphere. The significance of the doctrine was not immediately appreciated. Initial respect for it sprang primarily from the fact that the other European powers knew that Britain could use its naval mastery to protect Latin America, an area with which she enjoyed extensive, and growing, commercial ties.

Already, a couple of months before the statement, Canning had induced the French in the *Polignac Memorandum to disclaim any intention of invading the Spanish colonies. The Monroe Doctrine did not become an accepted part of international law, for it was never formally agreed to by the other powers. Nor did it end European influence in the Western Hemisphere. In 1850 the *Clayton–Bulwer Treaty between Britain and the United States recognized the former's presence in Central America.

A number of corollaries were subsequently attached to the doctrine. In 1845 President Polk declared that if any North American people desired to join the United States the matter would be one for them and the United States to determine 'without any further interposition'. He was here alluding to British and French efforts to prevent the recent annexation of Texas, to the dispute with Britain over Oregon and to suspicions that Britain might be bent on thwarting American ambitions in California. He also announced the opposition of the United States to the cession of any territory in North America to a European power. In the *Hay–Pauncefote Treaty (1901) Britain accepted an interpretation of the doctrine which precluded any country other than the United States from controlling the projected trans-isthmian canal. The Roosevelt Corollary (1904) notably transformed the Doctrine from a warning against European intervention into a justification for United States interference in Central and South America, describing the United States as 'an international police power' for the Americas. Since *World War II (1939–45) the Monroe Doctrine has assumed a new ideological significance, with the determination of the United States to protect Central and South America from the spread of Communist influence.

BEMIS, S. F., *John Quincy Adams and the Foundations of American Foreign Policy*, A. Knopf, New York, 1949.
MAY, E. R., *The Making of the Monroe Doctrine*, Harvard University Press, Cambridge, Mass., 1975.
PERKINS, D., *The Monroe Doctrine, 1823–26*, Harvard Historical Studies, Cambridge, Mass., 1927.

**MONTGOMERY,** Bernard Law, Viscount Montgomery of Alamein (1887–1976). Montgomery fought in *World War I (1914–18), including in the Battle of the *Somme (1916). Between the wars he saw service both in India and Palestine. In 1939 he commanded the Third Division of the *British Expeditionary Force. When General Gott was killed in 1942, Montgomery was appointed to succeed him as commander of the Eighth Army in the Western Desert. After careful preparation Montgomery launched the counter-attack on Rommel's Afrika Korps and won the crucial Battle of El *Alamein (1942). Montgomery went on to command the Eighth Army in the Allied invasion of Sicily and southern Italy, before returning to England to prepare Allied forces for *D-Day (1944). For the early part of Operation Overlord he was in charge of all land forces. However, his strategic conceptions did not always tie in with those of the Americans, including those of the Supreme Allied Commander, Eisenhower. His idea, for instance, for a direct thrust to Berlin was rejected. But he was made commander of 21 Army Group and in that capacity took the German surrender on Luneburg Heath. After the war he served as Commander-in-Chief of British forces in Germany, and in the senior military post of Chief of the Imperial General Staff. He retired in 1958 after serving as Deputy Supreme Allied Commander (Europe) in *NATO. His generalship, while popular in wartime, has come under more critical scrutiny in recent years.

CHALFONT, A. J., *Montgomery of Alamein*, Weidenfeld and Nicolson, 1976.
MONTGOMERY, VISCOUNT, *The Path to Leadership*, Collins, 1976.

**Montreux Convention** (1936). Signed with Turkey by Britain, France, Russia and Rumania on 20 July. It restored to the Turks the right to fortify the *Dardanelles, which had been demilitarized under the Treaty of *Lausanne (1923). It also set out new regulations under which warships of countries other than Turkey could enter the Black Sea in peacetime, during threat of war and wartime itself, along with similar regulations for the passage of Soviet warships into the Mediterranean. The Germans were not invited to participate and felt disadvantaged by its terms. The convention was the only important offer by a revisionist power to change the post-war settlement by peaceful means. The fact that the Turkish request came so soon after the remilitarization of the *Rhineland (March 1936) influenced the British decision to support her claim for revision. The demands made by Russia at the conference signified a revival of the *Eastern Question in the form of Russian pressure upon Turkey to dominate the Black Sea in a way which Britain considered prejudicial to her interests, and which made Allied aid to Rumania impossible when war broke out in 1939.

EVANS, S. F., *The Slow Rapprochement: Britain and Turkey in the Age of Kemal Ataturk, 1919–38*, Eothen, 1982.

**Moroccan Crises** (1905, 1911).
(1) At the beginning of the twentieth century Morocco was a focus of international rivalry. France was the dominant foreign presence and Britain accorded this role recognition in the *Anglo-French Entente (1904). While France publicly gave assurances that she supported the *Open Door principle she secretly arranged in agreements with Britain and Spain for the eventual partition of Morocco. The first crisis was precipitated when Kaiser William II landed at Tangier on 31 March 1905, proclaiming support for Moroccan independence and integrity.

Germany had a growing commercial interest there as well as burgeoning global ambitions (see: *Weltpolitik*). Her Chancellor, Bülow, and the Foreign Minister, Holstein had decided to test the strength of the Anglo-French Entente. The time seemed particularly propitious for this because of the defeats of Russia, France's ally, in the Russo-Japanese War (1904–5). The German government appeared to calculate that Britain would not be willing to go to war to uphold French colonial interests.

At first France declined the German suggestion of an international conference and the crisis continued through the summer and autumn. In the end a conference was held at *Algeciras (1906), by which time France had assured herself of British and American support. The outcome was a diplomatic defeat for Germany. The Anglo-French relationship was strengthened, not destroyed, and the crisis led to the *Anglo-French Military Conversations from 1906.

(2) The second Moroccan crisis followed the despatch by the Kaiser of the gunboat *Panther* to Agadir, a port on the Atlantic coast of Morocco, with the claim that he was protecting German interests. It was at once perceived by Britain and France as an attempt to weaken the Anglo-French Entente. It followed the French advance on Fez and German dissatisfaction with the working of the Franco-German

Morocco agreement of February 1909. Germany offered France control in Morocco, but in return for the whole of the French Congo, terms quite unacceptable to France.

The British, already very concerned at the growing naval dominance of Germany (see: *Anglo-German Navy Race) were alarmed that Germany might wish to establish a naval base close to *Gibraltar. On 21 July 1911, in the Mansion House speech, *Lloyd George (1863–1945), the Chancellor of the Exchequer, earlier considered as one of the ministers more favourably disposed towards Germany, caused a major stir by warning Germany. 'If a situation were to be forced upon us', he said, 'in which peace could only be preserved by the surrender of the great and beneficent position Britain has won by centuries of heroism and achievement, by allowing Britain to be treated, where her interests were vitally affected, as if she were of no account in the Cabinet of Nations, then I say emphatically that peace at that price would be a humiliation intolerable for a great country like ours to endure.'

Germany was enraged, but lowered her demands. As Britain made preparations for the contingency of war, France and Germany negotiated, producing a final agreement on 4 November which represented a substantial German climb-down. Germany conceded the French a free hand in Morocco and undertook not to oppose a French protectorate there. In return France ceded a small tract of the Congo connecting the German Cameroons with the Congo and Ubangi rivers. For the first time during this crisis arrangements were made to provide British troops for the French front in the event of war. Afterwards the Prime Minister, *Asquith (1852–1928) and the Foreign Secretary, *Grey (1862–1933) encouraged increased collaboration between British and French military and naval forces in which they now had the enthusiastic support, among others, of the new First Lord of the Admiralty, Winston *Churchill (1874–1965).

KENNEDY, P. M., *The Rise of the Anglo-German Antagonism, 1860–1914*, Allen and Unwin, 1980.

ROBBINS, K. G., *Sir Edward Grey*, Cassell, 1971.

STEINER, Z. S., *Britain and the Origins of the First World War*, Macmillan, 1977.

**MORRISON**, Herbert Stanley. Baron Morrison of Lambeth, (created 1959), (1888–1965). Morrison was educated at elementary school and worked as a shop assistant before entering Labour politics. He was Labour Member of Parliament for Hackney South (1923–4, 1929–31, 1935–45), for East Lewisham (1945–51) and South Lewisham (1951–9); and held office as Minister for Transport (1929–31), of Supply (1940) and Home Secretary (1940–5), and as Lord President and Leader of the Commons (1945–51). He was Foreign Secretary from March to October 1951. Lacking previous experience of foreign affairs, he wholly failed to appreciate their complexity or the time they required for study. Two of his seven months in office were spent away from London during major disputes with Egypt and Iran, where his hawkishness put him at odds with his Cabinet and Parliamentary colleagues. The same was true in the Far East, where he agreed to the extension of the Korean War by the United States; and in Europe where, after initial opposition, he came to support the Pleven Plan and the European Defence Community, a scheme which failed to materialize when the French Assembly refused to ratify it. Morrison's conduct of foreign affairs was widely recognized as inept and destroyed his hopes of succeeding *Attlee (1883–1967). He remained as Deputy Leader of the Labour Party (1951–5), retiring from politics in 1959.

MORRISON, H. S., *Herbert Morrison: An Autobiography by Lord Morrison of Lambeth*, Odhams, 1960.

SHLAIM, A., JONES, P. and SAINSBURY, K., *British Foreign Secretaries since 1945*, David and Charles, 1977.

**MOSLEY,** Sir Oswald Ernald (1896–1980). Politician and creator of the British Union of Fascists. In 1918, after military training and war service, he became Conservative MP for Harrow. In 1922, after disagreeing with his party over military expenditure and Irish affairs, he joined the opposition and was returned as Independent in the election of that year. In 1924 he joined the Labour Party and in 1926 was elected as Labour MP for Smethwick. In the Second Labour Government he became Chancellor of the Duchy of Lancaster with special responsibilities for the problem of unemployment. He advanced proposals for the direction of industry, control of foreign trade, and public works which conflicted with the orthodox financial policies of the Chancellor of the Exchequer, Snowden, and were rejected. In 1930 he accordingly resigned and, in the following year, launched the New Party. All of his candidates were defeated in the election of that year.

He became dissatisfied with the parliamentary system and, after a visit to Fascist Italy in 1932, set up the British Fascist Movement, among other things advocating a programme of economic reconstruction within an imperial framework. Originally based on the Italian model, from 1936 the Fascist movement in Britain started to take more inspiration from Nazi Germany than it did from Italy. From that time Mosley was avowedly pro-Nazi and mounted a peace campaign which continued after *World War II had started in September 1939. From 1940, for three years he and his wife were detained under Regulation 18B. This was not on grounds of treason, for Mosley called for the defence of the country if invaded. But they were preaching anti-war propaganda and anti-semitism and their views and activities at a time of grave national crisis were regarded as prejudicial to national morale.

After the war Mosley set out to justify his actions in *My Answer* (1946) and later, in 1968, in his autobiography. From 1947 until 1966 he led the Union Movement, aiming at European unity based on racial ideas, with the slogan 'Europe a Nation'. He was an early advocate of British participation in an economically united Europe.

GRIFFITHS, R., *Fellow Travellers of the Right: British Enthusiasts for Nazi Germany (1933–39)*, Oxford University Press, 1980.

MOSLEY, SIR O., *My Life*, Nelson, 1968.

MOSLEY, LADY D., *A Life of Contrasts*, Hamish Hamilton, 1977.

SKIDELSKY, R., *Oswald Mosley*, Macmillan, 1975.

**Most-Favoured-Nation Principle.** A clause frequently incorporated in bilateral trade agreements. It means that one, or both, signatories will have the same rights and privileges in the application of import and export duties and other trade regulations as accorded to any other treaty partner, thereby equalizing competition. The intention is not to make any single nation 'more favoured' commercially than any other, but equal treatment for all states. By ensuring past and future concessions to all contracting states, the clause encourages multilateralism in trade. In this way an otherwise discriminatory series of bilateral trade agreements can be turned into an outward-looking arrangement aimed at the general reduction of trade barriers. Before *World War I (1914–18) the Most-Favoured-Nation Principle led to a difference of opinion between Britain and the United States. Britain argued that the insertion of such a clause was unconditional in its implications, whereas the United States claimed it was conditional and did not include special conditions given to a nation. In 1923 the United States signalled acceptance of the British view.

**Munich Agreement** (1938). Concluded on 29–30 September 1938 between Britain, France, Italy and Germany, the Munich Agreement forced Czechoslovakia to cede the *Sudetenland, an area containing three-and-a-quarter million ethnic Germans, to Nazi Germany. It determined that the evacuation by stages of the districts claimed should be accomplished by 10 October 1938.

The background to this capitulation was Hitler's threat to go to war and the marked tension between the two countries since the spring of 1938 following the *Anschluss. The British Prime Minister Neville *Chamberlain (1869–1940) had made two earlier appeasing visits to Berchtesgaden (16 September) and Godesberg (22–24). The Munich Conference was convened on Mussolini's initiative, the proposals advanced to it having been drafted for him by the German Foreign Office. Neither Czechoslovakia nor the Soviet Union was represented. In an effort to avert war Britain and France had already persuaded the Czechs to transfer to Germany all territory in which more than half of the population were German-speaking. At Godesberg Hitler had declared that this was no longer adequate. At Munich Czechoslovakia had also to promise cessions of territory to Poland and Hungary. Once their minority populations had been ceded it was stipulated that Britain and France joined by Germany and Italy would guarantee the remainder of the Czech state. In fact this guarantee was never fulfilled. The promised plebiscites were not held in the disputed areas and within six months (on 13 March 1939) German troops occupied Prague and Czechoslovakia ceased to be an independent state, in spite of Hitler's avowal at Munich that he had no further territorial claims. The Munich concession had cost the Czechs one-third of their territory and population and it was immediately apparent that it had undermined the country's defensive and political viability. The Munich Agreement was accompanied by an Anglo-German pact in which the two powers agreed to renounce war as a means of settling their mutual disagreements.

Munich, which has entered the English language as a synonym for cowardly capitulation, was greeted with widespread relief by the British people, though it invited some prominent dissent. The best-known opponent was Winston *Churchill (1874–1965), who pronounced it 'a disaster of the first magnitude'. Duff *Cooper (1890–1954), First Lord of the Admiralty, resigned. It continues to be a controversial agreement. Chamberlain was not as gullible as his critics liked to make out. There was advantage, perhaps, in allowing Hitler further to discredit himself before world opinion. The attitude of the United States in particular in any war with Germany would be crucial. Munich gave Britain and France a further 12 months of rearmament. On the other hand it clearly encouraged Stalin in his distrust of the West's willingness to take an effective stand against the Nazi dictator, thereby leading him on to make his own arrangement with Germany (see: *Molotov–Ribbentrop Pact (1939) ). Moreover, Germany too was better prepared for war a year later.

BRÜGEL, J. W., *Czechoslovakia before Munich: The German Minority Problem and British Appeasement Policy*, Cambridge University Press, 1973.

DOUGLAS, R., *In the Year of Munich*, Macmillan, 1977.

TAYLOR, T., *Munich: The Price of Peace*, Doubleday, New York, 1979.

THORNE, C., *The Approach of War, 1937–39*, Macmillan, 1967.

**Mutual Assistance, Draft Treaty of** (1923). An unsuccessful attempt to strengthen the authority of the *League of Nations as a peace-keeping body by reconciling the requirements of French security against Germany with the British desire for general disarmament. The original submission was made in 1922 to the 3rd Assembly by the British representative Lord Robert *Cecil (1864–1958). It stipulated that each signatory power – provided it had reduced its level of armaments according to the general plan prescribed – would be entitled to immediate support against aggression from any other signatories in the same continent. The consequent proposed treaty was submitted in September 1923. It empowered the Council to name the aggressor in a conflict, to decree economic sanctions and to determine the military contributions of the signatory powers (though military action was not required by a power on another continent). The 4th Assembly did not accept these proposals. Only France proved wholeheartedly in favour. Britain, partly in response to pressure from the Empire, rejected the plan on 5 July 1924. She objected to the linking of proposals for disarmament with contingency preparations for armed action and was opposed to the idea of accepting a military commitment without the closest definition of the precise circumstances that might require it. Canada, to give an example of Dominion resistance to the treaty, had no wish to assume any obligation to wage war on the United States, or to impose economic sanctions against the neighbour on whom her economy so heavily depended. British rejection illustrates the role of imperial ties in British foreign policy and the extent to which the Dominions had gained *de facto* control over their own foreign policies since 1918 – something formally recognized in the *Statute of Westminster (1931).

MARKS, S., *The Illusion of Peace: International Relations in Europe 1918–33*, Macmillan, 1976.

ORDE, A., *Great Britain and International Security, 1920–26*, Royal Historical Society, 1977.

# -N-

**Nanking, Treaty of** (1842). Signed on 29 August 1842, this agreement ended the *Opium War (1839–42) between Britain and China. *Hong Kong was ceded to Britain and four further ports – Amoy, Foochow, Ningpo and Shanghai – were licensed for trade, consuls being recognized in each. Whereas, previously, British merchants had been confined to Canton and had no diplomatic representation, now British nationals acquired the legal status of *extraterritoriality. At the same time Shanghai quickly came to rival Canton in commerce. The treaty was regarded by China as the first of the 'unequal treaties' and its terms led to much subsequent friction. It heralded a considerable and growing Western influence over China – similar treaties were negotiated by France and the United States with China in 1844.

**Nassau Agreement** (1962). The result of discussions between Harold Macmillan (1894–1986) and President Kennedy in the Bahamas. The agreement was announced on 18 December 1962. This followed the British abandonment of their own air-to-ground missile project, 'Blue Streak' and the refusal of the United States to continue with their own air-to-ground 'Skybolt' programme. Britain had hoped to acquire 'Skybolt' and was now confronted with the loss of an 'independent' nuclear deterrent.

At this meeting Macmillan emphasized the crucial importance of Anglo-American collaboration and warned Kennedy of the likely wave of anti-Americanism in Britain if the United States was seen to be depriving Britain of her deterrent. He also hinted that the Conservative Government could fall on this issue and be replaced by one of neutralist inclination (see: *neutralism). At the same time, leading American newspapers reprimanded Kennedy for not showing greater concern for America's closest ally. The Nassau Agreement was a compromise. The United States promised to provide Britain with Polaris missiles (without warheads) for Royal Navy submarines normally operating under *NATO command. It was specified that these would be available to the British provided that the submarines would be in all circumstances used for the international defence of the Western Alliance 'except where Her Majesty's Government may decide that supreme national interests are at stake'. This formula, in a drafting which was conspicuously ambiguous, was intended to allow Macmillan to claim that he had saved the British deterrent while not contradicting the multilateralist policy advanced by Kennedy. The Nassau Agreement coincided with the British negotiations to join the *EEC and was one of the major reasons why De Gaulle vetoed the application in January 1953. This attempt to revitalize the Anglo-American special relationship was advanced by De Gaulle as proof that Britain was not convincingly orientated towards Europe and would be an untrustworthy partner. At the same time he rejected the offer of Polaris missiles to France, which he declared to be incompatible with national independence and a subordination to the United States.

BAYLIS, J., *Anglo-American Defence Relations*, 2nd ed., Macmillan, 1984.

NUNNERLEY, D., *President Kennedy and Britain*, Bodley Head, 1972.

NEUSTADT, R. E., *Alliance Politics*, Columbia University Press, New York, 1970.

**National Declaration on the League of Nations and Armaments,** see PEACE BALLOT (1934–5)

**National Self-Determination.** The right of a people to determine their own political destiny, to enjoy independence and have a government of their own choosing. The nationalist demand for self-determination became a dominant force during the nineteenth century, as witnessed for instance in the unification of Italy and Germany. Since then it has become so in the non-European, previously colonized, parts of the globe. It is based on the criteria of common language, race, cultural and religious traditions and the territorial delimitations of communities. The validity of the idea of self-determination was given prominent support in President Woodrow Wilson's *Fourteen Points, and found expression in the emergence of the *succession states following the collapse of the Habsburg Empire. In disputed areas the right of self-determination has commonly been exercised through plebiscites which afford the inhabitants the right to decide to which neighbouring state or states they wish to belong.

**NATO,** see NORTH ATLANTIC TREATY ORGANIZATION

**Navarino, Battle of** (1827). A major engagement in the western Peloponnesus on 20 October 1827, during the *Greek War of Independence (1821–9). A combined British, Russian and French fleet under Admiral Codrington defeated Ibrahim Pasha, almost destroying the Turkish–Egyptian fleet. This followed the Ottoman refusal to accept the Treaty of *London of July that year. It was the last great naval battle to be fought before the advent of steamships, ironclads and explosive shells.

While British public opinion was enthusiastic about the victory, the government was notably less so. They still hoped to offer mediation between Greece and Turkey. They wanted to maintain a *balance of power in the Eastern Mediterranean and to avert a Russo-Turkish war. From this standpoint it was a diplomatically inexpedient event. Navarino contributed significantly to the success of the Greek struggle against the Turks. Russian gains under the Treaty of *Adrianople (1829) so weakened

the Porte that Greek independence was assured. So too was the opportunity for Mehemet Ali later to rebel against the Sultan. The battle made a decisive contribution towards these later developments.

WOODHOUSE, C. M., *The Battle of Navarino*, Hodder and Stoughton, 1965.

**Navy Race,** see ANGLO-GERMAN NAVY RACE

**Nazi-Soviet Pact,** see MOLOTOV–RIBBENTROP PACT (1939)

**Neutralism.** A policy or attitude of independence and non-alignment in international relations which has become particularly prevalent since *World War II (1939–45) in the context of the *Cold War confrontation. It describes the position of those who wish to avoid being militarily, diplomatically or politically committed to either East or West. This policy of non-alignment has become particularly identified with Third World countries, and its impact has been particularly in evidence in the General Assembly of the *United Nations. The behaviour of states which follow such a path varies from relative withdrawal to positive attempts to arbitrate between the Communist and non-Communist worlds. Neutralism is to be distinguished from neutrality, the latter being a legal condition of impartiality which states, e. g. Switzerland, adopt in conflicts between other states. Moreover, neutralism can apply to attitudes of groups or individuals as well as to the policies of states. Traditionally, for instance, some members of the Labour Party in Britain have advocated dissociation from *NATO and a neutralist stance between the superpowers.

**Neutrality Act** (1939). Passed by United States Congress in November 1939, repealing features of earlier neutrality legislation and replacing it with general *Cash-and-Carry provisions. The Roosevelt Administration had campaigned for the repeal of the acts on the grounds that they encouraged Axis aggression. The passage of this act was clearly influenced by sympathy towards the British and French predicament at the beginning of *World War II (1939–45). It abolished the impartial arms embargo, stipulated that United States ships were on no account to enter the north European war zone nor any belligerent's port in Europe. This act was greatly welcomed by Britain and France and represented a reverse for the isolationist lobby in America. In November 1941 it was amended to permit armed United States merchant ships to voyage through the war zone to British ports. This was a move which would almost certainly have led to United States–German conflict had the Pearl Harbour attack not brought the United States into the war.

**Non-Belligerency.** The term used to describe the stance of United States policy in relation to Britain during 1940–1, in the period after the fall of France in which Britain stood alone against Nazi Germany. The United States was granting assistance in every way possible, short of militarily engaging herself against Germany. The phrase, which has been used by other powers in other circumstances, was introduced in this context by the British Ambassador to the United States, Lord *Lothian (1882–1940). He felt that the use of 'non-belligerency' rather than 'neutrality' would give a psychological boost to Britain at a time when it was clearly needed and when Winston *Churchill (1874–1965) was doing everything he could to commit the United States to the war effort.

**Non-Intervention.** The refusal to coerce an offending state into modifying its domestic or foreign policy through *intervention. Until the middle of the nineteenth century it was widely held that a state had the right to intervene in the affairs of another state in order to protect its own citizens, property and rights affected by the second state's inability or unwillingness to defend them. The contrary view that no sovereign state could have this right while still respecting the sovereignty of the other was incorporated in Article 1 of the 2nd Hague Convention in 1907. Britain has frequently pursued a non-interventionist foreign policy, for instance during the years immediately after the *Vienna Congress (1814–15), when she refused to participate in interventions against liberal uprisings, and during the *Spanish Civil War (1936–9) (see also: *Non-Intervention Committee).

**Non-Intervention Committee** (1936–9). Representing 27 states, this was formed in September 1936 to prevent external powers from becoming involved in the bitter *Spanish Civil War (1936–9) and to hold the ring by withholding military aid from both the Republic and the Nationalist rebel forces. It was proposed by Britain and France, both anxious to ensure that the conflict did not develop into a wider European war. The British *Foreign Office provided the administrative support for the committee, which had its headquarters in London. Throughout the civil war it served as a forum for diplomatic representations and the *League of Nations delegated questions to it. The committee, however, conspicuously failed to prevent large-scale Italian, German and Russian intervention and the sale and delivery of large quantities of military supplies. The British and French were careful not to threaten the Germans and Italians when they intervened for fear that those countries would withdraw from the committee.

In 1937–8 the committee was called on to support a naval and air patrol in the Mediterranean to counter the sinking of neutral shipping by Italian submarines. The result of the policy of non-intervention was that the Nationalists slowly wore down the Republican forces while Britain and France looked on. In any case public opinion was deeply divided over the issue in both countries. At the same time, the lack of British and French support had the effect of pushing the Spanish Republic into dependence on the Soviet Union, which began supplying aid in October 1936. Russian agents also helped to organize the groups of volunteers which became known as the *International Brigades. The Non-Intervention Committee was dissolved on 20 April 1939.

**Normandy Landings** (1944) (D-Day). Operation Overlord, the Allied invasion of Western Europe which began, after long preparation, on 6 June 1944 along a 50-mile stretch of the Normandy coast from the Cotentin Peninsula eastwards. The Allied forces were under the command of General Eisenhower. The Germans reacted slowly, reckoning that a major landing had still to come in the Pas-de-Calais. The British Second Army captured Caen on 20 July. The landing and subsequent engagements were very costly in human life, but the beachheads were secured and German resources, needed to cope with the Soviet advance in the east, the Allied advance through Italy and the strategic bombing of their own country, could ill afford such losses. Paris was liberated on 25 August and troops crossed the German frontier on 12 September 1944.

***Normanton* Incident** (1886). The diplomatic dispute which surrounded the sinking of the

British freighter *Normanton* off the coast of Wakayama Prefecture on 24 October 1886. The captain, John Drake, and his British crew escaped, but all 23 of the abandoned Japanese passengers drowned. At an initial hearing at the British Consulate in Kobe he was declared innocent. There was such a public outcry, however, that the Japanese Government appealed to the Consulate. The trial was then moved to Yokohama Consulate, where in December Captain Drake received a three-month prison sentence, though no compensation was granted for the victims. The furore over this incident contributed to the Japanese determination to revise the *Unequal Treaties with the Western Powers.

**North Atlantic Treaty Organization** (NATO). The military and political organization brought into existence by the North Atlantic Treaty of 4 April 1949, which was signed by the foreign ministers of Belgium, Britain, Canada, Denmark, France, Iceland, Italy, the Netherlands, Norway, Portugal and the United States. It was subsequently joined by Greece, Turkey, West Germany and Spain. The signatories are pledged to take such action as they consider necessary to assist a fellow member which is the victim of aggression and 'to safeguard the freedom, common heritage and civilization of their peoples founded on the principles of democracy, individual organization, liberty and the rule of law'. NATO was established on the initiative of the United States and resulted from the growing confrontation of the *Cold War, representing an important step in the evolution of the policy of *Containment. More immediately it was prompted by the *Berlin Blockade and Czech coup of 1948. The British Government in the late 1940s took the view that, without United States participation, a Western European alliance would not be able to counterbalance the military strength of the Eastern Bloc. The treaty was signed before the Soviet demonstration of a nuclear capability (August 1949) and to meet the problem posed by the imbalance of conventional forces in Europe. At various times clear differences of view have emerged between the United States and its European partners in NATO, between Europeanism and the American emphasis on strengthening the *Atlantic Community. For instance, President de Gaulle's suspicions of American intentions and his idea of a Europe 'from the Atlantic to the Urals' led him to

withdraw French forces from NATO in 1966 and resulted in the removal of its headquarters to Brussels (though France remained a member of the North Atlantic Treaty). More recently, tensions have arisen over nuclear arms policy in Europe with a strong revival of *unilateralism in Britain. NATO has remained an inter-governmental organization. Its supreme organ is the North Atlantic Council.

BAYLIS, J., *Anglo-American Defence Relations, 1939–84*, 2nd ed., Macmillan, 1984.
HENDERSON, N., *The Birth of NATO*, Weidenfeld and Nicolson, 1982.
OSGOOD, R., *NATO: The Entangling Alliance*, University of Chicago Press, Chicago, 1962.

**Northern Tier.** The *Cold War concept that Turkey, Iraq, Iran and Pakistan form a natural grouping for Middle Eastern defence. It evolved from a British wish to reaffirm relations with Iraq and from United States and Turkish desires to provide a regional defence system against the Soviet Union. The idea became a diplomatic reality (albeit short-lived) with the signing of the *Baghdad Pact (1955).

**North Sea Incident,** see DOGGER BANK INCIDENT (1904)

**Norwich, 1st Viscount,** see COOPER, ALFRED DUFF, (1890–1954)

**Nuclear Test Ban Treaty** (1963). Also known as the Limited (or Partial) Test Ban Treaty, it was signed in Moscow on 5 August 1963. It banned the testing of nuclear weapons in the atmosphere. This reflected the very widespread anxiety about the hazards of radioactive contamination for the human race. By this time, too, the advanced nuclear powers could afford to dispense with atmospheric testing. The original signatories were Britain, the United States and the Soviet Union. By the time it entered into force in October 1963 no fewer than 105 states had acceded to it. The most notable exceptions (both nuclear powers) were France and the People's Republic of China. The treaty also excluded testing under water, in outer space, or in any other place if such testing led to radioactive contamination outside a state's territorial limits. Underground testing of nuclear devices was still permitted.

**Nyon Conference** (1937). A diplomatic meeting held in the September of that year for the purpose of preventing the destruction of merchant shipping. In particular, British and Russian ships had been attacked by Italian submarines supporting the Nationalist cause in the *Spanish Civil War (1936–9). The hosts of the conference were Britain and France. Italy and Germany did not attend. The subsequent Nyon Agreements declared that the Mediterranean would be patrolled by various nations to protect shipping. The conference indicated that the British were to some extent willing to stand up to Italy and Germany, though the agreements reached and the patrols established did not prevent continuing depredations on neutral commercial shipping.

# —O—

**Octagon,** see QUEBEC CONFERENCE (1944)

**Oder–Neisse Line.** The western boundary of Poland since 1945, when the Soviet Union handed over to Polish administration the former German territories of Pomerania, Silesia and part of Brandenburg. The history of this demarcation dates from the wartime negotiations of Britain and the United States with the Soviet Union at the *Yalta Conference (1945). This had affirmed that Poland should receive 'substantial accessions of territory in the North and in the West' and agreed that the 'final delimitation of the Western Frontier of Poland should await the Peace Conference'. Before the *Potsdam Conference (1945) took place, however, the Soviet Union had transferred the administration of the Oder–Neisse provinces and southern East Prussia to the provisional Polish Government. Since a formal peace conference was never held the Yalta formula became the basis for a continuing East–West dispute about the significance of the Oder–Neisse boundary in international law. Both Winston *Churchill (1874–1965) and President Roosevelt spoke of these areas as 'compensation' to Poland for the territory she was forced to cede to the Soviet Union in the east. In the Warsaw Treaty of 1970 the German Federal Republic gave qualified endorsement to the border, but the West German position is that the boundaries do not preclude a peace treaty for Germany and do not establish a *de jure* foundation for the present-day frontiers.

**Open Diplomacy.** The first of President Woodrow Wilson's *Fourteen Points, a repudiation of the secret diplomacy which it was felt had contributed to the outbreak of *World War I (1914–18). It did not mean that all discussions and negotiations prior to concluding a treaty arrangement should be public, but that a treaty once agreed should be made public. As a consequence of this idea the Covenant of the *League of Nations stipulated that all treaties should be registered.

**Open Door Policy.** The policy of trading with all states on a basis of equality rather than through granting monopolies or preferences – free access to markets as contrasted with commercial *spheres of influence. Though it had already been applied in the *Berlin Congo Conference (1884–5), it was publicly enunciated by John Hay, the American Secretary of State, in 1899 to those governments, foremost among them the British and Japanese, which seemed bent on carving out monopolistic trade areas for themselves in China. At the time nations had marked out for themselves spheres of influence and were asserting rights of *extraterritoriality. Hay's circular note called for no nation to be given exclusive rights of commercial exploitation and stated (a year before the *Boxer Rising) that the policy of the United States was to 'preserve Chinese territorial and administrative entity' – though at the time China was not recognized as a sovereign state. Though the Open Door policy was accepted in principle by the European Great Powers and Japan, in practice it was ignored. A major reason for convening the *Washington Conference (1921–2) was to reaffirm the principle but the Japanese repudiated it with the invasion of Manchuria (see: *Manchurian Crisis (1931–3) ). After *World War II (1939–45) China's *de facto* position as a sovereign state was recognized.

**Opium War** (1839–42) A conflict between Britain and China arising from Chinese attempts to suppress the smuggling of opium in which many British merchants were involved. The measures taken included the burning of 20,000 chests of opium by the Chinese authorities. Anglo-Chinese trade dated back to the 1630s and had increased rapidly after the Manchu Court designated Canton as an open port. The main item of import for the British was tea, for which they paid the Chinese largely in silver. When the British found a market in China for the opium grown in Bengal, they were able to correct the imbalance of payments. By the 1830s the terms of trade had altered dramatically, with large quantities of silver leaving China. For the traders huge profits were involved. At the same time the colonial government of India derived revenue from it. There were wider issues in the conflict, too. The British were constantly pressing for freer trade while Confucian orthodoxy tended to oppose the idea of foreign trade. Following the refusal by the Chinese Government to pay compensation for the opium which they had confiscated, fighting broke out during which a British force bombarded Canton. The *Nanking Treaty (1842) concluded the war.
TWITCHETT, D. and FAIRBANK, J. K., *The Cambridge History of China*, Vol. X, Cambridge University Press, 1978.

**Oregon Boundary Dispute.** The diplomatic conflict between the United States and Britain over the western boundary between Canada and the United States. At various times this was complicated by Russian and Spanish claims. An Anglo-American convention drew the Canadian boundary to the Rocky Mountains, determined the boundary of Oregon and provided for the joint occupation of the latter by the signatories. By the 1840s, with the expansion of American settlements and British interests in the fur trade, rivalry came to a head. In spite, though, of acute tension (for instance, the aggressive slogan – 'Fifty-four Forty or Fight' – of the 1844 American election) the boundary question was finally resolved on 18 June 1846. As a result, the 49th Parallel was extended to the Pacific Coast. On 27 April 1846

Congress authorized the President, James Polk, to give Britain notice of the termination of the joint occupation treaty. The repeal of the Corn Laws in Britain at this time and the passing of the Walker Tariff in the United States, which were mutually beneficial to the two countries, helped to produce a favourable atmosphere for ending the dispute.
MERK, F., *The Oregon Question*, Harvard University Press, Cambridge, Mass., 1967.

**Ottawa Conference** (1932). British imperial economic conference convened between 21 July and 20 August 1932 on Canadian initiative. It secured mutual tariff preference to members of the British Commonwealth. Britain exempted some imports, mainly food and raw materials, from duties while the Dominions gave preferential tariffs to British manufactured goods. This had been preceded by the British switch to protectionism in February 1932. Ottawa, with the introduction of partial *Imperial Preference, was a response to the world economic depression. The following years saw a relative increase in trade between members of the Commonwealth as compared with the rate of increase in world trade. British imports from the Commonwealth rose from 25 per cent to nearly 38 per cent between 1930 and 1938, while British exports to the Commonwealth rose from 37·5 to 45·6 per cent over the same period. Acceptance of the Ottawa agreements forced the Free Traders in the Cabinet to recognize that the government would remain protectionist and in September the economically orthodox Liberals left it. It also, of course, enhanced the significance of imperial connections in the public mind, arguably at the expense of concern with the course of events in Europe.

**OWEN, Dr David Anthony Llewelyn** (1938– ). The youngest Foreign Secretary since *Eden (1897–1977), Dr Owen was educated at Bradfield College and Sidney Sussex College, Cambridge, and at St Thomas's Hospital, London. He entered the House of Commons in 1966 as Labour MP for Plymouth and was Under-Secretary of State for the Navy in the Ministry of Defence (1968–70). In 1972 he resigned as Opposition spokesman on defence because he disagreed with the Labour opposition to British membership of the *EEC. He was subsequently Minister for Health and Social Services (1974–6) and between 1977 and

1979 Foreign Secretary, where he combined enthusiasm for British membership of the Community with a belief in strong Anglo-American relations. The issue of Rhodesia was one of the major concerns of his period of office. In 1981 he left the Labour Party as one of the founder members of the Social Democratic Party, of which he has been leader since 1983. OWEN, D., *Human Rights*, Cape, 1978.

**Oxford, Earl of Oxford and Asquith,** see ASQUITH, HERBERT HENRY (1852–1928)

# P

**Pacifism.** The movement for the abolition or outlawing of war; repugnance for the use of armed force, particularly in relations between states. The appeal to mass support from public opinion and the growth of peace societies and campaigns became marked during the nineteenth century, especially in Britain, the United States, Germany and France. Nonconformist religious groups, notably the Quakers, were prominent in this. Advocates of political and economic change, free traders, socialists, and communists, for instance, argued that lasting peace would result from the universal acceptance of their ideas; some advanced the proposal for an international strike of the working class in the event of a war of nationalist or imperialist aggrandizement being declared. The growth of humanitarianism and, at the same time, the increased destructive potential of modern war also encouraged the growth of pacifism. The membership of peace societies in the pre-*World War I (1914–18) period was nevertheless limited, and while their development was significant it failed to restrain the arms race. The hostility of governments towards these movements, or at least scepticism, and the divisions between them helped to render them ultimately ineffective.

The ideas and initiatives of the pre-war period were considerably developed after World War I, which many hoped would be 'the war to end wars'. The *League of Nations reflected the hope that aggression could be outlawed by institutional means. The *Kellogg–Briand Pact (1928) proposed the renunciation of war as an instrument of national policy and attracted 65 signatory states. Many of the supporters of the League did not in fact renounce force as such. They wished to 'collectivize' it, to place it at the service of the international community, which could then through institutional means resist unprovoked aggression and militarism. They effectively accepted the distinction between 'just' and 'unjust' war. For this reason some would prefer to see them described as 'internationalists' rather than genuine pacifists. Others refused under any conditions to contemplate the use of armed force against another nation and considered the idea of a 'League with teeth', i.e. with military sanctions and an army at its disposal as a contradiction in terms for a 'League of peace'. Unconditional, absolute pacifism was represented amongst others by conscientious objectors in both World Wars. The widespread concern for peace, manifested in such initiatives as the *Peace Ballot (1935) was a significant influence on the policy of appeasement. Since *World War II (1939–45) the invention of nuclear weapons (first exploded in 1945) and the *balance of terror have given pacifist arguments a new dimension, both on humanitarian grounds and because of the self-defeating nature of a nuclear exchange, in which there would be no victor. A distinction is now made between conventional and nuclear war. The advocacy of the unilateral renunciation of nuclear arms (see: *unilateralism) is, therefore, now heard from numbers of people who would not consider themselves pacifist in relation to the issue of the waging of conventional war, or to that of conventional rearmament.

CEADEL, M., *Pacifism in Britain, 1914–45: The Defining of a Faith*, Clarendon Press, 1980.

HOWARD, M., War and the Liberal Conscience, Temple Smith, 1978.

MORRIS, A. J. A., Radicalism against War, 1906–14: The Advocacy of Peace and Retrenchment, Longman, 1972.

ROBBINS, K., The Abolition of War: The 'Peace Movement' in Britain, University of Wales Press, Cardiff, 1976.

**PALMERSTON,** Henry Temple, 3rd Viscount (1784–1865). Foreign Secretary 1830–4, 1835–41, 1846–51; Prime Minister 1855–8, 1859–65. Palmerston was appointed Secretary at War in 1809 and served under successive administrations, but in May 1828 he left office along with other followers of *Canning (1770–1827). In 1830 he became Foreign Minister in Grey's Whig ministry and was to remain the dominant influence in British foreign policy for the next 35 years.

Palmerston was aggressively concerned with the maintenance of British national interests, favouring the advance of liberal constitutionalism abroad because he believed this would improve international security and prosperity. Thus he could at times pose as the friend of liberty in opposition to Metternich's Austria. On the other hand, he was a firm advocate of the *balance of power, which he saw as 'a doctrine founded on the nature of man' and hence he was willing to take Britain into alliance with Austria over the *Eastern Question in order to prevent Russian expansion threatening vital British interests. He was a determined supporter of *Free Trade but differed from 'internationalists' like *Cobden (1804–65) and *Bright (1811–89) in his willingness to use force to uphold British commercial interests.

Palmerston's major concern in the 1830s was the revolt of Belgium against Dutch rule. He immediately recognized that Belgian independence was inevitable and set out to secure her freedom from interference from both France and the Netherlands. This objective was ultimately secured in 1839, after years of tedious negotiation and military intervention from both sides, when the five major powers agreed to guarantee Belgian neutrality. In both Spain and Portugal Palmerston successfully intervened to uphold constitutional monarchs and in April 1834 engineered the *Quadruple Alliance with France and the Iberian countries to keep reaction out of the peninsula. In the Middle East he unsuccessfully attempted to persuade the Cabinet to send help against the Sultan's unruly vassal, Mehemet Ali, the Pasha of Egypt. The Sultan therefore looked elsewhere, concluding on 8 July 1833 the Treaty of *Unkiar Skelessi with Russia. When a further crisis arose in 1839 Palmerston tried to secure united action by the Great Powers to support the Sultan, but France refused to cooperate. The subsequent disagreements in the Cabinet were resolved by *Melbourne (1779–1848), while Palmerston ultimately achieved a victory for British interests in the *Straits Convention of 13 July 1841, which limited French and Russian influence in the decaying Ottoman Empire and closed the *Dardanelles to foreign warships when Turkey was at peace. Meanwhile in China, Palmerston's defence of British trading interests led to the morally dubious *Opium War (1839–42), and in North America boundary disputes combined with British opposition to the slave trade to lead to deteriorating relations with the United States. Thus Palmerston's first period as Foreign Secretary saw substantial successes, but left the country in a state of potentially dangerous confrontation on several fronts.

Returning to office in 1846, Palmerston mishandled the *Spanish Marriages Crisis, failing to prevent the extension of French influence in the peninsula. He was an impotent observer of Austria's absorption of the Republic of Cracow, but in Switzerland helped to secure liberal victory in the civil war and averted intervention by the absolutist powers. In handling the revolutions of 1848 he was sympathetic to moderate liberal regimes but his primary concern was the maintenance of international order. This was especially evident in Italy, where he sought to diminish Austrian power while preventing French aggrandizement; in Hungary, where he showed little enthusiasm for the rebels against Austrian rule; and in Germany, where the limits of his support for the Frankfurt Assembly were apparent in his pro-Danish stance in the *Schleswig-Holstein question. This last issue was temporarily resolved in Denmark's favour by the Treaty of London in May 1852. Meanwhile at home Palmerston had encountered a rising tide of criticism of his policy centring on his bullying of Greece in the *Don Pacifico Affair (1850). He responded on 25 June 1850 with his famous 'Civis Romanus sum' speech, thus rallying the forces of popular *jingoism to his support, but his triumph was short-lived and, when he congratulated Louis Napoleon on seizing power in December 1851, *Russell (1792–1878) dismissed him.

In the Aberdeen coalition he served as Home Secretary, but was prominent in advocating a firm policy towards Russia. After *Aberdeen (1784–1860) resigned in January 1855 both *Derby (1799–1869) and Russell failed to form administrations and Palmerston became Prime Minister. The Treaty of *Paris (1856), which concluded the *Crimean War (1854–6), was largely the work of his Foreign Secretary, *Clarendon (1800–70), but Palmerston himself continued to take an active part in foreign affairs. His Chinese policy led again to war, this time over the *Arrow Incident (1856), but when in March 1857 *Cobden (1804–65) successfully carried a motion for a committee of enquiry against Palmerston, the Prime Minister appealed to the electorate and won a tremendous victory at the polls. However, he fell from power in February 1858 because of parliamentary condemnation of his agreement to strengthen the law against foreign conspirators on British soil following Orsini's assassination attempt on Napoleon III.

Palmerston returned to office in 1859 and held power until his death in 1865, working in close association with Russell, his Foreign Secretary. These years saw a decline in British influence in Europe: Palmerston found his bluff called by the Russians, who suppressed the Polish revolt in 1863, and by Bismarck, who occupied Schleswig-Holstein in 1864. Palmerston supported the unification of Italy, but the direction of British policy was muddled and the extent of his contribution to the *Risorgimento should not be exaggerated. Relations with the United States remained difficult and British neutrality in the American Civil War was by no means assured. Thus by 1865 gunboat diplomacy seemed to be running out of steam.

Palmerston had many failures and is open to the charges of undue abrasiveness and lack of finesse. His apparent inconsistencey however reflected his underlying belief that 'we have no eternal allies, and no perpetual enemies', a pragmatism which made him a clear-sighted guardian of his country's interests. At home he knew well how to manipulate public opinion through the Press and Parliament, achieving a popularity which reflected his standing as one of the greatest figures in British foreign relations.

BOURNE, K. *Palmerston: The Early Years 1784–1841*, Allen Lane, 1982.

BULLEN, R., *Palmerston, Guizot and the Collapse of the Entente Cordiale*, Athlone Press, 1974.
RIDLEY, J., *Lord Palmerston*, Constable, 1970.
SOUTHGATE, D., *The Most English Minister*, Macmillan, 1966.
WEBSTER, C. K., *The Foreign Policy of Palmerston, 1830–41*, Bell, 1951.

**Paris Conference** (1954). Between 20 and 23 October 1954 following the London Conference of 28 September to 3 October. It met after the French rejection of the European Defence Community (EDC) and resulted in the so-called Paris Agreements on European defence. The nine participating powers agreed that the occupation of the Federal Republic of Germany should be ended and that she be granted full sovereignty. It was further stipulated that she and Italy should sign the *Brussels Treaty (1948), to be renamed the *Western European Union (WEU). Western Germany was to make a contribution to *NATO, of which she was now to be a member, of 12 divisions. A European arms control agency was also to be created. Through these agreements the United States secured the West German rearmament which they saw as vital in presenting a credible conventional defence against the Soviet Union. The main stumbling block was France, understandably fearful of the revival of German militarism. In order to allay this fear the British government pledged to maintain a military presence on the Continent of four divisions and the Second Tactical Air Force. As such, Britain promised to go much further than she had been prepared to go in relation to the EDC, prompted by the desire to maintain the United States commitment in Europe. The French Assembly ratified these agreements in December 1954.

**Paris, Declaration of** (1856). Issued on 16 April 1856 by Britain, France, Russia, Austria, Prussia, Sardinia and Turkey to regularize the usages of naval warfare. It abolished privateering and defined the nature of contraband and blockade. It laid down the principle of 'free ships, free goods' (other than contraband of war) and stated that a blockade should be 'effective' in order to be binding on neutrals.

**Paris, 1st Peace of** (1814). Signed on 30 May by the Allies with King Louis XVIII of France after Napoleon's abdication. It allowed France to keep her frontiers of 1792, even with certain adjustments in her favour. The colonies annexed by Britain during the French Revolutionary and Napoleonic Wars were restored, with the exception of Tobago, St Lucia, Mauritius, Malta and the Ionian Islands. Of the conquered Dutch colonies Britain retained the Cape of Good Hope, Ceylon and British Guiana; and Denmark ceded Heligoland to her. France also recognized the freedom of shipping on the Rhine and Scheldt and promised to abandon the slave trade within five years.

**Paris, 2nd Peace of** (1815). Signed on 20 November 1815 after Napoleon's final defeat at *Waterloo (1815) and the second restoration of King Louis XVIII. On the whole it confirmed the settlement of the 1st Peace of *Paris (1814) and the decisions of the *Vienna Congress (1814–15), since both the Duke of *Wellington (1769–1852) and Tsar Alexander I regarded France as a potential future ally against their respective present allies. France was forced, though, to cede certain frontier districts – to Prussia (Saarland), Bavaria (Landau), Switzerland (Fort Joux), Savoy (Haute-Savoie), and the Netherlands (Bouillon, Philippeville, Mariembourg). She also had to return some of the art treasures looted in war and to pay a war indemnity of 700 million francs. To ensure compliance with these terms the Allies announced that troops would remain in France for five years. Since the indemnity was cleared in three years the occupation came to an end in 1818 at the Congress of *Aix-la-Chapelle.

**Paris Peace Conference** (1919–20) (see also *Versailles Treaty (1919) ). The meeting of the 'Allied and Associated Powers' between 18 January 1919 and 20 January 1920 to arrange a peace settlement with the defeated powers after *World War I (1914–18). The major territorial, economic and military decisions taken were imposed in a series of treaties. (1) *Versailles (28 June 1919), which was the settlement with Germany. (2) St Germain (10 September 1919), which confirmed the loss to Austria of all her non-German areas, as well as depriving her of about a third of her German population and forbidding the idea of unification with Germany (see: *Anschluss). (3) Neuilly (27 November 1919) by which Bulgaria lost Western Thrace to Greece, thereby being cut off from the Aegean Sea, ceded two areas to Serbia and conceded the incorporation of the Dobrudja by Rumania (which had taken it from

her in 1913). (4) Trianon (4 June 1920), the settlement with Hungary which made over two-thirds of her pre-war lands to her neighbours, Rumania, Poland, Czechoslovakia, Yugoslavia and Austria, reducing her population from a 1914 total of 21 million to 8 million. (5) *Sèvres (10 August 1920), the settlement with Ottoman Turkey which was never ratified.

This conference, its workings and its results, have attracted much criticism, of which an early and influential example was *The Economic Consequences of the Peace* (1919) by the British Treasury official and economist J. M.*Keynes (1883–1946). It was faced with formidable difficulties to resolve, though, consequent on the upheavals of war and the collapse of the German, Austrian, Russian and Ottoman empires. Until July its deliberations were dominated by the *Big Four, *Lloyd George (1863–1945) for Britain, President Woodrow Wilson for the United States, Clemenceau for France and Orlando for Italy. After this the decisions were taken by the 'Council of Heads of Delegations', usually Foreign Ministers. The issue of Turkish and Hungarian frontiers was entrusted to a Council of Ambassadors. The Paris Peace Conference revealed sharp differences of opinion and perspective between the representatives of the major powers, not least over the Rhineland, Poland, the Adriatic and the *League of Nations. Lloyd George was under considerable pressure to impose a more punitive settlement on Germany than he considered either wise or in Britain's national interest.

The durability of the post-war settlement was weakened by the United States' refusal to endorse the undertakings of their President and by the uncertainty of the situation in Eastern Europe following the Russian Revolution and Civil War. It was also early on undermined by the persistence of still-dissatisfied nationalist groups' taking the law into their own hands to secure disputed areas, for instance the seizure of Fiume by D'Annunzio in September 1919.

CALDER, K. J., *Britain and the Origins of the New Europe, 1914–18*, Cambridge University Press, 1976.

DOCKRILL, M. L. AND GOOLD, J. D., *Peace without Promise: Britain and the Peace Conferences, 1919–1923*, Batsford, 1981.

NICOLSON, H., *Peacemaking 1919*, Constable, 1933.

TEMPERLEY, H. W. V., *A History of the Peace Conference of Paris*, 6 vols., Hodder and Stoughton, 1920–4.

**Paris Treaty** (1856). Signed on 30 March 1856, the agreement ending the *Crimean War (1854–6). The powers undertook 'to respect the independence and territorial integrity' of the Ottoman Empire which was admitted to the Concert of Powers (see: *Concert of Europe) with the promise to introduce reforms for its Christian populations. The Russian protectorate over the Orthodox subjects of the Sultan was replaced by a European protectorate. The 'ancient rule' of the Ottoman Empire was reaffirmed, by which 'the Straits of the *Dardanelles and Bosphorus are closed to foreign ships of war, so long as the Porte is at peace'. According to the *Black Sea Clauses, which were repudiated by the Russians in 1870 during the Franco-Prussian War, neither Russia nor Turkey might maintain a navy in the Black Sea or fortresses along its shores. This principle of neutralization was also extended to the Aaland Islands in the Baltic. Free navigation of the Danube was guaranteed. Russia ceded south Bessarabia to Moldavia while Turkey promised self-rule to the Principalities (Moldavia and Wallachia).

The British wanted as far as possible to preserve the status quo and frustrated Napoleon III's ambitions at Paris to achieve a wider revision of the Vienna Settlement of 1815 (see: *Vienna, Congress of), particularly for Poland and Italy. For their part, the French prevented the British from pushing back the Russians as far as they would have liked. Nevertheless, the war and the treaty destroyed the old *balance of power in Europe and, with the consequent diplomatic isolation of Austria, favoured indirectly the emergence of Germany and Italy as nation-states between 1859 and 1871. The Treaty of Paris was followed by the Anglo-French–Austrian Treaty of 15 April 1856 by which the three powers agreed to regard any infringement of Ottoman independence and integrity as a *casus belli and undertook to concert measures to meet it.

ANDERSON, M. S., *The Eastern Question, 1774–1923*, Macmillan, 1966.

MOSSE, W. E., *The Rise and Fall of the Crimean System 1855–1871: The Story of a Peace Settlement*, Macmillan, 1963.

**Pax Britannica.** The phrase coined by Joseph *Chamberlain (1836–1914) to describe the stable peace achieved under British rule, comparable with the ancient Pax Romana. It has been used commonly to convey the global, imperial role of Britain during the years 1815–1914. In these years she was able to use her Great Power capability, conferred by commercial and industrial progress and naval supremacy, to stabilize the European *balance of power, and to police her empire and much of the remaining non-European world.

**Peace Ballot** (1934–5). Popular name for 'The National Declaration on the League of Nations and Armaments'. This was a nationwide private referendum organized by the *League of Nations Union in association with other groups following the breakdown of the *World Disarmament Conference (1932–4). There had been earlier, local polls in various parts of the country. The questionnaire was designed to demonstrate the support of British public opinion for the League and for the principle of *collective security. At this time the League's credibility as an organization capable of preserving world peace had been shaken by the *Manchurian Crisis (1931–3) and by Hitler's withdrawal of Germany from Geneva, the seat of the League. Thirty-eight per cent of the adult population of Britain replied to the poll. While it indicated overwhelming support in favour of the League and the reduction of armaments through international agreement, more than 10 million out of 11,640,066 endorsed the idea of imposing economic sanctions against an aggressor and 6,833,803 were willing to support military sanctions (2½ million opposed them and a similar number abstained on this question). The ballot showed that British public opinion demanded a policy based not on isolationism, nor on particular alliances, but on the collective system which they envisaged to be embodied in the League. This evidently influenced the tactics of the Baldwin government during the *Abyssinian Crisis (1935–6). Anxious to be seen as the party of peace, the Conservatives did not spell out the realities as they saw them during the general election of November 1935. They offered instead an insincere endorsement of the idea of collective security based on the League. This insincerity was exposed in the outcry over the *Hoare–Laval Pact (1935). At the same time it became increasingly clear to the public over the next year with the remilitarization of the *Rhineland

(1936) and the *Spanish Civil War (1936–9) as well as Mussolini's victory in Abyssinia that effective collective security now meant the very same policy of competing armaments and diplomatic encirclement which the League of Nations had been created to supersede.

BIRN, D., *The League of Nations Union, 1918–1945*, Oxford University Press, 1981.

CEADEL, M., *Pacifism in Britain, 1914–1945: The Defining of a Faith*, Clarendon Press, Oxford, 1980.

**Peaceful Coexistence.** A term first used in the mid-1950s in a period of comparative relaxation in East–West relations. It referred to the coexistence of the capitalist and communist states, particularly the United States and the Soviet Union, without war. The advent of nuclear weapons had forced a reappraisal of the earlier communist dogma of the inevitability of war between capitalism and communism. Used as a slogan, it led to ideological controversies between the national communist parties, particularly those of the Soviet Union and China, and was treated sceptically by the Western Powers. It was argued in the West that genuine peaceful coexistence was possible if both East and West were willing to contemplate necessary revisions of attitude. However, this was not the case: the Soviet Union had not renounced the prospect of, eventually, a world communist system, and it was stressed that Soviet military policies, foreign trade policies and anti-Western propaganda continued to threaten coexistence and endanger peace.

**Peace Movement,** SEE PACIFISM

**Pearl Harbour** (1941). The surprise attack on the United States naval base in Hawaii by Japanese air and naval forces on 7 December 1941. It was mounted without previous declaration of war and at a time when negotiations were going on between the two powers. Within two hours the Japanese had sunk or severely damaged 19 ships, destroyed 120 aircraft and killed 2,400 people. On the following day a Joint Resolution of Congress was adopted declaring war on Japan. On 11 December Hitler honoured his pledge to his partner in the Tripartite Pact (signed by Germany, Italy and Japan on 27 September 1940), by which the signatories undertook to assist each other if one of them was attacked by a power not already in the war when the pact was signed. The German declaration of war on the United States now gave the American government full justification for transforming the 'common-law' alliance with Britain into full military cooperation. Winston *Churchill (1874–1965) commented in his war memoirs on this turn of events: 'So we had won after all! . . . Once again in our long island history we should emerge, however mauled and mutilated, safe and victorious . . . Many disasters, immeasurable cost and tribulation lay ahead, but there was no more doubt about the end.'

THORNE, C., *Allies of a Kind: The United States, Britain and the War against Japan, 1941–45*, Oxford University Press 1978.

**PEEL,** Sir Robert (1788–1850). Conservative Prime Minister 1834–5, 1841–6. Peel served a brief apprenticeship as Under-Secretary for War and Colonies between 1810 and 1812, but throughout the major part of his career his interests and responsibilities lay primarily in domestic politics. Nevertheless, as Prime Minister between 1841 and 1846 he took an active interest in foreign affairs, generally urging more determined policies on *Aberdeen (1784–1860) and, in particular, manifesting a deep suspicion of France which contrasted with Aberdeen's more conciliatory attitude. Peel's economic policies had important consequences for Britain's role in the world: the Bank Charter Act of 1844 gave much-needed enduring stability to the currency, and the reduction of customs tariffs in 1842 and the repeal of the Corn Laws in 1846 were important moves towards *Free Trade. Peel's decision to act against the Corn Laws caused a split in the Conservative Party between Protectionists and Free Traders leading to the fall of the government.

GASH, N., *Mr Secretary Peel*, Longman, 1961. *Sir Robert Peel*, Longman, 1972.

PARKER, C. S., ed., *Sir Robert Peel from his Private Papers*, 3 vols., John Murray, 1891–9.

**Penjdeh Incident** (1885). A military conflict between Russian and Afghan forces in 1885 which threatened to lead to war between Britain and Russia over the latter's ambitions in Central Asia. The situation in this area following the Second *Afghan War remained unstable. Britain continued to be anxious about Russia's expansion southwards and the threat that this posed to India. In 1881 the Russians had declared that they had no hostile intent.

*Gladstone (1809–98) and Lord Ripon, the viceroy, had pursued a policy of defusing tension. However, in 1884 the Russians had occupied Merv and early in 1885 infiltrated troops into the Zulfiqar Pass, the key to the Afghan city of Herat. Then, in February of that year, in spite of earlier denying any such intention, they entered Penjdeh, which they had already openly recognized to be a symbol of Afghan sovereignty. Lord *Salisbury (1830–1903), now Prime Minister, opened negotiations with Germany in order to secure the latter's neutrality should an Anglo-Russian war break out. Bismarck, though, proved unwilling to alienate Russia, the lynchpin of his alliance system. This incident illustrates British diplomatic isolation at the time. As Salisbury commented, Gladstone's government had succeeded in creating a *Concert of Europe by 'uniting the Continent of Europe – against England'. At the same time Russia was not anxious for a major confrontation with Britain and the crisis was settled very largely in Britain and Afghanistan's favour. Russia was allowed to keep Penjdeh, but had to surrender areas south and respect the Oxus as an agreed barrier to further advance.

EDWARDES, M., *The West in Asia, 1850–1914*, Batsford, 1967.

GILLARD, D., *The Struggle for Asia, 1828–1914: A Study in British and Russian Imperialism*, Methuen, 1977.

**Perth, Earl of,** see DRUMMOND, SIR JAMES ERIC (1876–1951)

**Phony War.** Also called the 'Twilight War'; known in Germany as the 'Sitzkrieg'. The Phony War was the period of relative military inactivity in the West between Hitler's invasion of Poland at the beginning of September 1939 and the 'Blitzkrieg', his lightning war campaign from 9 April to 22 June 1940, during which German forces overran Denmark, Norway, Holland, Belgium and France. France was committed to a defensive strategy behind the Maginot Line and the British Government at this time pinned far more hope than was realistic on the likely effects of the economic blockade against Germany. During October and November Hitler made propagandistic peace overtures to Britain and France. In this period attention was to some extent distracted by the outbreak of the 'Winter War' (at the end

of November) with the Russian invasion of Finland.

**Polignac Memorandum** (1823). The diplomatic note from the French Ambassador to Britain, the Prince de Polignac, to the British Foreign Secretary George *Canning (1770–1827) in October 1823. It followed the French invasion of Spain, at a time when the fall of Cadiz seemed imminent and when rumours of pending French intervention in South America were rife. Canning had demanded information about France's attitude towards the Spanish Colonies and informed Polignac that Britain would recognize their independence if any attempt was made to restrict existing British trade with them. He further warned him against any French interference by either force or threat in the colonies. Polignac's memorandum stated that France did not believe Spanish America would be restored to Spain, that France had no plan to acquire any Spanish American colonies and that France opposed using force against the colonies in any case. It was not published until the following March, but it enabled Canning (at a time when the declaration of the *Monroe Doctrine (2 December 1823) might suggest otherwise) plausibly to represent Britain as the real guarantor of Latin-American liberty.

**Polish Corridor.** The stretch of land connecting Poland to the Baltic Sea which was granted her by the Treaty of *Versailles (1919) as a commercial outlet for what would otherwise have been a landlocked state. It aroused resentment in Germany since it divided East Prussia from the rest of the country. Throughout the interwar years (though these were for a while muted after the signing of the German–Polish Non-Aggression Pact (1934) ) there were German recriminations over the bisection of their country and on the grounds that in 1918 the ethnic composition of the area had been predominantly German. The Poles countered that this had originally belonged to Poland, and with the argument of commercial access, 80 per cent of their foreign trade being seaborne. It became a menacing international issue in March 1939 when Hitler demanded the return of *Danzig and advanced claims for an extraterritorial road across the Corridor. In August 1939 he insisted on the return of the whole Corridor. Britain attempted to negotiate over this issue but the invasion of Poland by Germany on 1 September 1939, following the

British and French guarantees to the Poles, precipitated *World War II (1939–45).

**Polish Government-in-Exile** (The 'London Poles'). After the German invasion of Poland in September 1939 the Poles established a government-in-exile in London which included, as Premier, General Sikorski and as Vice-Premier, Mikolajczyk. This supervised the activities of the clandestine Polish Home Army and the Polish Army-in-Exile. The German invasion of Russia in 1941 forced the government-in-exile to follow the Anglo-American policy of friendship towards the Soviet Union in spite of traditional Polish nationalist attitudes towards their eastern neighbour and the fact that the Soviet Union had appropriated eastern Poland in 1939. The discovery of the mass graves of Polish prisoners-of-war (see: *Katyn Forest Massacre (1940) ) and the clear indications of Soviet responsibility produced deep revulsion among the exiles. Stalin, however, used the Polish demand for a further enquiry into the massacre as an excuse for terminating relations with the 'London Poles'. Mikolajczyk became Premier in July 1943 following the death of Sikorski in an air crash at *Gilbraltar. He repeatedly sought Anglo-American assurances that Poland would be free and independent after the end of the war. The British and United States governments continued to support the 'London Poles' while the Russians backed the Lublin Committee. The Soviet military success in Eastern and Central Europe enabled Stalin to establish the Lublin group as the provisional government of Poland in January 1945.

KACEWICZ, G. V., *Great Britain, the Soviet Union and the Polish Government-in-Exile 1939–45*, Nijhoff, the Hague, 1979.

POLONSKY, A., ed., *The Great Powers and the Polish Question, 1941–45: A Documentary Study in Cold War Origins*, Orbis, 1976.

**Potsdam Conference** (1945). The last of the *Big Three wartime conferences, between 17 July and 2 August 1945, of Allied delegations led by *Churchill (1874–1965) (later *Attlee (1883–1967) ), Stalin and Truman. Except for the military details of Soviet entry into the Pacific war it dealt with the questions of the future of Germany and Eastern Europe. The concluding agreement established an *Inter-Allied Control Council in Berlin to deal with the administration of Germany. The defeated country was to be de-militarized and de-Nazified. Her major war criminals were to be tried. The declared purpose of the agreement was 'to prepare for the eventual reconstruction of German political life on a democratic basis and for eventual peaceful cooperation in international life by Germany'. Claims for *reparations were to be satisfied by the dismantling of industrial plant. Soviet and Polish claims were to be met from the Soviet zone and all other claims from the three Western zones. A quarter of all 'usable and complete' industrial equipment in the Western zones which was not required for Germany's peacetime economy was to be removed and handed to the Soviet Union.

The Soviets wanted to maximize reparations and freedom of action in their own zone while the United States was mainly interested in obtaining Russian aid in the Far East at no greater cost in concessions than those agreed at the *Yalta Conference (1945). Recognition of Soviet power in Eastern Europe was conceded, though Poland's boundaries were the subject of prolonged argument. At the eventual peace settlement Britain and the United States agreed they would support the Soviet annexation of the northern half of East Prussia. Peace treaties should be concluded with Bulgaria, Finland, Hungary, Italy and Rumania. The remaining German population in Poland, Czechoslovakia and Hungary was to be transferred to Germany. Stalin wished to include large portions of German Pomerania and German Silesia (since their military occupation by the Russians these territories had been administered by the Polish Provisional Government in Lublin and Warsaw) in Poland. It was finally agreed that, 'pending final determination of territorial questions at the peace conference', the disputed territory would be placed under the interim administration of Poland. Subsequently both the Soviet Union and Poland acted on the assumption that the powers at Potsdam had agreed in principle to establishing Poland's western frontier on the Oder and Western Neisse rivers with the Stettin area to the west of the Oder included in Poland (see: *Oder–Neisse Line). Potsdam, nicknamed 'Terminal', displayed the emerging East–West rift of the *Cold War. The Western powers were soon to condemn the Soviet flouting of the Potsdam decision that Germany should be treated as an economic unit. Churchill commented on this deterioration in relations: 'We British have had very early and increasingly to recognize the limitations of our own power and influence, great though it be, in the gaunt world arising from the ruins of this hideous war'. The *Potsdam Declaration demanded that Japan surrender unconditionally or be destroyed. Notification of the successful testing of the atomic bomb reached Truman during the conference.

FEIS, H., *Between War and Peace: The Potsdam Conference*, Princeton University Press, Princeton, N.J., 1960.

WHEELER-BENNETT, J. W. and NICHOLLS, A., *The Semblance of Peace*, Macmillan, 1972.

STRANG, LORD, 'Potsdam after Twenty-five Years' in *International Affairs*, 46:3, 1970, pp.441–89.

**Potsdam Declaration** (1945). A policy statement issued on 26 July 1945 by Britain, the United States and China which demanded *unconditional surrender by Japan. It threatened Japan with total destruction if she did not capitulate. Unknown to the Japanese, the United States was already in possession of the atomic bomb at this time. Originally drafted in Washington the document was amended at *Yalta to suit Britain. The declaration further announced that the Allies would dissolve the Japanese empire, demobilize the army and navy, mete out 'stern justice' to war criminals, impose a military occupation and reintroduce democracy there. After the atomic devastation of Hiroshima and Nagasaki, the Soviet Union's entry into the war and the Emperor Hirohito's personal intervention, the Japanese accepted the declaration on 14 August 1945.

**Pretoria Convention** (1881). Signed on 3 August 1881, ending the 1st *Boer War. British troops were withdrawn and the independence of the Transvaal recognized, though that territory was made responsible for debts incurred before and during the British occupation. The independence of the Transvaal was defined as being subject to the 'suzerainty of Her Majesty' and to certain 'reservations and limitations'. The more important of these related to the position of the native populations and to the Transvaal's relations with foreign powers. These terms were subsequently modified in the London Convention of 27 February 1884. The second agreement did not mention suzerainty; the Transvaal became the South African Republic and its frontiers were laid down precisely.

**Prinkipo Conference** (1919). One of several attempts made by the Western Allies after *World War I (1914–18) to deal with the situation in Russia following the Bolshevik seizure of power in 1917. On 3 January, in response to a Russian appeal for peace, the British Prime Minister *Lloyd George (1863–1945) suggested to the United States government that the Western Allies propose to the rival factions in Russia and to the 'governments of ex-Russian states' that they suspend hostilities during the *Paris Peace Conference (1919–20) and send representatives to negotiate a settlement. Woodrow Wilson the American President followed this up with an invitation to meet on Prinkipo in the Sea of Marmara. The only requirement stipulated for participation was that the governments were to lay down their arms by 15 February. The Bolsheviks accepted. The Whites on the other hand were incensed by the Council of Ten's proposal because it seemed to accord legitimacy to the Soviet Government and because the offer contradicted the simultaneous efforts of Britain and France to aid the White Russian cause. The British assured the Whites that Allied aid would not be cut off if they rejected the Prinkipo proposal. It is not surprising, perhaps, that the major anti-Bolshevik governments rejected the proposal out of hand. By March 1919 the project was dead. Lloyd George's hope that the 'Russian problem' might be resolved through discussion was disappointed, having proved unrealistic in the circumstances.

MAYER, A. J., *Politics and Diplomacy of Peacemaking: Containment and Counterrevolution at Versailles, 1918–19*, A. Knopf, New York, 1967.

**Pritchard Affair,** see TAHITI INCIDENT (1843)

**Protocol.** A word used in several senses in diplomacy. It may signify the official formulae to be observed in the drafting of treaties and other documents in relations between states. Alternatively, it can describe the form taken by an international agreement. Though this is by no means always the case, a protocol has often meant an agreement less formal than a convention or treaty. Protocols are frequently used to amend or clarify multilateral agreements, such as, in the interwar years, the *League of Nations. Sometimes protocols are simply a record of the minutes of a deliberative assembly of representatives of states.

**Protocol for the Pacific Settlement of International Disputes,** see GENEVA PROTOCOL (1924)

**Prussia, Britain and,** see GERMANY, BRITAIN AND

**PYM,** Francis Leslie (1922–    ). Educated at Eton and Magdalene College, Cambridge. Subsequently served in the African and Italian campaigns. Entering Parliament in 1961 for Cambridgeshire, as Conservative MP, he held office as Chief Whip (1970–3), when one of his major responsibilities was helping to secure the passage of the legislation for Britain's entry into the *EEC. In 1973–4 he was Secretary of State for Northern Ireland. With the return of the Conservatives to power in 1979 under Mrs *Thatcher (1925–    ) he became Secretary of State for Defence (1979–81), subsequently being Leader of the House of Commons. He became Secretary of State for Foreign and Commonwealth Affairs in April 1982, following the resignation of Lord *Carrington (1919–    ) in the wake of the Argentinian invasion of the *Falkland Islands. He was replaced by Sir Geoffrey *Howe (1926–    ) after Mrs Thatcher's re-election in 1983.
PYM, F., *The Politics of Consent*, Hamish Hamilton, 1984.

# —Q—

**Quadrant,** see QUEBEC CONFERENCE (1943)

**Quadruple Alliance** (1815). Signed on 20 November 1815 by Britain, Austria, Russia and Prussia to guarantee the 2nd Peace of Paris of the same date. The signatories agreed to maintain the provisions agreed at Vienna and Paris for 20 years. They further undertook permanently to exclude the Bonapartes from France and, if it should be necessary, to reimpose Allied occupation of France. This alliance, for which *Castlereagh (1769–1822) was particularly responsible, aimed at continuing wartime collaboration. Article 6 provided for periodic meetings of the powers, which resulted in the European congresses of 1818, 1820, 1821 and 1822 (see: *Congress System). The hope of permanent understanding between these powers was soon disappointed, however, by rivalries between them and by the marked divergence in attitude between Britain and the absolutist powers of the *Holy Alliance (1815).

**Quadruple Alliance** (1834). Signed on 22 April 1834, an alliance negotiated by *Palmerston (1784–1865) between Britain, France, Portugal and Spain. It was an attempt to alleviate Anglo-French tension, arising from fear of each other's intentions, during domestic dynastic conflicts in the Iberian Peninsula. The alliance forced the Pretenders, Miguel of Portugal and Carlos of Spain, to leave their countries. Anglo-French rivalry flared up again with the *Spanish Marriages Affair (1841–6).

**Quai d'Orsay.** The location of the French Ministry of Foreign Affairs since 1853 (with the exception of the Vichy period). Used as a synonym for the ministry.

**Quebec Conference** (1943). Between Winston *Churchill (1874–1965) and President Roosevelt, this conference (also known as Quadrant) was held between 19 and 24 August 1943, following the overthrow of Mussolini. The most important discussions involved the cross-Channel invasion – the Combined Chiefs of Staff agreed to an invasion by 29 divisions, Operation Overlord, proposed for May 1944, and this plan received the highest priority from this time on. A supplementary landing in the South of France by forces freed from the Italian campaign – Anvil – was also discussed. In the East it was agreed to mount an attack in northern Burma; plans were also advanced for air, naval and amphibious operations against various Japanese-held Pacific islands and for expanded operations in China.

**Quebec Conference** (1944). Held between 13 and 16 September 1944 (also known as Octagon) between Winston *Churchill (1874–1965) and President Roosevelt to discuss post-war policy for Germany and military plans for the war in the Pacific against Japan. It approved the (subsequently shelved) Morgenthau Plan for the 'pastoralization' (de-industrialization) of Germany. The Allies discussed the most effective strategy for the post-*D-Day push into Germany. The military situation for the Allies was markedly more favourable than at the time of the previous *Quebec Conference (1943). It was agreed that an Anglo-American Committee should work out details for *Lend-Lease on the assumption that the arrangement would continue after the anticipated defeat of Germany. In the war against Japan it was decided to capture the Philippines, effect landings on mainland China and Formosa and then undertake the invasion of Japan itself. At the same time the Allies would carry on the war in Burma and continue to supply the Soviet Union with matériel in the hope that, after the fall of Germany, she would assist in the defeat of Japan.

# R

**READING**, Rufus Daniel Isaacs, 1st Marquess of (created 1926) (1860–1935). Lord Chief Justice, Ambassador to the United States, Viceroy of India and, briefly, Foreign Secretary. Trained as a lawyer, he became Liberal MP for Reading in 1904; in 1910 he was appointed Solicitor-General and then Attorney-General. He was involved in the Marconi scandal. In 1913 he was appointed Lord Chief Justice, though his activities during *World War I (1914–18) carried him beyond the law courts. In 1915 he led the Anglo-French mission to the United States and succeeded in securing a loan of 500 million dollars for the war effort. He became a Viscount in 1916 and when a year later the United States entered the war against Germany, he returned to America as High Commissioner for Finance. Early in 1918 he became British Ambassador to Washington and his work there considerably accelerated the supply of food and the rapid deployment of troops to Europe. He took a leading part in coordinating the war effort, made a significant series of speeches which were calculated to sustain Anglo-American cooperation, and was also involved in the question of intervention in the Russian Civil War.

In 1921 he became Viceroy of India, his primary task there being to apply the Montagu–Chelmsford reforms of 1919. He was eventually forced, by the boycott by Congress and the increasing violence, to resort to harsh measures including the imprisonment of Gandhi. Returning to England in 1926, he subsequently played a prominent part in the Round Table Conference of 1930 and, from August to October 1931, was Foreign Secretary in the National Government.

JUDD, D., *Lord Reading: A Life of Rufus Isaacs, First Marquess of Reading, 1860–1935*, Weidenfeld and Nicolson, 1982.

HYDE, H. M., *Lord Reading: The Life of Rufus Isaacs, First Marquess of Reading*, Heinemann, 1967.

**Red Letter,** see ZINOVIEV LETTER (1924)

**Reparations.** Payments imposed on the loser in a war by the victorious power(s) to repair the damages resulting from the conflict and to reimburse the latter's costs. These were demanded by the Treaty of *Versailles (1919), the exact amount owing being calculated by a commission and by conferences of the powers. Justification for reparations was offered in the highly controversial *War Guilt Clause which stated that Germany and her allies were responsible for the war. In 1921 the sum payable by Germany was fixed at £6,600 million. The British economist and Treasury official J. M. *Keynes (1887–1946) was prominent among those who strongly criticized this arrangement. He argued that it would prove insupportable for Germany, would dislocate international trade and was also morally abhorrent. In 1922 hyperinflation forced Germany to withhold payments. This led to the invasion of the *Ruhr by France and Belgium in January 1923 and to German economic collapse. As a result, the reparation terms were modified in the *Dawes Plan (1924), terms which were further lightened in the *Young Plan (1929).

Reparations throughout this period were deeply resented by German public opinion, a fact which was powerfully exploited by the

Nazi Party. In July 1931 – in the face of general financial collapse – a moratorium was granted; the Lausanne Agreement of the following year stipulated a final sum. This was never paid. The question of reparations was a significant source of disagreement in Anglo-French relations (see: *Balfour Note (1922) ). In fact by the time of Hitler's accession to power Germany had paid only one-eighth of the sum originally demanded. On the other hand it had received loans equal to one-fifth. Reparations were also insisted on after *World War II (1939–45) following the Yalta agreement that 'Germany should make compensation in kind to the fullest possible extent for all damage caused to the United Nations'. These became an early source of dissension between the Soviet Union and the Western powers in the postwar years (see: *Yalta Conference (1945) ).

JORDAN, W. M., *Great Britain, France and the German Problem, 1918–39*, new ed. Cass, 1971.

MARKS, S., *The Illusion of Peace: International Relations 1918–33*, Macmillan, 1976.

TRACHTENBERG, M., *Reparation in World Politics: France and European Economic Diplomacy 1916–23*, Columbia University Press, New York, 1980.

**Rhineland, Remilitarization of the** (1936). An occupation begun on 7 March 1936, it was seen in retrospect to have been a crucial turning-point in the interwar years, the first of Hitler's moves to secure the revision of the territorial clauses of the Treaty of *Versailles (1919). This was the moment when, in the words of Duff *Cooper (1896–1954) 'Great Britain and France should have taken a firm line and insisted upon the withdrawal of the German troops as a preliminary to any discussion'. The post-war settlement had laid down that the Rhineland was to be occupied by Allied troops for 15 years and that a 30 mile wide demilitarized zone was to be created on the right bank of the Rhine. Britain had evacuated her zone of occupation in 1926, to be followed by France in 1930.

The invasion occurred at a time when public opinion had been distracted by the *Abyssinian War (1935–6). That Germany would at some stage attempt to alter the status of the Rhineland was accepted, and some in Britain tended to regard the demilitarization as one of the most unjust clauses in the Treaty. In the view of Sir Samuel *Hoare (1880–1959) 'three people out of four' were asking themselves in March 'what justification there could be for a European war to uphold an out-of-date clause of the Versailles Treaty and why should not the Germans have full sovereign rights in some of the most German territories in the Reich?' Hitler, arguing that the Franco-Soviet Pact (1935) justified his action, simultaneously suggested individual pacts of non-aggression with Germany's western neighbours, which could last either 25 or 50 years and be guaranteed by Britain and Italy.

While France pressed for economic and military sanctions, the motive in doing so seems to have been to secure a future commitment from Britain, rather than the expectation that they would take effective action then. Already on 27 February the French government had agreed that they could not act without the support of the other *Locarno signatories. In response to the occupation the French generals insisted that resistance was possible only if a large part of the French army were mobilized. This would take a fortnight and intervention by France would, it was reckoned, result in an early stalemate. In any case, the British government would not agree to such proposals for action. Sir Anthony *Eden (1897–1977) still hoped to secure an air pact, non-aggression treaties and the return of Germany to the *League of Nations. The result was verbal protests, including one from the League, but no action. Subsequently, Germany's refusal to make any concessions and French anxiety over the growing threat to security from the Nazi state led Britain, on Eden's insistence, to engage in staff conversations with France and Belgium, pending an understanding with Germany.

EMMERSON, J. T., *The Rhineland Crisis*, Temple Smith, 1977.

**RIBBENTROP,** Joachim von (1893–1946). Hitler's principal adviser on foreign affairs. He was successively head of the 'Ribbentrop Bureau', a Nazi foreign intelligence information service set up as a rival to the German Foreign Service, Ambassador in London (1936–8) and German Foreign Minister (1938–45). He also helped to negotiate the *Anglo-German Naval Agreement (1935), and as Ambassador hoped to further Anglo-German understanding, not least through informal contacts, such as with the Anglo-German Fellowship. He advised Hitler, wrongly, that he need not fear British support for

Poland in the event of a German attack on that country. As Foreign Minister he negotiated the *Molotov–Ribbentrop Pact (1939) and the Tripartite Pact (1940). Sentenced to death at the Nuremberg Trials, he was executed in October 1946.

RIBBENTROP, J. VON, *The Ribbentrop Memoirs*, trs. O. Watson, Weidenfeld and Nicolson, 1954.

**Risorgimento, Britain and the,** see ITALIAN UNIFICATION, BRITAIN AND

**Rome–Berlin Axis.** A term used to describe the relationship between Nazi Germany and Fascist Italy. It was coined by Mussolini in reference to the agreement between the powers concluded on 25 October 1936. Germany and Italy signed the *Anti-Comintern Pact in 1937 after the *Abyssinian War (1935–6). The Rome–Berlin Axis was further strengthened and institutionalized by the Pact of Steel (May 1939). Mussolini entered the war on Hitler's side on 10 June 1940. The Axis was a major element in German foreign policy, but ill prepared as she was for fighting a major war, Italy soon became a liability as an ally, a fact which led to Operation Axis.

**ROSEBERY,** Archibald Philip, 5th Earl of (1847–1929). Liberal Foreign Secretary 1886, 1892–4; Prime Minister 1894–5. Rosebery was endowed with striking looks, immense wealth and a capacity for sharp, compelling oratory – qualities which combined to make him one of the most charismatic political figures of the later Victorian period. He was also exceptionally well travelled, an obvious asset for a Foreign Secretary.

In early life Rosebery was friendly with *Disraeli (1804–81) whom in some ways he resembled, but he showed little hesitation in committing himself firmly to the Liberals in 1869. He rose to prominence in the party in 1879 by ably assisting *Gladstone (1809–98) in his Midlothian campaign, but only held junior office in the 1880 Liberal administration. In 1886, however, Granville's evidently failing powers combined with the loss of ministerial talent due to the secession of the Liberal Unionists to open the way to the *Foreign Office to Rosebery. He maintained continuity of policy on the lines laid down by *Salisbury (1830–1903) in the previous year and his careful diplomacy helped to prevent a major international crisis arising over Bulgaria.

During the 1880s Rosebery developed and propagated the Liberal Imperialist ideas particularly associated with his name. Although he had attacked the more extreme manifestations of 'Beaconsfieldism' he declared his commitment to 'sane' imperialism as distinguished from 'wild cat' imperialism. In a speech at Adelaide in January 1884 he enunciated his farseeing conception of the *Empire as 'a Commonwealth of Nations'.

In 1892 Rosebery, still depressed by the untimely death of his wife 18 months before, very reluctantly agreed to be Foreign Secretary again in Gladstone's last government. In a bitterly divided Cabinet Rosebery pursued an independent line which increasingly estranged him from Gladstone. He successfully advocated the annexation of Uganda and obtained Cabinet agreement to the strengthening of the army of occupation in Egypt in order to quell the restlessness of the Khedive. Like Salisbury Rosebery aimed to maintain good relations with the Triple Alliance (Germany, Austria-Hungary and Italy) without becoming committed to it, while he was distrustful of the French, with whom Britain clashed over Siam.

Rosebery was a firm advocate of increased naval expenditure in order to maintain the *balance of power in the Mediterranean and, when Gladstone resigned because of his opposition to the views of the rest of the Cabinet on this issue, Queen *Victoria (1819–1901) appointed Rosebery as his successor. As Prime Minister he was a disappointment: he was too aloof to retain the loyalty of his Cabinet while the Government's handling of foreign affairs, now entrusted to the diffident *Kimberley (1826–1902), was undistinguished. In the General Election of 1895 the Unionists obtained a landslide victory.

In October 1896 Rosebery resigned the leadership of the Liberal Party because of Gladstone's call for unilateral British action against Turkey over the *Armenian Massacres (1894–6), which Rosebery considered would lead to war or humiliation. Although still only 49 he was never to hold government office again. In December 1901 he made a notable call for magnanimity towards the Boers, thus helping to pave the way for a settlement of the *Boer War (1899–1902). For a time he remained a prominent figure on the imperialist wing of the Liberal Party, but he appeared quite content to leave the centre of the stage to *Asquith (1852–1928). Rosebery's obvious talents had earned him high office at a comparatively young age, but he was disadvantaged by a temperament which was, by turns, moody and impetuous and his career failed to maintain its early brilliance.

JAMES, R. R., *Rosebery*, Weidenfeld, 1963.

MATTHEW, H. C. G., *The Liberal Imperialists*, Oxford University Press, 1973.

**Ruhr Occupation** (1923). The leading mining and manufacturing region in Germany, the Ruhr was occupied by French and Belgian troops on 11 January 1923. It was in response to German failure to meet scheduled quota payments of *reparations imposed on her after *World War I (1914–18) that France and Belgium acted, and the occupation was sharply condemned by the British and the Americans, while it was met with passive resistance by the inhabitants of the Ruhr. The British Prime Minister *Bonar Law (1858–1923) had warned his opposite number in France, Poincaré, the year before that: 'no British government could agree to the occupation of the Ruhr to enforce demands which everyone regarded as impossible'.

Britain was by this time basically committed to a policy of conciliation with Germany while France continued to favour a policy of coercion. The event marked a culmination of those differences between Britain and France over Germany which had evolved since the Treaty of *Versailles (1919). The combination of industrial paralysis, the printing of money to keep the strike going and fast-rising imports soon led to economic collapse. The French made a failed attempt to take over the administration of the Ruhr. Passive resistance was called off on 26 September 1923. This grave dissension among the Allies was followed by a modification of the reparations schedule of payments in the *Dawes Plan (1924) and by the conciliation of *Locarno (1925).

MARKS, S., *The Illusion of Peace: International Relations in Europe, 1918–33*, Macmillan, 1976.

SCHMIDT, R. J., *Versailles and the Ruhr: Seedbed of World War II*, Nijhoff, The Hague, 1968.

WILLIAMSON, D. G., 'Great Britain and the Ruhr Crisis 1923–24', *British Journal of International Studies*, 3, 1977, pp. 70–91.

**Rush–Bagot Agreement** (1817). An Anglo-American agreement between the British Minister to the United States Charles Bagot and the United States Secretary of State James Rush. The war of 1812 had seen naval engagements between the powers in the Great Lakes and after the war an arms build-up had continued in the area. Agreement was reached in April 1817 and this was approved by the Senate a year later. Each side agreed to limit its naval forces to one ship in Lake Ontario, one in Lake Champlain and two in the upper lakes. They were to be used solely to enforce revenue laws. This agreement, which has been claimed to be the first instance of reciprocal naval disarmament in the history of international relations, was modified during *World War II (1939–45). This revision made by the United States and Canada allowed naval construction, training and testing to be carried out in the Great Lakes.

PERKINS, B., *Castlereagh and Adams*, University of California Press, Berkeley, 1964.

**RUSSELL,** Lord John, created Earl Russell (1861) (1792–1878). Whig Prime Minister (1846–52, 1865–6), Foreign Secretary (1852–3, 1859–65). During the first two decades of his long political career Russell was almost exclusively concerned with domestic politics, but in 1840 became involved in foreign affairs for the first time, opposing in the Cabinet Palmerston's anti-French policy in the Middle East. As Prime Minister from 1846 Lord John made unsuccessful efforts to open diplomatic relations with the Papacy in order to gain greater influence in Italy, but on the credit side, took steps leading to the foundation of Australia. He continued to have uneasy relations with *Palmerston (1784–1865) particularly as the Queen and the Prince Consort grew increasingly unhappy with the Foreign Secretary's conduct. Russell's dismissal of Palmerston in December 1851 shortly led to the fall of the Government.

Russell held the *Foreign Office under *Aberdeen (1784–1860) for only a few weeks purely in order to conform to constitutional proprieties following the formation of the ministry. His one significant decision was to bow to public pressure and send *Stratford Canning (1786–1880) back to Constantinople. Russell was a troublesome member of the Aberdeen coalition and his intrigues ultimately led to its downfall while discrediting Lord John himself. When Palmerston became Prime Minister in 1855 he sent Russell to negotiate peace at Vienna, but he was now more accommodating to the Russians than the government at home and, coming off worse in the subsequent disagreements, he was driven further into the political wilderness.

Nevertheless, Lord John returned to be Foreign Secretary again in 1859, although he held that office more because he considered it the only post worthy of the dignity of a former Prime Minister than because of any particular interest in foreign affairs. Now overshadowed by Palmerston, Russell did not perform with particular distinction. He supported Piedmont in the struggle for Italian unification and assisted Cobden's efforts for a Free Trade Treaty with France (see: *Cobden–Chevalier Treaty (1860) ). However, he badly mishandled relations with the United States, especially over the British-built ship *Alabama which he allowed to fall into Confederate hands. When Palmerston died in 1865, Russell succeeded him as Prime Minister, but his ministry only lasted nine months before it fell over the issue of parliamentary reform.

A shy and petulant man, Russell was better qualified for enunciating grand principles than for the handling of practical diplomacy. His most enduring contribution was the setting up in 1861 of the Select Committee on the Diplomatic Service which made important reforms in the Foreign Service. His involvement in foreign affairs was the least distinguished aspect of a career which, though not without some significant achievements, in general lacked the lustre of that of Palmerston or *Gladstone (1809–98).

PREST, J., *Lord John Russell*, Macmillan, 1972.
WALPOLE, S., *Life of Lord John Russell*, 2 vols., Longmans, 1889.

**Russia and the Soviet Union, Britain and.**
Though Britain and the Russian Empire emerged as triumphant allies in 1815 with the fall of Napoleon I, they were to become global rivals in the course of the rest of the century. Within 20 years of the Battle of *Waterloo (1815), Russophobia, the suspicion, fear and dislike of the Russian Empire and her system of government, had become a well-established factor in British political life, uniting Whigs, Radicals and Tories. This sentiment came to exercise considerable influence over British foreign policy. As Lord *Salisbury (1830–1903) was to comment: 'You must either disbelieve altogether in the existence of the Russians or you must believe they will be in Kandahar next

year. Public opinion recognizes no middle ground.' Hysterical fears were encouraged by, among others, the tireless pamphleteer, Urquhart, author among other things of *The Progress of Russia in the West, North and South*, who even accussed *Palmerston (1784–1865) (generally himself depicted as the archetypal Russophobe) of being in the pay of the Russians.

This growing animosity towards Russia sprang from territorial and commercial concerns and from ideological repugnance for the tsarist autocratic system. Pitt the Younger had sounded the first clear note of alarm at Russia's progress in south-eastern Europe. By the end of the eighteenth century her progressive drive southwards towards Constantinople and the Straits encountered the eastwards penetration of British economic interests and naval power. In British eyes this steady advance, prompted by the inexorable decline of the Ottoman Empire, posed a threat to British control in India and her lines of communication to it, a fear that was to be increased by Russian involvement in Persia and Afghanistan.

Though the struggle of the Greeks for independence between 1821 and 1829 brought Britain and Russia into collaboration, their deep-seated conflict of interest in the *Eastern Question set the pattern for relations between the two powers. Russia was able during the 1st *Mehemet Ali crisis to exploit the weakness of Turkey and by the *Unkiar–Skelessi Treaty (1833) to impose a virtual protectorate on the Sultan. At the same time, Russian intervention against liberal and nationalist uprisings aroused extreme indignation among Radicals, as during the repression in Poland in 1830 and the intervention to put down the Hungarian Revolution in 1849.

In fact Tsar Nicholas I showed considerable restraint and caution until the *Crimean War (1854–6) broke out. He hoped that British and Russian claims could be reconciled. This was certainly the impression he took away with him after his visit to Britain in 1844 to discuss the question of the Ottoman Empire with *Peel (1788–1850) and *Aberdeen (1784–1860). Both countries claimed to desire the continued existence of the Ottoman Empire. Russia, however, did not want to see the Porte strengthened. To have accepted a revived Ottoman Empire would have been a negation of the major objective of Russian policy for over a century. Britain, on the other hand, professed to believe in the possibility of effective reform in Turkey, a hope repeatedly to be disappointed. In January 1853 the Tsar tried to reach an understanding with Britain, putting forward a scheme for the partition of European Turkey. *Russell (1792–1878) replied that the British Government did not wish to discuss a hypothetical case. The anti-Russian faction in the Cabinet harried a hesitant and unconvinced Aberdeen into the Crimean War. This war was really an intervention by Britain, France and Piedmont-Sardinia in a conflict between Russia and Turkey. The ostensible objective of the Allies was to combat Russian claims to guardianship of Christians in the Ottoman Empire. Behind this, though, lay the crucial issue of the *balance of power and the determination of the Western Powers to ensure that Russia did not become the successor to the Ottoman Empire and controller of Constantinople and the Straits. Though hostility abated after the submission of Russia to the terms of the *Paris Treaty (1856), this did not resolve the underlying problem. The humiliation of the *Black Sea Clauses particularly rankled with the Russians. The Cretan Revolt of 1866 was openly encouraged by the Russians and there were frequent rivalries of interest between the powers in Persia and Afghanistan. In 1870, taking advantage of the distraction of Western Europe by the Franco-Prussian War, Russia renounced the Black Sea Clauses.

The crisis of 1853–4 was reproduced in 1875, though without this time leading to war between Britain and Russia. In the Eastern Crisis Russia was again denied Constantinople in its war with Turkey. But the events of these years, sparked off by revolts in Bosnia and Herzegovina, demonstrated the falsity of British hopes that the Sultan would be able to end Turkish misrule over Christian subjects in the Balkans, and the failure of the policy of bolstering up Turkey. Though the news of the *Bulgarian Massacres (1875–6) alienated British public opinion from the Turks, the stalward defensive action of the latter at Plevna in 1877 led to a dramatic resurgence of popular Russophobia. Britain resisted Russia over the *San Stefano Treaty (1878) and *Disraeli (1804–81), emboldened by the jingoistic outcry in Britain, forced Russia to accept the mediation of the *Berlin Congress (1878), which led to the abandonment of the idea of a 'Big Bulgaria' which would have considerably enhanced Russian influence had it been created.

In fact in the latter part of the nineteenth century the rivalry over the Balkans became increasingly a Russo-Austrian one. The focus of British attention shifted from the Straits to Egypt.

In Afghanistan and Persia an elaborate Anglo-Russian rivalry developed in the late Victorian period, in which the powers vied with each other to win over local rulers to their side (see, for instance,: *Afghan Wars). In retrospect we can see that the security of India and British control there was never in any real danger from Russia at this time, though the defence of the Indian border loomed large in defence calculations. At the same time, anxious for her commercial interests in China, Britain watched with apprehension Russia's appropriation of the Amur River provinces from China, which gave her a footing on the Pacific coast at Vladivostok. This was in the 1860s. By the end of the century Russia was encroaching on Manchuria and in 1898 she secured from Japan the Liaotung peninsula with the naval base at Port Arthur. The developing Anglo-Russian rivalry in the Far East was reflected in the *Anglo-Japanese Alliance (1902). Though this was also the result of wider imperial concerns, her general over-extension and her isolation, revealed clearly at the time of the 2nd *Boer War (1899–1902), its immediate object was to contain Russian expansion. It stipulated that if Britain were to fight Russia, Japan would remain neutral. In the event, in 1904–5 it was Japan who fought Russia and Britain who remained neutral. The defeat which Japan inflicted on Russia eliminated her as a major contender for power in the Pacific for 40 years.

The British wish to limit overseas defence liabilities was also reflected in the *Anglo-Russian Convention (1907), which set out to resolve the imperial rivalries of the two powers in Persia, Afghanistan and Tibet. This, together with the *Anglo-French Entente (1904) and the earlier Franco-Russian alliance produced the alignment of powers which faced Germany in 1914. In August 1914 Britain moved definitely to Russia's side in defence of Serbia. Later, when Turkey entered the war in November 1914, Britain joined France and Russia in agreements for the dismemberment of the Ottoman Empire, which she had been supporting against Russian advance for more than a hundred years. The core of these agreements was the proposed annexation by the Tsar of Constantinople and the Straits, described by the

British Foreign Secretary, Sir Edward *Grey (1862–1933) as the richest prize of the entire war. In fact the *Constantinople Agreements of May 1915 were repudiated by the Bolsheviks who seized power in November 1917.

## 1917–45

The most important fact about the fall of the Romanov dynasty in March 1917 and the subsequent revolution of November was, from the viewpoint of the British Government, considered to be their likely impact on the conduct of the war against Germany. It was strategic considerations rather than ideological ones which were uppermost. The revocation of the *secret treaties after the Bolshevik seizure of power was welcomed, but not Lenin's determination to make peace with Germany unless the Allies entered into peace negotiations. This Lenin and Trotsky did with the *Brest-Litovsk Treaty on 3 March 1918. The Allied intervention in the Russian Civil War (see: *Russian Civil War, Britain and the) was ill-fated and none of its objectives was achieved. Though some in Britain, most prominently Winston *Churchill (1874–1965) lobbied for the 'liberation of Russia'. (i.e. from the new revolutionary order), the original aim was to support by all possible means everyone in Russia willing to go on fighting the Germans, to prevent Allied supplies from falling into German hands and to make things difficult for those who wished to sue for peace. *Lloyd George (1863–1945) worked hard to break the deadlock in British relations with the new government. He called for a 'truce of God' in which the Bolsheviks would join the Paris talks on economic reconstruction and the revival of trade. This was strongly resisted both by Conservatives at home and by the French, whose Premier Clemenceau denounced Lenin and his supporters as a 'colony of lepers'. Lloyd George persisted in this policy until the Genoa Conference (1922), imagining that the New Economic Policy (NEP) introduced by Lenin in 1921 represented an ideological change of heart rather than simply a tactical retreat.

Nothing was achieved by way of reintegrating Russia into the economic life of the rest of Europe. The *Locarno Pacts (1925) were denounced by the Soviet Union, which had signed the Rapallo Treaty with Germany in 1922. In 1926 the General Strike in Britain brought charges of Soviet revolutionary interference,

followed by a breach of diplomatic relations. British grievances against the Soviet Union focused on two issues: confiscation of foreign property and the apparent determination of the Soviet Union to bring the capitalist world to its knees by propaganda and subversion. Comintern propaganda remained a standing source of British vexation, and British ministers were particularly concerned with the influence of communist ideas on anti-imperialist agitation in India. The British authorities during the 1920s charged the Soviet Union with repeated violations of the agreement of 1921 to refrain from 'hostile acts and propaganda'. The episodes of the *Zinoviev Letter (1925) and the *Arcos Raid (1927) illustrate the mood of distrust and hostility which presented such an obstacle to the regularization of relations between Britain and the Soviet Union.

With the rise to power of Hitler, Stalin saw the need for *collective security against Nazi Germany and in 1934 the Soviet Union became a member of the *League of Nations, an organization which she had previously consistently denounced. She called for a strengthening of the League Covenant and gave support to League sanctions over Abyssinia (see: *Abyssinian War (1935–6) ). Britain showed no inclination, though, to bring the Soviet Union into Western deliberations over the *Rhineland remilitarization (1936), the *Anschluss (1938), or at the time of the *Munich Agreement (1936). In the British Government's mind there appear to have been three essential objections to collaboration with the Russians: that the Soviet Union would be incapable of waging a successful offensive war against Germany (a doubt underlined by Stalin's purge of his army high command); that her regime and ideology were abhorrent; and, thirdly, that any suggestion of collaboration with Moscow would put an end to any hopes Neville * Chamberlain (1869–1940) or others might have that once Germany's grievances had been remedied she would settle down and become a respectable member of the international community. All of the Dominions with the exception of New Zealand were opposed to cooperation with the Soviet Union, while in Chamberlain's view the Russians were 'stealthily and cunningly pulling the strings behind the scenes to get us involved in war with Germany'.

Up till 1939 relations with Moscow took second place to the appeasers' pursuit of a 'general settlement' of European difficulties involving Britain, France, Germany and Italy. The subsequent pledges to Poland, Rumania and Greece bound Britain and France to go to war, if need be, in defence of the status quo on or near the borders of the Soviet Union. Britain refused to force Poland to allow Soviet forces to cross her territory in the event of a Nazi attack. Lord *Halifax (1881–1959) took the view that it was up to Stalin to allay his neighbours' fears in Eastern Europe, and this proved a major stumbling-block in half-hearted negotiations. By this time the Soviet Union was on the point of concluding the *Molotov–Ribbentrop Pact (23 August 1939).

When Britain and France went to war on 3 September 1939 the Soviet Union remained neutral. After her invasion of Finland she was castigated as a fellow-aggressor. The idea was even mooted in Britain of declaring war on her too, and in February 1940 the Supreme War Council went so far as to offer Finland 100,000 troops. By remaining neutral while Nazi Germany overran Western Europe in 1940, Stalin had helped to remove the *Second Front for which he so insistently called after Hitler launched his attack, Operation Barbarossa, against the Soviet Union (22 June 1941). Subsequent popular admiration for the heroism and sacrifices of the Soviet war effort did not, in fact, change the traditional distrust of the Soviet Union, at least at the official level. The Grand Alliance was an uneasy one. On the Soviet side the *Anglo-Soviet Alliance (1942) was regarded as an essential for Russian survival, rather than as something to be treated with either great trust or great gratitude. Stalin's aims in his relations with Britain were to ensure the fullest continuing commitment of Britain to the war effort against the *Axis and to elicit support for post-war Soviet claims in Eastern Europe once Germany had been defeated.

The war effort in common, therefore, suspended rather than bringing to an end the traditional antagonisms, territorial and ideological. On his way to the *Tehran Conference (1943) Churchill observed: 'Germany is finished . . . The real problem now is Russia. I can't get the Americans to see it.' For a while British and American statesmen had significantly different perceptions of Soviet intentions, but by the end of the war the East–West polarization was becoming increasingly apparent. Disputes over Poland, Germany and Iran were to signal the emergence of the post-war rivalry of the *Cold War.

## 1945–

The subsequent sharp confrontation of the Cold War and division between East and West were not initially perceived as inevitable by the British Government. British policy towards the Soviet Union at the end of the war envisaged alternatives. Ernest *Bevin (1881–1951), the Labour Foreign Secretary, repeatedly returned to the notion of three possible patterns of international order: a balance of power, a hegemony of one power, or a Concert of Powers of the *Big Three. His own preference was for a Concert of Powers. He made personal attempts to reduce post-war friction with the Soviet Union. He offered to extend the treaty of 1942 and insisted to the Americans that the Russians be given the opportunity to participate in the *Marshall Plan (1948–52) for economic recovery. Britain was not unaware of the Soviet need for security, particularly against a resurgent Germany, and of their apprehension over the Western monopoly of nuclear weapons.

Fear of the consequences of the military imbalance in Europe, the consolidation of Soviet control in Eastern Europe and the clash of interests in the Mediterranean and Middle East, in Iran, over Greece (though the Soviet Union refrained from direct support for the Greek Communists), impelled her towards the alternative of a balance of power with United States participation. The logic of Winston Churchill's *Iron Curtain Speech (1946), the alignment of Britain and Western Europe with the United States, assuaged the anxiety over security, but at the inevitable cost of a hardening of the East–West confrontation in opposed alliance systems. The *Truman Doctrine (1947) was precipitated by the British communication to the *State Department indicating that Britain could no longer afford to provide for the protection of Greece and Turkey. The Cold War was intensified with the *Berlin Blockade (1948–9) and the coup in Czechoslovakia (1948). The Soviet preponderance in conventional armed strength led to the *North Atlantic Treaty Organization (NATO) and, subsequently within it, to the rearmament of Western Germany.

Britain made new attempts after the death of Stalin to reach an understanding with the Soviet Union. These initiatives contributed to the armistice over Korea and the *Austrian State Treaty (1955). Sir Anthony *Eden (1897–1977) was instrumental in reviving East–West exchanges at top level and President Eisenhower was persuaded to participate in the *Geneva Summit Conference (1955). Eden called for German reunification to be followed by the establishment of a demilitarized zone in Central Europe, and for a European security pact, but was forced to drop these ideas by the other NATO partners.

The *Suez Crisis (1956) and the suppression of the Hungarian Revolution in the same year led to a sharp deterioration in relations, but by 1959 the tentative moves towards détente were renewed. The new Prime Minister, Harold *Macmillan (1894–1986) visited Moscow, associating himself with the Soviet leader, Khrushchev, in a declaration of common interest in the pursuit of arms limitation and troop withdrawals in agreed areas in Europe – the original Eden Plan which had been revised by the Polish Foreign Minister, Rapacki. The Macmillan era was the high point of Anglo-Soviet initiatives in the post-war period. His meeting prepared the way for the Paris Summit of May 1960, which nevertheless proved abortive, following the *U-2 Incident (1960). After the *Cuban Missile Crisis (1962) the *Nuclear Test Ban Treaty was signed (1963).

Subsequently, direct communication between the Soviet Union and the United States and vice versa has tended to be the pattern, as with the *Strategic Arms Limitation Talks (SALT). Britain's declining influence in this respect was clearly apparent in the failure of the attempts by Harold *Wilson (1916–    ) successfully to mediate in the Vietnam War. In January 1973 another avenue of relations with the Soviet Union opened up when the enlarged *European Community assumed powers to conduct commercial policy with the Eastern Bloc on behalf of its members. This removed from full national control an area of Anglo-Soviet relations of particular importance when the Soviet Union was rapidly increasing her international trade, and an area of political importance where commercial decisions are a not insignificant element in the response of the superpowers and their allies to one another.

ANDERSON, M. S., *The Eastern Question, 1774–1923*, Macmillan, 1966.

BOURNE, K., *The Foreign Policy of Victorian England, 1830–1902*, Oxford University Press, 1970.

COATES, W. P. AND Z., *A History of Anglo-Soviet Relations,* , Lawrence and Wishart, 1943.

GILLARD, D., *The Struggle for Asia, 1828–1914: A Study in British and Russian Imperialism*, Methuen, 1977.

GLEASON, J. H., *The Genesis of Russophobia in Great Britain*, Harvard University Press, Cambridge, Mass., 1950.

GORODETSKY, G., *The Precarious Truce: Anglo-Soviet Relations 1924–27*, Cambridge University Press, 1977.

KAZEMAZADEH, F., *Russia and Britain in Persia, 1864: A Study in Imperialism*, Yale University Press, New Haven, Conn., 1968.

MCNEILL, W. H., *America, Britain and Russia: Their Cooperation and Conflict, 1941–45*, Oxford University Press, 1953.

NORTHEDGE, F. S., *Descent From Power: British Foreign Policy 1945–73*, Allen and Unwin, 1973.

NORTHEDGE, F. S. AND WELLS, A., *British and Soviet Communism: the Impact of a Revolution*, Macmillan, 1982.

ULLMAN, R. H., *Anglo-Soviet Relations, 1917–21*, 3 vols., Princeton University Press, Princeton, N. J., 1961–72.

WHITE, S., *Britain and the Bolshevik Revolution*, Macmillan, 1980.

**Russian Civil War, British Intervention in the** (1918–20). At the time both of the overthrow of Tsar Nicholas II (8 March 1917) and of the subsequent Bolshevik seizure of power from the Provisional Government (6 November 1917) the primary interest of the British Government in the events in Russia was that her government should maintain the Eastern Front against Germany. British intervention in the war that broke out between the counter-revolutionary 'Whites' and the 'Red Army' was initially with the purpose of re-establishing their front and to prevent extensive stocks of military equipment and supplies, as at Murmansk and Archangel, from falling into the hands of the Germans. In April 1918 a small force of British marines landed at Murmansk and in June and July Allied troops occupied this area and Archangel. From December 1917 Britain in fact maintained contacts with the Bolsheviks while simultaneously supporting any anti-Bolshevik movement capable of removing Lenin from power.

At the same time, in southern Russia Britain threw her support behind the volunteer army of the White Russian General Denikin, who at one stage was able to penetrate to within 80 miles of Moscow. When the Red Army defeated him

Britain ordered him to negotiate surrender. On the refusal of his successor General Wrangel to implement the British order support was at once withdrawn. In the north the British prevailed upon the Baltic peoples, the Lithuanians, Latvians and Estonians to provide bases for an attack against Soviet-held Russia by the White armies in the Baltic under General Yudenich. This resulted in the independence of the Baltic states in the interwar years. British troops also intervened in the Caucasus and Trans-Caspian regions.

The hope that the Eastern Front could be re-established was thwarted by the *Brest-Litovsk Treaty (3 March 1918), yet after the German armistice in November the British Government continued to support the White Russian forces. Winston *Churchill (1874–1965), who had become War Minister in December 1918, campaigned for a decisive intervention to destroy the new revolutionary order, which had dissolved the Constituent Assembly, and to substitute a new constitutional, democratic regime along Western lines. Failing that, he argued, Britain should withdraw from the intervention altogether. In this he had the support of a large number of Conservative back-benchers.

The history of British involvement in the struggle of White *versus* Red does not support the view that it was a well-thought-out ideological crusade against Communism. Rather, it was confused, haphazard and half-hearted, following the line of least resistance. Troops were left in Russia simply because they were still there – in the end supporting White Russian leaders out of a residual sense of obligation derived from past services. *Lloyd George (1863–1945), the Prime Minister, took a very different view, recognizing that there was no benefit to Britain in an expensive and thorough intervention against the Bolsheviks. It was, in any case, only likely to strengthen the new order in Russia. He commented to Churchill: 'If we are committed to a war against a continent like Russia it is a road to bankruptcy and Bolshevism in these islands'. Lloyd George's search for an alternative policy at the *Paris Peace Conference (1919–20) led to the abortive *Prinkipo idea. He was unable to enforce negotiation with Lenin, being constrained by his French allies and by Conservative opinion at home. On 10 April 1919 he received a telegram bearing the signature of 200 Tory MPs on a motion rejecting any recognition for the Bolsheviks (at this time Churchill was advocating the use of German troops against the new Russia). At the same time, though, the Cabinet resolved to evacuate British troops from the losing White campaign. Lloyd George entertained the imaginative, though in the circumstances unrealistic notion of developing Russia by a European consortium. This, he hoped, would simultaneously, through rising prosperity, wean the Russians from Communism and provide a vast market for exports which would help to revive British industry. This plan remained a dead letter. Recognition of the new Soviet order was only finally accorded by Britain in January 1924.

BRADLEY, J., *Allied Intervention in Russia 1917–1920*, Weidenfeld and Nicolson, 1968.

MAYER, A., *Politics and Diplomacy of Peacemaking: Containment and Counterrevolution at Versailles, 1918–19*, A. Knopf, New York, 1967.

ULLMAN, R. H., *Anglo-Soviet Relations 1917–1921*, 3 vols., Princeton University Press, Princeton N.J., 1961–72.

**Russian Revolution and Britain,** see RUSSIA AND THE SOVIET UNION, BRITAIN AND, and also RUSSIAN CIVIL WAR, BRITISH INTERVENTION IN THE (1918–20)

# —S—

**SALISBURY,** Robert Gascoyne-Cecil, 3rd Marquess of (styled Lord Robert Cecil until 1865; Viscount Cranborne 1865–8) (1830–1903). Conservative Foreign Secretary (1878–80, 1885–6, 1887–92, 1895–1900); Prime Minister (1885–6, 1886–92, 1895–1902); Salisbury had one of the sharpest minds ever to be applied to the problems of British foreign policy. Like *Gladstone (1809–98), he had strong Christian convictions which caused him to view the conduct of foreign policy in moral terms. He thus abhorred war and human suffering, but while he was a vigorous critic of *Palmerston (1784–1865) and no admirer of Beaconsfield's bellicosity, he believed that the national interest and the cause of peace were best served by an active foreign policy. Accordingly, he was equally opposed to the inertia and *isolationism which afflicted British attitudes to the outside world in the period after Palmerston's death and were evident in the policies of *Derby (1799–1869) and *Granville (1815–91).

Salisbury, then styled Viscount Cranborne, first held Cabinet Office as Secretary for India in the 1866 Conservative government but resigned in 1867 because of his opposition to the Second Reform Act. He returned to the India Office in 1874 and was the principal British delegate to the abortive Constantinople Conference in 1876–7. Although Salisbury shared Beaconsfield's alarm at the threat from Russia he was sceptical as to the wisdom of supporting the Ottoman Empire in its existing form and favoured the partition of Turkey as the best long-term solution to the crisis. Initially he sided with *Derby (1826–93) in the Cabinet against the Prime Minister, but growing impatience with the *Foreign Secretary's ineffectual conduct had brought him round to support *Beaconsfield (1804–81) by the time Derby resigned. He was thus a logical choice to succeed to the *Foreign Office in March 1878.

The firmness of the new hand on the helm was immediately evident. Salisbury reasserted British objections to the Treaty of *San Stefano (1878) but expressed willingness to negotiate with Russia. Anglo-Russian Conventions were signed at the end of May 1878 and were followed by the Congress of *Berlin (1878). Here Beaconsfield was the man of the hour, but Salisbury played a major role in reaching a settlement. Meanwhile he endeavoured to obtain further safeguards for reform and stability in Turkey by negotiating a convention with the Sultan which enabled Britain to occupy Cyprus, and joining with the French in compelling the Khedive to accept essential reforms in Egypt. While these interventions were to alleviate the power vacuum in the Middle East they both led to long and troublesome commitments for Britain.

After Beaconsfield's death in 1881 Salisbury was able to establish himself as leader of the Conservative Party. He attacked the foreign policy of the 1880 Gladstone government and, when it fell in June 1885, he became Prime Minister. For most of the next 15 years Salisbury was Foreign Secretary as well as Prime Minister, and until 1895 he was the dominant influence on the formation of British foreign policy.

Salisbury immediately had to handle a new crisis in the Balkans. In September 1885 Eastern

Roumelia, which had been secured to Turkey at the Congress of Berlin, revolted and joined Bulgaria. Salisbury was initially alarmed by this fait accompli but subsequently accepted it as he considered that an enlarged Bulgaria would be an effective buffer against further Russian expansion. The underlying problem for Britain, highlighted by the Bulgarian crisis, was her strategic weakness in the Mediterranean, the consequences of which could only be alleviated by better relations with some of the other powers. Tensions with Russia in the Near East and with France in Egypt were for the present unavoidable, and hence Salisbury looked for an understanding with Germany and her partners in the Triple Alliance, Austria and Italy. This was achieved in the *Mediterranean Agreements of 1887, and good relations with Germany were confirmed in 1890 by the exchange of Heligoland for colonial concessions in Africa (see: *Heligoland–Zanzibar Treaty). However, the Government's suspicion of Bismarck and William II was too strong for them to be willing to make formal alliance. Salisbury was also anxious to reduce France's antagonism as far as possible.

After 1895 Salisbury's ascendancy was by no means as complete as it had been. Not only was he ageing rapidly, but the Unionists in the coalition government, notably *Lansdowne (1845–1927) at the War Office and Joseph *Chamberlain (1836–1914) at the Colonial Office, demanded a prominent share in the direction of policy. Chamberlain was an especially troublesome colleague, anxious for imperial expansion and an alliance with Germany. Unrest in the Ottoman Empire continued and, after Salisbury tried unsuccessfully to secure combined action by the European powers and recognized the hopelessness of independent action by Britain, the government abandoned the traditional policy of propping up Turkey, and fell back on Egypt. Thus the Mediterranean Agreements were allowed to lapse in 1897, a development which also represented a move away from alignment with the Triple Alliance. Consequent increased concern with the security of Egypt led Salisbury reluctantly to order *Kitchener to advance into the Sudan. After defeating the Mahdi at Omdurman on 3 September 1898 Kitchener found himself confronting a French army at *Fashoda on 19 September. This was a grave crisis in Anglo-French relations, but Salisbury's cool firmness enabled him to obtain a peaceful solution in Britain's favour. Elsewhere, however, Salisbury was unable to control the policy of his Cabinet: he could not halt the slide into war in South Africa (see: 2nd *Boer War (1899–1902) ), nor the acceptance of increased Russian interference in China, nor rapprochment with Germany both in the Far East and in Africa.

Salisbury was the last in the Victorian tradition of foreign secretaries who had kept Britain free from international alliances which could restrict her freedom of action, although he was well aware of the value of limited short-term cooperation. His commitment to peace combined with his concern for the maintenance of British prestige, within realistic limits, rendered him, in his prime, the most effective Foreign Secretary Britain had had since Palmerston's heyday. By 1900 his Cabinet colleagues were coming to consider that his policies were dangerously outmoded, but the events of the first quarter of the twentieth century were to show, retrospectively, the wisdom of Salisbury's shrewd caution.

CECIL, LADY, *Life of Robert, Marquis of Salisbury*, 4 vols., Hodder, 1921–32.

GRENVILLE, J. A. S., *Lord Salisbury and Foreign Policy*, Athlone Press, 1964.

LOWE, C. J., *Salisbury and the Mediterranean, 1886–1896*, Routledge, 1965.

**SALT,** see STRATEGIC ARMS LIMITATION TALKS

**San Francisco Conference** (1945). Otherwise known as the United Nations Conference on International Organization. It indicated a universal acceptance of the British and American wish for an international organization and the widespread concern to make it truly inclusive in its membership. Delegates from 50 countries, including Britain, met between 25 April and 26 June to finalize the Charter of the *United Nations. Draft proposals for this had already been presented at the *Dumbarton Oaks Conference (1944), and the proposed organization had been discussed at the *Yalta Conference (1945). A crucial point of debate was the veto power of the permanent members of the Security Council. Here the 'Yalta formula' was adopted. It is doubtful, despite the controversy over this during the discussions, whether any permanent member would genuinely have been willing to abandon the power of veto where enforcement action was contemplated which affected their vital interests. Another significant debate concerned the relationship between regional and universal organizations, particularly the Security Council. This reflected the desire especially of the countries of North and South America to be able to settle disputes in their own hemisphere amongst themselves. This was conceded in Article 51 of the Charter which permitted 'individual or collective self-defence against armed attack, until the Security Council has taken measures...'. Among its other initiatives, the San Francisco Conference created a new International Court of Justice and, to administer the *Trust Territories, a trusteeship Council.

NICHOLAS, H. G., *The United Nations as a Political Institution*, Oxford University Press, 1959.

WHEELER-BENNETT, J. W. AND NICHOLLS, A., *The Semblance of Peace*, Macmillan, 1972.

**San Stefano, Treaty of** (1878). The treaty ending the Russo-Turkish War of 1877–8 which was substantially modified by the *Berlin Congress (1878). Signed by the belligerents on 3 March 1878, San Stefano represented a conspicuous triumph for Panslavism and for the extension of Russian influence over the Ottoman Empire. It confirmed the independence of Serbia, Montenegro and Rumania and gave Russia gains in the Caucasus. Its most controversial clauses, though, specified the creation of a 'Big Bulgaria' including Macedonia and stretching to the Aegean. This was envisaged as an autonomous state under an elected prince and assembly. A Russian force of occupation of 50,000 troops was to remain in the territory for two years. Britain and Austria were very strongly opposed to the idea of such a 'Big Bulgaria'. *Disraeli (1804–81) took the view that such an entity would become a Russian client state, allowing the Russian Empire a stranglehold over Constantinople and access to the Mediterranean. As a result of strong protests and the threat of war between Britain and Russia, the Berlin Congress was convened to establish a *balance of power in the Balkans more generally acceptable to the Great Powers. This, among other things, divided the area which was to have constituted 'Big Bulgaria' into three. The northern part was to remain independent; Eastern Roumelia was created as a new province under Turkish suzerainty but with a Christian ruler, and the remaining areas were handed back to Turkey.

**Schleswig-Holstein Question.** A complex issue arising from the conflicting nationalist claims in the nineteenth century between Germans and Danes over the two Duchies. It involved Britain because of its possible implications for commerce and the *balance of power in the Baltic region. Schleswig-Holstein had been united since the Middle Ages with the King of Denmark as Duke of the Duchies. The composition of the Holstein population was almost wholly German, that of Schleswig only partly so. Further, the Danish King was a member of the German Confederation (Bund) though Schleswig lay outside it. During the revolutions of 1848 a Danish nationalist movement attempted to annex the Duchies, being opposed by the inhabitants and Prussian and other German forces with the blessing of the Frankfurt Assembly. *Palmerston (1784–1865) strongly objected to the German moves. Russia had already offered her support to Denmark and he was in particular afraid of the consequences for the balance of power of Russian and French intervention. Three campaigns between 1848 and 1852 resulted in the submission of the Duchies to the Danish Crown, and a compromise solution had the support of the powers in the Treaty of *London (1852).

The dispute was complicated by a dynastic wrangle resulting from the fact that the Danish Crown was due to pass through female descent to Christian of Glücksburg while the Salic Law recognized in the Duchies gave a preferential claim to the Duke of Augustenberg. On his accession in 1863 Christian IX accepted a constitution which incorporated Schleswig into Denmark, whereupon the Augustenburg claims were revived with German support in both Duchies. Through this issue the German Minister-President, Bismarck, set out to promote Prussian claims as the leading power in Germany, subsequently alleging that he had kept annexation of the Duchies in view from the very beginning. Palmerston assured Parliament that 'if any violent attempt were made to overthrow those rights and interfere with that independence, those who made the attempt would find in the result that it would not be Denmark alone with which they would have to contend'. This proved to be a bluff. Russia was preoccupied by the revolt in Poland and France was not interested in intervention. Britain could not go it alone and she contented herself with protests. As *Disraeli (1804–81) commented: 'We have threatened Prussia and Prussia has defied us'. Following the defeat of the Danes, it was agreed by the Convention of Gastein (1865) that the victorious powers, Prussia and Austria, should divide administrative control over the Duchies, with Holstein going to Austria and Schleswig to Prussia. Bismarck then used complaints of anti-Prussian agitation to provoke the Austro-Prussian War (1866), which brought Prussian mastery over North Germany. By the Treaty of Prague (1866) the Duchies were appropriated by Prussia and subsequently became part of the German Empire. After the collapse of Germany in *World War I (1914–18) the Treaty of *Versailles (1919) instituted plebiscites in Northern Schleswig where there was a large Danish population. As a result, the area north of Flensburg Fjord was annexed by Denmark in July 1920.

CARR, W., *Schleswig-Holstein, 1815–48*, Manchester University Press, 1963.

MOSSE, W. E., *The European Powers and the German Question, 1848–71*, Cambridge University Press, 1958.

**Schlieffen Plan.** The strategy worked out and amended by General Alfred von Schlieffen, who was Chief of the German General Staff between 1891 and 1905. It involved the violation of Belgian neutrality, which gave the British government, as co-guarantor of that neutrality, the *casus belli* for involvement in *World War I (1914–18). The plan was devised to meet the challenge of a two-front war against France and Russia (Bismarck's 'nightmare coalition') which Britain might join as an additional adversary.

The idea was to deploy maximum strength in the West and achieve a swift victory over France. It was hoped that if French power were broken early in a war her allies would offer little resistance. Secondly, French fortifications dictated that such a victory could only be attained by a flanking movement through Luxembourg, Belgium and Holland with a strong right wing encircling the French armies. The plan was modified by von Schlieffen's successor, the younger von Moltke. It was subsequently argued that the overlooking of the original injunction to 'keep the right wing strong' cost the Germans victory (see: *Marne, Battle of the (1914) ). This is over-simplistic. Britain could not in any case have tolerated the collapse of French power and the establishment of German hegemony over Europe. The strategy over-estimated the speed of German advance and underestimated the capacity of the French with their railway network for bringing up reserves. Nor did it take account of the British Expeditionary Force. Furthermore, since the plan had originally been devised the Russians had very considerably increased their military potential. The failure of this strategy of quick victory meant stalemate and the protracted war of attrition on the Western Front.

KENNEDY, P. M., ed., *The War Plans of the Great Powers, 1880–1914*, Allen and Unwin, 1979.

RITTER, G., *The Schlieffen Plan: Critique of a Myth*, tr. A. and E. Wilson, Oswald Wolff, 1958.

**Search, Right of** (see also: Blockade). The right to search and seize neutral shipping in order to enforce a *blockade or confiscate war contraband. This has been a frequently disputed issue between Britain and the United States and European countries. British naval supremacy after Trafalgar (1805) was such that collective action by other powers was needed if British searches were to be resisted. In 1812 the United States declared war on Britain after a British vessel opened fire on the *Chesapeake* for its refusal to submit to search. Attempts were made in the maritime clauses of the *Paris Treaty (1856), which Britain signed, and in the Declaration of London (1909), which she refused to ratify, to guarantee the free transit of shipping, except obvious contraband, in time of war. As *World War I (1914–18) showed, however, a country applying the laws of contraband and reprisal and mounting, therefore, a *de facto* blockade would not accept restraints on the right of search.

**SEATO**, see SOUTHEAST ASIAN TREATY ORGANIZATION

**Second Front.** A major issue of diplomatic and military dissension between the Soviet Union on the one hand and the Western Powers, Britain and the United States, on the other between 1941 and 1944. After Hitler's invasion of Russia on 22 June, 1941 the major Soviet objective in its relations with the Western Powers was to secure a second front in north-western Europe to relieve the pressure of German military might on Russia. A second front was first requested by Stalin in July 1941, but it did not materialize until the *Normandy

Landings in June 1944. The British did not wish to attempt a landing in northern France until both they and the Americans were sure of success. A major landing in 1942 or 1943 would certainly have been very hazardous, if not disastrous. So much seemed indicated by the fiasco of the Dieppe Raid of 19 August 1942. Britain was most reluctant to run the risk of a repeat of the experiences of *World War I (1914–18) and tended to favour a Mediterranean-Balkan strategy instead, attacking 'the soft under-belly of the Axis'. While the United States preferred a cross-Channel invasion because of the shorter distances involved and the simpler logistics, they, too, were well aware of the difficulties of operating against a fortified coast until they had sufficient numbers of troops, landing-craft and supplies. Impatience with the delay led to a vociferous 'Second Front Now' propaganda campaign in Left-wing circles in Britain. Stalin believed the delay was deliberate and that the Western Powers were not unhappy to see the Soviet Union weakened by taking the brunt of the war. This suspicion created considerable friction. The announcement of the principle of *unconditional surrender was made largely to reassure Stalin. In fact, had a successful landing taken place earlier, as he wished, it is unlikely that the Soviet Union would have gained such extensive control in Eastern Europe as it subsequently did with the collapse of Germany.

**Second World War,** see WORLD WAR II (1939–45)

**Secret Treaties** (World War I). The controversial pacts made by the Allies during the war apportioning the anticipated spoils of war. Between 1915 and 1917 secret engagements were entered into between Britain and France, Italy, Japan, Rumania, Russia, Serbia and Montenegro, covering a very large field of possible conquests. The most significant was the *London Treaty (1915). The details of the understandings with Tsarist Russia were discovered by the Bolsheviks after the Revolution and published. President Woodrow Wilson was strongly critical of the secret treaties and called for open diplomacy.

**Self-determination,** see NATIONAL SELF-DETERMINATION

**SELWYN-LLOYD,** John Selwyn Brooke Lloyd, 1st Baron (created 1976) (1904–78). Educated at Fettes and Magdalene College,

Cambridge. He was conservative MP for Wirral 1945–70, and Speaker of the House of Commons, 1971–6. As Minister of State at the *Foreign Office (1951–4), Lloyd developed a close political association with *Eden (1897–1977), who on becoming Prime Minister appointed him Minister of Defence in April 1955 and Foreign Secretary in December. Lloyd's lack of seniority and deference to Eden undoubtedly helped the latter get his way during the *Suez Crisis (1956): Lloyd supported all that Eden did, though he would have preferred to be much more open with the Americans. Lloyd survived the Suez débâcle and afterwards, with *Macmillan (1894–1986) concentrated on restoring good relations with the United States. This was necessary for maintaining the security of the Middle Eastern oil on which Britain depended, and for encouraging a détente between the superpowers – a process whose main result was the 1963 *Test Ban Treaty. Lloyd had shared Macmillan's reservations about joining the EEC and by the time he left the Foreign Office for the Treasury in July 1960 the radical policy options arising from economic and military decline, the end of empire and the loss of direction since 1956 were not yet apparent.

SELWYN-LLOYD, J., *Suez 1956: A Personal Account*, Cape, 1978.

SHLAIM, A., JONES, P., SAINSBURY, K., *British Foreign Secretaries Since 1945*, David and Charles, 1977.

**Sevastopol, Siege of** (1854–5). Major engagement during the *Crimean War (1854–6). This siege, which lasted for 349 days, was fought out between the Russian forces under Prince Menshikov defending the city and the besieging forces of the Allies, principally the British and French under Lord Raglan and General Canrobert respectively. Following the Battle of *Alma (1854) the Allies proceeded to bombard Sevastopol. They were too few in number to take the town by storm and a regular siege ensued, with the British blockading the harbour and leaving the Russians only the difficult northern route through which they could gain supplies. Tsar Alexander II sent forces to relieve the besieged and they were repulsed both at *Balaklava and *Inkerman. The siege was accompanied by a grave cholera epidemic and terrible hardship on both sides. The British lost 30 transports of essential supplies in a storm off Balaklava. This situation led to the fall of the British Government under Lord *Aberdeen

(1784–1860) and the arrival of Florence Nightingale, who organized nursing and relief work from Scutari, across the Bosphorus from Constantinople. In September 1855 the Malakov and Redan fortifications were captured. Prince Gorchakov, who had succeeded Menshikov, now abandoned Sevastopol, blowing up the defences and sinking the Russian ships. This was the last military engagement of the war, though the main Russian armies were undefeated. The allied victory at Sevastopol preserved the Ottoman Empire and halted the advance of Russian influence, as became apparent in the terms of the subsequent Treaty of *Paris (1856).

**Sèvres, Treaty of** (1920). Signed on 10 August by the victorious Allies with the defeated Ottoman Empire after *World War I (1914–18). The Sultan's government renounced all claims to non-Turkish territory. Smyrna and its hinterland were to be administered by Greece for five years, after which a plebiscite was to be held. The Dodecanese and Rhodes went to Italy while Thrace and the remainder of the Turkish islands in the Aegean were assigned to Greece. The *Straits were to be internationalized and the adjoining territory demilitarized. Armenia was recognized as independent, as was the Kingdom of Hijaz. Palestine and Mesopotamia (with Mosul) became British *mandates, while Syria became a mandate of France. The settlement was successfully resisted by the movement led by General Mustapha Kemal (later Atatürk), who proceeded to attack the Greeks. In 1921 France and Italy withdrew from their zones of occupation and, after the fall of Smyrna to Turkish forces, Britain also conceded the demand for a revision of the treaty terms. It is noteworthy that the recognition of the independence of non-Turkish peoples was not altered in the subsequent Treaty of *Lausanne (1923).

HELMREICH, P., *From Paris to Sèvres: The Partition of the Ottoman Empire at the Peace Conference of 1919–20*, Ohio State University Press, Columbus, 1974.

**Sextant,** see CAIRO CONFERENCE (1943)

**SIMON,** Sir John Allsebrook, 1st Viscount Simon (1873–1954). Educated at Fettes and Wadham College, Oxford, where he became a Fellow of All Souls in 1897. He was called to the Bar in 1899 and took silk only nine years later.

He became Liberal MP for Walthamstow in 1906 and entered the Cabinet in 1913 as Attorney-General. In August 1914 he originally favoured neutrality and was unhappy about the declaration of war. In May 1915 he became Home Secretary but, opposing *conscription, resigned in January 1916. Without the Lloyd George coupon, he lost his seat in 1918 but re-entered Parliament in 1922 as MP for Spen Valley, which he represented until his elevation to the Woolsack in May 1940.

It was Simon's formation and leadership of the Liberal National Party in 1931 that brought him into the Cabinet that November as Foreign Secretary. He was an unusual choice, and not one that *MacDonald (1866–1937) made willingly. He had not held ministerial office for 15 years, lacked experience of foreign affairs, and wanted to go to the Treasury; but he remained at the Foreign Office, despite friction with MacDonald, until June 1935. Most contemporaries and commentators agree that Simon was a failure as a Foreign Secretary, and Simon, in his otherwise unilluminating memoirs, implicitly acknowledged this himself: 'Responsibility ought to call out the best in a man, and I have never worked harder. But hard work may produce, alas! disappointing results.'

Behind this comment lay MacDonald's tendency to interfere unexpectedly and Simon's own inability to make up his mind and give a strong lead. He could master the details of a problem but he could not produce a policy. So in Cabinet he saw his role not as an initiator of policy but as an agent to be given instructions, while in the Foreign Office he was reluctant to arbitrate between different opinions. This exasperated Cabinet colleagues (especially Neville *Chamberlain (1869–1940)) and Foreign Office officials. Simon and the Permanent Under-Secretary, *Vansittart (1881–1957) did not get on, even though Simon's methods enhanced the position of Vansittart and other senior officials.

Simon's shortcomings were unfortunate at a time when the destabilizing effects of global economic depression were increasing the security risks to Britain and her empire. Simon's objectives during the *Manchurian Crisis of 1931–3 were incompatible: it was impossible to conciliate Japan and simultaneously to preserve China by working closely with the *League of Nations and the United States. The outcome was that Japan was alienated, the League humiliated and the United States

rendered indisposed to future cooperation with Britain. Simon assumed that world recovery and British recovery were dependent on European recovery; this required German recovery and therefore French consent which would not be given until France was satisfied about her own security. Hence the purpose of Simon's policies in Europe was to bring France and Germany together. *Reparations were ended in December 1932; but attempts to achieve a successful conclusion to the *World Disarmament Conference, which began in February 1932, all failed because France would neither disarm as Germany wanted nor allow Germany to rearm. Simon continued with an impartial approach to Franco-German disputes after Hitler's accession to power in 1933. In March 1935 he infuriated France and Italy by visiting Berlin only days after Hitler had flagrantly violated the *Versailles Treaty (1919) by announcing his intention to rearm. From June 1935 until May 1937 Simon was Home Secretary, and from May 1937 until May 1940 Chancellor of the Exchequer. Simon was closely involved with Chamberlain in conducting foreign affairs after 1937, but principally as a drafter of sensitive telegrams and as an advocate of government policy in Parliament, where he spoke with great effect. His advisory role was less important and he usually agreed with Chamberlain, although he showed considerable impatience at Chamberlain's tardiness in declaring war after the German invasion of Poland. He was Lord Chancellor in the Churchill wartime coalition (1940–5) and died in 1954.
SIMON, 1ST VISCOUNT, *Retrospect*, Hutchinson, 1952.

**Somme, Battle of the** (1916). A protracted series of frontal attacks in close formation by British and French divisions along a 20-mile stretch of the River Somme on strong German positions. It lasted for nearly five months (1 July–18 November). General *Haig (1861–1928) hoped for a breakthrough to end the stalemate on the Western Front. The Germans, who recognized that this was a turning-point in the war, because of the damage caused to them by losses, claimed that the front was in fact broken on 15 September, though this went unnoticed by the Allies. Tanks were used for the first time, though they achieved little because of unsuitable terrain and mechanical failure. Britain lost 400,000–500,000 men in this titanic engagement. There was a subsequent very major engagement on the Somme in 1918,

launched by Ludendorff in the hope of gaining a decisive victory in the west before the Americans could supply enough troops to cancel out the German advantage from the collapse of the Eastern Front.

**South African War,** see BOER WARS

**Southeast Asian Treaty Organization** (SEATO). Agreed by the Manila Pact of 8 September 1954 for the defence of Southeast Asia, SEATO came into existence on 9 February 1955. Though it attempted to base its character on *NATO, it did not have a unified military command, nor did it dispose of joint forces. It existed as a link in the global strategy of *Containment against Communism, but only provided for consultation in the event of emergency. Its membership consisted of Britain, the United States, France, Australia, the Philippines, New Zealand, Pakistan and Thailand. Its regional role was obviously weakened by the absence of India, Indonesia and Burma. At the same time, several members, including Britain, avoided unwelcome commitments to it. Britain, for instance, did not regard the Manila Pact as applying to Vietnam, Cambodia and Laos. In 1972 Pakistan withdrew after losing Bangladesh. France withdrew a year later. At the end of September 1975 ministers agreed to phase out the organization on the grounds of changed circumstances and conditions in the region, and on 30 June 1977 it was formally dissolved.

**Soviet Union, Britain and the,** see RUSSIA AND THE SOVIET UNION, BRITAIN AND

**Spain, Britain and,** see GIBRALTAR, POLIGNAC MEMORANDUM (1823), SPANISH CIVIL WAR, BRITAIN AND THE (1936–39), SPANISH MARRIAGES AFFAIR (1841–46)

**Spanish Civil War, Britain and the** (1936–1939). The Spanish Civil War broke out in July 1936 with the revolt of army commanders and units, led by Franco, commander of the troops in Morocco, against the Republican Government of Azaña. This war led to many hundreds of thousand dead, became the focus of wide international involvement and heated ideological controversy. The British Government's primary concern was that the struggle between Nationalists and Republicans should not be allowed to precipitate a major war between European powers. Soon Nazi Germany and Fascist Italy proceeded to aid the Nationalists with both troops and matériel. At the same time, the Soviet Union offered aid on a more limited scale to the Republic.

Opinions rapidly became polarized. On the one hand were those who saw Franco and his supporters as staunch defenders of Catholic and traditional Spain against the spread of Communism; on the other those, prominent among whom were the volunteers of the *International Brigades, who saw the war as a do-or-die struggle between democracy and Fascism. The role of France was obviously crucial. There the government of Léon Blum was under strong pressure to intervene on behalf of the Republic. Britain, for her part, made it clear that she would not come to the rescue of France if she involved herself in a European conflict as a result of involvement in Spain. The French Government therefore proposed that there should be an international agreement withholding all arms shipments from Spain. This idea was accepted with alacrity by the *Foreign Office. This led to the Non-Intervention Agreement, signed by 27 States, and the creation of the *Non-Intervention Committee in London. This was invested with the responsibility of investigating infringements – though it conspicuously lacked effective sanctions. The practical effect of this arrangement (admitted by the Prime Minister Stanley *Baldwin (1867–1947) to be 'a leaking dam') was to deprive the Spanish Republic of its international rights as a legally constituted government to buy arms.

The British Government essentially tried to hedge its bets over the Spanish Civil War. The strategic implications for *Gibraltar and the Canary Islands loomed large. It was clearly undesirable that these should become bases for a hostile power. There was a sizeable amount of British investment in Spain and some dependence on the supply of iron ore and pyrites from the Asturias. The Government was primarily interested that the territorial integrity of Spain and her possessions should be maintained and that, in the event of a European war, Britain should have a benevolently neutral Spain to deal with. Particular difficulties arose, though, from the blockades and submarine attacks against British and French shipping in the Mediterranean. These led to the *Nyon Conference (1937). Neville *Chamberlain (1869–1940) the new Prime Minister, was anxious to mend relations with Italy following the *Abyssinian War (1935–6). His readiness to make more concessions to Mussolini on the scheme to withdraw Italian troops from Spain than *Eden (1897–1977) considered appropri-

ate, without firm guarantees of good conduct from the Duce, became the issue over which the Foreign Secretary resigned.

The Spanish Civil War tended to distract British public opinion from the growing menace of German power. It also served to increase British Government suspicions of the intentions of the Soviet Union at a time when the logic of *collective security dictated their rapprochement. Franco gave Britain the assurance that Spain would remain neutral in the event of a European war. On 27 February 1939 the British Government recognized the Nationalists, to whom they had in fact already accorded a measure of *de facto recognition in 1937 when they sent a commercial agent, Sir Robert Hodgson, to Burgos. Madrid surrendered to the Nationalist forces on 28 March 1939.

EDWARDS, J., *The British Government and the Spanish Civil War, 1936–39*, Macmillan, 1979.
THOMAS, H., *The Spanish Civil War*, revised ed., Penguin, 1977.
WATKINS, K. W., *Britain Divided: The Effect of the Spanish Civil War on British Public Opinion*, Nelson, 1963.

**Spanish Marriages Affair** (1841–6). An issue which increased Anglo-French tension in the period following the *Straits Convention (1841). Britain was anxious to postpone the marriages of Isabella, Queen of Spain, and her sister, the Infanta, and to prevent the alliance of the son of the French King Louis Philippe and Isabella. After the failure of *Palmerston (1784–1865) to exclude the French from the negotiations, it was agreed that Isabella should marry the allegedly impotent Francis of Cadiz, and her sister the Duke of Montpensier (Louis Philippe's son). This interference was a conspicuous demonstration of Spanish weakness, and further undermined confidence in the regime.

In 1841 Prince *Albert (1819–61) and Lord *Aberdeen (1784–1860) had both declared that Britain would not intervene. In 1845 Louis Philippe had announced that 'he would never hear of Montpensier's marriage with the Infanta of Spain'. This pledge was jettisoned when Palmerston took over as Foreign Secretary in 1846. On 19 July 1846 he wrote a despatch to his Minister in Madrid in which he mentioned Leopold of Saxe-Coburg (first cousin to Queen *Victoria (1819–1901) and Prince Albert), as well as Isabella's two Spanish cousins, the Dukes of Seville and Cadiz, as being the only possible suitors for her. Palmerston stated unequivocally that the 'independence of Spain would be endangered, if not destroyed, by the marriage of a French Prince into the Royal Family of Spain'. The French had earlier told Aberdeen that Leopold's candidature would release them from their previous undertaking over Montpensier, and they now violently denounced Palmerston, who was presented as deliberately picking a quarrel with France. In the event the Duke of Seville proved unacceptable to either Queen Isabella or her government. Palmerston's proposals drove the Spaniards into the arms of France, and on 10 October 1846 the sisters married Cadiz and Montpensier. In the longer term, though, the Orléanist dynasty failed to gain Spain, by which time in any case (in the revolution of 1848) they had lost France.

JONES-PARRY E., *The Spanish Marriages, 1841–76*, Macmillan, 1936.

**Sphere of Influence.** A claim by a state to some degree of control or preferential status in a foreign territory or some region of the world. It may refer to military, political or economic claims or a mixture of these. The first agreement specifically to use the term was one concluded between Britain and Germany in 1885, defining their respective roles in the Gulf of Guinea. During the 1890s and the first decade of the twentieth century many agreements were concluded recognizing spheres of influence in China, Africa and the Middle East. China was the most conspicuous example, where Britain, France, Germany, Russia and Japan wished to enjoy monopolistic privileges in commerce and the exploitation of resources in their designated areas. In certain cases the powers appropriated for themselves political functions, usurping the role of Chinese authority. Spheres of influence may be proclaimed unilaterally, as with the hemispheric *Monroe Doctrine, or by agreement as between Britain and France in the *Anglo-French Entente (1904), in which Britain recognized French predominance in Morocco and France accepted Egypt as a British sphere of influence; or in the *Anglo-Russian Convention (1907) respecting spheres of influence in Persia. Since 1945 the term has tended to be applied most commonly to the hemispheric regions dominated by the superpowers.

**STANLEY,** Edward, 14th Earl of Derby (styled Lord Stanley 1834–51) (1799–1869). Conservative Prime Minister (1852, 1858–9, 1866–8). Stanley began his political career as a Whig and, when serving as Colonial Secretary in 1833, he carried the act for the abolition of slavery. In 1834 he resigned from the Government because of differences with his colleagues over Irish policy, and during the later 1830s, joined *Peel (1788–1850) in opposition. He returned to the Colonial Office in 1841 as a member of the Conservative Cabinet and in 1844 was raised to the Lords during his father's lifetime. He resigned over the repeal of the Corn Laws and in 1846 reluctantly assumed the leadership of the Protectionists. In the later 1840s he spoke frequently in the Lords on foreign affairs and his criticism of *Palmerston (1784–1865) reached a climax in 1850 when he carried a motion of censure against him over the *Don Pacifico affair. The government however obtained a contrary verdict in the Commons.

He succeeded to the earldom in 1851 and became Prime Minister in the next year. Following an inconclusive General Election Derby abandoned Protection in November 1852, but his government fell a few weeks later after only ten months in power. He attacked the 'fusion and confusion' which led to the *Crimean War (1854–6), but his own political position remained weak and he failed to form a government after the fall of *Aberdeen (1784–1860) in January 1855. Palmerston's discomfiture over the Orsini affair in 1858 enabled Derby to return to office. His second ministry lasted little more than a year. It saw much-needed reforms in the government of India and, in Italy, coolness towards the nationalist cause associated with unsuccessful endeavours to avert war between France and Austria.

In the early 1860s Derby was content to see Palmerston continue in office, although his isolationist and anti-imperialist instincts made him a frequent critic of Russell's foreign policy. When he became Prime Minister for the third time in 1866 he confirmed the shift towards non-intervention already evident in Clarendon's conduct of international relations in the short Russell ministry, and in his own son Lord *Stanley (1826–93) found a Foreign Secretary committed to the implementation of his principles. Failing health forced Derby to retire in February 1868. He had led the Conservatives for over 20 years and was distinguished by great ability as an orator, but the weakness of the party in the aftermath of the schism of 1846 meant that he had had little opportunity to exert a decisive influence on affairs.

JONES, W. D., *Lord Derby and Victorian Conservatism*, Oxford University Press, 1956.

**STANLEY,** Edward, 15th Earl of Derby (styled Lord Stanley 1851–69) (1826–93). Conservative Foreign Secretary (1866–8, 1874–8), the eldest son of Edward *Stanley, 14th Earl of Derby (1799–1869), Stanley differed from his father in having a shy, awkward personality. In his father's second ministry from 1858 to 1859 Stanley was Colonial Secretary and, after he had made a useful contribution in carrying the Government of India Act, he became the first Secretary of State for India.

In 1866 his father appointed him Foreign Secretary. It was generally accepted that he was an uninspiring choice, but there seemed to be no stronger candidate. His idealistic commitment to non-intervention, which reflected the views of his father, the Government and the country combined with his cautious nature to produce a policy of resolute irresolution. He watched from the sidelines while Bismarck imposed a peace settlement on Austria which greatly extended Prussian authority in Germany and destroyed the old European *balance of power. In the East he tried to bolster the Balkan states as buffers between Russia and Turkey, thus hoping to avoid commitments to the other powers, while he hesitated over the best response to the Cretan revolt (1866). However, in 1867 a dispute between France and Prussia over Luxembourg ultimately drove Stanley to agree to a conference in London on the issue. This only produced a meaningless guarantee of the Grand Duchy's neutrality. Stanley's attitude gave the impression that Britain could be discounted as a force in European affairs.

In 1874 Stanley, now Earl of Derby, returned to the *Foreign Office. His inertia came seriously to strain his friendship with *Disraeli (1804–81) and to infuriate Queen *Victoria (1819–1901) who, like the Prime Minister, favoured a vigorous interventionist foreign policy. As the crisis in the Balkans, sparked off by insurrections in Herzegovina and Bosnia in 1875, grew steadily more alarming, tension within the Cabinet grew apace. Derby was unable to develop a coherent policy. He made energetic efforts to achieve peace between Turkey and Serbia in autumn 1876 but otherwise merely floundered while his wife leaked Cabinet secrets to the Russians. When war between Russia and Turkey broke out in April 1877 Derby had the support of *Salisbury

(1830–1903) and Carnarvon in resisting Disraeli's scheme to seize the *Dardanelles in order to safeguard British interests. In the Treaty of *San Stefano of 3 March 1878 Russia imposed peace terms on Turkey which were unacceptable to Britain. Derby opposed exerting pressure on Russia to have the Treaty submitted to the scrutiny of the other powers. He found himself in a minority of one and resigned from the government. He moved to the Liberals and served *Gladstone (1809–98) as Colonial Secretary from 1882 to 1885 before joining the Liberal Unionists and serving as their leader in the House of Lords from 1886 to 1891.

It is hard to escape the conclusion that Derby was a man promoted beyond his competence on account of being his father's son, a friend of Disraeli and an important Tory magnate. The party also still lacked sufficient talent. Derby's general views on foreign policy were sound, albeit at variance with Disraeli's, but his personal deficiencies caused sensible caution to slide into dangerous indecision. He was one of the least successful foreign secretaries of the nineteenth century.

MILLMAN, R., *Britain and the Eastern Question, 1875–1878*, Oxford University Press, 1979
VINCENT, J., ed., *Disraeli, Derby and the Conservative Party: Journals and Memoirs of Edward Henry, Lord Stanley, 1849–69*, Harvester, 1977.

**State Department,** see DEPARTMENT OF STATE

*Status Quo,* see *Uti Possidetis* and *Status Quo*

**Sterling Area.** The free association of countries based on the use of sterling as an international financial medium. The commercial and financial supremacy of Britain before 1914 made sterling the key currency of world trade. Countries trading with Britain found it convenient to link their currencies with sterling and keep their reserves of foreign exchange in the form of sterling balances in London. It was only a loose association, however, until Britain went off the Gold Standard in 1931. On the outbreak of *World War II (1939–45) exchange controls were introduced, preserving the free circulation of sterling within the sterling area but limiting its convertibility into other currencies. During the war it shrank to include only the British *Commonwealth (though not Canada), Eire, Egypt, Sudan, Iraq, Jordan and Iceland. The sterling area was defined by statute in the Exchange Control Act of 1947. With the growing weakness of the international position of the British currency in the post-war years, particularly after the crisis leading to devaluation in 1967, many former members of the sterling area moved out of it. In 1977 an agreement was reached to help Britain run down her sterling balances and the so-called 'scheduled territories' were limited to Britain, including the Channel Islands and the Isle of Man, Gibraltar and Eire. In 1978 Eire left and in the following year the new Conservative government abolished exchange controls.

**STEWART,** Robert Michael Maitland (1906– ). Educated at Christ's Hospital and at St John's College, Oxford. After a teaching career he represented Fulham as Labour MP from 1945 to 1979, holding several junior posts in the Attlee Government and entering the Cabinet under Harold *Wilson (1916–   ) in October 1964 as Secretary of State for Education and Science. From January 1965 to August 1966 and from March 1968 to June 1970 he was Foreign Secretary, spending the intervening time at the Department of Economic Affairs. Accepting that Britain must adjust to being a major power of the second rank, Stewart was more willing than Wilson to think in European terms. Less enthusiastic than Wilson about the *Commonwealth, he hoped that Britain's considerable influence throughout the world could be used to enhance the United Nations's capacity to resolve disputes. In fact the *United Nations proved ineffective in many of the problems that Stewart faced: Rhodesia, Nigeria and, in particular, Vietnam, where British attempts to limit American commitment and promote peace were clumsy and resented in Washington. Convinced that Britain should join the *EEC to prevent France and Germany dominating Europe, Stewart could not persuade Wilson of this until after the 1966 election, but did much of the preparatory work for the unsuccessful negotiations led by George *Brown (1914–1985), and the successful ones of the Heath Government after 1970.
STEWART, M., *Life and Labour: An Autobiography*, Sidgwick and Jackson, 1980.

**STOCKTON,** Earl of, see MACMILLAN, (MAURICE) HAROLD, (1894–1986)

**Straits Convention** (1841). The international regulation of the Black Sea signed on 13 July 1841 by *Palmerston (1784–1965) and the representatives of Russia, Austria, Prussia, France and Turkey. It strategically weakened the position of Russia in the Near East by confirming the principle that foreign warships should be forbidden from entering the Straits while the Porte was at peace. In 1841 the terms of the Treaty of *Unkiar-Skelessi (1833) expired. The new arrangement, following second *Mehemet Ali crisis, for the first time created a regime of the Straits recognized by the powers as part of the international law of Europe. (See: *Straits Question.)

**Straits Question.** The major diplomatic issue between Britain and Russia over the rights of passage through the Bosphorus and Straits of the *Dardanelles between the Black Sea and the Mediterranean. The Treaty of Kutchuk-Kainardji (1774) had granted the Russian Empire freedom of navigation and passage for merchant ships through the Straits. Britain became progressively alarmed during the nineteenth century over Russian ambitions there, as did France and Austria. Britain in particular feared that Russian control of the straits would help to transform the *balance of power in the Eastern Mediterranean and endanger her interests in the Middle East and India, threatening her lines of communication. In 1833 the Treaty of *Unkiar-Skelessi was thought, wrongly, to give Russia a free passage through the Straits.

In 1841 in the *Straits Convention *Palmerston (1784–1865) amended this and brought about international recognition of the traditional Ottoman ruling which closed the Straits to all foreign warships while the Turkish Empire was at peace. The 'regime of the Straits', as it was called, remained a potential source of diplomatic tension and military conflict. It survived, though, until the end of *World War I (1914–18), when the defeat of Turkey and distraction of Russia in revolution and civil war allowed the Allies to establish control. The Treaty of *Sèvres (1920) proposed that the Straits should be controlled by an international commission and should be opened to all vessels, including ships of war, of all nations. The subsequent Straits Convention of 1923 modified this arrangement. It permitted free passage for merchant shipping and for warships under 10,000 tons in time of peace. It additionally set up an International Straits Commission at Istanbul. This was then rescinded by the *Montreux Convention (1936), which gave back control of the Straits to Turkey. The changes following World War I were consistently opposed by the Soviet Union, who considered them as a threat to her Black Sea coast. Strong pressure was brought to bear on Turkey in 1946 by the Soviet Union to persuade her to modify them. By then the future of Turkey, as of Greece, had become key considerations in the growing confrontation of the *Cold War (see: *Truman Doctrine).

ANDERSON, M. S., *The Eastern Question, 1774–1923*, Macmillan, 1966.

CLAYTON, G. D., *Britain and the Eastern Question: Missolonghi to Gallipoli*, Hodder and Stoughton, 1971.

**Strategic Arms Limitation Talks** (SALT). Armaments negotiations between the superpowers, undertaken in the hope that agreement on the most expensive nuclear weapons could lead to a general slowing-down of the arms race and a better international climate. The first round of these talks began in Helsinki in 1969. It was designed to place limits on strategic (intercontinental) nuclear weapons and to curb the development of anti-ballistic missile systems. Agreement was reached on limiting missile-delivery systems for five years and restricting the number of ABM systems to two in each country. Agreement was concluded in May 1972. Negotiations were resumed under the name of SALT II in November 1974. General guidelines on armaments ceilings were reached in the Vladivostok Accords. An agreement was signed in Vienna in June 1979 according to which the total number of strategic missiles and bombers on each side was to be reduced from 2,400 to 2,250 by 1981.

Latterly, opinion in the West hardened, questioning the seriousness of the Soviet Union's commitment to disarmament. Partly this was because of the Russian refusal to permit proper verification of Soviet missile sites and the involvement of the Soviet Union in, for instance, Ethiopia. There was also a fear that the Soviet union was exploiting *arms control to achieve a position of superiority in the nuclear race. President Carter's treaty with the Soviet Union was shelved when it was clear that it would not be ratified by the United States Senate. President Reagan indicated on taking office that he rejected the SALT II treaty because he felt the United States had negotiated from a position of weakness.

WOLFE, T. W., *The SALT Experience*, Ballinger, Cambridge, Mass., 1979.

**STRATFORD CANNING,** Viscount Stratford de Redcliffe (created 1852) (1786–1880). Arguably the greatest British diplomat of the nineteenth century, he was cousin of George *Canning (1770–1827), who helped to further his career in its early stages. He was first sent to the embassy in Constantinople in 1808 and, when still only 23, took charge of it in 1810. In 1812 he negotiated the Treaty of Bucharest between Turkey and Russia, thus averting the danger of a Turco-French alliance, establishing strong British influence in Turkey and freeing Russia to concentrate on the struggle against Napoleon.

After serving as Ambassador to Switzerland from 1814 to 1820, where he played an important part in setting up the federal government, and to the United States from 1820 to 1824, where he advanced Castlereagh's policy of conciliation in the aftermath of the war of 1812, Canning returned to Constantinople in 1825. He helped to bring about Greek independence (see: *Greek War of Independence 1821–29), but resigned his ambassadorship in 1829 as a result of a dispute with Lord *Aberdeen (1784–1860).

During most of the next ten years Canning was not actively involved in diplomacy, but instead tried to pursue a parliamentary career. However, it became clear to him that he was better equipped to be a diplomat than a politician, and in 1842 he once again became Ambassador to Turkey, holding the post, apart from short intervals, until he finally retired in 1858. During this period he exercised a strong influence on Turkish domestic affairs, encouraging much-needed reforms, while he became very popular at home as the man best able to contain Russian expansionism.

The most controversial phase of his career came when he played a central role in the crisis which led to the outbreak of the *Crimean War (1854–6). He has been accused of deliberately engineering conflict between Turkey and Russia, but modern research has served to exculpate him from this charge, stressing rather his persistent endeavour to avert war, which was frustrated by imperfect coordination of policy with the government at home and the bellicose attitudes of the protagonists. During the war he worked with remarkable energy and efficiency organizing invaluable logistical support for the army in the field. Stratford was popularly dubbed with the Turkish title of 'the Great Elchi' and gained a renown which gave a new dignity to the profession of diplomacy.

HERKLESS, J. L., 'Stratford, the Cabinet and the Outbreak of the Crimean War', *The Historical Journal*, vol. 18, 1975, pp. 497–525.

LANE-POOLE, S., *The Life of the Rt Hon Stratford Canning, Viscount Stratford de Redcliffe*, 2 vols, Longmans, 1888.

**STRATFORD DE REDCLIFFE,** Viscount, see STRATFORD CANNING

**Stresa Conference** (1935). A meeting of representatives from Britain (Ramsay *MacDonald (1866–1937) and Sir John *Simon (1875–1954) ), France and Italy between 11 and 14 April 1935. It followed the renunciation of the military clauses of the Treaty of *Versailles (1919) by Germany on 16 March and produced a strongly worded condemnation of Germany's actions, reaffirming the three powers' commitment to the *Locarno Pacts (1925) and to Austrian independence. The powers announced that they would oppose any further repudiation of Versailles which might endanger European peace. To reinforce its stand the British government persuaded the League Council to endorse the condemnation of Germany for its breaking of the arms limitation agreements. The so-called 'Stresa Front' was soon broken when Italy invaded Abyssinia (see: *Abyssinian War (1935–6) ). The British and French response to this, which included support for League sanctions against Mussolini, encouraged Italo-German rapprochement.

**Succession States.** The independent states which emerged from the break-up of the Austrian and Ottoman empires in 1918 and which succeeded to the sovereign rights previously possessed over their territories by the Habsburg Emperor and the Sultan. They included Austria, Czechoslovakia, Hungary, Poland, Rumania and Yugoslavia. Italy also incorporated areas of Habsburg territory (see: *irredentism). The potential vulnerability and instability of these states represented one of the major weaknesses of the settlement after *World War I (1914–18).

**Sudetenland.** The region of northern Bohemia along the German frontier. Though it had never been part of the German Empire founded in 1871, it became the focus of an irredentist campaign (see: *irredentism) on behalf of the three-and-a-quarter million German-speaking inhabitants there by the Nazi-backed Sudeten-deutsche Partei from the mid-1930s. The Sudetenland was assigned to the new *succession state of Czechoslovakia by the Treaty of St Germain (1919) after *World War I (1914–18). Hitler used the position of the Sudetendeutsch as a minority group in Czechoslovakia, occupying a part of the country that was both strategically and economically very important, to mount a sustained propaganda attack on the new state, which became conspicuously vulnerable after the *Anschluss (1938). The leader of the Sudeten Germans, Henlein, first put forward a demand for autonomy within the Czech state. When this was reluctantly granted by the Czechs after pressure from the British mediator Lord Runciman Hitler and Henlein increased their demand to one of outright cession of the area to Germany. In September 1938 the Czechs were forced by the *Munich Agreement of Britain, France, Germany and Italy to hand over the Sudentenland to Germany, its transfer involving also the surrender of the main line of Czech defence.

**Suez Canal.** The shipping lane between the Mediterranean and the Red Sea. It was constructed by the French engineer Ferdinand de Lesseps and financed by the Emperor Napoleon III and the Compagnie Universelle du Canal Maritime de Suez. The company was founded in 1858 and secured a 99-year concession for running the Canal. To start with the British government, Parliament and the Press strongly opposed the construction, seeing it as a French stratagem for extending her influence in the Middle East and, therefore, as a potential danger to British lines of communication with India. Consequently, not one of the 400,000 shares was taken up by British investors. The Canal was opened on 17 November 1869. In 1875, with a dramatic financial coup, the Prime Minister, *Disraeli (1804–81) purchased the shares of the bankrupt Khedive Ismail for £4 million (the money being advanced by Rothschild in anticipation of parliamentary approval). In this way Britain secured a control in this strategically highly important link.

The Treaty of *Constantinople (1888), signed by all European maritime nations, declared the Canal 'open to vessels of all nations' and 'free from blockade', a right which was suspended during the world wars. British troops were responsible for the defence of the Canal between 1883 and 1956, and a treaty of 1936 between Britain and Egypt created the

Suez Canal zone where British troops, withdrawn from Egypt proper, were concentrated. Following the recognition of the Canal as an integral part of Egypt in 1954, Britain finally evacuated the zone on 13 June 1956. However, on 26 June President Nasser of Egypt nationalized the Canal, an action which led to Anglo-French military intervention (see: *Suez Crisis (1956) ). In 1958 the Suez Canal Company recognized the nationalization in return for £28 million and changed its name to the Suez Financial Company.

BELL, K., 'British Policy towards the Construction of the Suez Canal. 1859–65', *Transactions of the Royal Historical Society*, Vol.15, 1965, pp. 121–43.

**Suez Canal Convention,** see CONSTANTINOPLE TREATY (1888)

**Suez Crisis** (1956). This developed in July 1956 when President Nasser of Egypt nationalized the *Suez Canal, an action precipitated by the cancellation of United States, British and World Bank aid for the construction of the Aswan Dam. He seized the Canal partly in order to use the income from its tolls to fund his project. The background to the crisis was one of sharply deteriorating relations. Arab–Israeli hostility had latterly been aggravated by Egyptian commando raids in Israel. At the same time, the British were growing apprehensive of the threat which, as they saw it, Nasser's aspirations, as leader of the Arab League, posed to their own position and that of their protégés in North Africa and the Middle East. Britain and France, both large stockholders in the Canal, additionally saw its nationalization as posing a threat to Western oil supplies. The British Prime Minister Anthony *Eden (1897–1977), seeing Nasser as a 'megalomaniacal dictator' and very conscious of the consequences of *appeasement in the 1930s, allowed British collaboration in a secret collusive understanding with France and Israel. The plan was for Israel (particularly anxious since large purchases of arms had been made by Egypt from the Eastern Bloc) to strike first at Egypt. After this the British and French were to repossess the Canal in the guise of peacemakers, separating the Israeli and Egyptian forces.

Following abortive efforts by the United States, among others, to forestall military action (for example, the mooted Suez Canal Users' Association), the Israelis launched a full-scale attack across the Egyptian border into the Sinai Peninsula on 29 October. An Anglo-French ultimatum was sent to the belligerents on 30 October, calling for a withdrawal of forces on each side of the Suez Canal. A further demand was made on the Egyptians that they allow Anglo-French troops to be moved 'temporarily' into certain key positions. These terms were unacceptable to Nasser. On 5 November paratroops were dropped on Port Said and Port Fuad and an invasion fleet arrived the following day. The United States (Washington had not been informed by the British of the impending invasion) moved swiftly with a series of political and economic manoeuvres to halt an operation which she regarded as very damaging to Western interests in the Middle East.

Britain now faced her worst financial crisis since 1945. The American government informed her that she would receive assistance for sterling only if the military campaign were called off. Accordingly, she and France almost immediately agreed to a ceasefire (7 November), under intense international pressure, including a Russian threat to use rockets. Eden also faced wide opposition at home to the use of force. The ceasefire was secured by a United Nations Emergency Force, with the backing, among others, of both the United States and the Soviet Union. The withdrawal demonstrated the limits of British capabilities in the face of world opinion and, more particularly, that of the United States. To much of the world the Anglo-French expedition was perceived as an 'imperialist' action, and its failure marked a dramatic loss of face in an area which had traditionally been one of British and French *spheres of influence. It also represented a post-war nadir in Anglo-American relations. Among *Commonwealth members only Australia and, less enthusiastically, New Zealand supported Eden, who resigned the premiership in poor health two months later. The furore over Suez additionally served to distract world opinion from the other major contemporary event – the suppression of the Hungarian Revolution by the Soviet Union.

BAYLIS, J., *Anglo-American Defence Relations: The Special Relationship 1939–84*, 2nd ed., Macmillan, 1984.

CARLTON, D., *Anthony Eden: A Biography*, Allen Lane, 1981.

JAMES, R. R., *Anthony Eden*, Weidenfeld and Nicolson, 1986.

NEUSTADT, R. E., *Alliance Politics*, Columbia University Press, New York, 1970.
NUTTING, SIR A., *No End of a Lesson: The Inside Story of the Suez Crisis*, Constable, 1967.
THOMAS, H., *Suez*, Weidenfeld and Nicolson, 1967.

**Summit Diplomacy.** Meetings of heads of state or government of the major powers, especially the superpowers, for the resolution of outstanding issues, promotion of mutual understanding and reduction of hostility, or in wartime for the coordination of policy and strategy between allies. The term was derived from the appeal by Winston *Churchill (1874–1965) for a 'parley at the summit' in 1950, but it has been used retrospectively to describe, for instance, the *Yalta and *Potsdam conferences of 1945. It could be argued that the decision of President Woodrow Wilson personally to participate in the *Paris Peace Conference (1919–20) inaugurated the modern era of summit conferences. On the one hand it represented a logical extension of wartime collaboration; on the other it reflected a distrust of pre-*World War I (1914–18) dependence on secret diplomacy. After *World War II (1939–45) summit diplomacy has tended to superimpose itself on the normal diplomatic processes. Post-war examples include the *Geneva Conference (1955), attended by Sir Anthony *Eden (1897–1977) for Britain and the abortive Paris Summit (1960) in which Harold *Macmillan (1894–1986) participated.

**Sykes–Picot Agreement** (1916). In 1914 Britain found herself at war with Turkey. In the past she had used the Ottoman Empire as a bulwark against Russian expansionism. Now she found herself taking part in the destruction of an empire she had hitherto sought to defend, as in the *Crimean War (1854–6), and in league with a Russia whose ambitions remained unaltered – one of which was the prize of Constantinople.

At the beginning of the war Britain annexed Egypt and Kuwait, which she had hitherto ruled, but doing so under the legal fiction of continuing Ottoman rule. In 1915 Russia reiterated her traditional demands. Britain and France agreed, but privately resolved not to allow Russia to have Constantinople and the Straits (see: *Straits Question). Anglo-French talks over partition began in November 1915 and it was decided that Britain would receive Transjordan, Iraq and northern Palestine while France would get Syria (including Lebanon), Cilicia and Mosul. Russia would be granted Turkish Armenia while southern Palestine would be under international control. Italy was also promised territory.

After preliminary agreement was reached in January the final accord was signed on 16 May by the two chief negotiators, Sir Mark Sykes (later chief adviser to the *Foreign Office on Near Eastern policy) and Georges Picot. The whole agreement was subject to Russian consent and the Bolshevik Revolution of 1917 nullified it. By the end of the war the situation had become confused by contradictory promises and changing events. The Arab Revolt had aroused nationalist sentiment and the British High Commissioner in Egypt, Sir Henry MacMahon, had promised Turkey's Arab lands to one of the leaders of the revolt, the Sharif of Mecca. Also in November 1917 the British Foreign Secretary Arthur *Balfour (1848–1930) had promised a Jewish national homeland in Palestine (see: *Balfour Declaration (Palestine) ). In the end Britain had done the lion's share of the fighting against Turkey and come away with the lion's share of the spoils. She obtained Iraq and eventually Mosul as well as Transjordan and the whole of Palestine as *Mandates – France receiving just Syria and Lebanon. Some, such as T. E. Lawrence, felt that the settlement had betrayed the Arabs. It left Britain the predominant power in the Middle East.

ADELSON, M., *Mark Sykes, Portrait of an Amateur*, Cape, 1975.
NEVAKIVI, J., *Britain, France and the Arab Middle East, 1914–20*, Athlone Press, 1969.

**Tahiti Incident** (1843). An Anglo-French colonial dispute which excited some popular agitation for war between the two countries. George Pritchard was a missionary from the London Missionary Society and British Consul in Tahiti. When the French Catholic missionaries attempted to land on Tahiti in 1836 Pritchard had intervened and forced the Queen of Tahiti, Pomare IV, to expel them. The French demanded retribution and the imposition of a French protectorate, to which Pritchard and the Queen had to accede. In 1842 he visited England in the hope of persuading the British government to annex the islands. When Queen Pomare, encouraged by Pritchard, tried to repudiate the convention the French admiral Dupetit-Thouars (without referring to Paris) deposed her and annexed Tahiti. Pritchard was arrested and then, in 1844, expelled from Tahiti by the French. In the following year the British government appointed him Consul in Samoa.

The Pritchard affair, as it is otherwise known, raised a storm of popular indignation in Britain and was magnified into a substantial issue of national pride. When the British government protested Guizot reversed the annexation but maintained the protectorate. At the same time, while the veto on Pritchard's return to Tahiti was upheld, France expressed regret at the manner of his expulsion and indemnified him for personal losses. British public opinion was already roused to hostility at this time because of French advances in North Africa, but calm negotiations between the governments produced an acceptable compromise, damping down popular belli-cosity over the issue. Tahiti was formally annexed by France in 1888.

**Tehran Conference** (1943). The first meeting of the *Big Three, *Churchill (1874–1965), Roosevelt and Stalin between 28 November and 1 December 1943. It was preceded by Soviet recriminations over the postponement of the Second Front and mutual suspicions between the Western Powers and the Soviet Union that each might be envisaging a separate peace with Hitler. Most of the discussions concerned military planning since operations 'Overlord' and 'Anvil' had been agreed upon. Churchill argued for a Mediterranean strategy, and there was considerable debate over the feasibility of bringing Turkey into the war. This idea received no support from Roosevelt and was regarded with suspicion by Stalin.

There were discussions about the 'Four Policemen' concept and a future world organization (later the *United Nations) about Soviet demands in Eastern Europe and the Far East and about Germany after the war. Final decisions on the later very contentious issue of Poland were postponed (*Eden (1897–1977) was to report to the Cabinet that Stalin had taken 'a very hard line' on Poland's eastern frontier). A separate protocol was signed by the Big Three promising to maintain Iran's independence. Tehran already suggested that harmony between the members of the Grand Alliance would be difficult to maintain after victory had been achieved, and that there would be considerable political differences between the Soviet Union and the Western Powers.

EUBANK, K., *The Summit Conferences, 1919–1960*, University of Oklahoma Press, Norman, 1966.

FEIS, H., *Churciill, Roosevelt, Stalin: The War they Waged and the Peace they Sought*, Princeton University Press, Princeton, N.J., 1957.

**Tel-el-Kebir, Battle of** (1882). On 13 September 1882 a British and Indian force under Sir Garnet Wolseley, acting under the authority of the Khedive Taufiq, defeated an Egyptian force of 10,000–15,000 under Arabi Pasha and went on to capture Cairo. Arabi was taken and sent into exile. British casualties were about 400 as against 4,000 Egyptian dead. This victory inaugurated the period of British control in Egypt, ending the Franco-British condominium.

**TEMPLEWOOD, Viscount,** see HOARE, SIR SAMUEL (1880–1959)

**THATCHER,** Margaret Hilda (1925–     ). Born in Grantham, educated at Somerville College, Oxford, subsequently qualifying as a lawyer in London, Margaret Thatcher was elected as MP for Finchley in 1959. From 1961 to 1964 she was joint parliamentary secretary for the Ministry of Pensions and National Insurance. When the Conservatives returned to power under Edward *Heath (1916–     ) she was appointed Secretary of State for Education and Science. Following Heath's double electoral defeat in 1974, she became leader of the Conservative Party and, in 1979, Prime Minister. Her foreign policy has been characterized by a forthright, and some would say abrasive, assertion of British national interests. This has been notably the case in relation to the other members of the EEC, where her attitude is in very marked contrast to that of her Conservative predecessor. She has consistently and firmly aligned Britain with United States foreign and defence policies, espousing a strongly anti-Soviet stance and giving priority to defence expenditure. Her most dramatic initiative was the despatch of a task force to the South Atlantic following the Argentinian invasion of the *Falkland Islands in April 1982 and the recapture of the islands, something which contributed to her re-election with a very large majority in Parliament in 1983.

COSGRAVE, P., *Margaret Thatcher: A Tory and her Party*, Hutchinson, 1978. *Thatcher: The First Term*, Bodley Head, 1985.

RIDDELL, P., *The Thatcher Government*, Martin Robertson, 1983.

**Ten Year Rule.** The instructions first issued by the coalition government under *Lloyd George (1863–1945) in 1919 that the defence estimates should be calculated on the assumption 'that the British Empire will not be engaged in any great war during the next ten years and that no expeditionary force will be required'. They were adopted at the suggestion of Winston *Churchill (1874–1965), then Secretary of State for War and Air. A later clarification allowed the Treasury to demand that everything requested by way of resources by the defence chiefs be justified in terms of immediate need, which was difficult in the relatively pacific scene of the 1920s. In the period of retrenchment which followed *World War I (1914–18) spending on the armed forces fell from £766 million in 1919–20 to £102 million in 1932. In 1928, as Chancellor of the Exchequer, Churchill persuaded the Cabinet and the *Committee of Imperial Defence to establish the Ten Year Rule on a permanent basis, but it remained in force only until 1932 when the implications of the Japanese aggression against Manchuria (see: *Manchurian Crisis (1931–3) ) forced its abandonment. In retrospect the consequences of the Ten Year Rule were perceived to be very damaging: the incapacity of British defence to meet the requirements of the Empire was one of the major considerations behind the strategy of *appeasement. Moreover, when rearmament began in earnest in the mid-1930s armaments factories, which in many cases had been adapted to other needs, found themselves understaffed for meeting the pressing demands made upon them.

**Tientsin Treaties** (1858). Treaties concluding the *Arrow* War which had started in 1856. They were signed between 26 and 29 June 1858 by China with Britain, Russia, France and the United States. The terms which were dictated to the Chinese by the victors greatly increased the scope of the imperialist powers in China. Ten new treaty ports were opened. Foreigners were granted freedom to travel anywhere in the interior of China. The tariff was fixed at five per cent and the opium trade was legalized. Furthermore, all foreign diplomats were to be allowed to reside in Peking. When the Chinese obstructed the ratification of the treaties in 1859 this led to a renewal of hostilities. The subsequent Peking Convention increased the burden of indemnity on China, added Tientsin to the treaty ports, ceded Kowloon to Britain, and granted the right of Catholic missionaries to own properties in the interior of China.

TWITCHETT, D. and FAIRBANK, J. K., eds., *The Cambridge History of China*, vol. X, Cambridge University Press, 1978.

**Treaty.** The most important type of international agreement which it is intended should be binding. The word is derived from the French *traiter* (to negotiate) and may be used in two senses, one general, the other restricted. In the wide sense, it may cover any international agreement which has an obligatory character. It can also mean a formal instrument of agreement by which two or more states establish or seek to establish a relationship between themselves under international law. Treaties having only two signatories are termed bilateral and those with more parties multilateral. Treaties may expire at the end of a stated period when certain conditions have been met, or by mutual agreement. Renunciation of a treaty by one or more of its parties may occur when a state of war exists or when conditions have been substantially altered.

**Trent Affair** (1861). A diplomatic crisis between Britain and the United States at the time of the American Civil War, which involved the disputed doctrine of the *freedom of the seas. It was caused by the capture of two Confederate diplomatic agents bound for Britain, James Mason and John Slidell, in November 1861. They were removed from the British mail packet *Trent* by the captain of the United States ship *San Jacinto*. Britain protested strongly against the action, viewing it as a demonstrable abuse of neutral rights at sea. With a strong outburst of anti-American feeling in Britain, war seemed, for a time, a possibility. Prince *Albert (1819–61) exercised a pacifying influence, moderating the belligerent demands made by *Palmerston (1784-1865). At the same time Britain rushed 8,000 troops to the defence of Canada and, for a while, prohibited the export of arms and ammunition.

The crisis was defused when the United States Secretary of State, on President Lincoln's prompting, sent a note 'cheerfully liberating' the commissioners on the grounds that the captain of the *San Jacinto* had failed to escort his prize to port for adjudication. In this way the United States was able to save some face diplomatically.

BOURNE, K., 'British Preparations for War with the North, 1861–2', *English Historical Review*, 1961, pp.600–32.

FERRIS, N. B., *The Trent Affair: A Diplomatic Crisis*, University of Tennessee Press, Knoxville, 1977.

**Trident Conference** (1943). Meeting between Winston *Churchill (1874–1965) and President Roosevelt together with the Combined Chiefs of Staff between 12 and 25 May 1943. They discussed military planning and harmonization of strategy against Germany, Italy and Japan. Churchill argued for a campaign to force Italy out of the war. The United States representatives inclined to the view that the Allies should establish themselves simply on Sicily. In the end it was agreed to invade the Italian mainland, but only to the extent that this effort did not detract from the success of the Second Front in France. The Allies also agreed that the offensive in the Pacific against Japan be stepped up and more support be given to the struggle in Burma.

**Tripartite Declaration** (Palestine) (1950). A British, French and United States guarantee of the status quo in Palestine. In May 1950 these powers bound themselves 'should they find that any of these states (the Arab states or Israel) was proposing to violate frontiers or armistice lines . . . immediately to take action, both within and outside the *United Nations, to prevent such violations'.

**Troppau Congress** (1820). Held in October 1820 following revolts in Naples and Spain. It was the second of the gatherings of the *Congress System and marked a clear rift between Britain and the autocratic powers of the *Holy Alliance (1815). In his State Paper of 5 May 1820 Lord *Castlereagh (1769–1822), the British Foreign Secretary, had already resisted the idea of involvement in Spain and criticized the whole notion of intervention advanced by the Eastern Courts. He had further told Metternich that he would not support a league of powers against the Neapolitan revolutionaries, whom he described as an 'Italian rather than a European problem'.

Metternich presented the Troppau Congress with a Protocol claiming that any state that had succumbed to revolution had ceased to be a member of the Holy Alliance and that the other powers were duty bound to coerce the wayward state 'back to the bosom of the Alliance'. This was welcomed by Tsar Alexander I who had pressed for the congress in the first place and by Prussia, but was vigorously opposed by Lord Stewart, half-brother of the Foreign Secretary, who had been sent to the congress as simply an observer rather than a plenipotentiary. Castlereagh then formally protested against the Protocol and against the idea of a combination of powers acting as policeman of the internal affairs of European states. The congress was adjourned and then, three months later, reconvened at Laibach. These two congresses marked the end of post-war cooperation, and Castlereagh's position in distancing himself from the Holy Alliance was strongly backed by parliamentary and public opinion in Britain.

KISSINGER, H., *A World Restored: Metternich, Castlereagh and the Problem of Peace 1812–22*, Weidenfeld and Nicolson, 1957.

WEBSTER, C. K., *The Foreign Policy of Castlereagh, 1815–22*, Bell, 1934.

**Truman Doctrine.** The announcement by the American President on 12 March 1947 pledging United States support to any country of 'free peoples who are resisting attempted subjugation by armed minorities or by outside pressures'. On 21 February Britain had given notice to the United States that she could no longer afford to send assistance to the Greeks and that she was dropping her aid programme to Turkey, a decision provoked by her post-war economic predicament which had been intensified by the very severe winter of 1946–7. Greece was faced with the insurgence of a communist-led guerrilla movement backed by neighbouring Balkan regimes, and the Soviet Union was applying diplomatic pressure on Turkey. The President explained that Britain had protected the two states against communist encroachment and subversion but that now – because of her economic condition – Britain was being forced to liquidate her overseas commitments 'in several parts of the world, including Greece'. The British decision had therefore faced the United States as 'the only country able to provide that help' with either taking on this responsibility or letting it go by default.

President Truman accordingly requested and obtained from Congress 400 million dollars of aid for Greece and Turkey. In fact the military and naval missions for which the Congressional support was enlisted were to be of an advisory nature. To begin with the British and American roles were complementary. The first shipload of United States aid to Greece did not arrive until August and very reluctantly Britain was forced to maintain 5,000 men in Greece until 1948. Though the crisis in the Eastern Mediterranean was specific, the ramifications of the Truman Doctrine were global. It deepened the East–West divide and placed the United States unequivocally at Britain's side. The announcement of an open-ended commitment stated the ideological basis for the strategy of *Containment which was soon to be tested in the Far East.

**Trust Territories.** The former *League of Nations *Mandates or non-self-governing territories placed under the trusteeship of the *United Nations, as provided in its Charter. All mandates which had not become independent (the B and C categories) became trust territories in 1946 with the exception of South-West Africa. The Union of South Africa refused to allow this territory to be put under the trusteeship system and, to all intents and purposes, incorporated it in 1949. Only one additional territory, Italian Somaliland, was placed under trust as a consequence of *World War II (1939–45). It was stipulated that a state which was appointed trustee should be accountable to the Trusteeship Council and to the inhabitants of the territory. Within 25 years all but two of the territories had either been granted independence or, following a plebiscite, merged with a neighbouring state. Of the trust territories under the *Commonwealth Togoland was united with Ghana in 1957, the Cameroons with Nigeria and the ex-French Cameroon Republic in 1971, and Tanganyika and Western Samoa became independent in 1961 and 1962 respectively.

**Two-Power Standard.** Naval strategic doctrine. It specified that the British Fleet should have a minimum margin of superiority. Its strength was to be 'at least equal to the naval strength of *any other* two countries'. The defence of British imperial interests was crucially dependent on the maintenance of naval dominance. As other major powers, in particular Germany, Japan and the United States, started to construct fleets of considerable size Britain was increasingly hard-pressed to retain her superiority in numbers and her technical advantage. The two-power standard was proposed in the Naval Defence Act of 1889. It proved increasingly difficult to maintain even though it applied only to first-class cruisers and battleships. In 1900 Lord Selborne removed the United States from the list of possible enemies to which this measure could apply. In 1912 Winston *Churchill (1874–1965), then First Lord of the Admiralty, abandoned it, substituting for it a new standard of superiority of at least 60 per cent higher than the size of the next biggest Dreadnought fleet.

# —U—

UDC, see UNION OF DEMOCRATIC CONTROL

**U-2 Incident** (1960). The shooting-down of an American high-altitude spy plane, piloted by Gary Powers, deep within Soviet territory. It led to the collapse of the Paris Summit between the United States, the Soviet Union, Britain and France, raised international tension and temporarily halted progress towards East–West *détente. Powers was shot down on 1 May 1960; he was sentenced to 10 years imprisonment and the United States indicted for 'aggressive acts'. (In fact he was released in a spy exchange in 1962.) The ostensible purpose of the U-2 flight was to provide the United States government with data on Soviet military activity. While it was condemned as a violation of international law, within a few years aerial spying with satellites would be recognized as legitimate, and it was accepted in the 1979 *SALT Treaty.

**Uitlanders.** The name given by the Boers to newcomers to the Transvaal in the late nineteenth century. They were mainly British subjects attracted by the discovery of gold in the Witwatersrand in 1886. The inferior status of the Uitlanders under the Transvaal Constitution and their agitation for equality with the Boers helped to precipitate the 2nd *Boer War (1899–1902) between Britain and the Boers.

**Ultimatum.** In diplomacy, a note or memorandum which a government or its representative conveys specifying the conditions on which it will insist. It commonly includes a demand for a prompt, clear and categorical reply and lays down a time limit within which this must be received. Usually also it implies a threat to use force if the demand is not met. A famous example in British diplomacy is the presentation by Lord *Palmerston (1784–1865) through the British minister at Athens of an ultimatum for the settlement of the dispute over *Don Pacifico (1850) within 24 hours. He warned that if the Greeks failed to comply their coast would be blockaded and merchant ships seized. The word 'ultimatum' can also bear a somewhat different sense in diplomatic relations. It may mean the maximum amount of concession that is envisaged in order to arrive at an agreement, where no resort to compulsion is contemplated in case of refusal.

**Unconditional Surrender.** The conclusion of armed conflict among nations on a basis which allows the victorious state(s) legally unlimited authority to impose whatever peace terms appear to them to be fitting on the defeated state(s). The policy of unconditional surrender was announced by Winston *Churchill (1874–1965) and President Roosevelt at the *Casablanca Conference (1943). Insisting on this for Germany and Japan, Roosevelt explained the term as meaning: 'not the destruction of the populace but the destruction of a philosophy which is based on conquest and subjugation of other people'. The origin of this demand can be traced to the clause in the *Atlantic Charter (1941) which envisaged 'the final destruction of the Nazi tyranny'. The policy was announced at a time when the promised *Second Front in the West had not yet come into existence, as a calculated reassurance, particularly to the Soviet Union, that the United States and Britain were determined to achieve total victory without compromises. It succeeded in boosting Allied morale, but the policy was used as propaganda by the Nazi hierarchy to convince the German people that they had no alternative but to fight to the bitter end. Critics have argued that it served to prolong the war. A further implication was that it helped to postpone serious negotiations on the terms of the post-war settlement with the Soviet Union until too late, when Eastern Europe was already under the control of the Red Army.

**Unequal Treaties.** The treaties imposed on China and Japan by the European colonial powers and the United States during the nineteenth century, granting one-sided privileges to the latter. The most important provisions of the Unequal Treaties were the imposition of external tariffs on the Chinese and Japanese (which represented both an affront to national sovereignty and a loss of revenue), of the *most-favoured-nation principle, and the granting of *consular jurisdiction. They sometimes included other rights as well, such as those concerning railway construction. The *Nanking Treaty at the end of the Anglo-Chinese *Opium War (1839–42) and the *Ansei Commercial Treaties (1858) are the best-known of the Unequal Treaties. The latter aroused strong nationalist resistance, so that in Japan the revision of these treaties became a major objective of the diplomacy of successive Japanese governments. The final abolition of these arrangements with China was not secured until the treaties of the British and the Americans with China in 1943.

**Unilateralism.** Voluntary renunciation of armaments by one side to a potential conflict. The word is currently most frequently used to describe the argument that Britain should renounce its own nuclear arsenal. This has been prominently advanced since the 1950s by the Campaign for Nuclear Disarmament (CND), a movement which at its peak has had more active supporters than any British mass movement since the Anti-Corn Law League. Launched under the leadership of the philosopher Bertrand Russell and Canon John Collins, it was adopted for a while as official party policy by the Labour Party Conference, though the Leader of the Opposition Hugh Gaitskell

reversed this. With divisions over tactics in the movement, a more militant wing of CND, the Committee of One Hundred, broke away in 1962. Since the end of the 1970s (particularly from the 1979 *NATO agreement on a 'twin-track strategy' with the siting of a new generation of missiles in Europe) the movement has markedly revived, particularly in resistance to the basing of Cruise missiles in Britain. The debate over unilateralism played a major part in the 1983 General Election campaign. Many contemporary unilateralists argue that not only should Britain not own nuclear weapons but neither should it allow them on its soil. Unilateralism does not necessarily imply *pacifism. Some unilateralists press for an increase in the level of conventional armaments.

**Union of Democratic Control.** A group set up only shortly after the outbreak of *World War I (1914–18) in September 1914 by a number of people who had opposed British entry into the war. The UDC pressed for democratic control over the conduct of foreign policy and the creation of an international system to guarantee an enduring peace and to ensure that this would be the war to end war. Among its best-known members were Ramsay *MacDonald (1866–1937) and Norman *Angell (1872–1967); its secretary was E. D. Morel, who for a while was imprisoned. The views of the UDC were shared by the Independent Labour Party. The UDC called for a large reduction of armaments and general nationalization of arms production. Rejecting the *balance of power, secret diplomacy and alliance systems, which its members regarded as inherently unstable, it advocated the preservation of peace by means of an international council of the powers. The study group which they set up to examine the possibility of a future world organization developed in 1915 into the League of Nations Society. During the war the UDC drew a distinction between German militarism and the German people. It called for an end to the war by negotiation and by a peace with no annexations. They were, accordingly, critical of the *Versailles Settlement (1919), seeing it as an 'imperialist' peace which perpetuated national injustices. In the inter-war years they continued to press for open and 'democratic' diplomacy and for substantial disarmament.

CLINE, C. A., *E. D. Morel*, Blackstaff Press, Belfast, 1980.

SWARTZ, M., *The Union of Democratic Control in British Politics During the First World War*, Oxford University Press, 1971.

**United Nations.** The international organization which developed from decisions taken by the *Big Three during *World War II (1939–45), at the *Dumbarton Oaks Conference (1944), and which was finally agreed at the *San Francisco Conference between April and June 1945. Its Charter became effective on 24 October 1945.

An association of sovereign states and successor to the *League of Nations, it was set up for the maintenance of international peace and security, and to achieve international cooperation in solving international problems of an economic or cultural nature. It was hoped that this would provide a more effective machinery than its predecessor for the prevention of war. The United Nations was constituted with six main organs: (1) the Security Council, with 15 members, five of which, Britain, China, France, the United States and the Soviet Union were to have permanent seats and a permanent power of veto; (2) the General Assembly, in which every member state was to have a vote; (3) the Trusteeship Council, which succeeded to the work of the *Mandates Commission of the League (see: *Trust Territories); (4) the International Court of Justice at the Hague, the world's supreme international court of judicial appeal; (5) the Economic and Social Council, devoted to welfare and culture (UNESCO); and (6) the Secretariat.

The main differences from the League of Nations were the stronger executive powers assumed by the Security Council, the wide range of specialized agencies and the requirement that member states should make available armed forces to serve as peacekeepers. However, any pretence of unanimity among the major powers ended with the emergence of the *Cold War. Frequent exercise of the veto power in the Security Council, which was treated as a common tactical ploy rather than an ultimate recourse, and disharmony among the powers, led both the Council and the Assembly to become arenas for propagandistic denunciations rather than convincingly effective bodies. Nevertheless, the United Nations has been continuously active since 1945 in preventive diplomacy, security operations, factfinding missions, peacekeeping and military operations. Major United Nations interventions have included those in the Middle East

crises, such as the *Suez Crisis (1956) and conflicts in the Congo, Cyprus and Indonesia. Peacekeeping has been confined to those areas where the superpowers have tacitly agreed to avoid a direct Cold War confrontation. The achievements of the United Nations also include the well-being promoted by its specialized agencies.

NICHOLAS, H. G., *The United Nations as a Political Institution*, Oxford University Press, 1976.

STOESSINGER, J. G., *The United Nations and the Superpowers*, 3rd ed., Random House, New York, 1973.

**United Nations Conference on International Organization,** see SAN FRANCISCO CONFERENCE (1945)

**United Nations Monetary and Financial Conference,** see BRETTON WOODS CONFERENCE (1944)

**United States, Britain and the.** After the conclusion of the Anglo-American war of 1812 in the *Ghent Treaty (1814) there was a progressive rapprochement between the two countries. It was now clear that Britain would not try to regain control over her lost colonies, and it seemed unlikely that the United States for her part would press seriously her claims to Canada. This rapprochement can be seen among other things in the limitation of naval armaments on the Great Lakes, the *Rush–Bagot Agreement (1817), in the *Webster–Ashburton Treaty (1842) and the *Oregon Treaty (1846). In 1830 Britain opened up the West Indies to American ships. While both countries had an interest in controlling any projected canal across the isthmus of Central America, the *Clayton–Bulwer Treaty (1850) arranged a compromise, providing joint control in the event of a canal being constructed.

Just before the declaration of the *Monroe Doctrine (1823) George *Canning (1770–1827) and Richard Rush had come close to an accord on a public announcement in favour of the independence of the Spanish colonies in Latin America. In the event the doctrine was announced unilaterally by the United States. During the first half of the nineteenth century the full implications of it for United States influence and control in the Western Hemisphere were by no means apparent. Initially the significant demands were those directed by

Britain to the other powers, to France that trade with the Spanish colonies must not be hampered, that outside powers must not interfere in Latin American struggles for independence and that the United States should be included in any discussion of Latin American affairs among Europeans. At this time the significant power in political consideration was the British navy, which alone was able to enforce the doctrine.

This period saw the development of a flourishing transatlantic trade. Britain purchased 80 per cent of her cotton in the United States. At the same time the United States was an important market for British goods. It was also a period of mass emigration to the New World. Nearly three million immigrants entered the United States from Britain between 1815 and 1860. Though tensions existed between Britain and the United States, they did not lead to war. Such differences as there were tended to be mitigated by a strong emergent sense of common interest, which in the twentieth century was to attract the much-debated and analysed description of 'the special relationship'. The point is that as American economic and naval power developed, it was essentially accommodated rather than resisted by Britain. The development of the United States was, in any case, far removed from the central arenas of British diplomatic concern, Europe and the Near East.

During the American Civil War there was a fair degree of British sympathy for the Confederacy, particularly among trading groups and the aristocracy. In June 1861 troops were despatched to guard Canada against any wild action by the anti-British faction in the Union. The *Trent Affair (1861) and the *Alabama Incident (1862) threatened to precipitate war, but this was avoided in the first case when President Lincoln ordered the release of two Confederate diplomats who had been removed from the British ship, and the second was subsequently settled by arbitration, with the *Washington Treaty (1871) awarding more than 15 million dollars to the American claimants. The British did not break the Union blockade. Further, the secession of the South allowed the British and the Union to agree to searches of one another's ships in African waters to eradicate the slave trade. Southern objections along with the traditional antagonism of the United States to British searches had hitherto blocked such an agreement.

In the years following the Civil War the United States became the recipient of large amounts of British capital investment. British governments had come to recognize that it was not possible for Britain to rival the United States in the Americas and preserve its position vis-à-vis the rivalry of the European powers. By the end of the 1870s British troops had been withdrawn from Canada. The Americans were secure in their isolation and the British in their, as yet, unchallenged naval power across the globe. Disputes with the United States, such as those over the Newfoundland fisheries and the *Bering Sea (1889) were settled by arbitration and without undue recrimination. As the United States became increasingly protectionist, however, as for instance with the McKinley Tariff, British commercial alarm was aroused.

The most serious diplomatic episode was the *Venezuela Boundary Dispute (1895), during which President Cleveland accused the British of violating the Monroe Doctrine and demanded arbitration. After a considerable delay, during which the threat of war loomed, Britain finally accepted arbitration. In truth, Britain's concern for the boundaries of British Guiana was relatively small, as compared with her interests and anxieties elsewhere. By this time she was increasingly aware of her imperial vulnerability and isolation – a fact emphasized by the 2nd *Boer War (1899–1902). More particularly, she was growing nervous of German aspirations. As Lord *Clarendon (1800–70) had observed in 1869 when there were rumours of United States designs on Canada: 'the unfriendly state of our relations with America ... paralyses our action in Europe. There is not the slightest doubt that if we were engaged in a Continental quarrel we should immediately find ourselves at war with the United States.' In 1902 there was another retreat from Venezuela following expressions of American concern over British and German use of force to make Venezuela pay her debts (see: *Venezuelan Crisis (1902)). After this Britain conspicuously avoided any challenge to American influence in the Western Hemisphere. In the *Hay–Pauncefote Treaty (1901) she acceded to the abrogation of the Clayton–Bulwer Treaty. On the other side, the benevolent neutrality displayed by the United States towards Britain during the 2nd *Boer War was very welcome in Britain, which was widely criticized for its campaign.

Anglo-American relations in the Far East were also essentially harmonious. In 1899 John Hay proclaimed the *Open Door policy in China, by which the freedom of the powers to intervene in the economic affairs of China and other nations would be preserved. Though the *Anglo-Japanese Alliance (1902) was a potential embarrassment to Anglo-American relations, Britain let it be known that the alliance would never commit them to fight the United States, and this was emphasized again in the revision of the treaty in 1905.

In August 1914, following the *July Crisis and the German infringement of Belgian neutrality, Britain declared war on Germany. The United States' entry on the Allied side followed the German resort to unrestricted submarine warfare in 1917. It was clear, though, that it would not be in the American interest to see the opposite shores of the North Atlantic dominated by a Germany which had defeated Britain and France and gained control of their naval power. Britain had recognized the need not to alienate the United States through blockade. As Sir Edward *Grey (1862–1933) was to note in his memoirs: 'It was better . . . to carry on the war without blockade than to incur a break with the United States . . . The object of diplomacy, therefore, was to secure the maximum of blockade that could be enforced without a rupture with the United States.' America joined the war as an 'associated' rather than an 'allied' power: though there was joint naval command under a British admiral, the American army kept itself together as an operational unit, rather than disposing its men into the British and French armies as the Allies had wanted. Similarly, President Woodrow Wilson was only very reluctantly drawn into the Allied intervention in Russia after the Revolution (see: *Russian Civil War, British Intervention in the, 1918–20).

### 1918–45

Early in 1918 President Woodrow Wilson had enunciated his *Fourteen Points as the basis for a subsequent peace settlement. These and the Four Principles were lofty guidelines for the chaotic situation which confronted the Allies in November of that year, with the collapse of four empires. The incompatibility of Allied aims was soon apparent. During the *Paris Peace Conference (1919–20) the President tried to resist Allied demands for new acquisitions and large-scale reparations. The attempt to translate the principle of *national self-determination into reality was to present numerous difficulties. In the event the United States Senate did not ratify the *Versailles Treaty (1919) and, in spite of Woodrow Wilson's fervent advocacy of a league of peace, refused to participate in the *League of Nations. With this decision, the mooted Anglo-American guarantee of French security also disappeared.

While the United States withdrew into political *isolationism during the following years the unresolved and interlinked questions of war debts, loans and reparations served to cast a shadow over transatlantic relations as well as to contribute to the world-wide depression of the 1930s. In retrospect we can see that *World War I (1914–18) marked a significant turning-point in Anglo-American economic relations. By 1919 the dollar had displaced sterling as the dominant world currency. As a consequence of her war expenditures Britain had become a debtor nation (in 1932 the British Treasury was to inform a not overjoyed United States that it would be better for all concerned if the British war debts went unpaid). The American need for British exports was also declining (between 1920 and 1950 British imports likewise fell from 19 to 3½ per cent of the American market). Britain was now compelled, too, to recognize and adjust to the reality of the United States as a major naval power. At the *Washington Naval Conference (1921–2) she accepted parity in large capital ships. Under United States influence the Anglo-Japanese Alliance was allowed to lapse.

In the later 1930s President Roosevelt followed a policy of what he described as 'watchful waiting' as far as events in Europe were concerned. He lent an ear to his Secretary of State, Cordell Hull's, argument that a grand programme of trade liberalization was the best road to peace. The latter argued that freer access to markets and raw materials should remove the grievances of the revisionist powers and encourage not only economic growth, but also disarmament and respect for the rule of law in international affairs. Such proposals received an unenthusiastic response from Britain. The British feared that the Americans were trying to dilute *Imperial Preference and to secure other economic advantages for themselves. Neville *Chamberlain (1869–1940) was determined to yield no more economically than the bare minimum to the United States. Roosevelt's relations with Chamberlain were distant and isolationism in the United States remained strong. Chamberlain was doubtful of the prospect of American assistance in the event of a European war and accorded *appeasement of Nazi Germany a higher priority than Anglo-American cooperation.

On the outbreak of war in September 1939 Roosevelt was initially wary of concrete measures to aid Britain. Though his support for Britain and France was not in doubt, public opinion had to be brought to a consensus if the United States were to go to war. His first significant visible move was to trade 50 destroyers for eight naval bases in Newfoundland and the British West Indies (see: *Destroyer–Bases Deal (1940) ). Following the warning by *Churchill (1874–1965) that Britain had almost exhausted the financial resources she needed to purchase American goods, United States *Lend-Lease Aid began in 1941. After the fall of France the British Empire needed American support for survival, let alone victory. At the same time, however, though perhaps less obviously, the United States needed Britain. The Royal Navy was regarded in Washington as America's 'front line' against German expansion into the Atlantic, and the British Empire was acknowledged as a source of key raw materials in the struggle against Japanese aggression in Asia.

Once fully involved in the war after *Pearl Harbour (1941), the United States fought in close cooperation with Britain, though the alliance was not without rivalries and tensions between British and American commanders in Europe, North Africa and Burma. Winston *Churchill (1874–1965), who had left no stone unturned in order fully to involve the United States in the war effort, voiced clear differences of opinion with the United States. Perhaps the most important source of friction was the future of the British Empire. The United States posed a challenge to the British imperial position both from an ideological (traditionally anti-colonialist) and a self-interested, commercial standpoint. Churchill and Roosevelt took opposite views, as can very plainly be seen in their divergent interpretations of the extent to which the principle of self-government, as expressed in the *Atlantic Charter (1941), should be applied. During the war the United States used economic leverage to force open some of Britain's colonial markets and to coerce

Britain's agreement to post-war economic arrangements, conspicuously reflecting the relative decline of British power.

## 1945–

The ending of the war placed additional strains on the Anglo-American relationship. The cancellation of Lend-Lease came as a most unwelcome shock. Anticipating a faster economic recovery than Britain could in the circumstances achieve, the United States drove what the British regarded as hard economic bargains. There was a well-established conflict of interest here. Since the *Ottawa Conference (1932) Britain had inclined towards a protectionist policy while, from 1934, the United States had sought to dismantle trading barriers, especially those of a discriminatory nature – and British *Imperial Preference was at the top of their list.

There was also a halt in the collaboration between the two countries over atomic weapons. Churchill had reached an agreement at the *Quebec Conference (1943), but the McMahon Act (1946) stipulated that atomic secrets should be kept in American hands. The sharing of such information was later resumed, but only after Britain had exploded her own hydrogen bomb. Another issue which aroused contention was that of Palestine where there was, in British eyes, a marked failure of the Americans to appreciate the difficulties of the British position. As Britain worked with increasing desperation for an agreement between Jews and Arabs which would allow her an honourable exit from her responsibilities, President Truman intervened to press the Jewish case, while refusing any ultimate responsibility for making the settlement work. The State of Israel came into existence on 14 May 1948 when the British *Mandate ended.

Circumstances had already by the end of 1946 aligned Britain and the United States against the Soviet Union – with the breakdown of relations over Poland, over the previous agreement to treat Germany as an economic unit and over the continued presence of Soviet forces in northern Iran. In 1947 Britain notified the United States that because of her weakened economic position, she could no longer assume responsibility for Greece and Turkey. This led to the *Truman Doctrine (1947) which specified aid for these countries as well as articulating the general principle of *Containment.

In 1948 the *Marshall Plan (European Recovery Programme) granted massive aid to Western Europe. Britain gave the United States permission for atomic bases on British soil. In 1949 Britain and the United States joined other European nations in the *North Atlantic Treaty Organization (NATO). The development of the Marshall Aid programme and NATO were both very much Anglo-American joint enterprises. The British government, particularly the Foreign Secretary, Ernest *Bevin (1881–1951), regarded an American commitment to European defence as essential in the post-war situation, with deteriorating East–West relations and the numerical superiority of Soviet conventional forces.

British and United States interests converged more closely in Europe than they did in Asia and the Middle East. The Americans wanted a strong line towards Communism in Asia and (without changing policy towards Israel), a more moderate stance towards the Arab states. British governments did not, for their part, want to see the United States distracted from what they saw as the essential priority of containing Soviet power in Europe. The difference of perspective was inevitable since the United States had become quite as much a Pacific as an Atlantic superpower. It was illustrated by Britain's refusal to toe the United States line over non-recognition of China in 1949–50 and by her pressure on Washington against the extension of the Korean War to Chinese territory. Britain was particularly apprehensive that the Korean War might escalate to the point where the United States retaliated with the atomic bomb. From the American standpoint in these years British colonialism and economic rivalry continued to strain the relationship. The Anglo-American divergence was also, and most dramatically, revealed during the *Suez Crisis (1956). There the resistance of the Eisenhower Administration to the Franco-British invasion of Egypt doomed the expedition at once. It was clear for all to see that a comparatively minor exercise of American leverage could have decisive consequences for Britain, and that there was no longer any question of partnership on the basis of equality with the United States. It also showed that despite the closeness of the alliance (though *Eden (1897–1977) and Dulles did not have a good working relationship) there was still the possibility of great error, misjudgement and misperception between the allies. After

Suez Britain did not again embark on a major departure in foreign policy without first carefully consulting with the United States.

The new Prime Minister, Harold *Macmillan (1894–1986) and President Eisenhower subsequently proceeded to rebuild Anglo-American trust. Indeed, Macmillan gave the highest priority to an improved understanding with the United States. In return Eisenhower was accommodating towards Britain in amending the McMahon Act in the Atomic Energy Act of 1958, and allowing the sharing of nuclear information between the two countries. In the same year Britain and the United States co-operated in the intervention in Lebanon and Jordan to prevent the spread of the Iraq revolution.

Relations were further consolidated by the British decision to seek entry to the *Common Market (see: *Western Europe, Britain and since 1945). In the post-war years American administrations had consistently encouraged Western European integration. The United States considered that British membership would provide a guarantee that the EEC would remain anchored in the Western Alliance. The cancellation of 'Skybolt' at this time though posed a major, if short-lived dilemma, since Britain was determined to retain an 'independent' nuclear deterrent. Only after some hard negotiation with President Kennedy was this resolved by the *Nassau Agreement (1962) with the offer of 'Polaris' to Britain. This arrangement was presented by General de Gaulle as evidence that Britain was insufficiently European in her orientation and was offered as a justification for his refusal to support her admission to the EEC in 1963.

During the 1960s the United States became progressively embroiled in the Vietnam War, in which, in spite of some American encouragement to do so, Britain refused to become militarily involved. Vietnam was perceived in Britain as an American problem and from the start there was considerable official scepticism over American policy there. Harold *Wilson (1916–    ) made a number of attempts to bring the belligerents to the negotiating table, an exercise in mediation which, on balance, irritated the United States more than anything else, particularly when it was combined with Labour condemnation of the bombing of North Vietnam. Under the 1954 accords Britain and the Soviet Union were co-chairmen of the Geneva Conference on Indochina. Now, by the mid–1960s, Britain was only capable of a peripheral role. While the United States appeared to press Britain to take more responsibility in the Far East (a change from the earlier critical attitude towards the British colonial presence), British economic resources were no longer able to sustain it. After the sterling devaluation of November 1967 the Wilson government indicated that it intended the east-of-Suez capability to be surrendered by the end of 1971 (see: *East of Suez).

By 1973 Britain was a member of the EEC. This was also Henry Kissinger's 'Year of Europe' and the year of the Arab–Israeli war. Tensions between the United States and Western Europe have presented, and continue to present (as over the American attack on Libya in April 1986) Britain and her historic relationship with the United States with a dilemma. Since 1945 the *Cold War has served to bring Britain and the United States closer together. On the other hand, greater dependence on the United States, associated with Britain's declining international role, has inevitably changed the nature of the relationship.

Until perhaps the early 1960s the relationship remained one of partnership, though with the United States as unmistakably the senior partner. In recent years the special role of Britain has been less manifest and the divergence in status, power and influence more so – between the global superpower and the economically hard-pressed, essentially regional power. The decline of the British role can be gauged if one thinks back to her major participation in the test ban negotiations in the early 1960s and contrasts it with her status in the contemporary East–West dialogue over nuclear armaments. Since 1979 Mrs *Thatcher (1925–   ) has strongly reaffirmed the relationship with the United States, to which she accords priority in foreign policy over relations with Western Europe. The nuclear relationship has been re-emphasized with the agreements of 1980 by which 'Trident' is to replace 'Polaris' in the 1990s, and by the acceptance of Cruise missiles. For her part, the United States gave Britain vital logistical assistance at the time of the invasion of the *Falkland Islands (1982).

ALLEN, H. C., *Great Britain and the United States, 1783–1952*, Odhams, 1954.
BAYLIS, J., *Anglo-American Defence Relations, 1939–1984*, 2nd ed. Macmillan, 1984.
BELOFF, M., ' "The Special Relationship": An Anglo-American Myth' in GILBERT, M., ed., *A Century of Conflict, 1850–1950: Essays for A. J. P. Taylor*, Hamish Hamilton, 1966.
BOURNE, K., *Britain and the Balance of Power in North America, 1815–1908*, Longmans, 1967.
CAMPBELL, C. S., *From Revolution to Rapprochement: The United States and Great Britain, 1783–1900*, Wiley, New York, 1974.
GOWING, M., *Britain and Atomic Energy, 1939–45*, Macmillan, 1964.
JONES, W. D., *The American Problem in British Diplomacy, 1841–61*, Macmillan, 1974.
MCNEILL, W. H., *America, Britain and Russia: Their Cooperation and Conflict, 1941–46*, Oxford University Press, 1953.
NICHOLAS, H. G., *Britain and the U.S.A.*, Johns Hopkins Press, Baltimore, 1963. *The United States and Britain*, University of Chicago Press, Chicago, 1975.
PERKINS, B., *The Great Rapprochement: England and the United States, 1895–1914*, Atheneum, New York, 1968.
REYNOLDS, D., *The Creation of the Anglo-American Alliance, 1937–41: A Study in Competitive Cooperation*, Europa Publications, 1982.
THORNE, C., *Allies of a Kind: The United States, Britain and the War against Japan*, Hamish Hamilton, 1978.
WATT, D. C., *Succeeding John Bull: America in Britain's Place, 1900–75*, Cambridge University Press, 1984.

*Unkiar-Skelessi, Treaty of (1833). The Russo-Turkish defensive alliance which followed the first *Mehemet Ali crisis. The Russians had intervened in April with 30,000 troops, saving Asia Minor, Constantinople and the Straits for the Sultan against the Pasha of Egypt. Signed on 3 July 1833 and valid for eight years, the treaty contained a secret clause closing the Straits to warships of all nations. This agreement was the price paid for Russian assistance by the Ottoman Empire and it was intended to reduce Anglo-French influence at Constantinople and to give Russia exclusive control over Turkey. It gave Russia the guarantee that, if she were to find herself at war with Britain, her Black Sea coast would be safe from British bombardment. This was an advantage she had never enjoyed before. *Palmerston (1784–1865) in particular was afraid that Russia might be able to send her warships into the Mediterranean, threatening British interests. Britain was, however, able substantially to retrieve her position in the *Straits Convention (1841), after the second Mehemet Ali crisis.

CLAYTON, G. D., *Britain and the Eastern Question: Missolonghi to Gallipoli*, Hodder and Stoughton, 1971.

*Uti Possidetis* and *Status Quo.* These terms may commonly be used interchangeably. They denote actual possession by right of conquest, occupation, or by some other right. In the proposals for treaties, and clauses in them, such rights have to be identified with as much exactitude as possible. While the first term relates to territorial possessions, the term 'status quo' may be used to refer to the existing state of affairs in other matters.

# —V—

**VANSITTART,** Robert Gilbert, 1st Baron Vansittart of Denham (1881–1957). British diplomat and prominent critic of Germany in the 1930s and 1940s. In his earlier career he was posted to Cairo, Stockholm and Paris and between 1920 and 1924 he acted as secretary to Lord *Curzon (1859–1925). As Permanent Under-Secretary at the *Foreign Office (1930–8) he was a vigorous opponent of the policy of *appeasement. He was accused of fostering hostility towards Germany in the face of the government's efforts to the contrary. In 1938 he was as a consequence effectively demoted to the specially created post of Chief Diplomatic Adviser to H.M. Government. During *World War II (1939–45) his name was taken to describe the contemporary mood of hostility towards Germany – 'Vansittartism'. He ascribed the conflict to the German national character which in his view was inherently vicious and which had been responsible for no fewer than five European wars since 1864, rather than simply to Nazism. His writings at this time helped to change the climate of opinion in Britain which came to see the war not only as an ideological war against Hitler and Nazi tyranny, but as a national conflict with Germany.

COLVIN, I., *Vansittart in Office: An Historical Survey of the Origins of the Second World War Based on the Papers of Sir Robert Vansittart,* Victor Gollancz, 1956.

ROSE, N., *Vansittart: Study of a Diplomat,* Heinemann, 1978.

VANSITTART, BARON, *Lessons of my Life,* Hutchinson, 1943. *The Mist Procession,* Hutchinson, 1958.

**Venezuelan Crisis** (1895). Anglo-Venezuelan boundary dispute. When Britain annexed the territory of British Guiana in 1814 there was no clearly defined boundary along the western side. Later in the century the British accepted a line drawn by an agent, Robert Schomburgk, as its claim. Venezuela made a counter-claim for territory including two-thirds of the British colony. In 1885–6 Britain laid claim to a further 30,000 square miles to the west of the Schomburgk line, an area in which finds of gold were reported. This led the Venezuelan government to break off diplomatic relations with Britain in 1887. The United States then intervened to demand *arbitration, offering the *Monroe Doctrine (1823) as justification for this intervention. For a while Britain and the United States seemed to be moving towards war over the issue.

Lord *Salisbury (1830–1903) initially refused, but then President Cleveland requested Congress for authority to appoint a commission. In the event Britain climbed down, being unwilling to alienate the United States, particularly at a time when the growth of German ambitions was starting to preoccupy her. In 1899 the arbitrators awarded Venezuela the land claimed by Britain in 1885–6 but also effectively reaffirmed the Schomburgk line.

BOYLE, T., 'The Venezuela Crisis and the Liberal Opposition, 1895–6', *Journal of Modern History,* 50: 3, 1978.

PERKINS, B., *The Great Rapprochement: England and the United States, 1895–1914,* New York, Atheneum, 1968.

**Venezuelan Dispute** (1902). In December 1902 Britain, Germany and Italy blockaded major

Venezuelan ports and sank part of that country's navy. This was in reprisal for the Venezuelan dictator Cipriano Castro's refusal to settle his country's debts or treat equitably the nationals of several European countries, British subjects included. The United States brought strong pressure to bear to persuade the European nations to agree to *arbitration. This crisis gave rise to the *Drago Doctrine (1903), which repudiated the right of *intervention for purposes of debt collection. In the following year the Hague Court declared that the intervening powers did have preferential rights to the first Venezuelan payments. Since this seemed an invitation to foreign intervention, this ruling helped to provoke the Roosevelt Corollary to the *Monroe Doctrine in 1904, which justified United States intervention in the Western Hemisphere as a means of forestalling European or other foreign intervention.

BEALE, H. K., *Theodore Roosevelt and the Rise of America to World Power*, Johns Hopkins, Baltimore, 1956.

PLATT, D. C. M., 'The Allied Coercion of Venezuela 1902–3: A Reassessment', *Inter-American Economic Affairs*, 15: 4, 1962, pp. 3–28.

**Vereeniging, Treaty of** (1902). This treaty, which was signed on 31 May, marked the end of the 2nd *Boer War (1899–1902). The Orange Free State and the Transvaal agreed to accept British sovereignty. They were promised representative institutions, however, as soon as circumstances should permit and this promise was honoured in 1906–7. The Boers were exonerated from paying war reparations to the British and were granted £3 million to repair and restock their farms. There were to be no prosecutions of leading Boers, except those held guilty of atrocities, and civilian administration was to be installed as soon as possible. English was to be the official language, but Dutch was allowed continued use in schools and the law courts. As a result of this settlement many leading Boers such as Smuts and Botha were persuaded to support a policy of cooperation with the British. This led to Dominion status for a united South Africa under predominantly Boer influence in 1910 in the South Africa Act.

**Verona Congress** (1822). The last meeting of the *Congress System to be attended by Britain. It was held in October 1822 following the revolt in Spain against Ferdinand VII. By this time the community of interest between Britain and the other powers of the *Quadruple Alliance (1815) had been considerably weakened. Lord *Castlereagh (1769–1822) had distanced her from the *Holy Alliance powers over the question of international intervention in the internal affairs of European states (see: *Troppau Congress (1820) ). He had drawn up similar instructions for Verona shortly before his suicide in August. When the British representative at Verona, the Duke of *Wellington (1769–1852) informed the British government that the Austrians and Russians, in conformity with the counter-revolutionary imperatives of the autocratic monarchies and the spirit of the Troppau Protocol, supported the sending of a French force to suppress the revolution in Spain, he was instructed by the new Foreign Secretary, George *Canning (1770–1827), to protest and to withdraw from the congress. The French army invaded Spain in 1823, provoking further British remonstrance.

KISSINGER, H., *A World Restored: Metternich, Castlereagh and the Problem of Peace 1812–22*, Weidenfeld and Nicolson, 1957.

SKED, A., ed., *Europe's Balance of Power 1815–48*, Macmillan, 1979.

**Versailles, Treaty of** (1919). The peace settlement concluded with Germany by the Allies after *World War I (1914–18), signed on 28 June 1919 in the Hall of Mirrors at Versailles. Major terms among the 440 articles included cession by Germany of Alsace-Lorraine to France; Eupen-Malmédy to Belgium; and West Prussia, Posen and, after a plebiscite, part of Upper Silesia to Poland, thus creating the 'Polish Corridor' – with *Danzig becoming a free city under the *League of Nations. After much debate among the Allies it was decided that the Rhineland should be demilitarized (rather than be allowed to become an independent state) and occupied by the Allies for 15 years. At the same time, France was given the right to exploit the coal mines of the Saar for 15 years. Germany's union with Austria was forbidden, contradicting the principle of *self-determination (see: *Anschluss). She lost in all 13.5 per cent of her territory, 13 per cent of her economic productive capacity and 10 per cent of her population through these changes. The first part of the treaty dealt with the Covenant of the League of Nations and established *Mandates under the League for the colonies confiscated from Germany. The German army was reduced to 100,000 men; conscription was forbidden; the navy was allowed to maintain only six old battleships; military aircraft, submarines, tanks and heavy artillery were also proscribed (though most of these clauses were fairly soon evaded, partly with the assistance of the Soviet Union).

The clause subsequently most exploited by the enemies of the treaty (and the most controversial) was the *War Guilt Clause (Article 231), which forced Germany and her allies to accept responsibility for all the loss and damage caused by the war. The following article required her to accept liability for all costs incurred by the victors during the war, including war pensions. Total costs of reparations were set at £6,600,000,000 in 1921, though they were subsequently reduced in the *Dawes Plan (1924) and the *Young Plan (1929) and later repudiated altogether by Nazi Germany. Germany's very strong hostility to the imposed peace, the 'Diktat' of Versailles, was reflected in Britain and the United States in the feeling that its terms were excessively harsh and should be moderated. The economic and financial implications were bitterly castigated by the British Treasury official and economist J. M. *Keynes (1883–1946) in his celebrated tract *The Economic Consequences of the Peace*, which contributed to this feeling of guilt.

*Lloyd George (1863–1945), the British Prime Minister, occupied a middle position between Clemenceau, the French representative, and President Woodrow Wilson. He wanted a peace which, above all, would not through excessive harshness sow the seeds of a new war and which would allow the speedy revival of European prosperity on which British trade depended. His particular contribution to the treaty was to place Danzig under the League of Nations and obtain a plebiscite for the inhabitants of Upper Silesia and the Saar. The concept of the League never received his wholehearted support. Not only did Lloyd George not wish to see the German economy gravely weakened, he also in the Fontainebleau Memorandum of March 1919 warned against what he regarded as the potentially disastrous incorporation of millions of Germans within new boundaries in Eastern Europe. His rhetorical support for the 'Hang the Kaiser' mood during the Coupon Election did not reflect his real assessment – which was the imperative need for moderation.

In the end the treaty represented an unhappy compromise between idealism and power politics. When the United States Senate in March 1920 refused to ratify the treaty the settlement was substantially weakened. Britain now also considered herself no longer bound by her offer of an alliance in support of France. The treaty gravely humiliated Germany but it did not in fact cripple her economically and militarily in the longer term. Britain and France were in fundamental disagreement as to how the settlement should be applied. Britain pressed for gradual revision in order to secure the cooperation of the defeated power and the French continued to argue that peace could only be guaranteed by the strict enforcement of the treaty. At the same time, Hitler's strident denunciation of Versailles and of subsequent reparations payments was to contribute to Nazi success in Germany and to prepare for the dismantling of the treaty during the 1930s.

DOCKRILL, M. L. and GOOLD, J. D., *Peace without Promise: Britain and the Peace Conferences 1919–1923*, Batsford, 1981.
ELCOCK, H., *Portrait of a Decision: The Council of Four and the Treaty of Versailles*, Eyre Methuen, 1972.
MARKS, S., *The Illusion of Peace: International Relations in Europe 1918–1933*, Macmillan, 1976.

**VICTORIA,** Queen of Great Britain (1819–1901) (reigned 1837–1901). The reign of Victoria was a watershed in the history of the British monarchy between the active political involvement of the Hanoverian kings and the much more limited role played by twentieth-century sovereigns. However, foreign affairs were, together with the Church, the main area of policy in which the Queen clung tenaciously to her prerogatives and exerted a significant influence. In addition to insisting on her constitutional right to be consulted by her own government, her family connections gave her a wide range of contacts with foreign sovereigns which grew ever wider as the reign went on. She was thus extremely well informed and also able to pursue a kind of dynastic diplomacy of her own, whose results, though essentially intangible, can have been far from negligible in an age when absolute monarchy still prevailed extensively on the Continent.

Victoria's relations with her successive Prime Ministers are the staple of historical legend: she adored *Melbourne (1779–1848) and

*Disraeli (1804–81), admired *Salisbury (1830–1903), came to like *Peel (1788–1850), tolerated *Russell (1792–1878) and, eventually, *Palmerston (1784–1865), but detested *Gladstone (1809–98). To some extent those varying reactions can be explained in personal terms. Melbourne's fatherly protection of the young girl who had inherited awesome responsibilities and, much later, Disraeli's attentive flattery of the lonely widow, contrasted with Gladstone's stiff moralism and his tendency to treat her as an institution rather than a person. Nevertheless her attitudes reflect her views on policy, which were very pronounced although they changed with the years.

The reign can be divided into three main periods. In the first, until shortly after the death of the Prince Consort in 1861, she was much influenced by his non-interventionist views and thus had stormy relations with Palmerston. Secondly, from the mid–1860s to 1885, she came to favour more aggressive policies, despising *Granville (1815–91), Gladstone and the 15th Earl of *Derby (1826–93) for what she conceived to be a spiritless approach, while her obstructiveness diminished their chances of success. Her *jingoism and almost pathological fear of Russia were at times too strong even for Disraeli. Finally, after 1885, she found in Salisbury a Prime Minister whose general course of policy she could approve. Although her increasing age weakened her energy for active involvement she still made her views forcefully known, particularly in supporting the Liberal Imperialists against Gladstone. During this period her prestige, enhanced by the Royal Titles Act of 1877 which made her Empress of India and by the jubilees of 1887 and 1897, was at its height, and she had great symbolic importance as the 'grandmother of Europe' and the ceremonial focus of the British *Empire.

Queen Victoria's involvement in foreign policy extended over a period longer than that of any of her subjects with the exception of Palmerston and Gladstone. Her activity was at its height in the months which preceded Palmerston's dismissal in 1851; in the *Schleswig-Holstein crisis of 1863–4 when her pro-German sympathies caused her to quash moves by her Cabinet towards intervention in favour of Denmark and in relation to the *Eastern Question between 1875 and 1878. However, she was always a force to be reckoned with, serving as a spur to those of whom she approved and an embarrassing check on the plans of those who sought to defy her wishes.

CECIL, A., *Queen Victoria and her Prime Ministers*, Eyre and Spottiswoode, 1953.

HARDIE, F., *The Political Influence of Queen Victoria 1861–1901*, Oxford University Press, 1935.

LONGFORD, E., *Victoria R. I.*, Weidenfeld and Nicolson, 1964.

**Vienna, Congress of** (1814–15). The international gathering of monarchs and diplomats between 18 September 1814 and 9 June 1815 to re-establish the European order after the French Revolutionary and Napoleonic Wars. Convened by the Austrian Chancellor, Metternich, it was attended by representatives of all the powers concerned but it never met in full conference except for the signing of the Final Act, the Treaty of Vienna. The main work of the Congress was accomplished by Britain, Austria, France, Russia and Prussia meeting informally and in committee. The underlying political principles of the Congress were international stability, resistance to revolutionary movements and legitimism. The leading British representatives were Lord *Castlereagh (1769–1822) and the Duke of *Wellington (1769–1852). Castlereagh played a decisive role in its deliberations, wishing to pacify France and at the same time to contain French or Russian expansionism. The chief aims of the British statesmen were the restoration of the *balance of power in Europe and the security of the Empire, which meant guarantees of the sea- and land-routes, particularly to India. These aims were already clearly embodied in the 1st Peace of *Paris (1814). Britain retained the Cape of Good Hope, Ceylon, Malta, Heligoland, Tobago, St Lucia and Mauritius. She was also given a protectorate over the Ionian Islands, to last until 1863.

Britain retained Hanover, which was now raised to the status of a kingdom, enlarged by the addition of Osnabruck, Hildesheim, East Frisia and several enclaves. The containment of France was secured by the enlargement of the Netherlands to include Belgium and Luxemburg, the establishment of Prussia in Rhineland-Westphalia, the enlargement of Savoy-Sardinia by the incorporation of Genoa (with the Austrian Empire taking control of Lombardy and Venetia), and the guarantee of Swiss neutrality. The British notion of reviving

Poland to block the spread of Russian influence proved impracticable. Russia, insisting on the acquisition of Poland, and Prussia, laying claim to the whole of Saxony, were even prepared to countenance war against Britain and Austria if their demands were resisted. This led Britain and Austria to conclude an alliance with France on 3 January 1815 (see: *Franco-Austrian–British Treaty (1815) ). The unity of the Allies was only restored by Napoleon's escape from Elba and the *Hundred Days (1815). In the end Russia was given 'Congress Poland' and Prussia was compensated with parts of Saxony, Westphalia and Rhineland.

Britain successfully resisted the Austrian Chancellor's scheme for an Italian League under Austrian protection, but supported the creation of the German Confederation (Bund), which was placed under the guarantee of the Great Powers. The settlement arrived at in Vienna was subsequently strongly criticized because of its alleged failure to satisfy nationalist aspirations, particularly in Italy, Germany and Poland, and because of its support for the autocratic principle. In fact Britain as a constitutionalist power soon diverged from the monarchies of the *Holy Alliance on this point. This later censure tends to overlook the fact that the statesmen and diplomats at Vienna were cosmopolitan, European rather than nationalist in outlook, and the fact that they were primarily concerned to prevent further revolutionary outbreaks and ensure international peace and stability. The force of nationalism only became really prominent and widespread later in the nineteenth century. Nor was the Vienna Settlement devoid of liberal elements. For instance, *minority treaty guarantees were granted in the Netherlands and the declaration against the slave trade, proposed by Britain, was accepted. Vienna established the principle of free navigation on the Rhine and the Meuse. The regulation of the precedence and classification of diplomatic representatives was also a by-product of this congress, which gave Europe political stability until the emergence of united Italy and Germany in 1859–71. The settlement remained virtually unchanged for 40 years and no European-wide war occurred for nearly a century.

KISSINGER, H., A World Restored: Metternich, Castlereagh and the Problems of Peace, 1812–22, Weidenfeld and Nicolson, 1957.

NICOLSON, H., The Congress of Vienna: A Study in Allied Unity, 1812–1822, Constable, 1946.

SKED, A., ed., Europe's Balance of Power 1815–1848, Macmillan, 1979.

WEBSTER, C. K., The Foreign Policy of Castlereagh, 1812–15, Bell, 1931.

**War Guilt Clause.** Article 231 of the Treaty of *Versailles (1919), which placed responsibility on Germany and its allies for causing all the loss and damage of *World War I (1914–18). It served as a legal basis for *reparations and was highly resented by all sections of German public opinion. From 1919 a special department of the German Foreign Office organized a campaign against the so-called 'war guilt lie' and attempted to prove the essential innocence of pre-war German foreign policy. The War Guilt Clause served to poison international relations during the interwar years and continues to provoke major historical controversy.

**War-In-Sight Crisis** (1875). A diplomatic crisis in April 1875 sparked off by the publication of an article in the German *Die Post* with the title 'Is War in Sight?'. This was followed by the indiscreet defence of the idea of preventive war by Radowitz, one of the German Chancellor's confidential agents, in discussion with the French Ambassador Gontaut. There was at this time some German military pressure for a preventive war against France, who was strengthening her army in the wake of the humiliation of the Franco-Prussian War (1870). France approached Britain and Russia (an article, 'The French Scare' appeared in *The Times*) and both powers jointly brought pressure to bear on Bismarck, forcing him to disclaim the affair as a false alarm. Lord *Derby (1826–93) made it clear that Britain would not tolerate a weakening of France's position in the European balance, and Russia hastened to assure Britain that her expansion in Central Asia which was offending Britain would be halted. The crisis represented an early anticipation of the grouping of powers, the Triple Entente, which was to confront Germany in 1914.

**Washington Conference** (1921–22). Convened on the initiative of the United States Secretary of State, Hughes, to discuss naval disarmament and to resolve tensions between the powers in the Far East. It met between 21 November 1921 and 6 February 1922 and was attended by representatives from Britain, Belgium, China, France, Italy, Japan, the Netherlands, Portugal and the United States. In December Britain, France, Japan and the United States concluded the Four-Power Pact, in which they guaranteed each other's existing Pacific possessions and agreed to consult with one another in times of crisis. This agreement was particulary significant for Britain because it supplanted the *Anglo-Japanese Alliance, signed in its original form in 1902. In February all the powers present joined in the Nine-Power Pact, which at the same time guaranteed the integrity of Chinese territory and upheld the *Open Door principle. This was followed by the most important interwar disarmament agreement, the *Five-Power Treaty (February 1922), otherwise known as the Washington Naval Limitation Treaty. This was abandoned by Japan in 1934.

BIRN, D. S., 'Open Diplomacy at the Washington Conference, 1921–2: The British and French Experience'. In *Comparative Studies in Society and History*, vol. 12, 1970, pp. 297–319.

ROSKILL, S., *Naval Policy between the Wars,,* Vol. 1: *The Period of Anglo-American Antago-nism,* Collins, 1968.

**Waterloo, Battle of** (1815). Fought on 18 June 1815, 11 miles from Brussels, Waterloo was the final defeat of the Emperor Napoleon I, following his return from Elba. The contest was between the hammer tactics of the French and the resilient defensive formations of the British forces under *Wellington (1769–1852). Napoleon sent column after column against the British line, trying to force his way through to Brussels which lay to the north. In the afternoon the Prussian forces under Blücher appeared. With the linking of the two allies the French Army disintegrated. Napoleon fled to Paris, abdicating four days later.

**WAVELL,** Archibald Percival, 1st Earl Wavell (1883–1950). Soldier and scholar, Wavell served in the 2nd *Boer War (1899–1902) in 1901 and in France during *World War I (1914–18), as well as in the Caucasus and Palestine. He held various staff appointments between the wars and in 1939 was made Commander in Chief in the Middle East. Here he took command of the war in the Western Desert. To begin with, British forces enjoyed major success in driving back *Axis forces. But the need to send troops to Greece, in the unsuccessful attempt to save that country, severely drained resources at a crucial time. British forces lost ground heavily and Wavell, whose relations with *Churchill (1874–1965) had never been close, was transferred to the post of Commander in Chief, India. There he had the further misfortune to be made Supreme Allied Commander in the South West Pacific at the zenith of the Japanese advance. In 1943 he became the penultimate Viceroy of India, an essentially political post, involving complex negotiations with Congress and Muslim League leaders for which his military back-ground had not clearly prepared him. He released the Congress leaders when the war ended, but the Cabinet mission to India in 1946 failed. He retired in 1947.

LEWIN, R., *The Chief: Field-Marshall Lord Wavell: Commander in Chief and Viceroy, 1939–47,* Hutchinson, 1980.

**Webster–Ashburton Treaty** (1842). Agreement settling the Maine–Canada northeast boundary dispute. Daniel Webster was the United States

Secretary of State and Lord Ashburton was British Minister to the United States. The United States ceded much of the disputed territory, though receiving 7,000 square miles. The treaty also contained provisions for extradition. A compromise agreement, it was accompanied on both sides of the Atlantic by a 'battle of the maps'. Both Britain and the United States assuaged domestic opposition by pointing to the conflicting evidence of early maps and maintaining that concessions in both directions were more than fair.

JONES, H., *To the Webster-Ashburton Treaty: A Study in Anglo-American Relations, 1783–1843,* University of North Carolina Press, Chapel Hill, 1977.

**WELLINGTON,** Arthur Wellesley, Duke of (1769–1852). Tory Prime Minister 1828–30; Foreign Secretary 1834–5. During the first phase of his career Wellington rose to eminence as a soldier, initially serving in India and, following an interlude as Chief Secretary for Ireland between 1807 and 1809, assuming the command of the force sent to the Iberian Peninsula. In 1813 he ultimately succeeded in driving the French back across the Pyrenees and, after Napoleon's return from Elba, routed his army at *Waterloo on 18 June 1815. For the next three years Wellington commanded the Allied army of occupation in France, executing Castlereagh's policy of avoiding unduly harsh treatment of the defeated power.

In general the Duke was to remain a firm disciple of *Castlereagh (1769–1822), upholding the *Concert of Europe and non-intervention. Returning to England in 1818 he entered the Cabinet as Master-General of the Ordnance. He was instrumental in securing Canning's appointment to succeed Castlereagh in 1822 in order to bolster the popularity of the government. *Canning (1770–1827) used him on diplomatic missions, notably at the Congress of *Verona in 1822 where he opposed French military intervention in Spain, and in negotiating in 1826 the St Petersburg Protocol with Tsar Nicholas I which contained an agreement that Greece would form an autonomous state, although providing inadequate checks upon Russian ambitions. Wellington became thoroughly disillusioned with Canning, believing that his policies threatened the Concert of Europe set up by Castlereagh, and he refused to serve under him in 1827. Wellington himself became Prime Minister in 1828 against a background of conflict between Russia and Turkey which enabled the former considerably to extend her influence in the Near East. His government also weakened British influence in Portugal and seemed to be moving into a condition of uncomfortable isolation. Wellington fell from power in November 1830 but, enjoying immense prestige at home and abroad, he remained an important figure in relation to foreign affairs, offering opposition to *Palmerston's interventionist policies in the 1830s and evincing strong hostility to all manifestations of democracy. He was himself Foreign Secretary in Sir Robert *Peel's short-lived administration of 1834–5 and exercised a significant influence on policy while *Aberdeen (1784–1860) was Foreign Secretary between 1841 and 1846.

LONGFORD, E., *Wellington, The Years of the Sword*, Weidenfeld and Nicolson, 1971. *Wellington, Pillar of State*, Weidenfeld and Nicolson, 1972.

**Weltpolitik.** Term for German imperial policy, involving persistent intervention in world affairs. The claim by Germany for world power status and 'a place in the sun' was advanced in the period leading to *World War I (1914–18) (the term was first used by the Kaiser in 1896). It involved her in the construction of a large fleet (see: *Flottenpolitik*) and a forward colonial policy in addition to her older demand for dominance in Central Europe (*Mitteleuropa*). It was regarded by other powers as reckless and provocative (see, for instance, 1st and 2nd *Moroccan Crises (1905, 1911) ). The German aspiration to rival the British Empire and to attain its scale of global power and influence was regarded in Britain as a threat to essential British interests.

**Western European Union.** The basis of this alliance, which includes Britain, France, the Federal Republic of Germany, Italy, Luxembourg and the Netherlands, was laid in the *Dunkirk Treaty (1947) between Britain and France, and it evolved through the *Brussels Treaty (1948), signed by Britain, France, Luxembourg and the Netherlands. The latter was concluded for a period of 50 years and numbered among its aims the strengthening of economic, cultural and social ties between the countries concerned and mutual assistance in maintaining international peace and security. Following the rejection of the European Defence Community treaty by France, the Brussels Treaty was amended and expanded in the Paris Agreements of September–October 1954. Italy and West Germany were included in the Pact. It was to determine maximum force levels. Protocol III imposed restrictions on the armaments of the Federal Republic (significantly amended over the years) while Protocol IV set up an agency for the control of armaments. The Western European Union came into force on 5 May 1955. It has concentrated on harmonizing the interests of defence and arms control in Western Europe. It has also dealt with political issues, such as East–West relations and the institution of democracy in Spain and Portugal.

**Western Europe since 1945, Britain and.** Britain emerged from *World War II (1939–45), though greatly weakened, with a global status which in subsequent years has progressively diminished as her relative economic power has shrunk and the territories of the British *Empire have been granted independence. She was still in the 1940s and 1950s the world's third major state in her economic, military and nuclear capability. She had been one of the victors, though at tremendous cost, while most of the nations on the Continent had been either defeated, or occupied and humiliated. The British Empire and Commonwealth in 1945 was still largely intact. As one of the *Big Three Britain was to play a very important part in putting into effect the *Marshall Plan (1948–52) for the economic recovery of Europe and in forging the *North Atlantic Treaty Organization (NATO) (1949). She was therefore disposed to follow her traditional policy towards the Continent, which was one of influence without close commitment. After the war the advantages of an American alignment as against a much closer association with Western Europe, or participation in it, seemed indisputable. Winston *Churchill (1874–1965) in his Zürich speech of September 1946 called for 'a kind of United States of Europe', but with Britain and the United States acting as outside sponsors. Britain's policy, then, was to encourage collaboration between the Western European nations, but essentially to keep her distance.

The Conservative Party thought in terms of Great Power status based on the Commonwealth and with a special relationship with the United States. The Labour Party shared their scepticism over Continental involvement, though for other reasons. They feared commitment to a Europe which, they felt, if they participated, would put at risk the socialist planned economy and social welfare. Some saw such an alignment with Western Europe as an unwelcome, and decisive, step away from a lasting understanding with the Soviet Union. Clement *Attlee (1883–1967) and his colleagues were, additionally, strong believers in the constructive contribution which the Commonwealth could make to world affairs. In general the British argued that the movement towards European economic integration, which was to characterize the post-war period, was a protectionist movement, contrary to the principles accepted in the *General Agreement on Tariffs and Trade (GATT). While Britain encouraged the OEEC, the *Brussels Treaty (1947) and NATO she either boycotted, or only very reluctantly joined, organizations with more explicit supranational overtones, such as the Council of Europe, the European Coal and Steel Community and the European Economic Community (*EEC). In fact in its early years the European integration movement had only a marginal impact upon British politics. The decisions to abstain from the negotiations over the Schuman Plan and the Pleven Plan were based on the expectation that the plans would not succeed, combined with a confidence that if they should, Britain would have another chance to join the integration movement at a later date. Traditionalism and pragmatism strongly reinforced British nationalism and attachment to national sovereignty.

Churchill refused to join the European Defence Community (EDC). Following the final collapse of this scheme, with the refusal of the French Assembly to ratify it in 1954, Britain, accepting the pressing United States demand for rearmament, including the rearmament of West Germany, produced the *Western European Union plan. This, set up in what came to be known as the Paris Agreements, was ratified by nine countries. *Eden (1897–1977) played a leading role in this, using it as a means of promoting defence cooperation without involving surrender of British sovereignty. It was agreed to admit West Germany and Italy and to make the Brussels Treaty the basis of a new defensive arrangement which would be tied to NATO. Eden pledged the retention of four British divisions and an air force contingent on the Continent, to be withdrawn only if the other Brussels Treaty powers consented.

The British did not participate in the Messina talks which preceded the formation of the EEC. They merely sent a 'representative' from the Board of Trade. The Treaty of Rome was signed by the Six in 1957 and the Community institutions were established in 1958 with an agenda for building increasing collaboration and structural linkage among the member nations. The Rome Treaty was intended, by some at any rate, as a step towards political integration which, it was hoped, would ensue from the functional integration of the economies. Britain, while welcoming the creation of *Free Trade for industrial goods, was determined to protect her special trade relationship with the Commonwealth and to resist not only the supranational political ambitions of the new *European Community, but many of the economic ones as well. She consequently set about building up the *European Free Trade Association (EFTA). The purpose of this was not to establish a continuing trading organization but to lever concessions out of the EEC. In fact EFTA proved insufficiently powerful to make the EEC accept the idea of a general Western European Free Trade association.

The close diplomatic link established between the French President, General de Gaulle, and the German Chancellor, Adenauer, worried Harold *Macmillan (1894–1986). As soon as the Rome Treaty was signed he sounded the alarm: 'Let us be under no delusions, by far the biggest danger would be if this great European unit came into being and we did nothing about it and were left outside'. Confronted, therefore, with the failure of British attempts to weaken or dilute the EEC, he announced at the end of July 1961 that an effort would be made formally to join the organization and that this would involve a greater sacrifice of independence than Britain had hitherto been willing to make. By this time, in fact, the Commonwealth was fast losing importance for Britain, while the Six were showing impressive economic growth rates, as contrasted with the relatively modest post-war economic performance of Britain. The United States was also by this time very much in favour of Britain joining the EEC.

The Prime Minister told the Commons that Britain stipulated three conditions for membership: (1) that satisfactory arrangements could be made to safeguard British interests in general; (2) that Commonwealth interests, primarily New Zealand's, could be taken care of; (3) that the interests of Britain's EFTA partners could be provided for. The Commonwealth presented an enormous barrier to agreement. British domestic farming presented an even more contentious area. The Community farm producers, particularly the French, were afraid that, with their system of generous agricultural subsidy, British farmers would undersell them. While the British in the event were willing to conform to normal EEC arrangements on subsidies, they insisted on a much longer period of transition than the EEC members were willing to grant.

In January 1963 at a press conference General de Gaulle sealed the rejection of Britain's application. He declared that the British were insufficiently European in their orientation, and too closely tied to the United States. The informal, but strong, bonds of the Anglo-Saxon community, he believed, made it impossible for the British to be reliable members of the European organizations. British entry would mean that Europe would have a subordinate status in an Anglo-American-dominated alliance. Also, it was argued, Britain's economic structure and problems were very different from those of the Six. The *Nassau Agreement (1962) between Harold Macmillan and President Kennedy over Polaris seemed to offer timely substance to General de Gaulle's arguments – as a clear illustration of Britain's reliance on the United States. There was a clear division between France and the other five over the exclusion of Britain, but unanimity was essential for the admission of a new member.

In November 1966 the Labour Prime Minister, Harold *Wilson (1916–    ) announced that a new effort would be made to enter the Community. By this time domestic and external developments had converged to weaken Britain's position; by 1967 the balance-of-payments crisis had led to the devaluation of sterling and withdrawal from *east of Suez. The relationship between Britain and the United States was less clearly a 'special' one. At the same time, the compromise Luxembourg Agreement (1966) had rendered the institutional implications of the EEC less intimidating for member states. In November 1967, however, General de Gaulle declined to reopen negotiations, declaring that Britain would be an economic liability and reiterating his belief that Britain's links were primarily outside Europe.

The election in 1970 of Edward *Heath (1916–    ) and the Conservatives gave Britain a leader deeply determined to take her into the Community. He had been the negotiator for Harold Macmillan in 1961–3. At the same time, there was a French change of heart, prompted not least by the desire to counterbalance the growing power of West Germany in the Community. Britain was admitted on 1 January 1973. This was 12 years since her original application and 15 after the Rome Treaty.

Popular opinion in Britain had never registered great enthusiasm for British participation in the Community. As the terms negotiated with the Six became known the unpopularity of Mr Heath's European policy spread. Membership of the Community was the culmination of a long-term effort to help bring British foreign policy more closely in line with political realities. But popular misgivings over rising prices, the burdens of EEC contributions and the long-standing reluctance of the Labour Left to entertain closer relations, even with their political opposite numbers across the Channel, induced Mr Wilson as Leader of the Opposition to stand out against the terms. He claimed that if he won the next election he would either renegotiate those terms or, if this were not possible, bring Britain out again. He also declared that the question should be settled 'once and for all' by means of a popular referendum.

After Labour regained power in 1974 Wilson and his Foreign Secretary, James *Callaghan (1912–    ) entered on a lengthy process of negotiation with other Community members. The new agreement was not substantially different from the existing one. The referendum was held in June 1975 and the division of opinion cut across normal party lines with Labour deeply split. However, there was a substantial majority in favour of continued membership and it appeared to have settled the question of membership once and for all. Nevertheless, this has not meant greater willingness on the the the part of subsequent governments to make major concessions to the larger European institutional structure. There has been disillusionment of earlier hopes, such as those entertained by federalists, that a strong, independently viable, political community could be formed among the European states. The conspicuous pro-Europeanism of Mr Heath has very clearly not been reflected in the attitude of Mrs *Thatcher (1925–    ).

Sharp differences of opinion and policy have continued to surface with other Community members, not least in the area of budget contributions and energy policy.

BARKER, E., *Britain and a Divided Europe, 1945–70*, Weidenfeld and Nicolson, 1971.

BELOFF, N., *The General Says No: Britain's Exclusion from Europe*, Penguin, 1963.

CAMPS, M., *Britain and the European Community, 1955–63*, Oxford University Press, 1964.

FRANKEL, J., *British Foreign Policy, 1945–73*, Oxford University Press, 1974.

JOWELL, R. and HOINVILLE, G., eds., *Britain into Europe: Public Opinion and the EEC, 1961–75*, Croom Helm, 1976.

KITZINGER, U., *Diplomacy and Persuasion: How Britain Joined the Common Market*, Thames and Hudson, 1973.

NEWHOUSE, J., *De Gaulle and the Anglo-Saxons*, Viking, New York, 1970.

NORTHEDGE, F. S., *Descent from Power: British Foreign Policy, 1945–73*, Allen and Unwin, 1974.

WATT, D. C., *Britain Looks to Germany: British Opinion and Policy towards Germany since 1945*, Oswald Wolff.

**Westminster, Statute of** (1931). Passed by Parliament on 11 December 1931, this statute provided legal recognition of the self-governing Dominions as 'autonomous communities within the British Empire, equal in status . . . united by common allegiance to the Crown, and freely associated as nations of the British Commonwealth of Nations'. Giving the Dominion parliaments as much control over their own constitutions as they wished to take, it repealed certain imperial statutes which had become obsolete with the changing relationship between Britain and the Dominions, such as that of 1865 governing the validity of colonial law. The principles underlying the Statute of Westminster and its specific provisions had been discussed at the Colonial Conference of 1926 which adopted the *Balfour Declaration (Empire) (1926) and set up a committee for further study. The report produced by the committee was adopted at the Colonial Conference of 1930.

**Wilhelmstrasse.** The location of the Reich Chancellery and German Foreign Ministry in Berlin between 1871 and 1945. It is commonly used as a synonym for the German Foreign Ministry.

**WILSON,** (James) Harold, Baron Wilson of Rievaulx (created 1983) (1916–     ). Harold Wilson was educated at Wirral Grammar School and Jesus College, Oxford. He was Labour MP for Ormskirk (1945–50) and for Huyton (1950–79), and was leader of the Labour Party (1963–76). He entered the Attlee Cabinet as President of the Board of Trade in October 1947, resigning over the introduction of prescription charges to pay for rearmament in April 1951. He was Prime Minister from October 1964 to June 1970, and from March 1974 to March 1976.

Wilson assumed in 1964 that foreign affairs would continue much as they had done under the Conservatives, if with slight changes of emphasis. To develop the global influence of a socialist Britain, the *Commonwealth was to be revitalized by the setting up of a Ministry of Overseas Development to channel aid to needy Commonwealth countries, and the Commonwealth Secretariat. Economic weakness and political instability in the newly independent African states, fighting between India and Pakistan, and Rhodesia's Unilateral Declaration of Independence in 1965 together frustrated this objective. Rejecting the use of force against Rhodesia, Wilson himself negotiated with the Rhodesian Prime Minister, Ian Smith, in 1966 and 1968, to no avail. Rhodesia exposed Wilson to backbench criticism from both sides of the House. So did Vietnam. Wilson would not condemn American involvement, but there was pressure from the Labour Left that he should intervene to stop it. His clumsy attempts to mediate were resented in Washington. This displeasure increased with his decision to withdraw from *East of Suez. Wilson had taken this with deep regret when the 1967 balance-of-payments crisis appeared to leave no choice. The prospect of continuing economic decline had by then led Wilson to abandon his opposition to entering the *Common Market, and he manoeuvred his doubtful party into agreeing that Britain should join. De Gaulle prevented this happening in the 1960s. Britain joined in 1973. Back in government in 1974, the increasingly strong anti-marketeer lobby in the Labour Party waged a determined campaign to take Britain out. Wilson managed to continue guarded support for continued membership with keeping his party together during the 1975 referendum on the issue which approved British membership. Financial constraints and diminishing world influence led

Wilson to conclude that the relatively cheap nuclear deterrent was worth keeping. Britain remained a nuclear power when Wilson surrendered the premiership in 1976. He left the Commons in 1979.

WILSON, H., *The Labour Government, 1964–70: A Personal Record*, Penguin, 1974. *Final Term: The Labour Government, 1974–6*, Weidenfeld and Nicolson, 1979.

**World Disarmament Conference** (1932–4). The international conference which met on 2 February 1932 at a time of rising international tension accompanied by economic collapse. Article 8 of the Covenant of the *League of Nations which was incorporated in the Versailles Treaty (1919) had specified that the Council of the League would 'formulate plans' for 'the reduction of national armaments to the lowest point consistent with national safety and the enforcement by common action of international obligations'. Following the *Locarno Treaties (1925) (which re-emphasized this principle), the Council set up a preparatory commission for a disarmament conference. In 1930 a draft convention was put forward which provided for Germany to remain at the level of disarmament specified by the peace treaty. This was rejected by Germany, who demanded equality. On 24 January 1931 the Council, therefore, convened a 'Conference for the Reduction and Limitation of Armaments' to meet the next year. It was presided over by Arthur *Henderson (1863–1935) and attended by representatives of 59 states. Its sessions were riven by deep-seated and fundamental disagreements. The British emphasized qualitative limitations, the reduction of armaments according to category rather than quantity – with a distinction made between offensive and defensive armaments. It proved impossible for the powers to reach agreement over definitions or to build an effective organization for control. France stressed in particular the need for the latter, to assist the League. Germany continued to insist on military parity and her 'equality' was recognized by a declaration of the Great Powers on 11 December 1932; on 16 March 1933 the British Prime Minister Ramsay *MacDonald (1866–1937) presented a draft convention of 96 articles providing for substantial disarmament and for the substitution of this convention for Part V of the Versailles Treaty. On 14 October Hitler recalled German representatives from the conference. It proved impossible to reconcile German demands with French insistence on guarantees for her security. There was a conspicuous inclination of the powers to put forward schemes which would enable them to keep their own weapons while their neighbours disarmed. Britain was not blameless in this respect. With a strong interest in aerial disarmament, not least because of large concentrations of urban population, she added to her proposal for this the proviso that she could keep some bombers for policing rebellious tribesmen on the boundaries of empire. The collapse of the World Disarmament Conference made rearmament very hard to avoid and justified the warnings of the pessimists.

WALTERS, F. P., *A History of the League of Nations*, 2 vols., Oxford University Press, 1952.

***World War I** (1914–18). The outbreak of war followed the *July Crisis (1914). Sparked off by the spread of Balkan nationalism, a local conflict became a European and then a global war, fought on land, sea and in the air. Austria-Hungary declared war on Serbia on 28 July 1914. This led to the mobilization of Serbia's ally, Russia, on 29 July. Germany declared war on Russia on 1 August and on France, Russia's ally, on 3 August. Naval rivalry and trade competition had been dominant factors in the deterioration of Anglo-German relations in the preceding period. Britain had a moral obligation to France in the *Anglo-French Entente (1904) and had also reached an agreement with Russia in the *Anglo-Russian Convention (1907). Britain had been engaged in military conversations with France since 1906. What brought the Liberal Government round to support a declaration of war, though, was the German infringement of Belgian neutrality which was inevitable if the *Schlieffen Plan was to be followed. Britain entered the war on 4 August. While Belgium was the *casus belli*, members of the Government, particularly Sir Edward *Grey (1862–1933) calculated that whatever the outcome of war, whether a German or a Franco-Russian victory, Britain's interests would not be served by neutrality. There was an early optimistic assumption that the war would 'be over by Christmas'. Instead it was to drag on for four years at the end of which, with the collapse of four empires, the German, Austro-Hungarian, Ottoman and Russian, the distribution of power in the world was to be dramatically altered.

The Schlieffen Plan did not succeed. German troops were halted at the *Marne (7–9 September 1914), and both sides constructed defensive positions on the Western Front. The deadly war of attrition, with attacks from behind trench lines, which was the most marked feature of the war in the West now began. For three-and-a-half years there was a stalemate with massive loss of life, something not broken by the introduction of new instruments of war, such as poison gas and tanks (the British first used tanks at the Battle of the *Somme in 1916).

The British involvement was, in the main, on the Western Front and in the war against the Ottoman Empire. Support for the war in the latter region was urged by the 'Easterners', who felt that a thrust through the Dardanelles and into the Balkans would lead to victory. Their argument gained strength because of the colossal losses in the West. The situation there was worsened by shortages of shells and by the unimaginative leadership of generals such as French and *Haig (1861–1928), who was in conflict with the political leadership in London. At the Somme, for example, there were 420,000 casualties. Giving way to Conservative pressure following an outcry over munitions, *Asquith (1852–1928) formed a coalition government in 1915 and was replaced by *Lloyd George (1863–1945) in the following year (6 December 1916).

The Royal Navy blockaded the German navy, captured German merchant ships and intercepted neutral ships taking war materials to Germany. The one major naval encounter was the inconclusive Battle of *Jutland in the North Sea in 1916, after which the German High Seas Fleet never again ventured out to sea again in strength. The German naval threat, however, became dangerous with the start of unrestricted U-boat warfare in February 1917. Although this brought the United States into the war on Britain's side and the convoy system helped to reduce Allied losses, Britain lost nearly half the tonnage of shipping it had possessed in 1914.

The attempt of the 'Easterners' to end the war through the Balkans met with disaster at *Gallipoli (1915). In Egypt, however, the British offensive against the Ottoman Levantine possessions was more successful. British forces under Allenby reversed the setback at Kut by invading Palestine. Jerusalem was captured in December 1917 and further successes, aided by the activities of T. E. Lawrence and the *Arab Revolt (1916) then followed.

The President of the United States, Woodrow Wilson, was originally keen to keep America out of the war. The *House–Grey Memorandum of February 1916, though, indicated that she might enter the war on the Allied side if the Germans rejected United States peace overtures. The *Zimmermann Telegram (1917) swayed neutral American opinion against Germany. The United States declared war on Germany on 1 April. This brought financial and economic aid to the Allies, but no military aid until the following year. Their entry, nevertheless, decisively shifted the balance against Germany. The Allies on the Western Front, now under the command of General Nivelle, launched an abortive thrust against the Germans in April 1917, which failed in May. Haig launched his own attack in July, the Third Battle of Ypres, but this petered out in November. In the East the new Bolshevik government of Lenin sued for peace, which led to the draconic *Brest-Litovsk Treaty (1918). Britain, together with the other Allies, attempted to keep Russia in the war against Germany (see: *Russian Civil War, Britain and the).

In January 1918 Woodrow Wilson announced his *Fourteen Points. In March–April the German offensives under Ludendorff failed, and again in July. In September Bulgaria asked for an armistice and the Turks followed in October. Germany gave in on 11 November following negotiations by Prince Max of Baden which had begun on 3 October. A mutiny had already broken out at Kiel on 29 October. Germany abandoned all her conquests and Allied forces occupied the Rhineland. The myth was subsequently, and very effectively, propagated in Germany that she had not been defeated but 'stabbed in the back'. British Empire casualties during the war were 996,230 killed and died and 2,289,860 wounded. The first air raid against Britain was in 1914. *Conscription was introduced in 1916 and food rationing began in 1918.

As a result of the *Paris Peace Conference (1919–20) the *Versailles Treaty was signed by Germany (28 June 1919), that of St. Germain by Austria (10 September 1919), The Trianon Treaty by Hungary (20 June 1920), that of Neuilly by Bulgaria (27 November 1919) and those of *Sèvres (10 August 1920) and *Lausanne (24 July 1923) with Turkey.

JOLL, J., *The Origins of the First World War*, Longmans, 1984.

KENNEDY, P. M., ed., *The War Plans of the Great Powers 1880–1914*, Allen and Unwin, 1979.

ROBBINS, K., *The First World War*, Oxford University Press, 1984.

ROTHWELL, V. H., *British War Aims and Peace Diplomacy 1914–18*, Oxford University Press, 1971.

TAYLOR, A. J. P., *The First World War*, Hamish Hamilton, 1963.

*World War II (1939–45). The immediate cause of World War II was Hitler's invasion of Poland on 1 September 1939, following the *Molotov–Ribbentrop Pact on 23 August, which freed Hitler from the prospect of a major war on two fronts. Britain and France were pledged to assist Poland (see: *Anglo-Polish Alliance (1939) ) and they declared war on Germany on 3 September. The earlier stage of the war is known as the *'phony war', and Hitler's conquest of Poland was speedy and unhindered. Ministries of Shipping, Information, Food and Economic Warfare were set up in Britain. Neville *Chamberlain (1869–1940) immediately formed a War Cabinet, making Winston *Churchill (1874–1965), earlier the leading opponent of his policy of *appeasement, First Lord of the Admiralty. Having declined to allow the Soviet Union facilities on their territory, the Finns were invaded by the Soviet Red Army. Britain agreed to send rifles and ammunition and for a while there was some official enthusiasm for the idea of declaring war on the Soviet Union as well, though the Finns made peace in March 1940.

On 8 April 1940 the German assault on Scandinavia began, Norway and Denmark both falling within a month. After the debacle of Narvik Chamberlain resigned, succeeded by Churchill, who brought the Labour leader *Attlee (1883–1967) and some of his colleagues, most importantly *Bevin (1881–1951) into the Cabinet, forming a coalition to win the war. During the night before Churchill's appointment Germany invaded Holland and Belgium. Seven weeks of lightning-war led to the fall of France and the evacuation of *Dunkirk, in which almost all the *British Expeditionary Force were saved. (Germany had avoided the Maginot Line and invaded through the Ardennes.) Italy, hitherto neutral, joined the Germans on 10 June and the French were forced to sue for an armistice on the 22nd of that month.

In Britain a million men joined the Home Guard and absolute priority was given to fighter aircraft production. Britain was now alone, but her position was arguably less precarious than contemporaries imagined. Hitler had not anticipated having to move against the British so quickly and was not ready. To invade Britain he needed air superiority. The ensuing *Battle of Britain between British fighter divisions and the Luftwaffe was fought in the summer and autumn of 1940, largely over London and Southern England. The British success frustrated Hitler's invasion plans, though Churchill was aware that the British position depended crucially on the role of the United States in this conflict, and worked tirelessly to secure their support. Caution dictated (until 1944) a twofold British approach. Germany was to be weakened by strategic bombing and British initiatives in North Africa and the Mediterranean area. A major assault in Northwest Europe was not to be contemplated until Germany was sufficiently weakened to ensure its success.

In the Balkans Rumania and Hungary, whose fear of the Soviet Union exceeded their distrust of Nazi Germany, acceded to the *Axis in November 1940, the former's oil supplies falling into German hands (Bulgaria was to join in March 1941). Allied forces attempted to come to the rescue of Greece which had been invaded by Italy, but in so doing the British severely prejudiced their campaign against Italy in North Africa. When Yugoslavia declared for the Allies Germany invaded it and Greece, in April 1941, both countries falling swiftly into Axis hands. With the arrival of Rommel in North Africa the British were forced out of Cyrenaica, with the exception of Tobruk.

In March 1941 the lifeline of *Lend-Lease was instituted, guaranteeing United States supplies to Britain. Already in November 1940 the United States had decided on a Europe-first policy should she find herself at war with the Axis powers. The continued independence of Britain was perceived on the other side of the Atlantic as a vital American strategic interest. The *Atlantic Charter was signed in August 1941. By then another dimension had been added to the war with the German attack on the Soviet Union on 22 June 1941 (Operation Barbarossa). The Japanese attack on Pearl Harbour on 7 December of that year, which led Hitler to declare war on the United States, also transformed the war into a genuinely global conflict, leading to the emergence of the Grand Alliance of Britain, the United States and the Soviet Union.

The early months of 1942 were very grave for Britain. After the British declaration of war on Japan the British commander in Singapore was forced to surrender with 60,000 British and Commonwealth troops. The Japanese followed this with an attack on Burma, and India appeared to be threatened. The Battle of the *Atlantic, which had begun in December 1939 with the encounter between HMS *Exeter* and the *Graf Spee* was also going badly, with major U-boat successes scored against British shipping. The fall of Tobruk was a particular humiliation for Churchill, and a large slump in support for the Government was registered at the time. The tide of defeat started to turn with Montgomery's victory at El *Alamein in October–November 1942, which was the prelude to a major offensive driving Germany from North Africa (by May 1943 the Allies had effectively defeated the Germans in this theatre). On the Russian front the German forces suffered a very major humiliation at Stalingrad in the winter of 1942. Then, in July 1943, in arguably one of the most decisive battles of the war at Kursk, they suffered a further defeat at the hands of the Red Army. By mid-1943, too, the effectiveness of the German campaign in the Atlantic was slowly diminishing.

At the *Casablanca Conference in January 1943 the British and Americans pledged themselves to demand *unconditional surrender of the enemy. The major motive here was to disabuse the Soviet Union of any apprehension that the Western Powers were willing to make a separate peace with Nazi Germany. Another purpose was to avoid the repetition of a German 'stab-in-the back' legend after the war was over. Britain at this stage resisted the idea of a *Second Front in Northern Europe – until, that is, the success of such an operation could be guaranteed. Roosevelt agreed to make Sicily the next target for invasion. It was invaded on 1 July and Mussolini fell in the same month, though the Allied success provoked the German entry into Italy. At the same time planning began for Operation Overlord, the *Normandy landings, something discussed at the *Tehran Conference (1943), the first meeting of the *Big Three.

Already it was apparent that there would be problems over Poland, since the Soviet Union wished to maintain their post-1939 borders (the evidence of the Soviet execution of Polish army officers in the *Katyn Forest Massacre had been uncovered the previous April). Stalin also wished to retain the Baltic republics he had seized in 1940 and to take northeastern Prussia. Churchill had grave misgivings over Russian intentions, but by January 1944 Russian troops were already crossing the borders of pre-1939 Poland.

June was a victorious month for the Allies. Rome fell. In the Far East British forces defeated the Japanese at Imphal. Above all, on 6 June, the D-Day landings began the reconquest of Northern Europe. British forces maintained a prolonged action before Caen which allowed the Americans to break out of the Cotentin Peninsula. Paris was reached on 25 August and Brussels on 2 September. In the latter month, though, the Allied advance began to slow down. The British parachute drop on Arnhem was a disaster. The Allies suffered a setback with the Battle of the Bulge. *Montgomery (1887–1976) was attracted by the idea of a swift offensive across the North German plain, but this was not acceptable to the Americans.

Warsaw was captured by the Soviet forces in January 1945 and by the end of that month Russian armies were only 40 miles from Berlin, a fact which put Stalin in a particularly strong bargaining position by the time of the *Yalta Conference (February 1943). British and American armies crossed the Rhine in March 1945, reaching the Elbe on 11 April. Though Montgomery had wanted Western forces to capture Berlin it had been agreed by the Allies to let the Russians take the city. On 30 April Hitler committed suicide and on 8 May war in Europe was over.

The war in the Far East still continued, however. Preparations were made for the invasion of Japan, which it was anticipated would cost many casualties. Following the dropping of the atomic bomb on Hiroshima and Nagasaki, Japan surrendered unconditionally on 14 August, formally capitulating to General MacArthur on 2 September.

The total of British casualties in World War II was lower than that in 1914–18, but in all other major respects the costs for Britain were higher. Britain had lost a quarter of her pre-war wealth and was in the unenviable position now of being the world's largest debtor nation. The war accelerated an inevitable retreat from empire, as became almost immediately apparent. Victorious, but greatly weakened, and faced with the now incontestable superiority of the United States and the Soviet Union, Britain's position in the world was to undergo a major transformation from a genuinely global role to that of an essentially regional power over the next 40 years.

CALVOCORESSI, P. and WINT, G., *Total War*, Allen Lane, 1972.

COLLIER, B., *A Short History of the Second World War*, Collins, 1967.

HOWARD, M., *The Continental Commitment: the Dilemma of British Defence Policy in the Era of Two World Wars*, Temple Smith, 1972.

ROTHWELL, V., *Britain and the Cold War, 1941–48*, Cape, 1982.

THORNE, C. G., *Allies of a Kind, the United States, Britain and the War against Japan, 1941–45*, Hamish Hamilton, 1978.

WOODWARD, E. L., *British Foreign Policy in the Second World War*, 5 vols., HMSO, 1962–76.

Yalta Conference (1945). Between 4 and 11 February 1945, a meeting of the leaders of the Grand Alliance, *Churchill (1874–1965), Stalin and Roosevelt. The *Big Three discussed the question of Poland and the other states of Eastern Europe, the fate of post-war Germany and the terms for the prospective entry of the Soviet Union in the war against Japan which at this time, it was officially estimated, might last a further 18 months. They also dealt with the question of voting on the Security Council of the *United Nations. It was agreed that a conference should be convened to set up this organization (see: *San Francisco Conference (1945)), and the Russians inserted the controversial veto which allowed a dissenting permanent member of the Security Council to defeat majority decisions. Poland was to be re-established within new frontiers: the Russo-Polish border was moved westwards to the *Curzon Line with Poland promised territory in compensation from Germany. The Soviet government agreed that the pro-communist Lublin government would be re-organized along more representative lines with free elections to be held in the near future. Germany was to be divided into four zones of occupation, including a French zone; an *Inter-Allied Control Council was to be set up in Berlin. She was also to be disarmed and made to pay reparations (the specific arrangements over the latter were subsequently to be a vexed issue between the Soviet Union and the West). At Yalta after heated debate it was agreed to allow a Reparations Commission to determine the amount, using the Soviet figure of 20 billion dollars as 'a basis for discussion'.

While Churchill was increasingly preoccupied by the post-war implications of the Soviet advance in Eastern Europe and wanted his American counterpart vigorously to take up the question of the non-communist Poles, Roosevelt's main priority was to secure by concessions, some at China's expense, a Russian commitment to enter the war against Japan. Stalin pledged that his country would join this war two or three months after the surrender of Germany, in return for the cession of the Kurile Islands, Lower Sakhalin, leaseholds on Port Arthur and Dairen, control of the main Manchurian railways and recognition of Outer Mongolia's independence from China. Yalta also specified the independence of Korea after a period of joint occupation by American and Soviet forces.

Yalta has provided much ground for subsequent debate. The United States introduced a 'Declaration on Liberated Europe', partly to counter the agreement which Churchill had made with Stalin for the division of *spheres of influence in Southeast Europe, the 'percentages deal'. While Roosevelt was anxious at Yalta not to be seen to side with Britain against the Soviet Union and was very keen to secure Soviet participation in the United Nations, the public and non-public agreements reached at Yalta soon became the object of opposed interpretations and mutual charges of bad faith between East and West. The Declaration, which reasserted the principles of the *Atlantic Charter (1941) and committed the three powers to consult each other on the formation of new governments within the liberated areas, was soon a dead letter. There was mounting criticism in the West that Eastern Europe in particular had been surrendered to a new tyranny. On the other hand it can be argued that the Western Powers conceded nothing that was not under the control of the Red Army already, or soon would be, and that the earlier decisions effectively to postpone a territorial settlement until Germany had been defeated rendered this situation inevitable.

CLEMENS, D. S., *Yalta*, Oxford University Press, 1972.

DOUGLAS, R., *From War to Cold War, 1942–48*, Macmillan, 1981.

FEIS, H., *Churchill, Roosevelt, Stalin: The War they Waged and the Peace they Sought*, Princeton University Press, Princeton, N.J., 1957.

ROTHWELL, V., *Britain and the Cold War 1941–47*, Jonathan Cape, 1982.

**Yangtse Agreement** (1900). During the last decade of the nineteenth century Britain dominated the Yangtse valley. This agreement between Britain and Germany (signed on 10 October 1900), provided for the maintenance of the *Open Door in 'all Chinese territory as far as they (the contracting powers) can exercise their influence', and it disallowed all territorial claims by other European nations. Both powers were willing to relinquish further territorial advantages in the interest of guaranteeing trade in those parts of China where they could exert influence. In the event of the other powers using the upheaval of the *Boxer Rising (1900) to their own ends, Germany and Britain were to confer with each other on counter-measures. This agreement, which was a result among other things of growing British anxiety over Russian designs in the Far East, was acceded to by the other major powers.

**Young Plan** (1929). The modification of German *reparations payments proposed by the committee under American businessman Owen D. Young on 7 June 1929. It proposed that Germany pay 37 annuities averaging £100 million (the *Dawes Plan (1924) had stipulated £125 million), followed by 22 smaller payments equal in total to the war debts owed the United States. It abolished the foreign controls established over German finances by the Dawes Plan and transferred from the Allies to Germany the responsibility for converting reparations payments into foreign currencies. It also abolished the Reparations Commission.

Adoption of the plan was complicated by Anglo-French conflict over the percentage each country was to receive, though it was finally approved on 20 January 1930 and put into effect on 17 May 1930. This arrangement did not survive the Depression. All payments were suspended by the Hoover Moratorium (1931) and in practice ended by the Lausanne Conference (1932), which relieved Germany of all payments for a period of three years. Hitler, who came to power in 1933, repudiated all further payments.

MARKS, S., 'The Myth of Reparations', *Central European History*, 11:3, 1978, pp. 231–55.

# Z

**Zimmermann Telegram** (1917). Written on 16 January 1917 by the German Under-Secretary of State and sent to the German Minister in Mexico. It contained the proposal that Mexico should ally with Germany in the event of the United States joining in *World War I (1914–18) against Germany. In return for this they would receive financial aid and regain 'the territory lost . . . in Texas, New Mexico and Arizona' (the Mexican Cession). It also suggested that Japan should be brought into the alliance and further proposed that Mexico sign an offensive alliance with Japan, should the United States join the war. The telegram was intercepted by British Intelligence and passed on to the United States where, from the British point of view, it had the desired effect of confirming the growing hostility of the Woodrow Wilson administration towards the Germans (so much so that some historians have argued that it was a hoax designed by the British to push the United States into war on their side). The telegram was made public on 28 February, a few weeks after Germany had announced that she was resuming unrestricted submarine warfare. Wilson hesitated a while before releasing it to the press in the hope that peace was still possible (Germany had not yet sunk any United States vessels). However, after the isolationists in Congress refused his request for authority to arm merchant vessels he issued the telegram, and public opinion in the United States was promptly excited to a war fever.

TUCHMAN, B., *The Zimmermann Telegram*, Viking, New York, 1966.

**Zinoviev Letter** (1924). Also known as the 'Red Letter' — a communication of disputed authenticity from Grigori Zinoviev, the first president of the Third International (Comintern) in Moscow to the British Communist Party. Calling for armed struggle against capitalism and sedition among the forces, its publication on 25 October, four days before polling, helped to rob Ramsay MacDonald (1866–1937) of victory in the General Election. Copies of the letter had reached both the *Foreign Office and the *Daily Mail* and it was published together with a Foreign Office protest to the Soviet Union. It was believed by Labour leaders that it was a forgery planted to ensure the return of a Conservative government. Its content and tone were typical of Comintern propaganda. At the same time, émigré organizations were circulating forged documents to discredit the Soviet Union. Strictly speaking, the letter had nothing to do with the Labour Party, but its publication enabled the Conservatives to play on the deep suspicions of British public opinion over the Bolsheviks. It increased disquiet aroused by the Anglo-Soviet treaty awaiting ratification and cast doubt on the wisdom of entrusting power to a Labour government again, whose members might sympathize with the Soviet Union. In the General Election about 100 Liberal candidates stood down to ensure a united front against socialism.

ANDREW, C., 'More on the Zinoviev Letter', *Historical Journal*, 22, 1979, pp. 211–14.

CARR, E. H., 'The Zinoviev Letter', *Historical Journal*, 22, 1979, pp. 209–10.

CHESTER, L., FAY, S. and YOUNG, H., *The Zinoviev Letter*, Heinemann, 1967.

**Zulu War** (1879). The Zulus were one of the most warlike and militarily successful of the great tribes of South Africa in the nineteenth century, with an army of 45,000 warriors. The Zulu threat to the Transvaal had become a grave one and the Boer President, Burger, had warned the British Government that unless they came to his aid he would be compelled to go to Germany for support. A bankrupt Transvaal was annexed by Britain in 1877 and the new High Commissioner, Frere, persuaded a reluctant Cabinet in London to send more troops to the area. On 11 December 1878 Frere sent an impossible demand to Cetewayo, the Zulu chief. The Zulu boundary had been adjusted in his favour on condition that he disbanded his army. In order to enforce this agreement British troops invaded Zululand on 12 January 1879. A large part of the British force was massacred at Isandhlwana, though the post at Rorke's Drift was successfully defended with conspicuous bravery. When the defeat became known the Cabinet ordered more men and supplies, making Wolseley commander-in-chief. In July he defeated the Zulus at Ulundi and the war was over. The annexation of the Transvaal was to cause much Boer unrest, leading subsequently to war.

# Chronological Table

*(Events, treaties etc., in which Britain participated or was significantly involved are entered in capital letters.)*

1815   3 JANUARY: SECRET TREATY BETWEEN AUSTRIA, BRITAIN AND FRANCE
1 MARCH: Napoleon landed at Cannes
8 JUNE: GENERAL ACT OF THE CONGRESS OF VIENNA
18 JUNE: BATTLE OF WATERLOO
22 JUNE: Second abdication of Napoleon
26 SEPTEMBER: The Holy Alliance
20 NOVEMBER: THE SECOND PEACE OF PARIS AND THE QUADRUPLE ALLIANCE

1817   28 APRIL: RUSH–BAGOT AGREEMENT

1818   29 SEPTEMBER–21 NOVEMBER: THE CONGRESS OF AIX-LA-CHAPELLE
15 NOVEMBER: THE QUINTUPLE ALLIANCE

1819   20 SEPTEMBER: Carlsbad Decrees sanctioned by the Diet at Frankfurt

1820   OCTOBER: CONGRESS OF TROPPAU
8 DECEMBER: CIRCULAR NOTE OF TROPPAU

1821   FEBRUARY–MARCH: Opening of Greek rebellion. Rising against Turks in Wallachia, Moldavia and the Morea

1822   12 AUGUST: DEATH OF CASTLEREAGH, REPLACED BY CANNING
20 OCTOBER–14 DECEMBER: CONGRESS OF VERONA

1823   13 JANUARY: Greek Assembly declared Greek independence
APRIL: French intervention in Spain
9 OCTOBER: POLIGNAC MEMORANDUM
2 DECEMBER: Monroe Doctrine

1824   19 APRIL: BYRON'S DEATH AT MISSOLONGHI

1825   FEBRUARY: Egyptian intervention in Greece
18 FEBRUARY: ANGLO-RUSSIAN CONVENTION
13 DECEMBER: Death of Tsar Alexander I, succeeded by Tsar Nicholas I

1826   4 APRIL: ST PETERSBURG PROTOCOL

1827   6 JULY: TREATY OF LONDON
8 AUGUST: DEATH OF CANNING
20 OCTOBER: BATTLE OF NAVARINO

1828   22 JANUARY: WELLINGTON BECAME PRIME MINISTER
26 APRIL: Opening of Russo-Turkish War

1829   22 MARCH: AUTONOMY FOR GREECE BY LONDON PROTOCOL
14 SEPTEMBER: Treaty of Adrianople

1830   3 FEBRUARY: NEW LONDON PROTOCOL
28 JULY: Revolution in France
25 AUGUST–OCTOBER: Belgian revolt
NOVEMBER: Polish rebellion against Russia
4 NOVEMBER: LONDON CONFERENCE ON BELGIUM

1831   MARCH: Austrian intervention in Papal States
8 SEPTEMBER: Polish rebellion ended with Russian capture of Warsaw
NOVEMBER: Mehemet Ali declared war on the Sultan
15 NOVEMBER: TREATY OF LONDON, CONFIRMING BELGIAN INDEPENDENCE

1832   MARCH: French occupation of Ancona
APRIL: Ottoman Empire declared war on Mehemet Ali
JULY: Turkey finally accepted Greek independence
21 DECEMBER: Egyptian victory at Konieh

1833   20 FEBRUARY: The Sultan having asked Russians for protection, a Russian squadron arrived in the Bosphorus
8 JULY: Treaty of Unkiar-Skelessi between Russia and Turkey
18 SEPTEMBER: Münchengrätz agreement (between Russia and Austria)

**1834**   22 APRIL: QUADRUPLE ALLIANCE OF
BRITAIN, FRANCE, SPAIN AND
PORTUGAL
18 AUGUST: ADDITIONAL ARTICLES TO
THE QUADRUPLE ALLIANCE

**1839**   19 APRIL: TREATY OF LONDON
GUARANTEEING BELGIAN NEUTRALITY
21 APRIL: Sultan declared war on
Mehemet Ali
24 JUNE: Egyptian victory at Nizib
JUNE: BRITISH FLEET IN ACTION IN
EASTERN MEDITERRANEAN
27 JULY: FIVE-POWER NOTE WARNED
EGYPTIANS
SEPTEMBER–DECEMBER: BRUNNOW
MISSION TO LONDON
3 NOVEMBER: OUTBREAK OF OPIUM
WAR

**1840**   15 JULY: TREATY OF LONDON:
BRITAIN, AUSTRIA, RUSSIA AND
PRUSSIA AGREED TO FORCE A
SETTLEMENT ON MEHEMET ALI
9 SEPTEMBER: BRITISH FLEET
BOMBARDED BEIRUT
10 OCTOBER: BEIRUT CAPTURED
3 NOVEMBER: ACRE BOMBARDED AND
CAPTURED
27 NOVEMBER: MEHEMET ALI MADE
PEACE

**1841**   13 JULY: STRAITS CONVENTION,
SIGNED BY BRITAIN, FRANCE, AUSTRIA,
RUSSIA AND PRUSSIA

**1842**   9 AUGUST: WEBSTER–ASHBURTON
TREATY WITH THE UNITED STATES
29 AUGUST: TREATY OF NANKING

**1844**   JUNE: TSAR NICHOLAS VISITED
BRITAIN, CONVERSATIONS WITH
ABERDEEN
SEPTEMBER: NESSELRODE
MEMORANDUM

**1846**   15 JUNE: OREGON BOUNDARY TREATY
WITH THE UNITED STATES

**1848**   12 JANUARY: Revolt in Sicily
22 FEBRUARY: Revolution in Paris
13 MARCH: Metternich resigned
17 MARCH: King of Prussia, Frederick
William IV, granted Constitution
22 MARCH: Outbreak of war in
Northern Italy: Venice proclaimed
Republic
18 MAY: German National Assembly
met at Frankfurt

22 JULY: Radetzky defeated
Piedmontese at Custozza
26 AUGUST: Treaty of Malmö
2 DECEMBER: Louis Napoleon
Bonaparte assumed presidency of
Second French Republic

**1849**   9 FEBRUARY: Mazzini proclaimed
Republic in Rome
23 MARCH: Piedmontese were defeated
at Novara
28 MARCH: Frankfurt parliament
offered crown of a 'small Germany' to
King of Prussia
25 APRIL: French army entered Papal
States
17 JUNE: Russian troops suppressed
revolt in Hungary
4 JULY: Pope restored to his temporal
power

**1850**   JANUARY–APRIL: THE DON PACIFICO
AFFAIR
19 APRIL: CLAYTON–BULWER TREATY
28 NOVEMBER: Olmütz agreement

**1852**   8 MAY: TREATY OF LONDON
(SCHLESWIG-HOLSTEIN)

**1853**   JANUARY: TSAR NICHOLAS I'S
CONVERSATIONS WITH LORD GEORGE
SEYMOUR, BRITISH AMBASSADOR
FEBRUARY: Menshikov mission to
Constantinople
MAY: Menshikov mission ended in
failure
13 JUNE: BRITISH FLEET TO BESIKA BAY
2 JULY: Russian troops entered
Moldavia and Wallachia
28 JULY: VIENNA NOTE
7 SEPTEMBER: Russia repudiated
Vienna Note
23 SEPTEMBER: BRITISH FLEET
ORDERED TO CONSTANTINOPLE
4 OCTOBER: Turkey declared war on
Russia
30 NOVEMBER: Turkish fleet destroyed
at Sinope

**1854**   3 JANUARY: BRITISH AND FRENCH
FLEETS ENTERED THE BLACK SEA
27 FEBRUARY: ANGLO-FRENCH
ULTIMATUM TO RUSSIA
12 MARCH: ANGLO-FRENCH ALLIANCE
WITH TURKEY
28 MARCH: BRITAIN AND FRANCE
DECLARED WAR ON RUSSIA
20 APRIL: Austro-Prussian treaty

8 AUGUST: THE VIENNA FOUR POINTS
Russia evacuated Moldavia and
Wallachia
14 SEPTEMBER: LANDINGS OF THE
ALLIED TROOPS AT EUPATORIA
20 SEPTEMBER: BATTLE OF ALMA
17 OCTOBER: FIRST BOMBARDMENT OF
SEVASTOPOL
26 OCTOBER: BATTLE OF BALACLAVA
5 NOVEMBER: BATTLE OF INKERMAN
2 DECEMBER: TRIPLE ALLIANCE OF
AUSTRIA, BRITAIN AND FRANCE

1855 26 JANUARY: Piedmontese troops
entered war
2 MARCH: Accession of Tsar Alexander
II
11 SEPTEMBER: Russia evacuated
Sevastopol
28 DECEMBER: Austrian ultimatum to
Russia

1856 1 FEBRUARY: RUSSIA AGREED TO
PRELIMINARY PEACE TERMS AT VIENNA
25 FEBRUARY–30 MARCH: CONGRESS
OF PARIS
15 APRIL: ANGLO-FRENCH–AUSTRIAN
TREATY UPHOLDING TURKISH
INDEPENDENCE
8 OCTOBER: 'ARROW' INCIDENT LEADS
TO ANGLO-CHINESE HOSTILITIES

1857 10 MAY: THE INDIAN MUTINY BEGAN

1858 14 JANUARY: Orsini attempted to
assassinate Napoleon III
26–29 JUNE: TREATIES OF TIENTSIN
20 JULY: Meeting of Napoleon and
Cavour at Plombières

1859 23 APRIL: Austria sent ultimatum to
Piedmont
29 APRIL: Outbreak of war in
Northern Italy
12 MAY: France entered the war
4 JUNE: Battle of Magenta
14 JUNE: Prussian mobilization began
24 JUNE: Battle of Solferino
11 JULY: Truce of Villafranca
10 NOVEMBER: Treaty of Zürich

1860 23 JANUARY: COBDEN–CHEVALIER
TREATY BETWEEN BRITAIN AND FRANCE
13–15 MARCH: Plebiscites in Parma,
Modena, Romagna and Tuscany
resulted in vote for annexation to
Piedmont
24 MARCH: Treaty of Turin ceded Nice
and Savoy to France

11 MAY: Garibaldi and the Thousand
landed in Sicily
22 AUGUST: Garibaldi crossed the
Straits of Messina
18 SEPTEMBER: Battle of
Castelfidardo: Piedmontese troops
occupied Papal States

1861 17 MARCH: Kingdom of Italy
proclaimed by the first Italian
Parliament: Victor Emmanuel II
declared King of Italy
8 NOVEMBER–25 DECEMBER: THE
TRENT AFFAIR

1862 22 SEPTEMBER: Bismarck appointed
Minister-President of Prussia

1863 JANUARY: Warsaw uprising
Polish rebellion crushed by Russia
8 FEBRUARY: Alvensleben Convention
7 JUNE: French troops occupied
Mexico City
18 NOVEMBER: Christian IX signed
new constitution affecting Schleswig
and Holstein

1864 16 JANUARY: Austro-Prussian alliance
1 FEBRUARY: Austria and Prussia
occupied Schleswig and Holstein
25 APRIL: CONFERENCE OF LONDON
BEGAN
26 JULY: Austria and Prussia renewed
war against Denmark
30 OCTOBER: Treaty of Vienna ended
the war

1865 14 AUGUST: Convention of Gastein
OCTOBER: Napoleon and Bismarck
met at Biarritz

1866 8 APRIL: Italian–Prussian alliance
12 JUNE: Austria agreed to cede
Venetia to France
14 JUNE: Outbreak of Austro-Prussian
War
JUNE–AUGUST: The Seven Weeks War
3 JULY: Austrian defeat at Sadowa
26 JULY: Preliminary peace of
Nikolsburg
23 AUGUST: Peace of Prague

1867 APRIL: Luxembourg crisis
7–11 MAY: LONDON CONFERENCE ON
LUXEMBOURG
19 JUNE: Execution of the Emperor
Maximilian in Mexico
9 SEPTEMBER: TREATY OF LONDON

1869   17 NOVEMBER: Suez Canal opened

1870   JUNE: Hohenzollern candidature crisis
13 JULY: Ems Telegram
18 JULY: Declaration of Papal
Infallibility
19 JULY: Outbreak of Franco-Prussian
War
30 AUGUST: Battle of Sedan:
Capitulation of Napoleon III
1 SEPTEMBER: Italian forces occupied
Rome
31 OCTOBER: RUSSIA RENOUNCED
BLACK SEA NEUTRALIZATION

1871   18 JANUARY: German Empire
proclaimed at Versailles
13 MARCH: LONDON PROTOCOL
MARCH–MAY: The Paris Commune
8 MAY: TREATY OF WASHINGTON
10 MAY: Treaty of Frankfurt

1873   6 MAY: Russo-German military
convention
6 JUNE: Austro-Russian Schönbrunn
Convention
22 OCTOBER: Three Emperors' League
(*Dreikaiserbund*) formed

1875   8 APRIL: 'WAR IN SIGHT' CRISIS
PRECIPITATED BY ARTICLE IN BERLIN
*POST*
JULY: Revolt in Herzegovina
25 NOVEMBER: BRITISH PURCHASE OF
THE SUEZ CANAL SHARES
DECEMBER: Balkan Revolt spread to
Bosnia
30 DECEMBER: Andrässy Note

1876   MAY–SEPTEMBER: Bulgarian revolt
13 MAY: BERLIN MEMORANDUM
REJECTED BY BRITAIN
30 JUNE: Montenegro and Serbia at
war with Turkey
8 JULY: Reichstadt agreement between
Austria and Russia
6 SEPTEMBER: GLADSTONE'S
'BULGARIAN HORRORS' PAMPHLET
12 DECEMBER: CONSTANTINOPLE
CONFERENCE BEGAN: NEGOTIATIONS
BETWEEN LORD SALISBURY AND COUNT
NICHOLAS IGNATIEV

1877   20 JANUARY; CONSTANTINOPLE
CONFERENCE ABANDONED
FEBRUARY–17 MARCH: Ignatiev
mission to western capitals
24 APRIL: Russian declaration of war
on Turkey

6 MAY: BRITISH WARNING TO RUSSIA
10 DECEMBER: Fall of Plevna

1878   31 JANUARY: Russo-Turkish armistice:
Russians had reached the outskirts of
Constantinople
15 FEBRUARY: BRITISH FLEET ARRIVED
AT CONSTANTINOPLE
3 MARCH: San Stefano Treaty
1 APRIL: LORD SALISBURY'S CIRCULAR
MAY–JUNE: BRITISH MEMORANDUM
CONDEMNING SAN STEFANO; ANGLO-
RUSSIAN (30 MAY), ANGLO-AUSTRIAN
(6 JUNE) AND ANGLO-TURKISH (4 JUNE)
AGREEMENTS
13 JUNE: CONGRESS OF BERLIN BEGAN
13 JULY: TREATY OF BERLIN

1879   4 SEPTEMBER: DUAL CONTROL
(BRITISH AND FRENCH) ESTABLISHED
IN EGYPT
7 OCTOBER: Austro-German Dual
Alliance

1881   12 MAY: Treaty of Bardo established
the French Protectorate of Tunis
18 JUNE: League of Three Emperors
28 JUNE: Secret treaty between Austria
and Serbia

1882   20 MAY: Triple Alliance between
Austria, Germany and Italy
11 JULY: BRITISH BOMBARDED
ALEXANDRIA
13 SEPTEMBER: BATTLE OF TEL-EL-
KEBIR; BRITISH OCCUPATION OF EGYPT

1883   30 OCTOBER: Austro-German–
Rumanian agreement

1884   15 SEPTEMBER: Skiernewice meeting of
the Three Emperors
15 NOVEMBER: BERLIN CONFERENCE
ON AFRICAN AFFAIRS BEGAN

1885   APRIL: PENJDEH INCIDENT,
FOLLOWING RUSSIAN ATTACK ON
AFGHAN FORCES (30 MARCH)
18 SEPTEMBER: Revolution in Eastern
Roumelia
13 NOVEMBER: Serbia declared war on
Bulgaria

1886   3 MARCH: Treaty of Bucharest between
Serbia and Bulgaria
14 JULY: General Boulanger appointed
Minister for War in France
7 SEPTEMBER: Russians forced
abdication of Alexander of Battenburg
in Bulgaria

1887   12 FEBRUARY: 1ST MEDITERRANEAN
AGREEMENT
20 FEBRUARY: Triple Alliance renewed
24 MARCH: Austro-Hungary acceded
to the Mediterranean Agreement
4 MAY: Spain acceded to the
Mediterranean Agreement
22 MAY: DRUMMOND–WOLFF
CONVENTION
18 JUNE: Reinsurance Treaty between
Germany and Russia
7 JULY: Ferdinand of Saxe-Coburg-
Kohäry elected Prince of Bulgaria
12 DECEMBER: SECOND
MEDITERRANEAN AGREEMENT

1888   13 MAY: Italy acceded to the Austro-
Roumanian alliance
29 OCTOBER: SUEZ CANAL
CONVENTION

1890   18 MARCH: Bismarck dismissed
1 JULY: ANGLO-GERMAN
HELIGOLAND–ZANZIBAR TREATY

1891   4 JULY: WILLIAM II'S STATE VISIT TO
LONDON
21 AUGUST: Franco-Russian Entente

1893   JULY: ANGLO-FRENCH CRISIS OVER
SIAM

1894   4 JANUARY: Franco-Russian Dual
Alliance
1 AUGUST: Outbreak of war between
China and Japan

1895   17 APRIL: Treaty of Shimonoseki
between Japan and China
29 DECEMBER: JAMESON RAID

1896   3 JANUARY: KRUGER TELEGRAM
1 MARCH: Italians defeated at Adua by
the Ethiopians

1898   17 JANUARY: SALISBURY'S
UNSUCCESSFUL OVERTURE TO RUSSIA
FOR CO-OPERATION IN CHINA
25 MARCH: BRITAIN DECIDED TO
LEASE WEI-HAI-WEI FROM CHINA
29 MARCH: CHAMBERLAIN'S BID FOR
ANGLO-GERMAN ALLIANCE
24 APRIL: Spanish–American War
began
4 MAY: SALISBURY'S 'DYING NATIONS'
SPEECH
13 MAY: CHAMBERLAIN'S BID FOR
FRIENDSHIP OF U.S.A. AND GERMANY
(BIRMINGHAM SPEECH)

14 JUNE: ANGLO-FRENCH CONVENTION
OVER WEST AFRICA
30 AUGUST: ANGLO-GERMAN
AGREEMENT ON PORTUGUESE
COLONIES
2 SEPTEMBER: BATTLE OF OMDURMAN
SEPTEMBER–NOVEMBER: FASHODA
CRISIS
10 DECEMBER: Spanish–American
War ended

1899   21 MARCH: ANGLO-FRENCH
CONVENTION OVER CENTRAL AFRICA
(France excluded from the Valley of
the Nile)
18 MAY: FIRST HAGUE PEACE
CONFERENCE BEGAN
9 OCTOBER: OUTBREAK OF THE 2ND
BOER WAR
30 NOVEMBER: CHAMBERLAIN
PROPOSED TRIPLE ALLIANCE
(LEICESTER SPEECH)
10 DECEMBER: BEGINNING OF 'BLACK
WEEK' IN BOER WAR

1900   17 MAY: RELIEF OF MAFEKING
13 JUNE: BOXER RISING AND SIEGE OF
LEGATIONS IN PEKING
14 AUGUST: BOXER RISING ENDED
16 OCTOBER: ANGLO-GERMAN
YANGTSE AGREEMENT

1901   12 MARCH: LANSDOWNE'S DRAFT
ALLIANCE FOR GERMAN CO-OPERATION
IN THE FAR EAST
25 OCTOBER: CHAMBERLAIN
DEFENDED BRITISH POLICY IN SOUTH
AFRICA (EDINBURGH SPEECH)
16 DECEMBER: US SENATE APPROVED
HAY–PAUNCEFOTE TREATY WITH
BRITAIN
19 DECEMBER: LANSDOWNE AGAIN
APPROACHED GERMANY
UNSUCCESSFULLY

1902   30 JANUARY: ANGLO-JAPANESE TREATY
31 MAY: PEACE OF VEREENIGING IN
SOUTH AFRICA
9 AUGUST: FOURTH COLONIAL
CONFERENCE
DECEMBER: VENEZUELAN CRISIS
18 DECEMBER: FIRST MEETING OF
COMMITTEE OF IMPERIAL DEFENCE

1903   1 MAY: EDWARD VII'S STATE VISIT TO
PARIS
15 MAY: LANSDOWNE WARNED RUSSIA
OFF PERSIAN GULF

6 JULY: VISIT OF LOUBET AND
DELCASSÉ TO LONDON

**1904** 8 FEBRUARY: Outbreak of Russo-
Japanese War
8 APRIL: ANGLO-FRENCH ENTENTE
7 SEPTEMBER: ANGLO-TIBETAN TREATY
21 OCTOBER: DOGGER BANK INCIDENT

**1905** JANUARY: Revised Schlieffen Plan (for
a German attack upon France through
Belgium)
2 JANUARY: Fall of Port Arthur to
Japanese
22 JANUARY: Outbreak of revolution
in Russia
31 MARCH: German Emperor visited
Tangier: FIRST MOROCCAN CRISIS
BEGAN
27 MAY: Destruction of Russian fleet at
Tsushima
24 JULY: German and Russian
Emperors signed agreement at Björkö
12 AUGUST: ANGLO-JAPANESE
ALLIANCE RENEWED
5 SEPTEMBER: TREATY OF
PORTSMOUTH (ended Russo-Japanese
War)
15 DECEMBER: ANGLO-FRENCH STAFF
TALKS BEGAN

**1906** 10 JANUARY: GREY AUTHORIZED ARMY
GENERAL STAFF CONVERSATIONS
16 JANUARY: ALGECIRAS CONFERENCE
OPENED
10 FEBRUARY: FIRST DREADNOUGHT
LAUNCHED
7 APRIL: ALGECIRAS ACT SIGNED

**1907** 1 JANUARY: EYRE CROWE
MEMORANDUM
16 MAY: ANGLO-FRANCO-SPANISH
AGREEMENT (on Mediterranean status
quo)
15 JUNE: SECOND HAGUE PEACE
CONFERENCE OPENED
31 AUGUST: ANGLO-RUSSIAN ENTENTE
15 OCTOBER: SECOND HAGUE PEACE
CONFERENCE ENDED

**1908** 16 FEBRUARY: ACCELERATION CRISIS:
WILLIAM II WROTE TO LORD
TWEEDMOUTH ABOUT BRITISH AND
GERMAN NAVAL TENSION
12 JUNE: EDWARD VII AND NICHOLAS
II MET AT REVAL
5 JULY: Young Turk revolution began

6 OCTOBER: Austrian annexation of
Bosnia and Herzegovina
28 OCTOBER: 'DAILY TELEGRAPH'
AFFAIR
4 DECEMBER: LONDON NAVAL
CONFERENCE

**1911** 21 MAY: French occupied Fez
1 JULY: 'PANTHER' SENT TO AGADIR
21 JULY: LLOYD GEORGE'S MANSION
HOUSE SPEECH
4 NOVEMBER: Franco-German accord
over Morocco

**1912** 8 FEBRUARY: HALDANE VISITED BERLIN
13 MARCH: Serbia and Bulgaria
formed Balkan League
18 MARCH: CHURCHILL PROPOSED
REDISTRIBUTION OF FLEET
4 JULY: ANGLO-FRANCO-RUSSIAN
NAVAL AGREEMENT
15 OCTOBER: Treaty of Lausanne
(ended Italo-Turkish War)
18 OCTOBER: Outbreak of First Balkan
War
21 OCTOBER: GREY-CAMBON LETTERS
EXCHANGED
3 DECEMBER: Armistice between
Turkey and Balkan states
5 DECEMBER: Triple Alliance renewed
16 DECEMBER: AMBASSADORIAL
CONFERENCE OPENED IN LONDON

**1913** 26 MARCH: CHURCHILL PROPOSED
'NAVAL HOLIDAY'
30 MAY: TREATY OF LONDON (ended
First Balkan War)
29 JUNE: Outbreak of Second Balkan
War
11 AUGUST: TREATY OF BUCHAREST
(ended Second Balkan War)
18 OCTOBER: CHURCHILL AGAIN
PROPOSED 'NAVAL HOLIDAY'
NOVEMBER: Liman Von Sanders crisis
began

**1914** 15 JUNE: ANGLO-GERMAN BAGHDAD
RAILWAY AGREEMENT
28 JUNE: Assassination of Archduke
Franz Ferdinand
20 JULY: Poincaré and Viviani visited
St Petersburg
23 JULY: Austrian ultimatum to Serbia
24 JULY: GREY CONSULTED CABINET
ON AUSTRO-SERBIAN CRISIS
28 JULY: Austria declared war on
Serbia

29 JULY: GREY'S WARNING TO
LICHNOWSKY; BETHMANN-HOLLWEG'S
BID FOR BRITISH NEUTRALITY
30 JULY: Austria-Hungary ordered
general mobilization
Russia ordered general mobilization
31 JULY: Both mobilizations took
effect; Kaiser proclaimed 'state of
imminent war'
German ultimatum to Russia
1 AUGUST: Germany declared war on
Russia and mobilized
2 AUGUST: CABINET AGREED TO
PROTECT NORTH COAST OF FRANCE
AND CHANNEL AGAINST GERMAN
ATTACK
Germany invaded Luxembourg
Germany sent ultimatum to Belgium
3 AUGUST: Germany declared war on
France
Belgium rejected German ultimatum
BRITISH MOBILIZED ARMY
CABINET AGREED TO SEND ULTIMATUM
TO GERMANY
4 AUGUST: Germany invaded Belgium
BRITISH ULTIMATUM EXPIRED AT
MIDNIGHT
6 AUGUST: Austria-Hungary declared
war on Russia
CABINET AGREED TO SEND BEF TO
FRANCE
12 AUGUST: BRITAIN DECLARED WAR
ON AUSTRIA-HUNGARY
23 AUGUST: Japan declared war on
Germany
29 OCTOBER: Turkey allied to
Germany against Russia

**1915** FEBRUARY: NAVAL ATTACKS AT
DARDANELLES
APRIL: TROOP LANDINGS ON
GALLIPOLI PENINSULA
26 APRIL: TREATY OF LONDON (Britain,
France, Russia and Italy)
23 MAY: Italy declared war on
Austria-Hungary
AUGUST: FURTHER TROOP LANDINGS
ON GALLIPOLI PENINSULA
OCTOBER: ANGLO-FRENCH LANDING AT
SALONIKA

**1916** 22 FEBRUARY: HOUSE–GREY
MEMORANDUM
16 MAY: SYKES–PICOT AGREEMENT ON
MIDDLE EAST
JUNE: Arab revolt began

27 AUGUST: Rumania declared war on
Austria-Hungary
28 AUGUST: Italy declared war on
Germany
12 DECEMBER: German peace note
20 DECEMBER: Wilson's peace note

**1917** 10 JANUARY: ALLIES REPLY TO WILSON
31 JANUARY: Germany announced
unrestricted submarine warfare
MARCH: BAGHDAD CAPTURED
15 MARCH: Abdication of Tsar
Nicholas II of Russia
6 APRIL: USA declared war on
Germany
19 JULY: Reichstag peace motion
15 AUGUST: Pope's peace note
published
2 NOVEMBER: BALFOUR DECLARATION
ON PALESTINE
7 NOVEMBER: Bolsheviks seized power
in Russia
29 NOVEMBER: FIRST MEETING OF
SUPREME WAR COUNCIL

**1918** 5 JANUARY: LLOYD GEORGE STATED
ALLIED PEACE AIMS
8 JANUARY: Wilson's Fourteen Points
17 FEBRUARY: BRITISH FORCES
LANDED IN TRANSCAUCASUS
3 MARCH: Treaty of Brest-Litovsk
23 JUNE: BRITISH FORCES LANDED AT
MURMANSK
4 OCTOBER: German peace note to
Wilson
30 OCTOBER: TURKEY SIGNED
ARMISTICE
3 NOVEMBER: Austria-Hungary signed
armistice with Italy
6 NOVEMBER: PRE-ARMISTICE
AGREEMENT WITH GERMANY
9 NOVEMBER: William II abdicated
11 NOVEMBER: GERMANY SIGNED
ARMISTICE
12 NOVEMBER: Emperor Charles
abdicated

**1919** 18 JANUARY: PARIS PEACE
CONFERENCE OPENED
14 FEBRUARY: LEAGUE OF NATIONS
COVENANT APPROVED
4 MARCH: Comintern established
24 MARCH: COUNCIL OF FOUR BEGAN
7 MAY: VERSAILLES TREATY PRESENTED
TO GERMANY
19 MAY: landing of Mustapha Kemal
at Samsun

28 JUNE: TREATY OF VERSAILLES (with Germany)
31 JULY: Constitution of German Republic approved in Weimar
10 SEPTEMBER: TREATY OF ST-GERMAIN-EN-LAYE (with Austria)
12 SEPTEMBER: D'Annunzio seized Fiume
12 OCTOBER: BRITISH EVACUATED MURMANSK
19 NOVEMBER: U.S. Senate failed to ratify the peace treaty with Germany
27 NOVEMBER: TREATY OF NEUILLY (with Bulgaria)

1920 10 JANUARY: VERSAILLES TREATY (INCLUDING COVENANT OF THE LEAGUE) CAME INTO FORCE
16 JANUARY: FIRST MEETING OF LEAGUE COUNCIL
16 MARCH: ALLIES OCCUPIED CONSTANTINOPLE
18–16 MARCH: SAN REMO CONFERENCE (produced Mandates settlement for Turkey-in-Asia, France had Lebanon and Syria, Britain had Palestine and Iraq)
25 MARCH: Polish offensive against Russia
4 JUNE: TREATY OF TRIANON (with Hungary)
6 JULY: Russian offensive against Poland
16 JULY: SPA PROTOCOL (on reparations)
10 AUGUST: TREATY OF SÈVRES (with Turkey)
14–16 AUGUST: Poles defeated Russia at Warsaw
15 NOVEMBER: FIRST ASSEMBLY OF LEAGUE OF NATIONS

1921 19 FEBRUARY: Franco-Polish alliance
16 MARCH: ANGLO-SOVIET TRADE AGREEMENT
18 MARCH: Treaty of Riga (between Poland and Russia)
20 MARCH: Plebiscite in Upper Silesia
5 MAY: LONDON SCHEDULE OF PAYMENTS ANNOUNCED
12 NOVEMBER: WASHINGTON CONFERENCE BEGAN
6 DECEMBER: IRISH TREATY
13 DECEMBER: FOUR-POWER PACT

1922 6–13 JANUARY: CANNES CONFERENCE
6 FEBRUARY: WASHINGTON

CONFERENCE ENDED WITH FIVE-POWER NAVAL LIMITATIONS TREATY NINE-POWER PACT (on China) FOUR-POWER TREATY (on Pacific Islands)
10 APRIL: OPENING OF GENOA ECONOMIC CONFERENCE
16 APRIL: Treaty of Rapallo (between Germany and Russia)
19 MAY: GENOA ECONOMIC CONFERENCE ENDED
1 AUGUST: BALFOUR NOTE (on war debts)
SEPTEMBER–OCTOBER: CHANAK CRISIS

1923 1 JANUARY: USSR formally established
11 JANUARY: Franco-Belgian occupation of the Ruhr
19 JANUARY: German passive resistance began
19 JUNE: BRITAIN SIGNED AGREEMENT ON WAR DEBTS WITH USA
24 JULY: TREATY OF LAUSANNE
31 AUGUST: Italy occupied Corfù
12 SEPTEMBER: Draft Treaty of Mutual Assistance
26 SEPTEMBER: Germany abandoned passive resistance in the Ruhr
20 NOVEMBER: German currency stabilized
Adjustment of Sèvres and new Straits settlement
Capitulations ended
Recognition of Kemal's government

1924 1 FEBRUARY: BRITAIN RECOGNIZED USSR
9 APRIL: DAWES PLAN ON GERMAN REPARATIONS REPORTED
5 JULY: BRITAIN REJECTED DRAFT TREATY OF MUTUAL ASSISTANCE
16 JULY: LONDON CONFERENCE OPENED
16 AUGUST: LONDON CONFERENCE APPROVED THE DAWES PLAN
2 OCTOBER: GENEVA PROTOCOL FOR PACIFIC SETTLEMENT OF INTERNATIONAL DISPUTES
25 OCTOBER: PUBLICATION OF ZINOVIEV LETTER

1925 12 MARCH: BRITAIN REJECTED GENEVA PROTOCOL
3 APRIL: BRITAIN RETURNED TO THE GOLD STANDARD
1 DECEMBER: LOCARNO TREATIES SIGNED IN LONDON

**1926** 10 SEPTEMBER: Germany entered the League

**1927** 2–23 MAY: WORLD ECONOMIC CONFERENCE AT GENEVA
27 MAY: BRITAIN BROKE OFF DIPLOMATIC RELATIONS WITH USSR
20 JUNE–4 AUGUST: GENEVA NAVAL CONFERENCE

**1928** 27 AUGUST: KELLOGG–BRIAND PACT

**1929** 7 JUNE: YOUNG REPORT ISSUED ON GERMAN REPARATIONS
6–31 AUGUST: HAGUE CONFERENCE ADOPTED YOUNG PLAN
3 OCTOBER: BRITAIN REOPENED RELATIONS WITH USSR
29 OCTOBER: Wall Street crash

**1930** 3–20 JANUARY: SECOND HAGUE CONFERENCE
22 APRIL: LONDON NAVAL TREATY
9 MAY: DAWES PLAN SUPERSEDED BY YOUNG PLAN
17 MAY: Briand memorandum on United States of Europe
30 JUNE: EVACUATION OF THE RHINELAND COMPLETED
14 SEPTEMBER: Nazis won 107 seats in the Reichstag

**1931** 21 MARCH: Proposal for Austro-German customs union
11 MAY: Failure of Credit-Anstalt
11 AUGUST: LONDON PROTOCOL ON HOOVER MORATORIUM
18 SEPTEMBER: Mukden incident (beginning of Japanese conquest of Manchuria)
21 SEPTEMBER: BRITAIN ABANDONED THE GOLD STANDARD
11 DECEMBER: STATUTE OF WESTMINSTER

**1932** 2 FEBRUARY: WORLD DISARMAMENT CONFERENCE OPENED
9 MARCH: Manchukuo proclaimed
11 MARCH: THE LEAGUE ADOPTED POLICY OF NON-RECOGNITION
16 JUNE–9 JULY: LAUSANNE CONFERENCE
21 JULY–20 AUGUST: OTTAWA CONFERENCE
25 AUGUST: Russo-Polish non-aggression pact
31 AUGUST: Nazis won 230 seats in Reichstag

4 OCTOBER: LYTTON COMMISSION REPORT ON MANCHURIA MADE PUBLIC

**1933** 30 JANUARY: Hitler became Chancellor of Germany
24 FEBRUARY: LEAGUE ADOPTED LYTTON REPORT ON MANCHURIAN CRISIS
27 MARCH: Japanese withdrew from League
17–27 JUNE: WORLD ECONOMIC CONFERENCE (in London)
15 JULY: FOUR-POWER PACT SIGNED IN ROME
14 OCTOBER: Germany withdrew from the World Disarmament Conference and the League
16 NOVEMBER: USA recognized USSR

**1934** 26 JANUARY: German–Polish non-aggression pact signed
11 JUNE: EFFECTIVE END OF THE DISARMAMENT CONFERENCE
25 JULY: Murder of Dollfuss in Vienna
18 SEPTEMBER: Russian entry into the League
9 OCTOBER: Assassination of King Alexander I of Yugoslavia and Barthou
29 DECEMBER: Japan denounced Washington naval treaty of 1922

**1935** 7 JANUARY: Franco-Italian agreement
17 JANUARY: Plebiscite in the Saar
27 JANUARY: PEACE BALLOT
1 MARCH: Saar returned to Germany
16 MARCH: Germany reintroduced conscription
11–14 APRIL: STRESA CONFERENCE
2 MAY: Signature of Franco-Soviet pact
18 JUNE: ANGLO-GERMAN NAVAL AGREEMENT
3 OCTOBER: Italy invaded Ethiopia
11 OCTOBER: LEAGUE ASSEMBLY DECIDED TO IMPOSE SANCTIONS ON ITALY
18 NOVEMBER: LEAGUE IMPOSED SANCTIONS ON ITALY
8 DECEMBER: HOARE–LAVAL PLAN
LONDON NAVAL CONFERENCE OPENED

**1936** 15 JANUARY: JAPAN WITHDREW FROM LONDON NAVAL CONFERENCE
7 MARCH: Germany reoccupied the Rhineland and denounced Locarno pacts
25 MARCH: SECOND LONDON NAVAL TREATY

9 MAY: Italy annexed Ethiopia
4 JULY: LEAGUE ASSEMBLY
RECOMMENDED END TO SANCTIONS
15 JULY: SANCTIONS ON ITALY LIFTED
17 JULY: Beginning of the Spanish
Civil war
20 JULY: MONTREUX CONVENTION
14 OCTOBER: Belgium announced
return to neutrality
1 NOVEMBER: Mussolini proclaimed
existence of Rome–Berlin Axis
25 NOVEMBER: Germany and Japan
signed Anti-Comintern Pact

**1937**   2 JANUARY: BRITAIN AND FRANCE
AGREED TO MAINTAIN STATUS QUO IN
MEDITERRANEAN
ANGLO-ITALIAN GENTLEMEN'S
AGREEMENT
7 JULY: Beginning of Sino-Japanese
war
10–14 SEPTEMBER: NYON CONFERENCE
6 NOVEMBER: Italy joined Anti-
Comintern pact
19 NOVEMBER: HALIFAX VISITED
HITLER
11 DECEMBER: Italian withdrawal
from the League

**1938**   20 FEBRUARY: RESIGNATION OF EDEN
9 MARCH: Austrian plebiscite
announced
11–13 MARCH: Austrian Anschluss
16 APRIL: ANGLO-ITALIAN AGREEMENT
20 MAY: Rumours of German troop
movements against Czechoslovakia
23 JULY: LORD RUNCIMAN 'INVITED'
TO CZECHOSLOVAKIA
7 SEPTEMBER: 'THE TIMES' FOLLOWED
THE LEAD OF 'THE NEW STATESMAN' IN
SUGGESTING THE CESSION OF THE
'SUDETENLAND'
15 SEPTEMBER: CHAMBERLAIN FLEW
TO MEET HITLER AT BERCHTESGADEN
19 SEPTEMBER: ANGLO-FRENCH
ADVICE TO BENEŠ TO CEDE AREAS
CONTAINING 50% OR MORE GERMANS
20 SEPTEMBER: Czech refusal
21 SEPTEMBER: ANGLO-FRENCH
ULTIMATUM TO BENEŠ ACCEPTED
22 SEPTEMBER: CHAMBERLAIN AND
HITLER MET AGAIN AT GODESBERG
27 SEPTEMBER: BRITISH FLEET
MOBILIZED
CHAMBERLAIN BROADCAST TO THE
NATION

28 SEPTEMBER: Hitler accepted
Mussolini's proposal of Four-Power
talks
29–30 SEPTEMBER: MUNICH
CONFERENCE
30 SEPTEMBER: Polish ultimatum to
Czechoslovakia
5 OCTOBER: Beneš resigned
2 NOVEMBER: Vienna award gave
southern Slovakia and part of
Ruthenia to Hungary
16 NOVEMBER: ANGLO-ITALIAN
AGREEMENT RATIFIED

**1939**   11–14 JANUARY: CHAMBERLAIN AND
HALIFAX TO ROME
15 MARCH: German occupation of
Prague
Hungary began occupying Ruthenia
16 MARCH: Germany announced
protectorate over Bohemia and
Moravia
19 MARCH: BRITAIN REJECTED SOVIET
PROPOSAL FOR FIVE-POWER TALKS ON
ROUMANIA
28 MARCH: Spanish Civil War ended
31 MARCH: ANGLO-FRENCH
GUARANTEE TO POLAND
7 APRIL: Italy invaded Albania
13 APRIL: ANGLO-FRENCH
GUARANTEES TO GREECE AND RUMANIA
17 APRIL: USSR PROPOSED ALLIANCE
TO BRITAIN AND FRANCE
28 APRIL: HITLER DENOUNCED ANGO-
GERMAN NAVAL AGREEMENT
8 MAY: BRITAIN REJECTED SOVIET
PROPOSAL FOR TRIPARTITE ALLIANCE
12 MAY: ANGLO-TURKISH MUTUAL
ASSISTANCE DECLARATION
22 MAY: Pact of Steel signed
1–2 JULY: Scare over Danzig
4–6 AUGUST: Danzig–Polish customs
crisis
12 AUGUST: BRITAIN AND FRANCE
BEGAN MILITARY TALKS WITH RUSSIA
IN MOSCOW
21 AUGUST: ANGLO-FRENCH-SOVIET
MILITARY TALKS SUSPENDED
22 AUGUST: BRITAIN REAFFIRMED ITS
PLEDGE TO POLAND
23 AUGUST: Signature of Nazi–Soviet
pact
24 AUGUST: Danzig–Polish custom
talks broken off
25 AUGUST: ANGLO-POLISH TREATY
SIGNED

HITLER OFFERED LASTING FRIENDSHIP WITH BRITISH EMPIRE
Mussolini informed Hitler that he could not participate in a general conflict
Hitler demanded Danzig, Corridor and parts of Silesia
29 AUGUST: POLAND PERSUADED BY BRITAIN AND FRANCE TO POSTPONE FULL MOBILIZATION
1 SEPTEMBER: Germany invaded Poland
Italy announced her neutrality
BRITAIN AND FRANCE WARNED GERMANY
2 SEPTEMBER: French activity in support of Italian-sponsored conference
ANGRY SCENES IN HOUSE OF COMMONS
3 SEPTEMBER: BRITAIN AND FRANCE DECLARED WAR ON GERMANY
4 SEPTEMBER: Mutual Assistance Protocol between Poland and France
17 SEPTEMBER: USSR invaded Poland
27 SEPTEMBER: Warsaw fell
Tripartite pact between Germany, Japan and Italy
28 SEPTEMBER: German–Soviet Boundary Treaty (Germany and USSR divided Poland)
19 OCTOBER: TRIPARTITE TREATY BETWEEN BRITAIN, FRANCE AND TURKEY
30 OCTOBER: French divisions drew back
30 NOVEMBER: USSR invaded Finland
14 DECEMBER: USSR expelled from the League

**1940** 9 APRIL: German troops invaded Denmark and Norway
10 MAY: beginning of German offensive in the West
28 MAY: FRANCO-BRITISH FORCES RESCUED OFF DUNKIRK
16 JUNE: REJECTION OF FRANCO-BRITISH UNION
22 JUNE: France signed armistice with Germany
25 JUNE: French armistice came into force
3 JULY: 'OPERATION CATAPULT' AT MERS-EL-KEBIR
7 AUGUST: AGREEMENT BETWEEN FREE FRENCH AND BRITISH GOVERNMENT
8 AUGUST: BEGINNING OF THE BLITZ

2 SEPTEMBER: ANGLO-AMERICAN DESTROYER – BASES DEAL
27 SEPTEMBER: Tripartite pact signed between Germany, Italy and Japan
8 OCTOBER: German forces entered Roumania
28 OCTOBER: Italy invaded Greece

**1941** 11 MARCH: LEND-LEASE ACT
6 APRIL: Germany invaded Yugoslavia and Greece
27 MAY: BRITAIN SANK THE 'BISMARCK'
31 MAY: FIRST MASSIVE RAF RAID ON GERMANY
22 JUNE: Germany invaded USSR
12 JULY: ANGLO-SOVIET AGREEMENT
14 AUGUST: PUBLICATION OF ATLANTIC CHARTER
25 AUGUST: BRITISH AND SOVIET TROOPS OCCUPIED IRAN
5 DECEMBER: EDEN ARRIVED IN MOSCOW
7 DECEMBER: Japanese attack on Pearl Harbour
8 DECEMBER: US AND BRITAIN DECLARED WAR ON JAPAN
11 DECEMBER: Germany and Italy declared war on the United States

**1942** 29 JANUARY: ANGLO-SOVIET-IRANIAN TREATY
15 FEBRUARY: Japanese seized Singapore
26 MAY: BRITISH–SOVIET TREATY
18–20 JULY: 'OPERATION TORCH' PLANNED
12–15 AUGUST: CHURCHILL'S FIRST VISIT TO MOSCOW
4 OCTOBER: Battle of Stalingrad began
22 OCTOBER: MONTGOMERY'S COUNTER-OFFENSIVE IN EGYPT
3 NOVEMBER: ROMMEL DEFEATED AT EL ALAMEIN
8 NOVEMBER: ALLIES LANDED IN FRENCH NORTH AFRICA
19 NOVEMBER: BEGINNING OF TUNISIAN CAMPAIGN

**1943** 14–26 JANUARY: CHURCHILL AND ROOSEVELT MET AT CASABLANCA
31 JANUARY: Germans surrendered at Stalingrad
11 MARCH: LEND-LEASE ACT EXTENDED
19 APRIL: Uprising in Warsaw ghetto
26 APRIL: USSR broke off diplomatic

relations with the Polish government-in-exile in London
12 MAY: GERMAN SURRENDER IN TUNISIA
22 MAY: Comintern dissolved
10 JULY: ALLIED LANDING IN SICILY
25 JULY: Fall of Mussolini
19 AUGUST: QUEBEC CONFERENCE (QUADRANT)
3 SEPTEMBER: ITALY SIGNED ARMISTICE
19–30 OCTOBER: FOREIGN MINISTERS' CONFERENCE IN MOSCOW
26 NOVEMBER: TEHRAN CONFERENCE

**1944** 5 JANUARY: Soviet troops entered Poland
21 JANUARY: Leningrad was relieved
15 FEBRUARY: BATTLE OF MONTE CASSINO BEGAN
4 JUNE: ROME TAKEN
6 JUNE: ALLIED LANDINGS IN NORMANDY – 'D-DAY'
1–22 JULY: BRETTON WOODS MONETARY CONFERENCE
20 JULY: Assassination attempt on Hitler failed
1 AUGUST: Warsaw Rising began
21 AUGUST–7 OCTOBER: DUMBARTON OAKS CONFERENCE
2 SEPTEMBER: ALLIED FORCES LIBERATED BRUSSELS
11–19 SEPTEMBER: QUEBEC CONFERENCE (OCTAGON)
12 SEPTEMBER: American 1st Army crossed the German frontier
2 OCTOBER: Warsaw Rising crushed
9–18 OCTOBER: CHURCHILL'S SECOND VISIT TO MOSCOW
23 OCTOBER: ALLIES RECOGNIZED COMMITTEE OF NATIONAL LIBERATION AS PROVISIONAL GOVERNMENT OF FRANCE
16–25 DECEMBER: BATTLE OF THE BULGE

**1945** 4–11 FEBRUARY: YALTA CONFERENCE
12 APRIL: Death of Roosevelt
25 APRIL: SAN FRANCISCO CONFERENCE
28 APRIL: Death of Mussolini
30 APRIL: Death of Hitler
1 MAY: Battle of Berlin
8 MAY: VE-DAY
17 JULY–2 AUGUST: POTSDAM CONFERENCE

6 AUGUST: First atomic bomb dropped on Hiroshima
8 AUGUST: USSR declared war on Japan
9 AUGUST: Second atomic bomb dropped on Nagasaki
15 AUGUST: OFFICIAL END OF WAR IN FAR EAST
2 SEPTEMBER: Japan signed formal capitulation
24 OCTOBER: UNITED NATIONS CAME INTO EXISTENCE

**1946** JANUARY–APRIL: IRAN CRISIS WITH SOVIET UNION
5 MARCH: CHURCHILL'S 'IRON CURTAIN' SPEECH (FULTON, MISSOURI)
29 JULY: PARIS PEACE CONFERENCE BEGAN TO DRAFT TREATIES WITH MINOR AXIS NATIONS
30 SEPTEMBER: INTERNATIONAL TRIBUNAL AT NUREMBERG ANNOUNCED ITS JUDGMENTS
2 DECEMBER: CREATION OF BIZONIA

**1947** 4 MARCH: TREATY OF ALLIANCE BETWEEN BRITAIN AND FRANCE
12 MARCH–24 MARCH: COUNCIL OF FOREIGN MINISTERS IN MOSCOW
12 MARCH: TRUMAN DOCTRINE
4 JUNE: MARSHALL PLAN ANNOUNCED
5 JULY: INDIAN INDEPENDENCE BILL
12 JULY: MARSHALL PLAN ARRANGEMENTS MADE AT PARIS CONFERENCE
15 AUGUST: INDIA BECAME INDEPENDENT
29 OCTOBER: Customs Union set up (between Belgium, Netherlands and Luxembourg)
25 NOVEMBER: COUNCIL OF FOREIGN MINISTERS IN LONDON

**1948** 30 JANUARY: Gandhi assassinated
25 FEBRUARY: Communist coup in Czechoslovakia
17 MARCH: BRUSSELS TREATY (BETWEEN BRITAIN, FRANCE, BELGIUM, NETHERLANDS AND LUXEMBOURG)
16 APRIL: ORGANIZATION FOR EUROPEAN ECONOMIC COOPERATION (OEEC) INAUGURATED
14 MAY: END OF BRITISH MANDATE IN PALESTINE: PROCLAMATION OF THE STATE OF ISRAEL
JUNE–JULY 1949: War between Israel and the Arab League

JUNE–MAY 1949: BERLIN BLOCKADE

**1949**   13 MARCH: Economic Union between Belgium, Netherlands and Luxembourg
4 APRIL: NORTH ATLANTIC TREATY SIGNED (NATO)
8 APRIL: OCCUPATION STATUTE FOR WEST GERMANY
5 MAY: COUNCIL OF EUROPE ESTABLISHED
23 MAY: German Federal Republic came into being

**1950**   9 MAY: Schuman Plan proposed
25 JUNE: OUTBREAK OF WAR IN KOREA

**1951**   18 APRIL: Schuman Plan adopted by France, West Germany, Italy, Belgium, Netherlands, Luxembourg
1 SEPTEMBER: ANZUS pact signed
12 SEPTEMBER: IRANIAN GOVERNMENT SENT ULTIMATUM TO BRITISH GOVERNMENT
27: IRAN OCCUPIED ABADAN
2 OCTOBER: FIRST BRITISH ATOM BOMB TESTED

**1952**   26 MAY: BONN CONVENTIONS
27 MAY: Charter of European Defence Community signed
1 JULY: Schuman Plan came into effect

**1953**   27 JULY: EFFECTIVE DATE OF KOREAN TRUCE
4–8 DECEMBER: BERMUDA CONFERENCE

**1954**   25 JANUARY–18 FEBRUARY: BIG FOUR FOREIGN MINISTERS' CONFERENCE IN BERLIN
1 MARCH: US tested hydrogen bomb
26 APRIL–21 JULY: GENEVA CONFERENCE
30 AUGUST: French national assembly rejected EDC treaty
3 OCTOBER: LONDON CONFERENCE: AGREEMENT TO ALTERNATIVE TO EDC

**1955**   18 FEBRUARY: BAGHDAD PACT
5 MAY: German Federal Republic gained sovereign status
7 MAY: WESTERN EUROPEAN UNION DEFENSIVE ALLIANCE
15 MAY: AUSTRIAN STATE TREATY
25 MAY: Rome Treaty signed; European Atomic Community established

**1956**   13 JUNE: BRITISH OCCUPATION OF SUEZ CANAL ENDED
26 JULY: NASSER ANNOUNCED 'NATIONALIZATION' OF SUEZ CANAL
24 OCTOBER: Soviet troops brought in to quell uprising in Hungary
29 OCTOBER: Israel attacked Egypt
30 OCTOBER: INTERVENTION OF BRITAIN AND FRANCE IN EGYPT – SUEZ CRISIS
6 NOVEMBER: ACCEPTANCE OF UN ORDER TO CEASE FIRE
Eisenhower re-elected
22 DECEMBER: BRITISH–FRENCH EVACUATION OF SUEZ COMPLETED

**1957**   9 MARCH: Eisenhower Doctrine enunciated
13 AUGUST: Syrian Crisis

**1958**   1 JANUARY: Rome Treaty came into force

**1959**   19 FEBRUARY: AGREEMENT FOR INDEPENDENCE OF CYPRUS
24 MAY: ANGLO-SOVIET TRADE AGREEMENT
1 DECEMBER: ANTARCTIC TREATY

**1960**   1 MAY: US U-2 shot down over USSR
3 MAY: EUROPEAN FREE TRADE ASSOCIATION (EFTA) SET UP

**1961**   3 JANUARY: US severed diplomatic relations with Cuba
17 APRIL: 'Bay of Pigs' débâcle
18 APRIL: Khrushchev promised aid to Cuba
31 MAY: SOUTH AFRICA BECAME A REPUBLIC
JULY: BERLIN CRISIS
13 AUGUST: Berlin Wall built

**1962**   22 OCTOBER: Cuban Missile crisis began
20 NOVEMBER: US ended blockade of Cuba

**1963**   29 JANUARY: FRANCE VETOED BRITAIN'S ENTRY INTO THE EEC
20 JUNE: East–West 'hot line' installed
5 AUGUST: NUCLEAR TEST BAN TREATY
22 NOVEMBER: Assassination of J. F. Kennedy

**1964**   14 FEBRUARY: REQUEST FOR INTERNATIONAL PEACE-KEEPING FORCE IN CYPRUS

**1966** 11 MARCH: decision of French government to withdraw troops from NATO command and to request all NATO bases be removed from French soil by 1 April 1967

**1967** 27 JANUARY: TREATY OF PRINCIPLES (governing the activities of states in the exploration and use of outer space – signed by 62 nations)
11 MAY: BRITAIN, IRELAND AND DENMARK APPLIED FOR MEMBERSHIP OF THE COMMUNITY
16 MAY: DE GAULLE AGAIN VETOED BRITISH MEMBERSHIP OF EEC
5–10 JUNE: Outbreak of Arab–Israeli Six Day War
3 NOVEMBER: UN RESOLUTION CALLING ON BRITAIN TO USE FORCE AGAINST RHODESIA

**1968** 19 JANUARY: BRITISH–SOVIET AGREEMENT ON SCIENCE AND TECHNOLOGY
12 JUNE: UN approved Nuclear Non-Proliferation Treaty submitted by its disarmament committee
20–21 AUGUST: Occupation of Czechoslovakia by Warsaw Pact forces

**1969** 3 JUNE: CONCLUSION OF BRITISH–SOVIET TRADE TREATY
25 JULY: Nixon Doctrine announced
17 NOVEMBER: Strategic Arms Limitation Talks (SALT) began at Helsinki
24 NOVEMBER: ratification of Non-Proliferation Treaty
25 NOVEMBER: unilateral pledge by US not to engage in germ warfare or use chemical weapons except in self-defence (germ weapons to be destroyed)

**1970** 17 NOVEMBER: SECURITY COUNCIL CALLED ON BRITAIN TO TAKE URGENT ACTION AGAINST RHODESIA
22 NOVEMBER: UN vote on admission of Communist China

**1971** 3 SEPTEMBER: FOUR-POWER BERLIN AGREEMENT SIGNED

**1972** 22 JANUARY: TREATY OF ACCESSION TO EUROPEAN COMMUNITY SIGNED (BY BRITAIN, IRELAND AND DENMARK)
30 MARCH: BRITISH GOVERNMENT SUSPENDED STORMONT, ASSUMED DIRECT RULE IN NORTHERN IRELAND
10 APRIL: BRITAIN AND SOVIET UNION SIGNED AGREEMENT TO OUTLAW BIOLOGICAL WEAPONS
22–29 MAY: SALT I signed
3 JUNE: SIGNING OF THE BERLIN AGREEMENT BY THE FOUR POWERS

**1973** 1 JANUARY: BRITAIN, IRELAND AND DENMARK BECAME MEMBERS OF EEC
27 JANUARY: Vietnam peace treaty signed in Paris
6 OCTOBER: Yom Kippur War

**1974** 20 JULY: Turkish invasion of Cyprus

**1975** 29 APRIL: Surrender of Saigon government to North Vietnamese and Vietcong: end of Vietnam War
16 JUNE: SIMONSTOWN NAVAL AGREEMENT ENDED (BETWEEN BRITAIN AND SOUTH AFRICA)
30 JULY–1 AUGUST: HELSINKI CONFERENCE ON EUROPEAN SECURITY

**1979** 1 JANUARY: European Monetary System (EMS) set up
7–10 JUNE: FIRST DIRECT ELECTIONS TO THE EUROPEAN PARLIAMENT
25 DECEMBER: Soviet invasion of Afghanistan

**1980** 17 APRIL: RHODESIA BECAME INDEPENDENT STATE OF ZIMBABWE

**1981** 13 DECEMBER: Introduction of martial law in Poland

**1982** 2–3 APRIL: ARGENTINIAN INVASION OF FALKLAND ISLANDS
14 JUNE: SURRENDER OF PORT STANLEY TO BRITISH

**1984** 1 AUGUST: ANGLO-CHINESE ACCORD OVER FUTURE OF HONG KONG

# —MAPS—

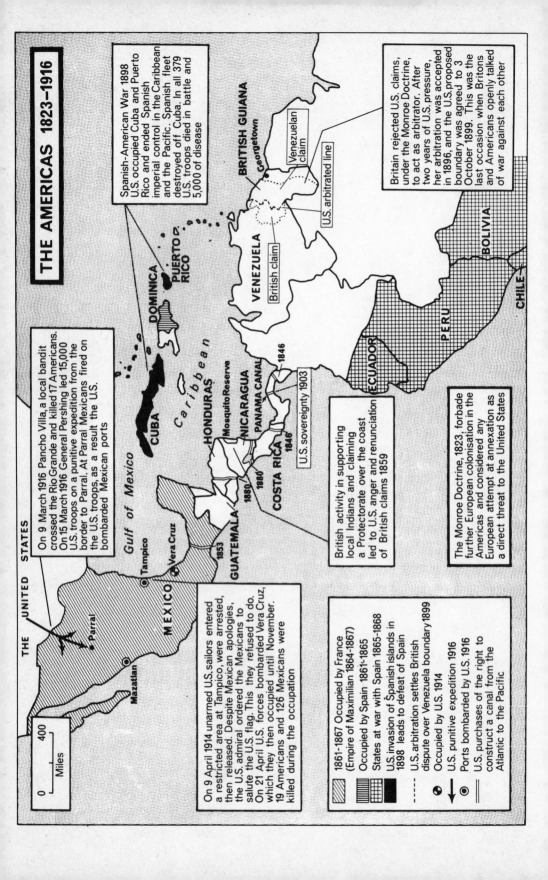

# THE AMERICAS 1823–1916

THE UNITED STATES

**MEXICO**

Mazatlan
Parral
Tampico
Vera Cruz

Gulf of Mexico

On 9 March 1916 Pancho Villa, a local bandit crossed the Rio Grande and killed 17 Americans. On 15 March 1916 General Pershing led 15,000 U.S. troops on a punitive expedition from the border to Parral. At Parral Mexicans fired on the U.S. troops, as a result the U.S. bombarded Mexican ports

On 9 April 1914 unarmed U.S. sailors entered a restricted area at Tampico, were arrested, then released. Despite Mexican apologies, the U.S. admiral ordered the Mexicans to salute the U.S. flag. This they refused to do. On 21 April U.S. forces bombarded Vera Cruz, which they then occupied until November. 19 Americans and 126 Mexicans were killed during the occupation

1853

**GUATEMALA**
**HONDURAS**
Mosquito Reserve
**NICARAGUA**
1860
1880
PANAMA CANAL
**COSTA RICA**
1846
1846
U.S. sovereignty 1903

Caribbean

**CUBA**

**DOMINICA**

**PUERTO RICO**

Spanish-American War 1898 U.S. occupied Cuba and Puerto Rico and ended Spanish imperial control in the Caribbean and the Pacific. Spanish fleet destroyed off Cuba. In all 379 U.S. troops died in battle and 5,000 of disease

**BRITISH GUIANA**
Georgetown

Venezuelan claim

U.S. arbitrated line

**VENEZUELA**

British claim

Britain rejected U.S. claims, under the Monroe Doctrine, to act as arbitrator. After two years of U.S. pressure, her arbitration was accepted in 1896, and the U.S. proposed boundary was agreed to 3 October 1899. This was the last occasion when Britons and Americans openly talked of war against each other

**ECUADOR**
**PERU**
**BOLIVIA**
**CHILE**

British activity in supporting local Indians and claiming a Protectorate over the coast led to U.S. anger and renunciation of British claims 1859

The Monroe Doctrine, 1823, forbade further European colonisation in the Americas and considered any European attempt at annexation as a direct threat to the United States

0    400
Miles

1861-1867 Occupied by France (Empire of Maximilian 1864-1867)

Occupied by Spain 1861-1865

States at war with Spain 1865-1868

U.S. invasion of Spanish islands in 1898 leads to defeat of Spain

- - - U.S. arbitration settles British dispute over Venezuela boundary 1899

Occupied by U.S. 1914

U.S. punitive expedition 1916

Ports bombarded by U.S. 1916

U.S. purchases of the right to construct a canal from the Atlantic to the Pacific